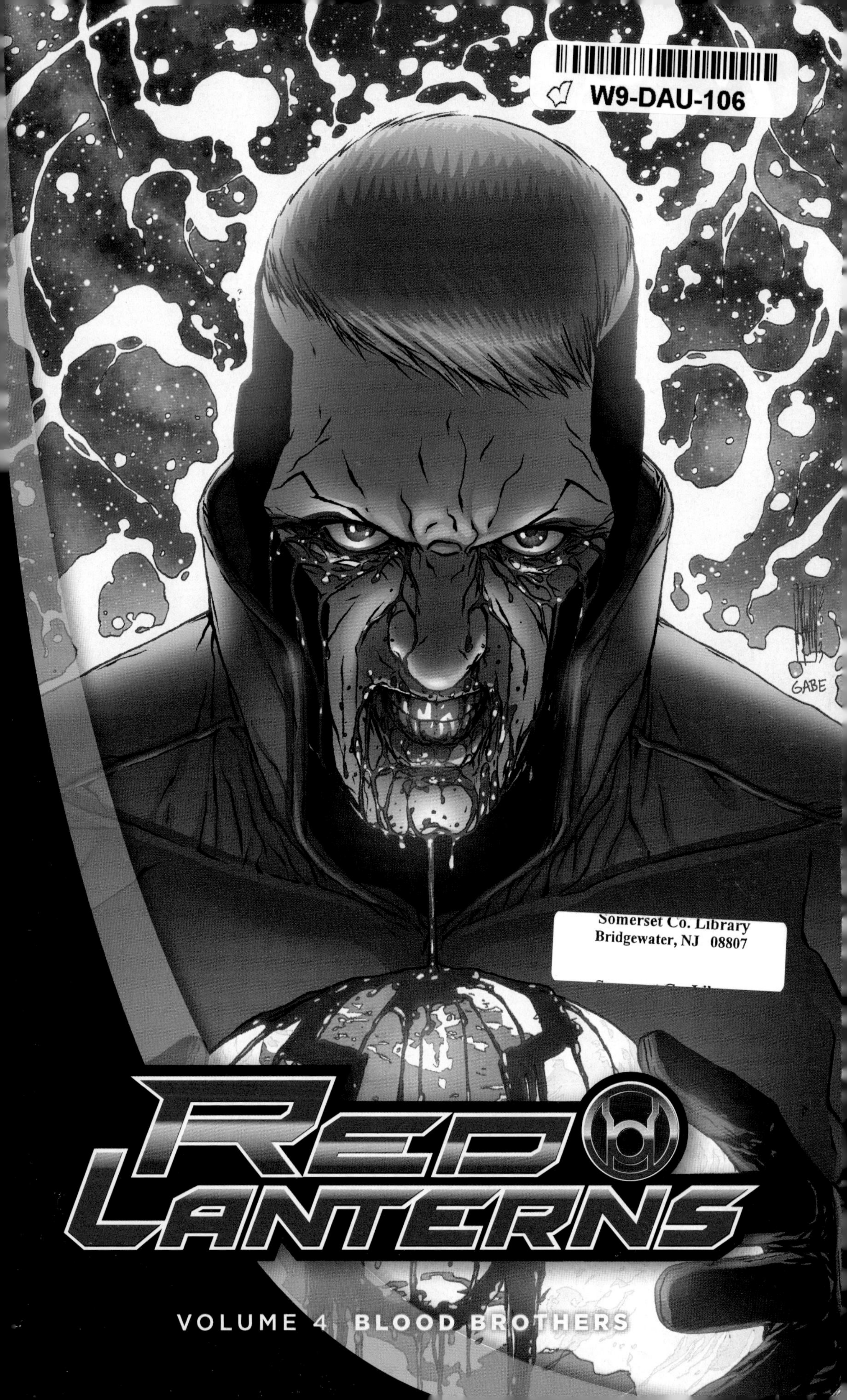
GABE

RED LANTERNS

VOLUME 4 BLOOD BROTHERS

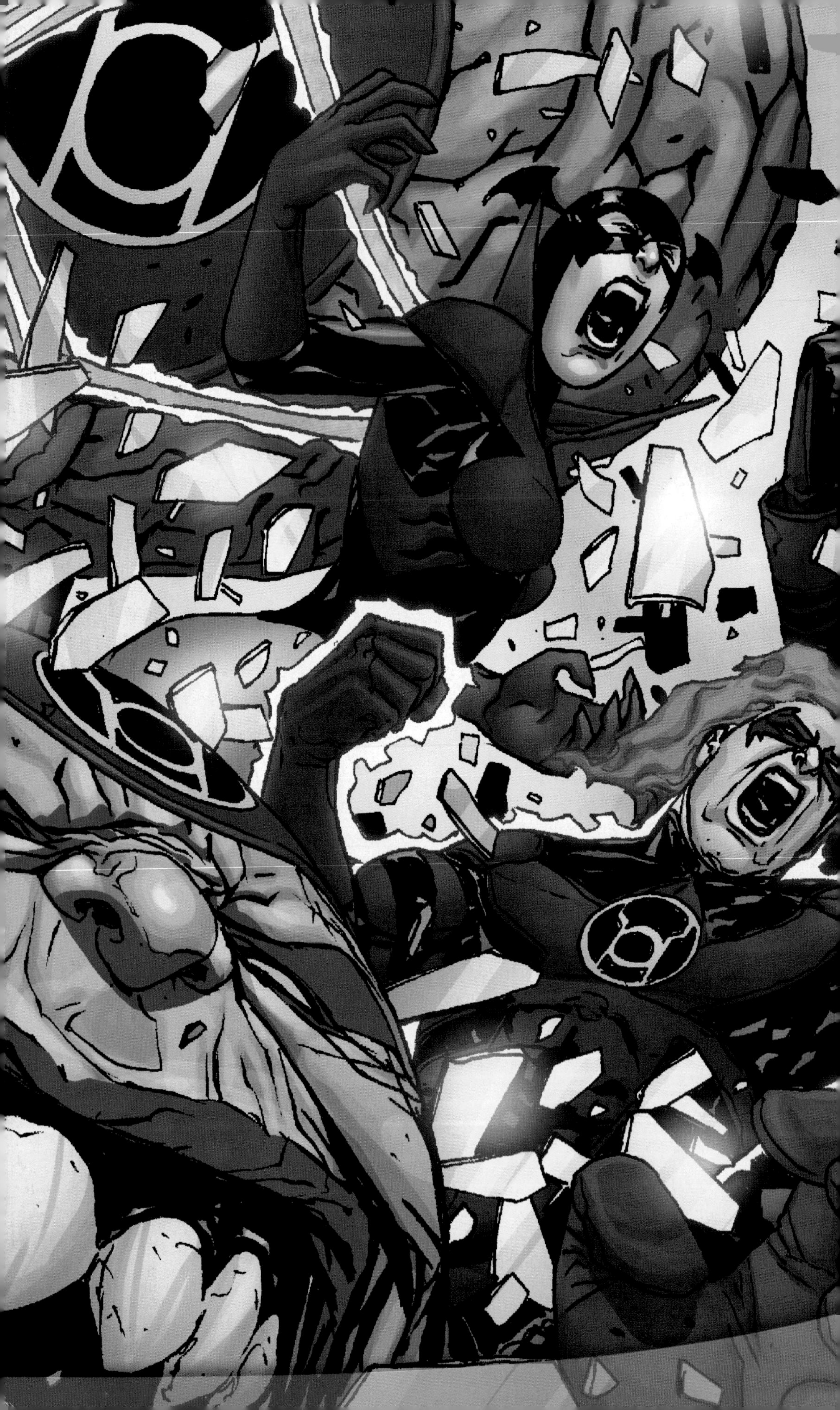

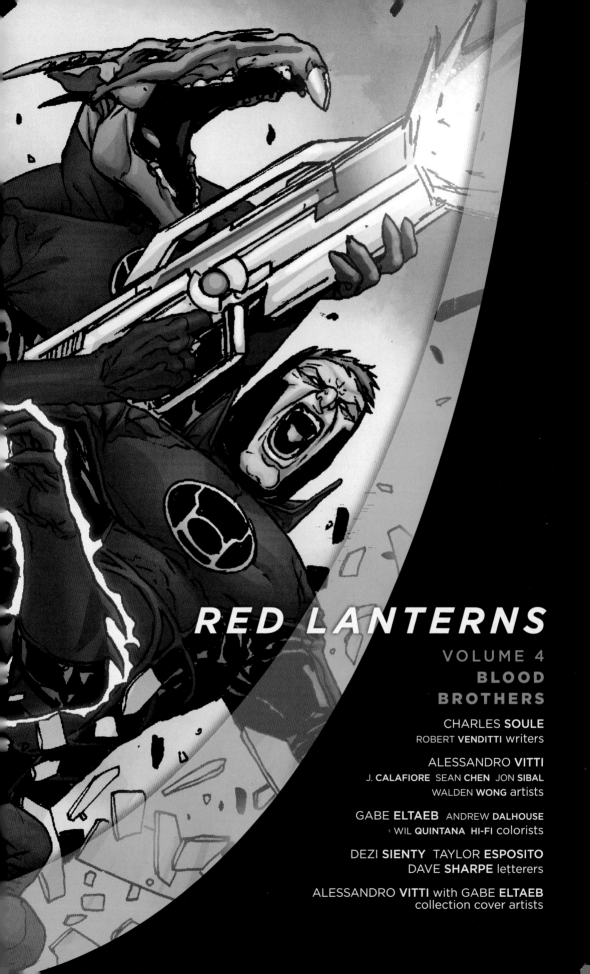

RED LANTERNS

VOLUME 4
BLOOD
BROTHERS

CHARLES **SOULE**
ROBERT **VENDITTI** writers

ALESSANDRO **VITTI**
J. **CALAFIORE** SEAN **CHEN** JON **SIBAL**
WALDEN **WONG** artists

GABE **ELTAEB** ANDREW **DALHOUSE**
WIL **QUINTANA** HI-FI colorists

DEZI **SIENTY** TAYLOR **ESPOSITO**
DAVE **SHARPE** letterers

ALESSANDRO **VITTI** with GABE **ELTAEB**
collection cover artists

CHRIS CONROY Editor – Original Series ROBIN WILDMAN Editor
ROBBIN BROSTERMAN Design Director – Books ROBBIE BIEDERMAN Publication Design

BOB HARRAS Senior VP – Editor-in-Chief, DC Comics

DIANE NELSON President DAN DIDIO and JIM LEE Co-Publishers
GEOFF JOHNS Chief Creative Officer
JOHN ROOD Executive VP – Sales, Marketing and Business Development
AMY GENKINS Senior VP – Business and Legal Affairs NAIRI GARDINER Senior VP – Finance
JEFF BOISON VP – Publishing Planning MARK CHIARELLO VP – Art Direction and Design
JOHN CUNNINGHAM VP – Marketing TERRI CUNNINGHAM VP – Editorial Administration
ALISON GILL Senior VP – Manufacturing and Operations HANK KANALZ Senior VP – Vertigo and Integrated Publishing
JAY KOGAN VP – Business and Legal Affairs, Publishing JACK MAHAN VP – Business Affairs, Talent
NICK NAPOLITANO VP – Manufacturing Administration SUE POHJA VP – Book Sales
COURTNEY SIMMONS Senior VP – Publicity BOB WAYNE Senior VP – Sales

RED LANTERNS VOLUME 4: BLOOD BROTHERS

DC Comics, 1700 Broadway, New York, NY 10019
A Warner Bros. Entertainment Company.
Printed by RR Donnelley, Salem, VA, USA. 4/25/14. First Printing.

ISBN: 978-1-4012-4742-3

Library of Congress Cataloging-in-Publication Data

Soule, Charles, author.
Red Lanterns. Volume 4, Blood Brothers / Charles Soule ; [illustrated by] Alessandro Vitti.
pages cm. — (The New 52!)
ISBN 978-1-4012-4742-3 (paperback)
1. Graphic novels. I. Vitti, Alessandro, 1978- II. Title. III. Title: Blood Brothers.
PN6728.R439S68 2014
741.5'973—dc23
2014008600

SUSTAINABLE
FORESTRY
INITIATIVE

Certified Chain of Custody
20% Certified Forest Content,
80% Certified Sourcing
www.sfiprogram.org
SFI-01042
APPLIES TO TEXT STOCK ONLY

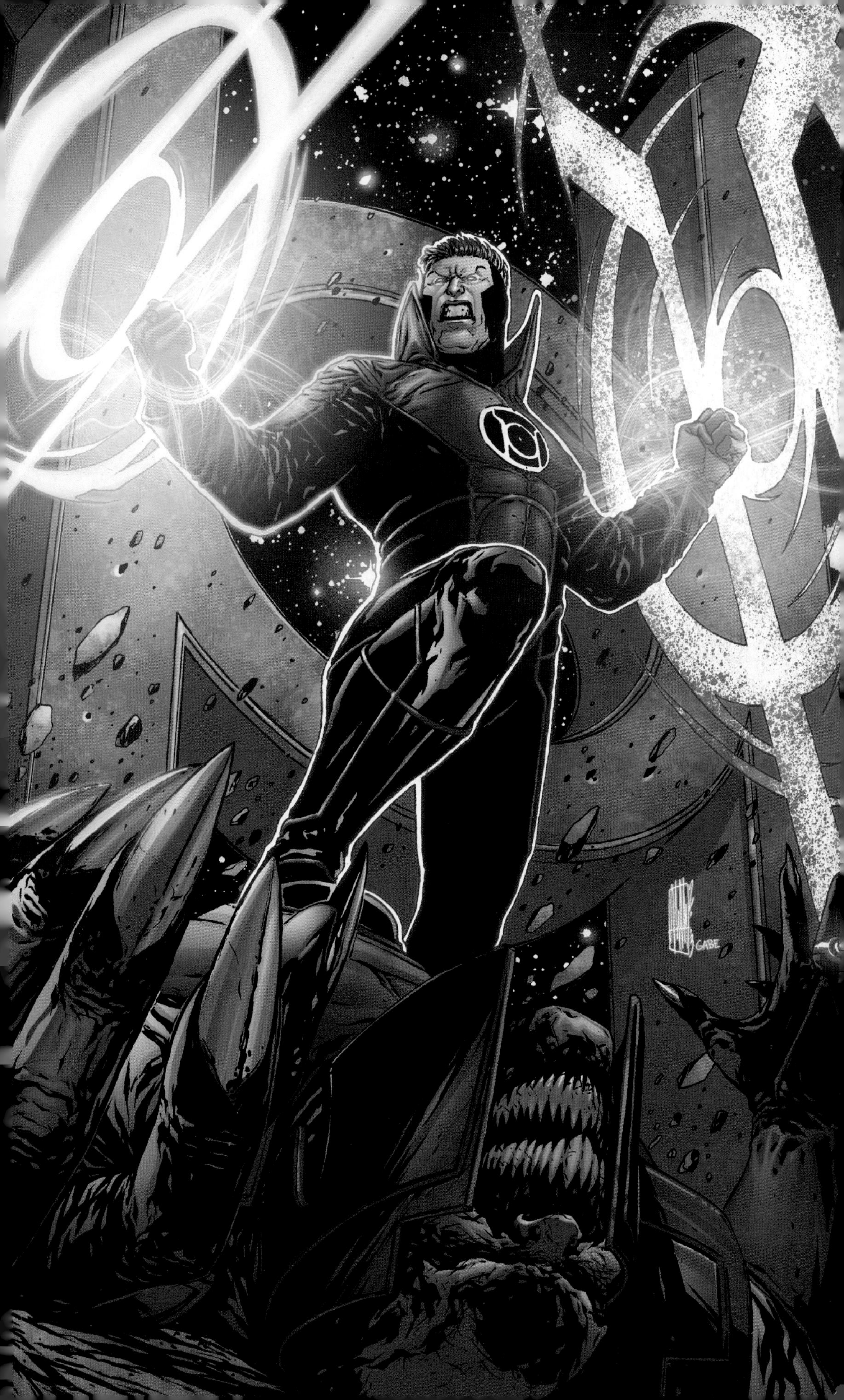
GABE

THE NEW BLOOD

CHARLES SOULE writer ALESSANDRO VITTI artist GABE ELTAEB colorist cover art by ALESSANDRO VITTI with GABE ELTAEB

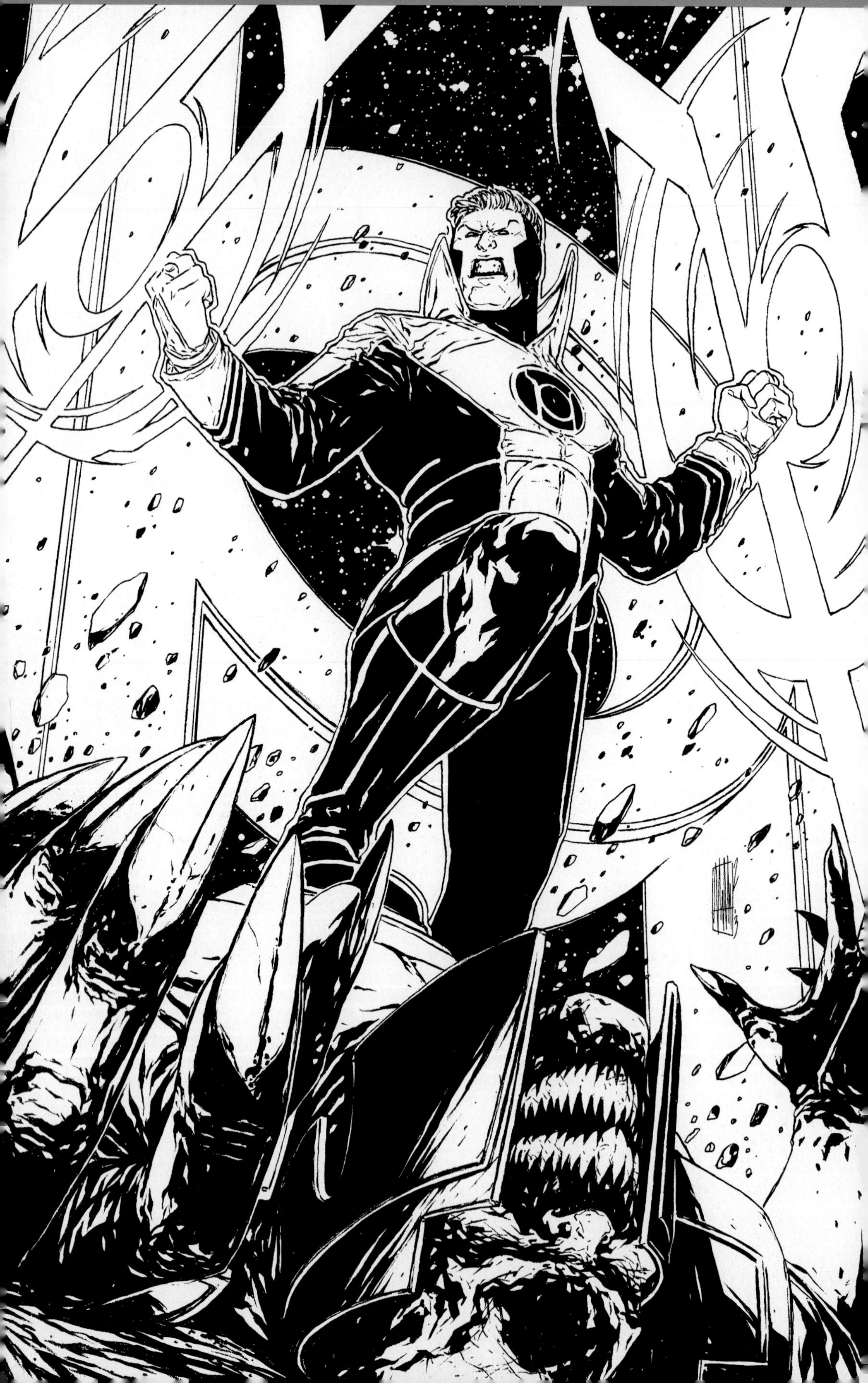

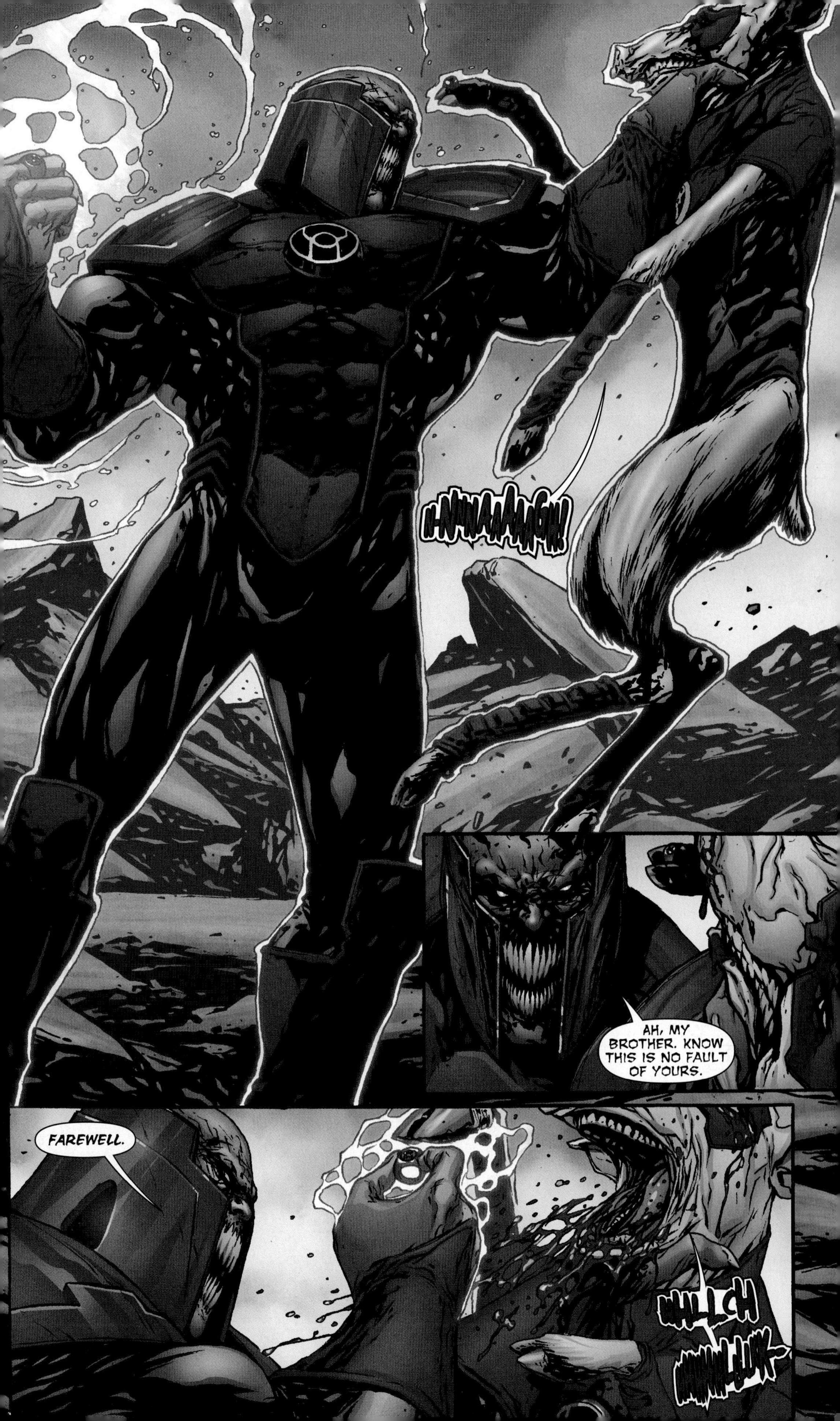

UHNNNAAAAAAGH!
AH, MY BROTHER. KNOW THIS IS NO FAULT OF YOURS.
FAREWELL.
WHLLCH
WHNNNLLUK

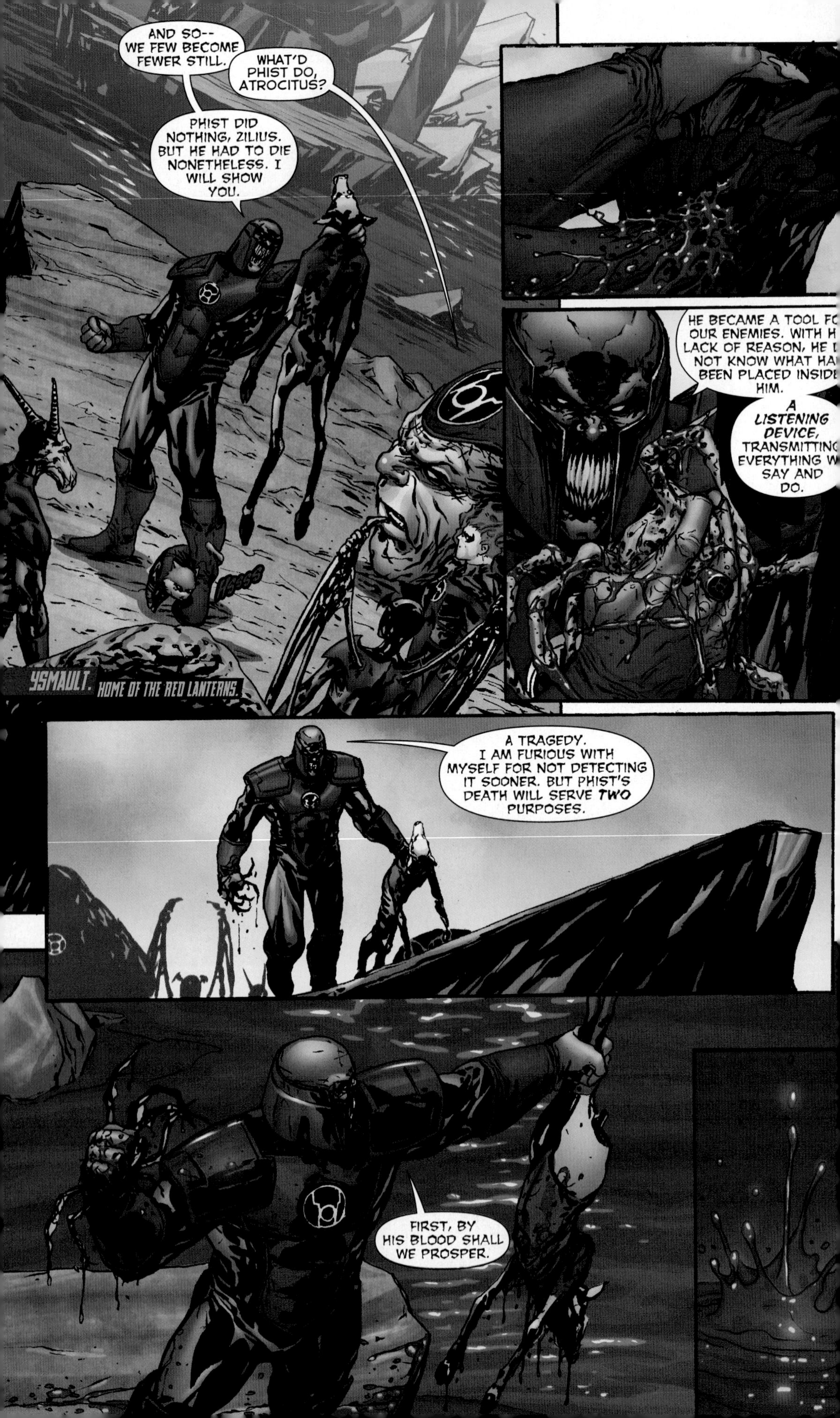
YSMAULT. HOME OF THE RED LANTERNS.
AND SO-- WE FEW BECOME FEWER STILL.
WHAT'D PHIST DO, ATROCITUS?
PHIST DID NOTHING, ZILIUS. BUT HE HAD TO DIE NONETHELESS. I WILL SHOW YOU.
HSSSS
HE BECAME A TOOL FO OUR ENEMIES. WITH H LACK OF REASON, HE D NOT KNOW WHAT HA BEEN PLACED INSIDE HIM.
A LISTENING DEVICE, TRANSMITTING EVERYTHING W SAY AND DO.
A TRAGEDY. I AM FURIOUS WITH MYSELF FOR NOT DETECTING IT SOONER. BUT PHIST'S DEATH WILL SERVE TWO PURPOSES.
FIRST, BY HIS BLOOD SHALL WE PROSPER.

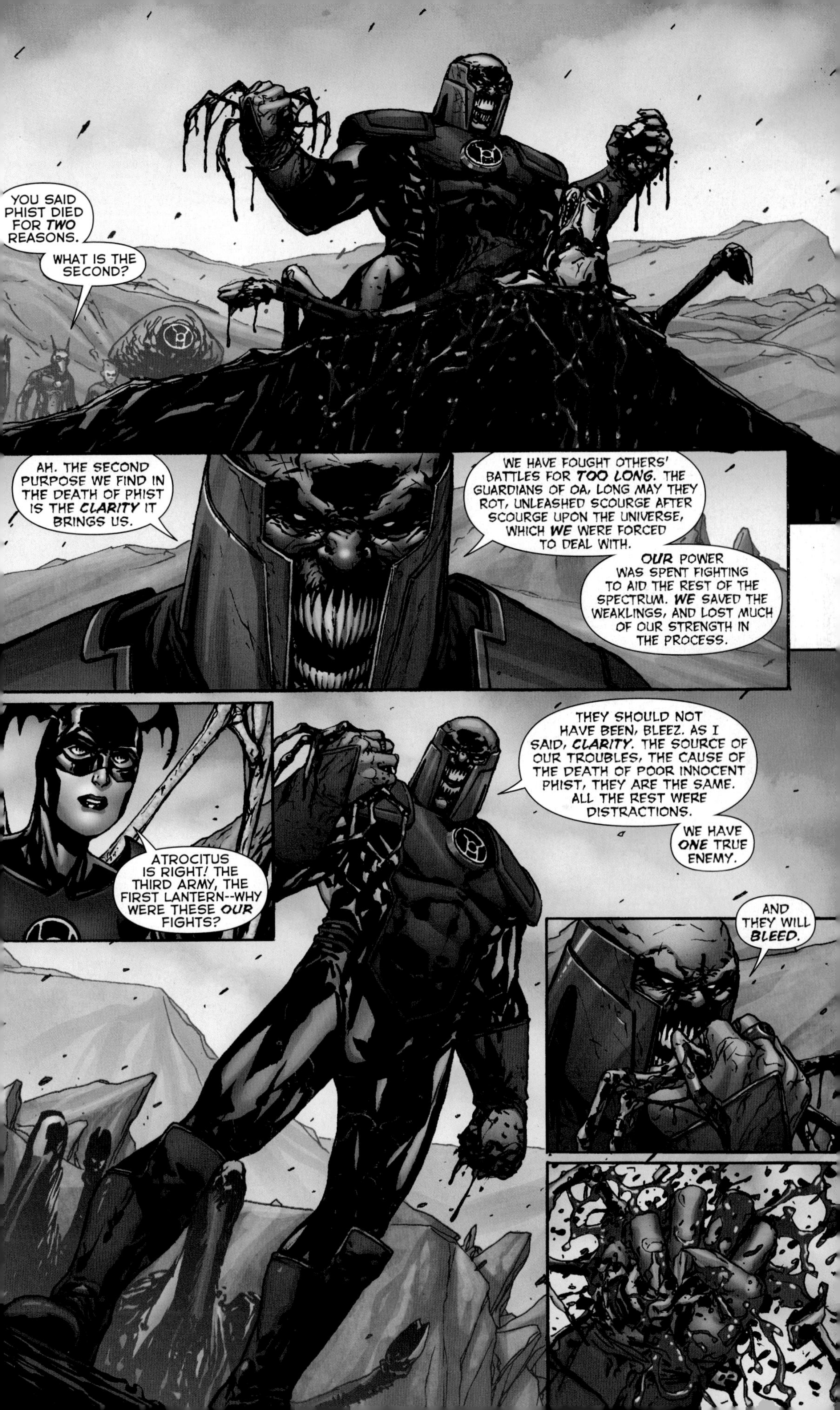
YOU SAID PHIST DIED FOR TWO REASONS.
WHAT IS THE SECOND?
AH. THE SECOND PURPOSE WE FIND IN THE DEATH OF PHIST IS THE CLARITY IT BRINGS US.
WE HAVE FOUGHT OTHERS' BATTLES FOR TOO LONG. THE GUARDIANS OF OA, LONG MAY THEY ROT, UNLEASHED SCOURGE AFTER SCOURGE UPON THE UNIVERSE, WHICH WE WERE FORCED TO DEAL WITH.
OUR POWER WAS SPENT FIGHTING TO AID THE REST OF THE SPECTRUM. WE SAVED THE WEAKLINGS, AND LOST MUCH OF OUR STRENGTH IN THE PROCESS.
ATROCITUS IS RIGHT! THE THIRD ARMY, THE FIRST LANTERN--WHY WERE THESE OUR FIGHTS?
THEY SHOULD NOT HAVE BEEN, BLEEZ. AS I SAID, CLARITY. THE SOURCE OF OUR TROUBLES, THE CAUSE OF THE DEATH OF POOR INNOCENT PHIST, THEY ARE THE SAME. ALL THE REST WERE DISTRACTIONS.
WE HAVE ONE TRUE ENEMY.
AND THEY WILL BLEED.

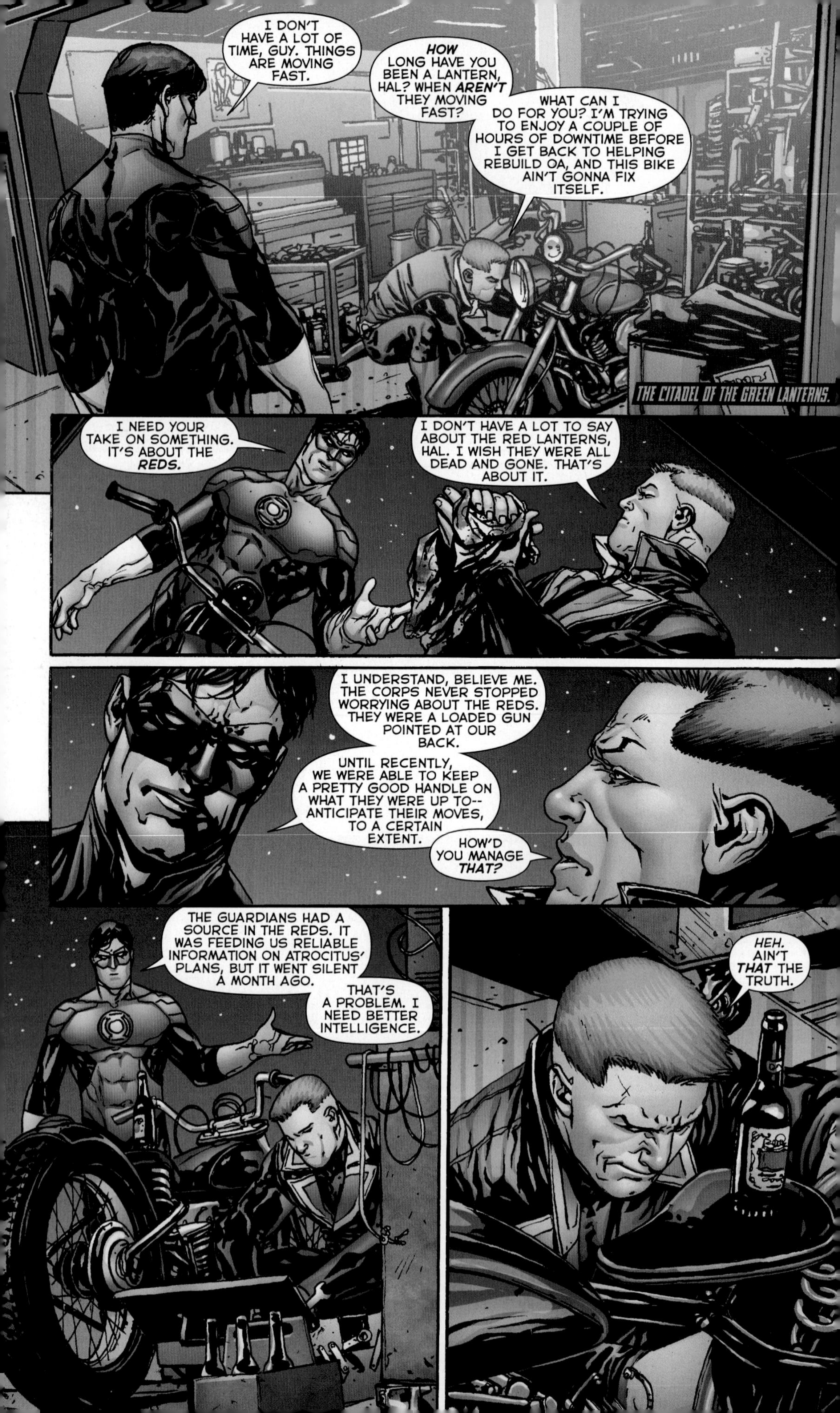
I DON'T HAVE A LOT OF TIME, GUY. THINGS ARE MOVING FAST.
HOW LONG HAVE YOU BEEN A LANTERN, HAL? WHEN AREN'T THEY MOVING FAST?
WHAT CAN I DO FOR YOU? I'M TRYING TO ENJOY A COUPLE OF HOURS OF DOWNTIME BEFORE I GET BACK TO HELPING REBUILD OA, AND THIS BIKE AIN'T GONNA FIX ITSELF.
THE CITADEL OF THE GREEN LANTERNS.
I NEED YOUR TAKE ON SOMETHING. IT'S ABOUT THE REDS.
I DON'T HAVE A LOT TO SAY ABOUT THE RED LANTERNS, HAL. I WISH THEY WERE ALL DEAD AND GONE. THAT'S ABOUT IT.
I UNDERSTAND, BELIEVE ME. THE CORPS NEVER STOPPED WORRYING ABOUT THE REDS. THEY WERE A LOADED GUN POINTED AT OUR BACK.
UNTIL RECENTLY, WE WERE ABLE TO KEEP A PRETTY GOOD HANDLE ON WHAT THEY WERE UP TO-- ANTICIPATE THEIR MOVES, TO A CERTAIN EXTENT.
HOW'D YOU MANAGE THAT?
THE GUARDIANS HAD A SOURCE IN THE REDS. IT WAS FEEDING US RELIABLE INFORMATION ON ATROCITUS' PLANS, BUT IT WENT SILENT A MONTH AGO.
THAT'S A PROBLEM. I NEED BETTER INTELLIGENCE.
HEH. AIN'T THAT THE TRUTH.

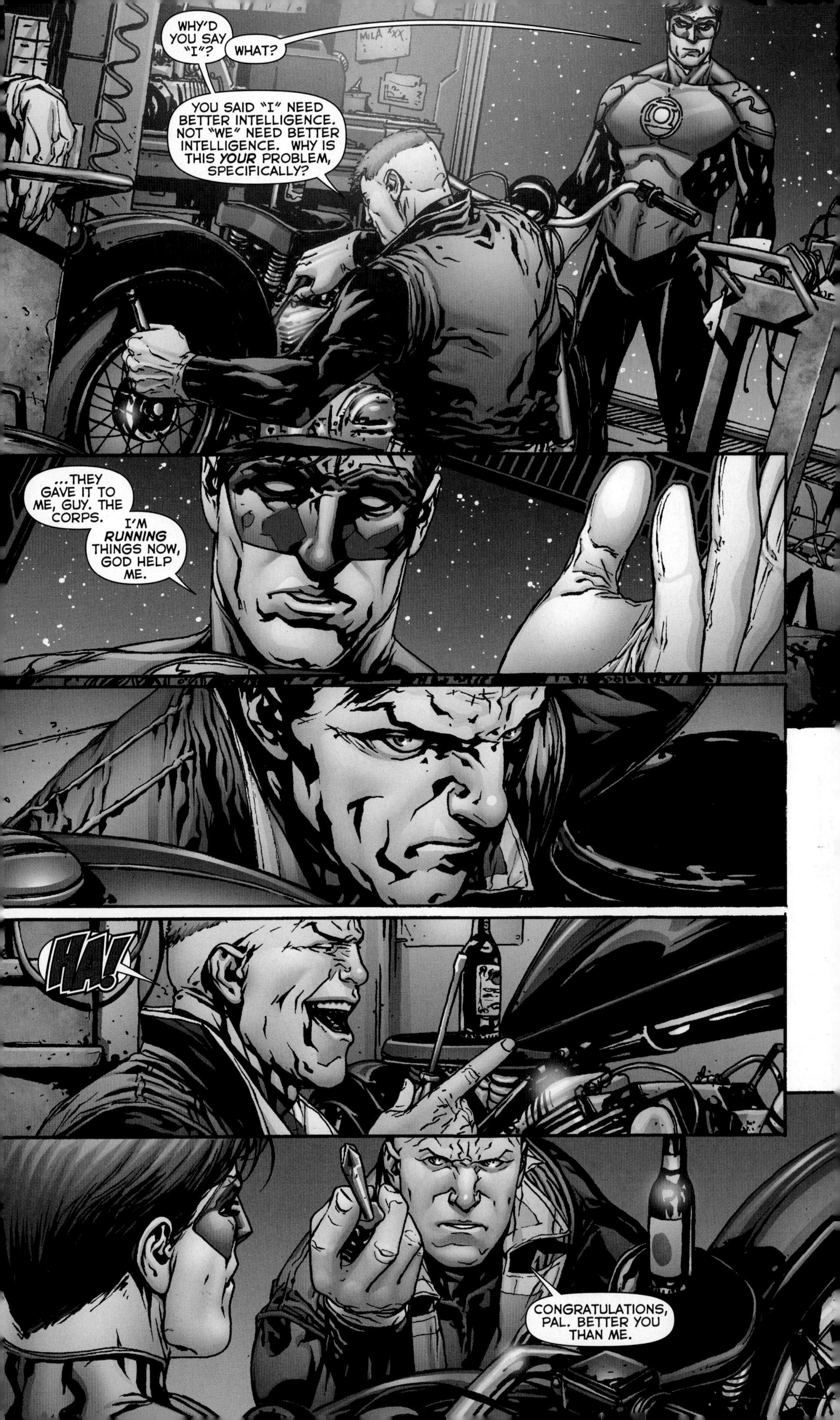
WHY'D YOU SAY "I"?
WHAT?
YOU SAID "I" NEED BETTER INTELLIGENCE. NOT "WE" NEED BETTER INTELLIGENCE. WHY IS THIS *YOUR* PROBLEM, SPECIFICALLY?
...THEY GAVE IT TO ME, GUY. THE CORPS.
I'M *RUNNING* THINGS NOW, GOD HELP ME.
HA!
CONGRATULATIONS, PAL. BETTER YOU THAN ME.

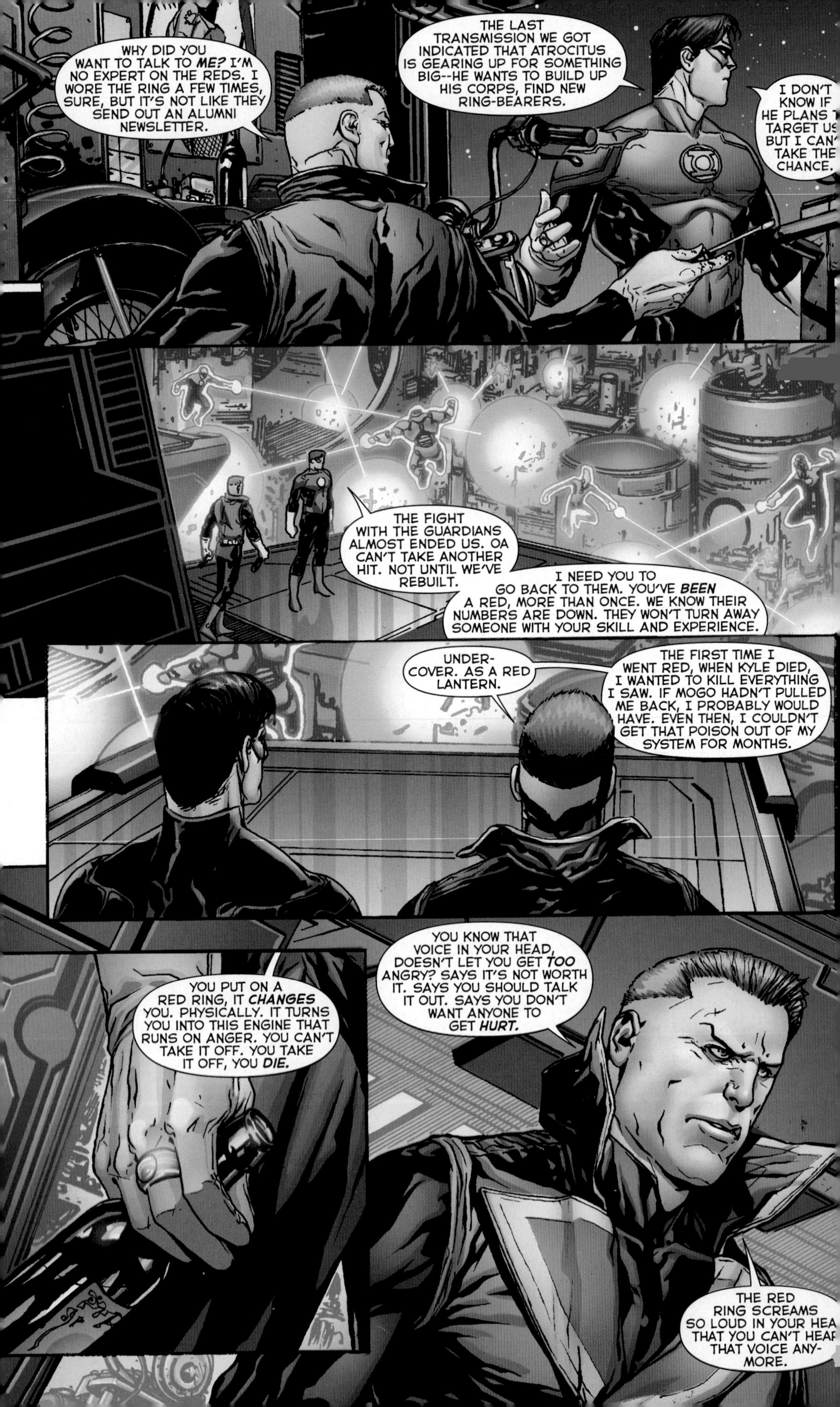
WHY DID YOU WANT TO TALK TO ME? I'M NO EXPERT ON THE REDS. I WORE THE RING A FEW TIMES, SURE, BUT IT'S NOT LIKE THEY SEND OUT AN ALUMNI NEWSLETTER.
THE LAST TRANSMISSION WE GOT INDICATED THAT ATROCITUS IS GEARING UP FOR SOMETHING BIG--HE WANTS TO BUILD UP HIS CORPS, FIND NEW RING-BEARERS.
I DON'T KNOW IF HE PLANS TO TARGET US BUT I CAN'T TAKE THE CHANCE.
THE FIGHT WITH THE GUARDIANS ALMOST ENDED US. OA CAN'T TAKE ANOTHER HIT. NOT UNTIL WE'VE REBUILT.
I NEED YOU TO GO BACK TO THEM. YOU'VE BEEN A RED, MORE THAN ONCE. WE KNOW THEIR NUMBERS ARE DOWN. THEY WON'T TURN AWAY SOMEONE WITH YOUR SKILL AND EXPERIENCE.
UNDER-COVER. AS A RED LANTERN.
THE FIRST TIME I WENT RED, WHEN KYLE DIED, I WANTED TO KILL EVERYTHING I SAW. IF MOGO HADN'T PULLED ME BACK, I PROBABLY WOULD HAVE. EVEN THEN, I COULDN'T GET THAT POISON OUT OF MY SYSTEM FOR MONTHS.
YOU PUT ON A RED RING, IT CHANGES YOU. PHYSICALLY. IT TURNS YOU INTO THIS ENGINE THAT RUNS ON ANGER. YOU CAN'T TAKE IT OFF. YOU TAKE IT OFF, YOU DIE.
YOU KNOW THAT VOICE IN YOUR HEAD, DOESN'T LET YOU GET TOO ANGRY? SAYS IT'S NOT WORTH IT. SAYS YOU SHOULD TALK IT OUT. SAYS YOU DON'T WANT ANYONE TO GET HURT.
THE RED RING SCREAMS SO LOUD IN YOUR HEAD THAT YOU CAN'T HEAR THAT VOICE ANY-MORE.

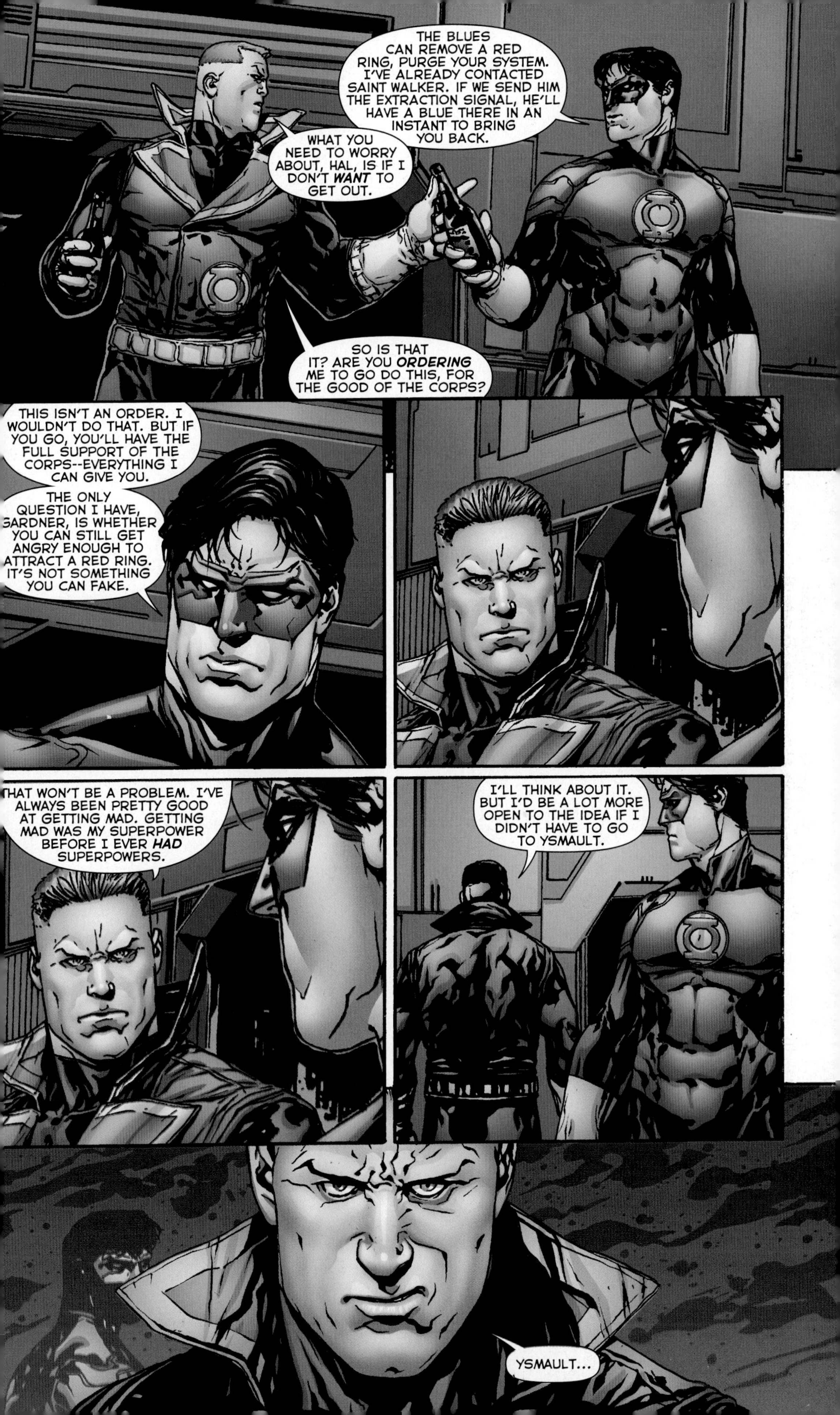
THE BLUES CAN REMOVE A RED RING, PURGE YOUR SYSTEM. I'VE ALREADY CONTACTED SAINT WALKER. IF WE SEND HIM THE EXTRACTION SIGNAL, HE'LL HAVE A BLUE THERE IN AN INSTANT TO BRING YOU BACK.
WHAT YOU NEED TO WORRY ABOUT, HAL, IS IF I DON'T *WANT* TO GET OUT.
SO IS THAT IT? ARE YOU *ORDERING* ME TO GO DO THIS, FOR THE GOOD OF THE CORPS?
THIS ISN'T AN ORDER. I WOULDN'T DO THAT. BUT IF YOU GO, YOU'LL HAVE THE FULL SUPPORT OF THE CORPS--EVERYTHING I CAN GIVE YOU.
THE ONLY QUESTION I HAVE, GARDNER, IS WHETHER YOU CAN STILL GET ANGRY ENOUGH TO ATTRACT A RED RING. IT'S NOT SOMETHING YOU CAN FAKE.
THAT WON'T BE A PROBLEM. I'VE ALWAYS BEEN PRETTY GOOD AT GETTING MAD. GETTING MAD WAS MY SUPERPOWER BEFORE I EVER *HAD* SUPERPOWERS.
I'LL THINK ABOUT IT. BUT I'D BE A LOT MORE OPEN TO THE IDEA IF I DIDN'T HAVE TO GO TO YSMAULT.
YSMAULT...

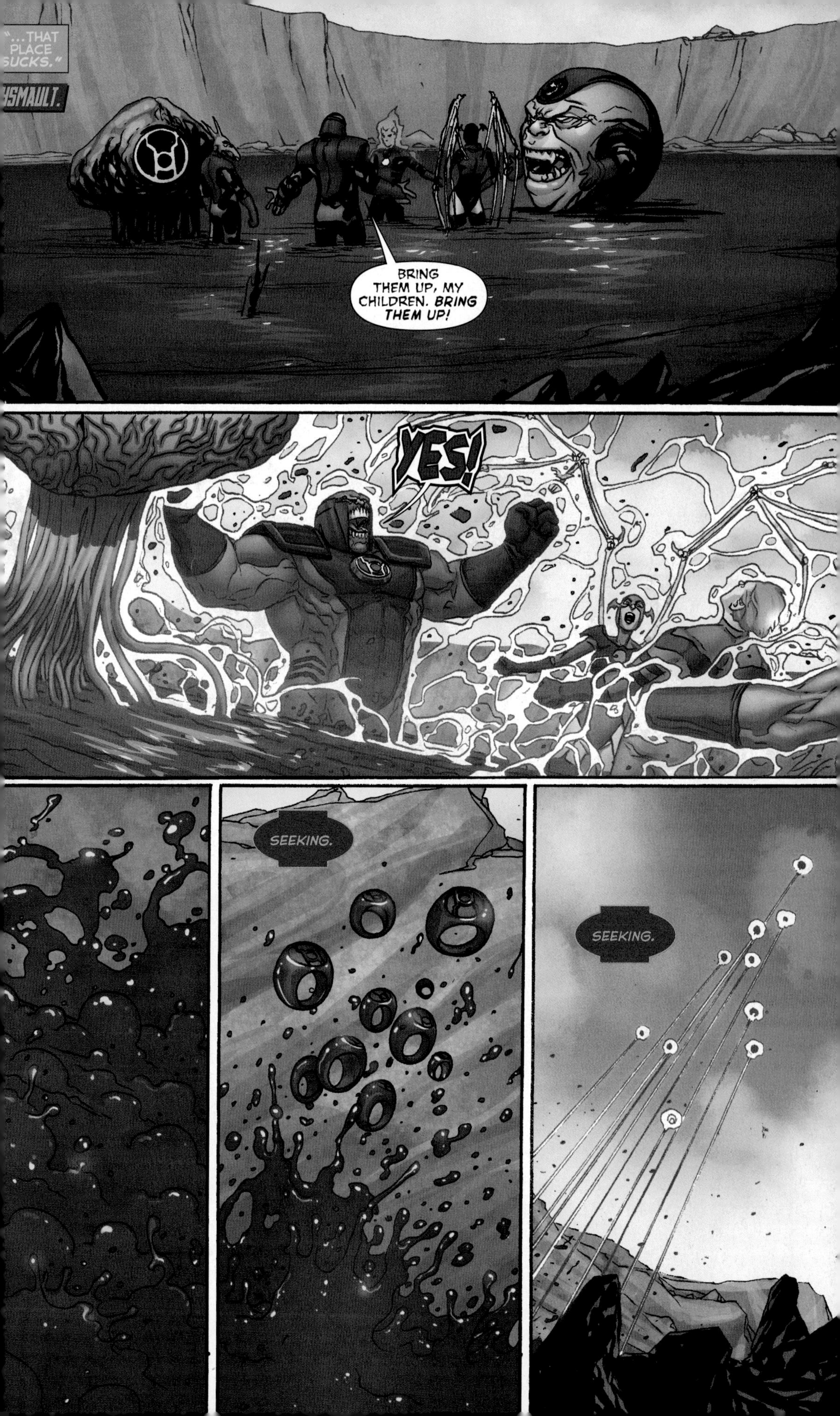
"...THAT PLACE SUCKS."
YSMAULT.
BRING THEM UP, MY CHILDREN. BRING THEM UP!
YES!
SEEKING.
SEEKING.

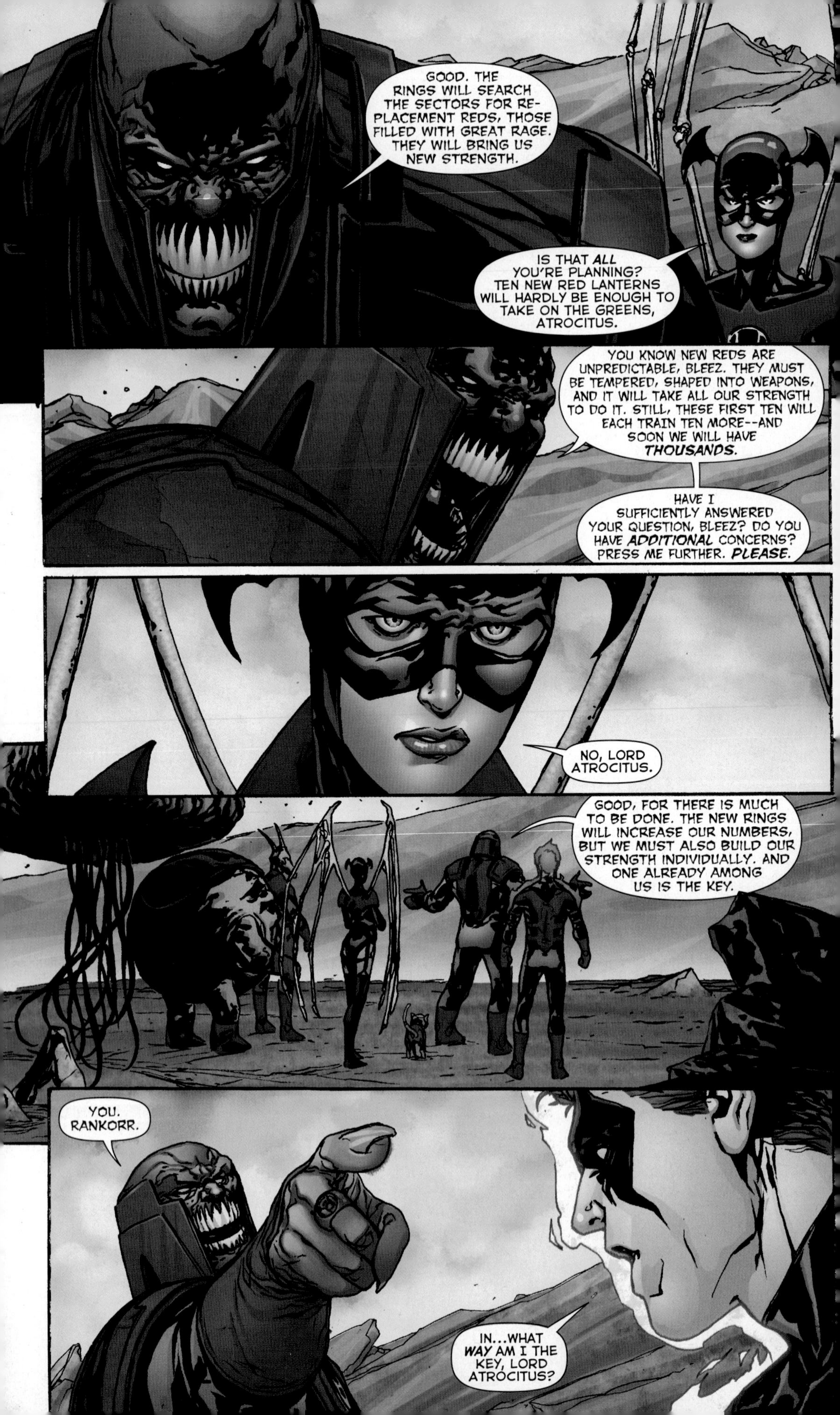
GOOD. THE RINGS WILL SEARCH THE SECTORS FOR RE-PLACEMENT REDS, THOSE FILLED WITH GREAT RAGE. THEY WILL BRING US NEW STRENGTH.
IS THAT *ALL* YOU'RE PLANNING? TEN NEW RED LANTERNS WILL HARDLY BE ENOUGH TO TAKE ON THE GREENS, ATROCITUS.
YOU KNOW NEW REDS ARE UNPREDICTABLE, BLEEZ. THEY MUST BE TEMPERED, SHAPED INTO WEAPONS, AND IT WILL TAKE ALL OUR STRENGTH TO DO IT. STILL, THESE FIRST TEN WILL EACH TRAIN TEN MORE--AND SOON WE WILL HAVE ***THOUSANDS.***
HAVE I SUFFICIENTLY ANSWERED YOUR QUESTION, BLEEZ? DO YOU HAVE ***ADDITIONAL*** CONCERNS? PRESS ME FURTHER. ***PLEASE.***
NO, LORD ATROCITUS.
GOOD, FOR THERE IS MUCH TO BE DONE. THE NEW RINGS WILL INCREASE OUR NUMBERS, BUT WE MUST ALSO BUILD OUR STRENGTH INDIVIDUALLY. AND ONE ALREADY AMONG US IS THE KEY.
YOU. RANKORR.
IN...WHAT ***WAY*** AM I THE KEY, LORD ATROCITUS?

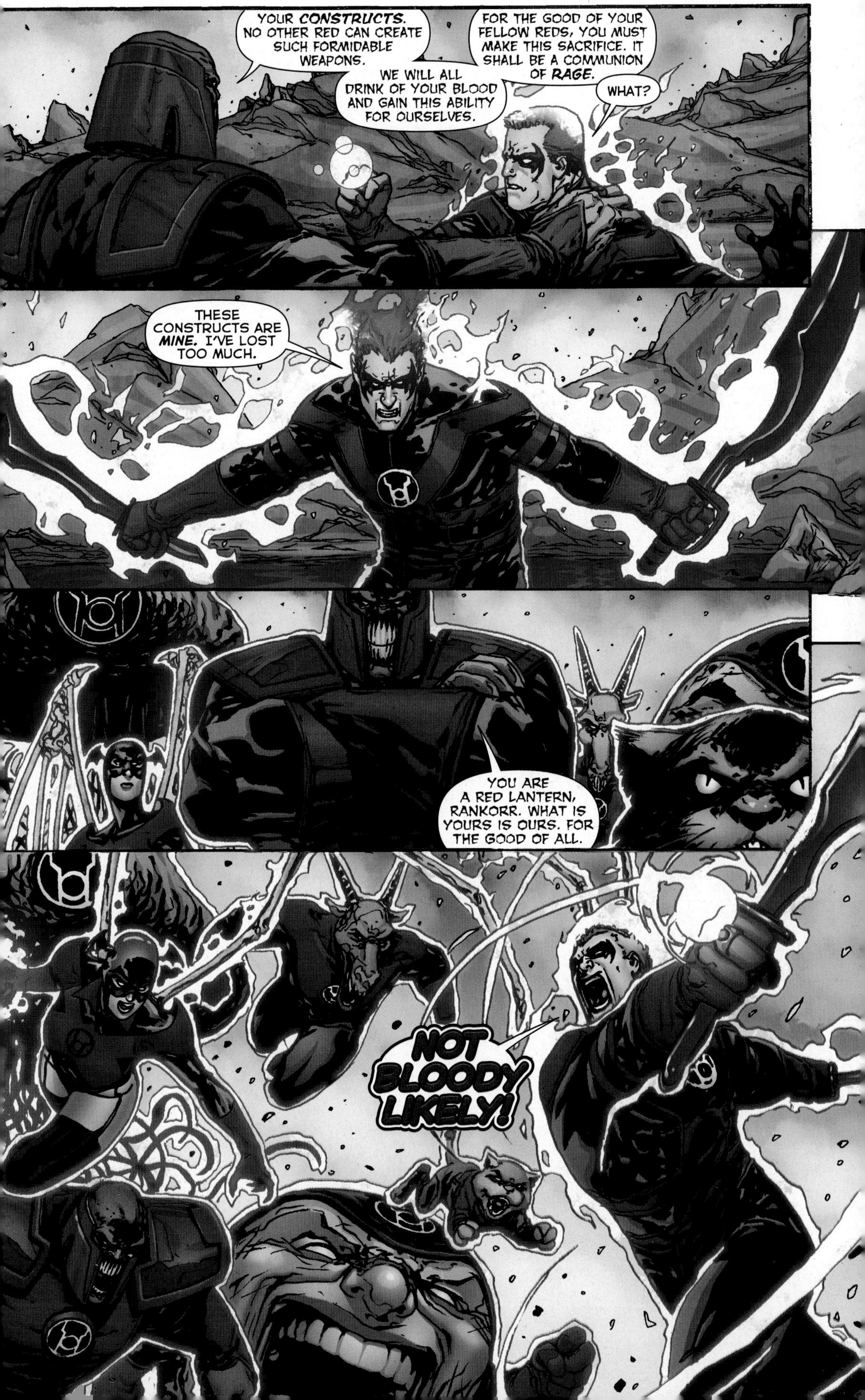
YOUR CONSTRUCTS. NO OTHER RED CAN CREATE SUCH FORMIDABLE WEAPONS.
WE WILL ALL DRINK OF YOUR BLOOD AND GAIN THIS ABILITY FOR OURSELVES.
FOR THE GOOD OF YOUR FELLOW REDS, YOU MUST MAKE THIS SACRIFICE. IT SHALL BE A COMMUNION OF RAGE.
WHAT?
THESE CONSTRUCTS ARE MINE. I'VE LOST TOO MUCH.
YOU ARE A RED LANTERN, RANKORR. WHAT IS YOURS IS OURS. FOR THE GOOD OF ALL.
NOT BLOODY LIKELY!

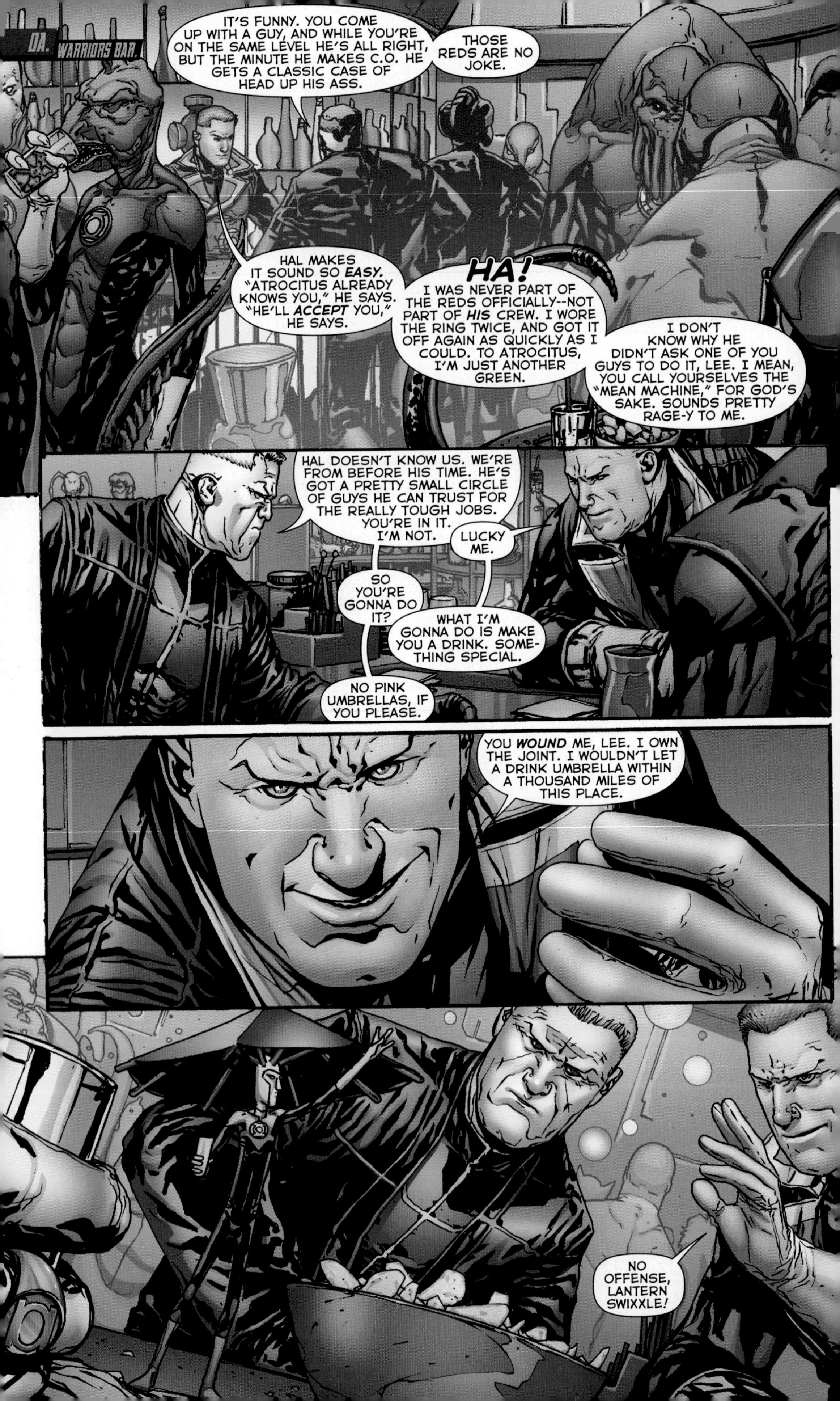
OA. WARRIORS BAR.
IT'S FUNNY. YOU COME UP WITH A GUY, AND WHILE YOU'RE ON THE SAME LEVEL HE'S ALL RIGHT, BUT THE MINUTE HE MAKES C.O. HE GETS A CLASSIC CASE OF HEAD UP HIS ASS.
THOSE REDS ARE NO JOKE.
HAL MAKES IT SOUND SO EASY. "ATROCITUS ALREADY KNOWS YOU," HE SAYS. "HE'LL ACCEPT YOU," HE SAYS.
HA! I WAS NEVER PART OF THE REDS OFFICIALLY--NOT PART OF HIS CREW. I WORE THE RING TWICE, AND GOT IT OFF AGAIN AS QUICKLY AS I COULD. TO ATROCITUS, I'M JUST ANOTHER GREEN.
I DON'T KNOW WHY HE DIDN'T ASK ONE OF YOU GUYS TO DO IT, LEE. I MEAN, YOU CALL YOURSELVES THE "MEAN MACHINE," FOR GOD'S SAKE. SOUNDS PRETTY RAGE-Y TO ME.
HAL DOESN'T KNOW US. WE'RE FROM BEFORE HIS TIME. HE'S GOT A PRETTY SMALL CIRCLE OF GUYS HE CAN TRUST FOR THE REALLY TOUGH JOBS. YOU'RE IN IT. I'M NOT.
LUCKY ME.
SO YOU'RE GONNA DO IT?
WHAT I'M GONNA DO IS MAKE YOU A DRINK. SOMETHING SPECIAL.
NO PINK UMBRELLAS, IF YOU PLEASE.
YOU WOUND ME, LEE. I OWN THE JOINT. I WOULDN'T LET A DRINK UMBRELLA WITHIN A THOUSAND MILES OF THIS PLACE.
NO OFFENSE, LANTERN SWIXXLE!

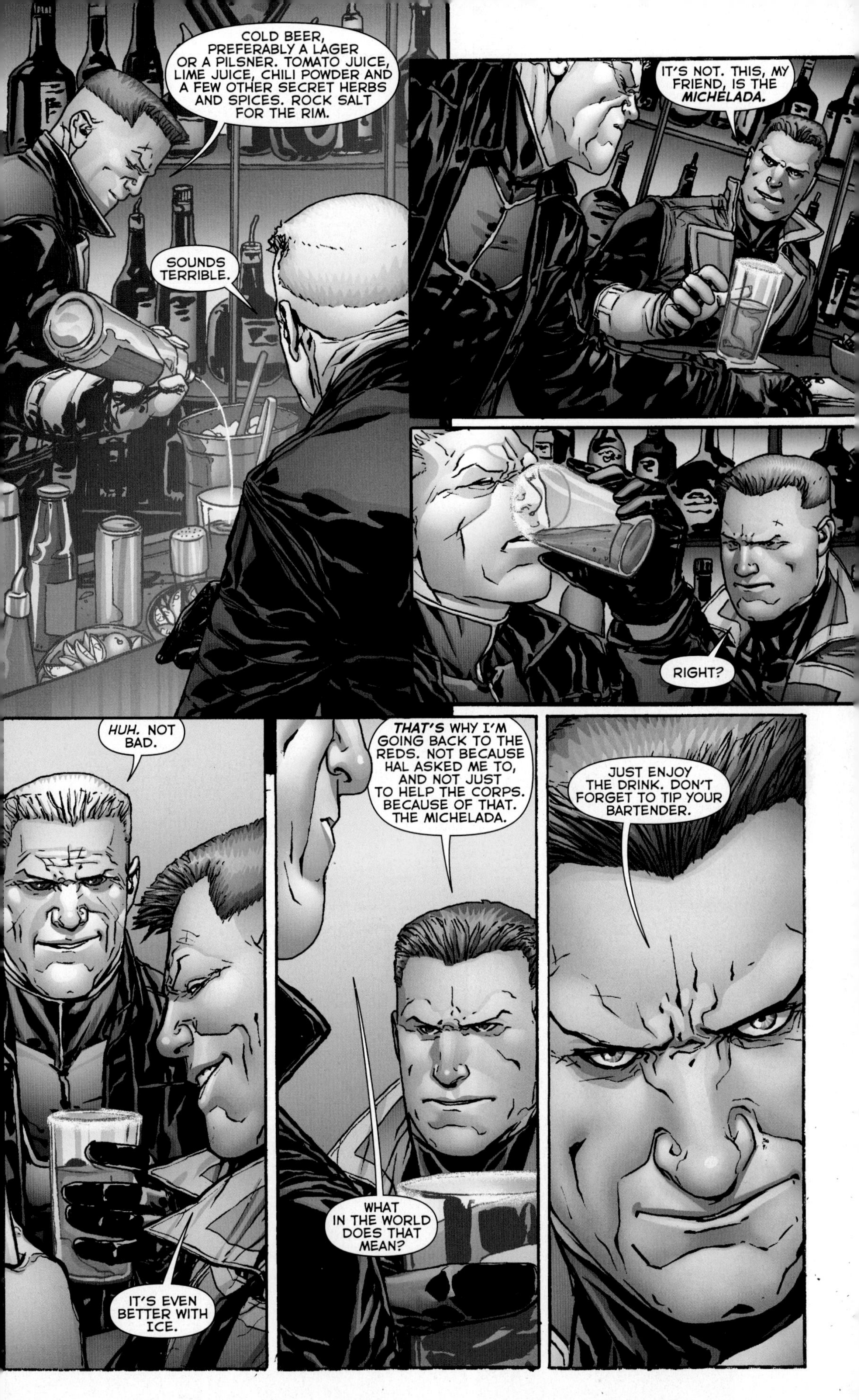
COLD BEER, PREFERABLY A LAGER OR A PILSNER. TOMATO JUICE, LIME JUICE, CHILI POWDER AND A FEW OTHER SECRET HERBS AND SPICES. ROCK SALT FOR THE RIM.
SOUNDS TERRIBLE.
IT'S NOT. THIS, MY FRIEND, IS THE *MICHELADA.*
RIGHT?
HUH. NOT BAD.
IT'S EVEN BETTER WITH ICE.
THAT'S WHY I'M GOING BACK TO THE REDS. NOT BECAUSE HAL ASKED ME TO, AND NOT JUST TO HELP THE CORPS. BECAUSE OF THAT. THE MICHELADA.
WHAT IN THE WORLD DOES THAT MEAN?
JUST ENJOY THE DRINK. DON'T FORGET TO TIP YOUR BARTENDER.

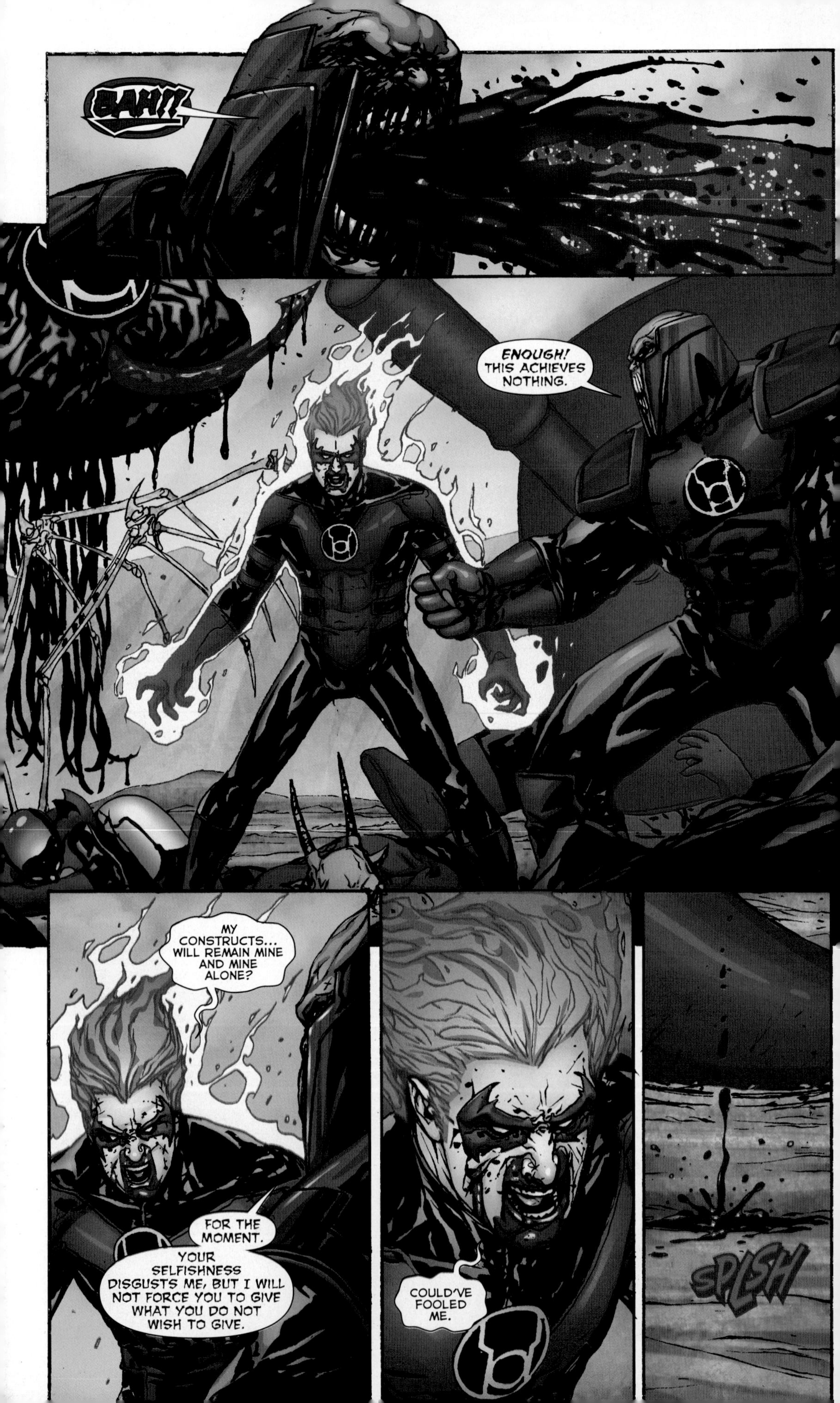
BAH!!
ENOUGH! THIS ACHIEVES NOTHING.
MY CONSTRUCTS... WILL REMAIN MINE AND MINE ALONE?
FOR THE MOMENT.
YOUR SELFISHNESS DISGUSTS ME, BUT I WILL NOT FORCE YOU TO GIVE WHAT YOU DO NOT WISH TO GIVE.
COULD'VE FOOLED ME.
SPLSH

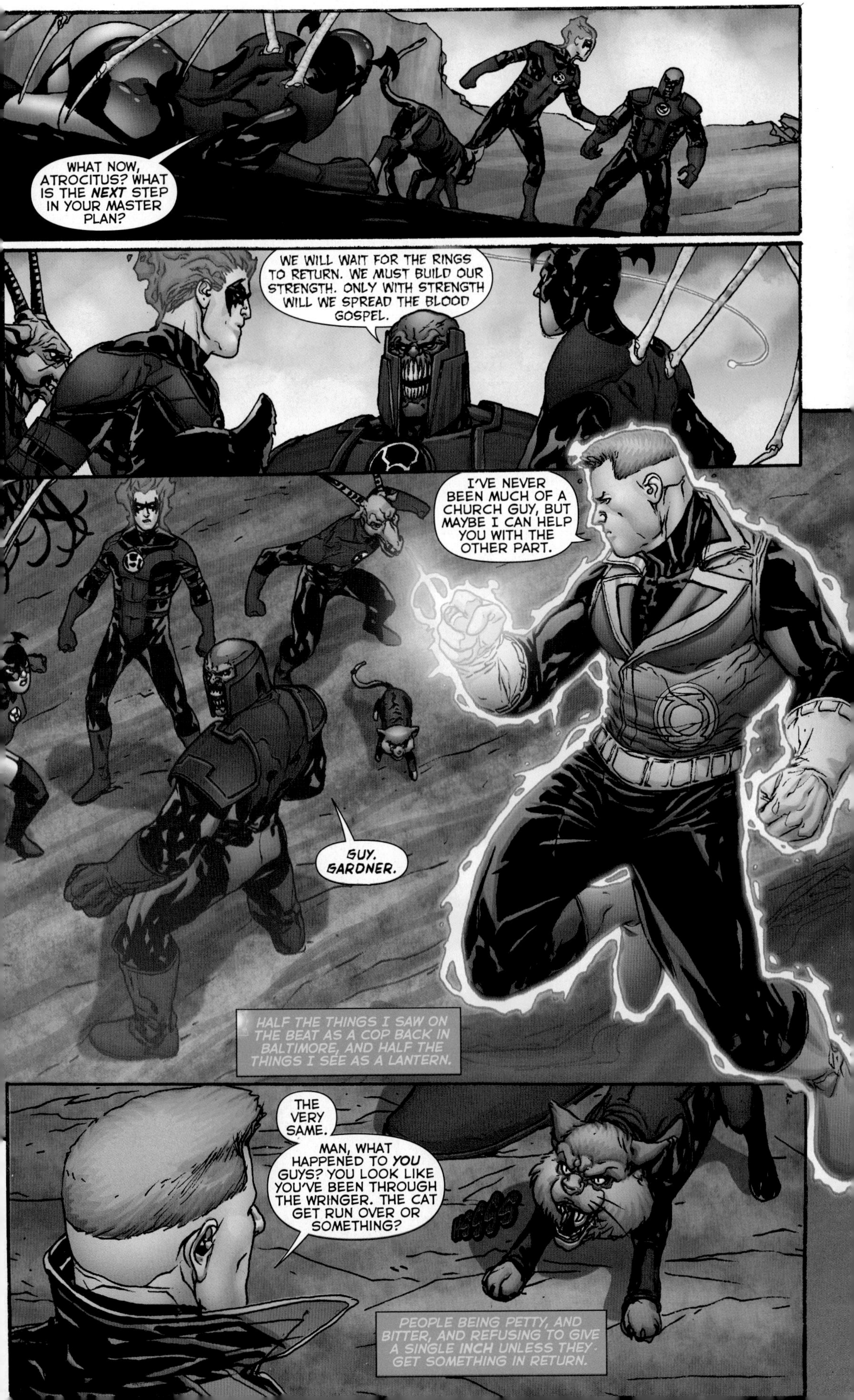
WHAT NOW, ATROCITUS? WHAT IS THE *NEXT* STEP IN YOUR MASTER PLAN?
WE WILL WAIT FOR THE RINGS TO RETURN. WE MUST BUILD OUR STRENGTH. ONLY WITH STRENGTH WILL WE SPREAD THE BLOOD GOSPEL.
I'VE NEVER BEEN MUCH OF A CHURCH GUY, BUT MAYBE I CAN HELP YOU WITH THE OTHER PART.
HALF THE THINGS I SAW ON THE BEAT AS A COP BACK IN BALTIMORE, AND HALF THE THINGS I SEE AS A LANTERN.
GUY. GARDNER.
THE VERY SAME.
MAN, WHAT HAPPENED TO *YOU* GUYS? YOU LOOK LIKE YOU'VE BEEN THROUGH THE WRINGER. THE CAT GET RUN OVER OR SOMETHING?
PEOPLE BEING PETTY, AND BITTER, AND REFUSING TO GIVE A SINGLE INCH UNLESS THEY GET SOMETHING IN RETURN.

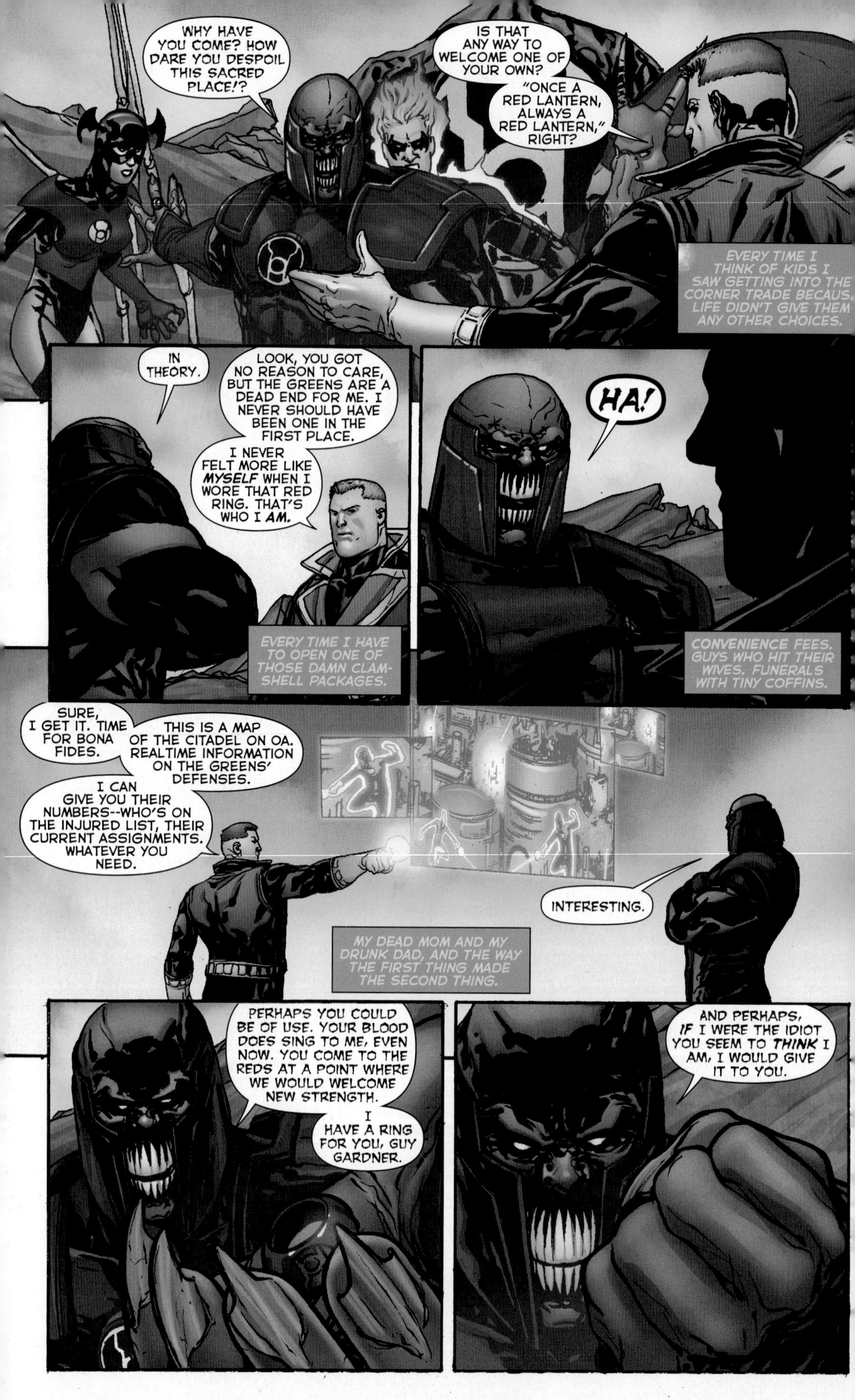

WHY HAVE YOU COME? HOW DARE YOU DESPOIL THIS SACRED PLACE!?
IS THAT ANY WAY TO WELCOME ONE OF YOUR OWN?
"ONCE A RED LANTERN, ALWAYS A RED LANTERN," RIGHT?
EVERY TIME I THINK OF KIDS I SAW GETTING INTO THE CORNER TRADE BECAUS LIFE DIDN'T GIVE THEM ANY OTHER CHOICES.
IN THEORY.
LOOK, YOU GOT NO REASON TO CARE, BUT THE GREENS ARE A DEAD END FOR ME. I NEVER SHOULD HAVE BEEN ONE IN THE FIRST PLACE.
I NEVER FELT MORE LIKE MYSELF WHEN I WORE THAT RED RING. THAT'S WHO I AM.
EVERY TIME I HAVE TO OPEN ONE OF THOSE DAMN CLAM-SHELL PACKAGES.
HA!
CONVENIENCE FEES. GUYS WHO HIT THEIR WIVES. FUNERALS WITH TINY COFFINS.
SURE, I GET IT. TIME FOR BONA FIDES.
THIS IS A MAP OF THE CITADEL ON OA. REALTIME INFORMATION ON THE GREENS' DEFENSES.
I CAN GIVE YOU THEIR NUMBERS--WHO'S ON THE INJURED LIST, THEIR CURRENT ASSIGNMENTS. WHATEVER YOU NEED.
INTERESTING.
MY DEAD MOM AND MY DRUNK DAD, AND THE WAY THE FIRST THING MADE THE SECOND THING.
PERHAPS YOU COULD BE OF USE. YOUR BLOOD DOES SING TO ME, EVEN NOW. YOU COME TO THE REDS AT A POINT WHERE WE WOULD WELCOME NEW STRENGTH.
I HAVE A RING FOR YOU, GUY GARDNER.
AND PERHAPS, IF I WERE THE IDIOT YOU SEEM TO THINK I AM, I WOULD GIVE IT TO YOU.

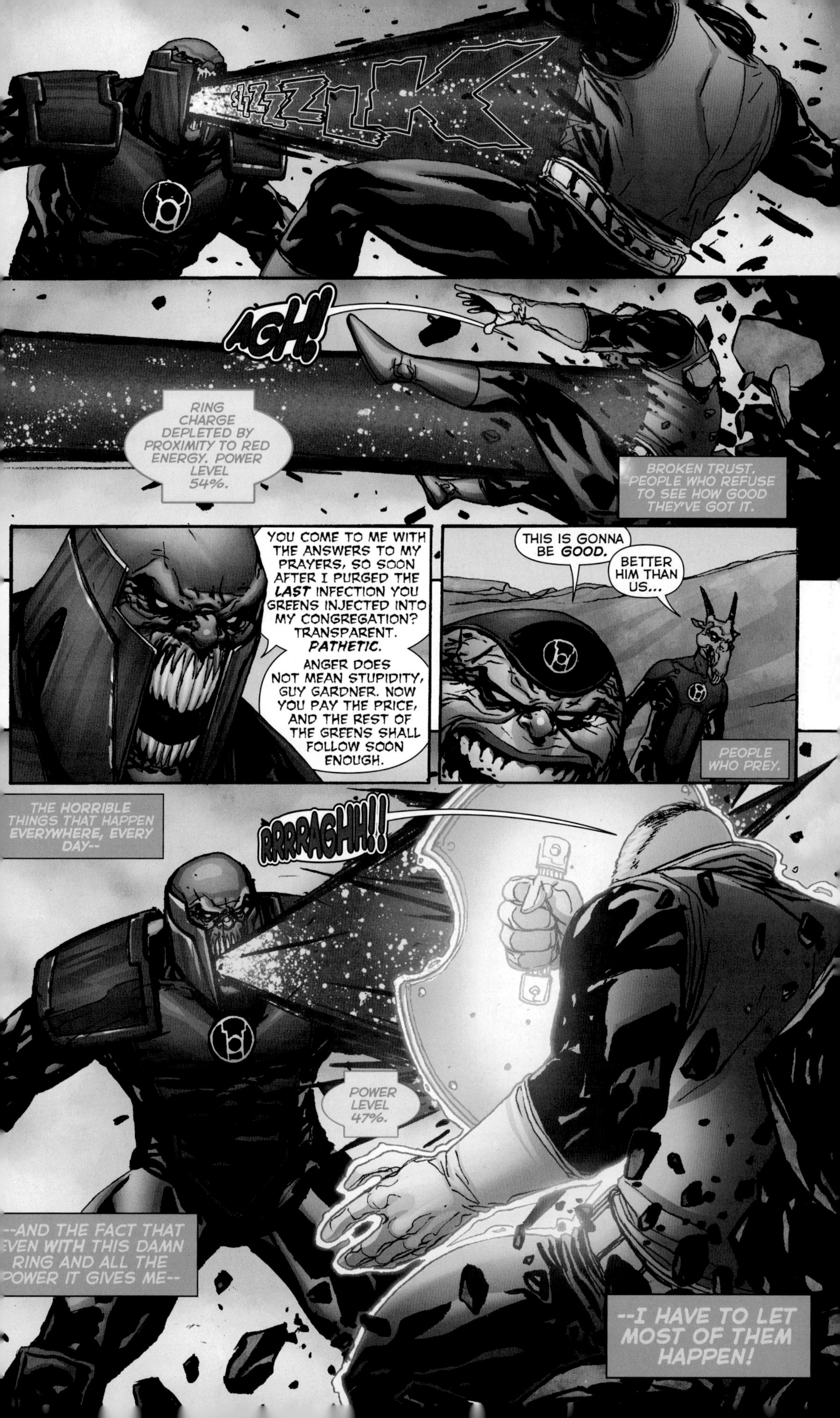
AGH!
RING CHARGE DEPLETED BY PROXIMITY TO RED ENERGY. POWER LEVEL 54%.
BROKEN TRUST. PEOPLE WHO REFUSE TO SEE HOW GOOD THEY'VE GOT IT.
YOU COME TO ME WITH THE ANSWERS TO MY PRAYERS, SO SOON AFTER I PURGED THE *LAST* INFECTION YOU GREENS INJECTED INTO MY CONGREGATION? TRANSPARENT. ***PATHETIC.***
ANGER DOES NOT MEAN STUPIDITY, GUY GARDNER. NOW YOU PAY THE PRICE, AND THE REST OF THE GREENS SHALL FOLLOW SOON ENOUGH.
THIS IS GONNA BE **GOOD.**
BETTER HIM THAN US...
PEOPLE WHO PREY.
THE HORRIBLE THINGS THAT HAPPEN EVERYWHERE, EVERY DAY--
RRRRAGHH!!
POWER LEVEL 47%.
--AND THE FACT THAT EVEN **WITH** THIS DAMN RING AND ALL THE POWER IT GIVES ME--
--I HAVE TO LET MOST OF THEM HAPPEN!

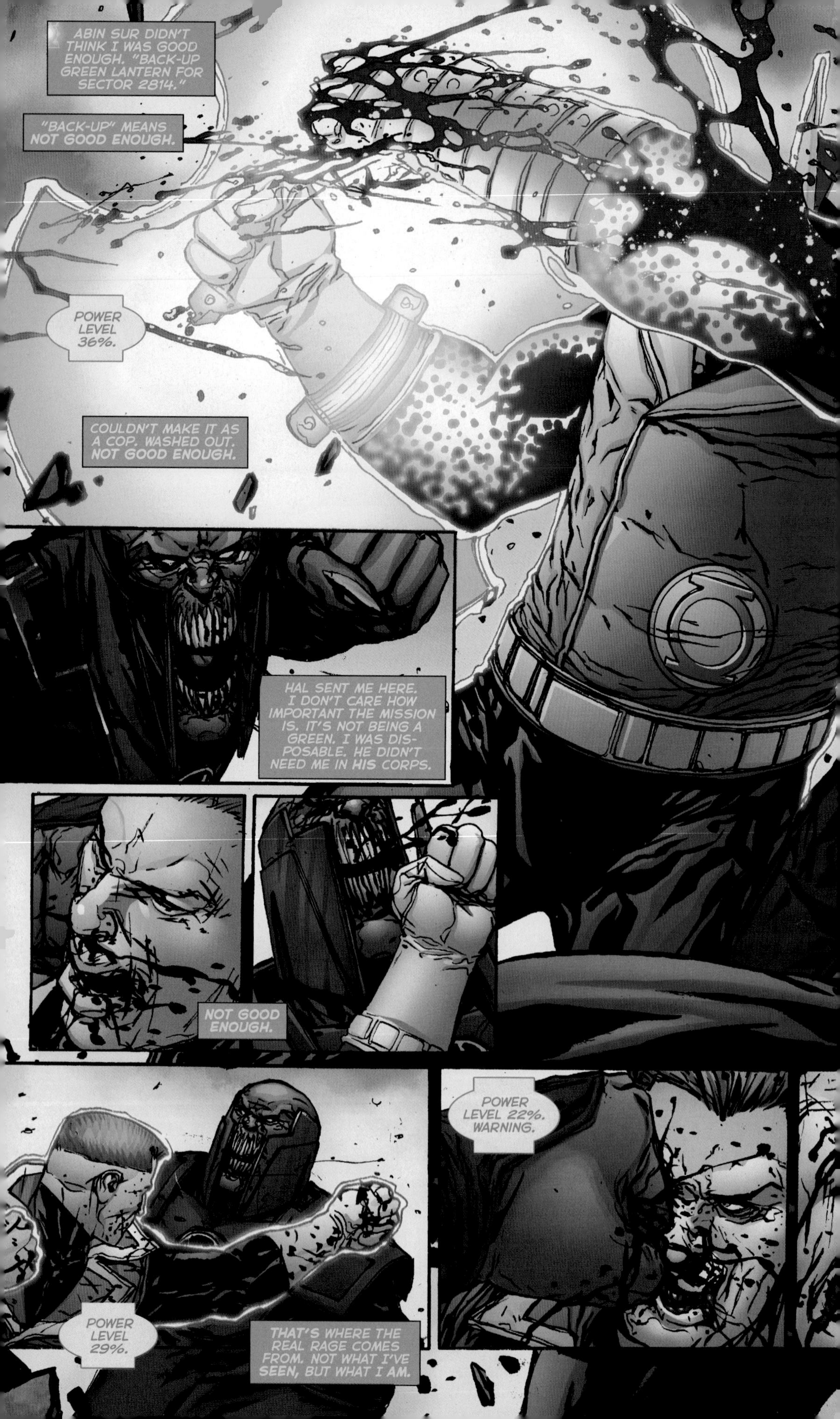

ABIN SUR DIDN'T THINK I WAS GOOD ENOUGH. "BACK-UP GREEN LANTERN FOR SECTOR 2814."
"BACK-UP" MEANS NOT GOOD ENOUGH.
POWER LEVEL 36%.
COULDN'T MAKE IT AS A COP. WASHED OUT. NOT GOOD ENOUGH.
HAL SENT ME HERE. I DON'T CARE HOW IMPORTANT THE MISSION IS. IT'S NOT BEING A GREEN. I WAS DISPOSABLE. HE DIDN'T NEED ME IN HIS CORPS.
NOT GOOD ENOUGH.
POWER LEVEL 29%.
THAT'S WHERE THE REAL RAGE COMES FROM. NOT WHAT I'VE SEEN, BUT WHAT I AM.
POWER LEVEL 22%. WARNING.

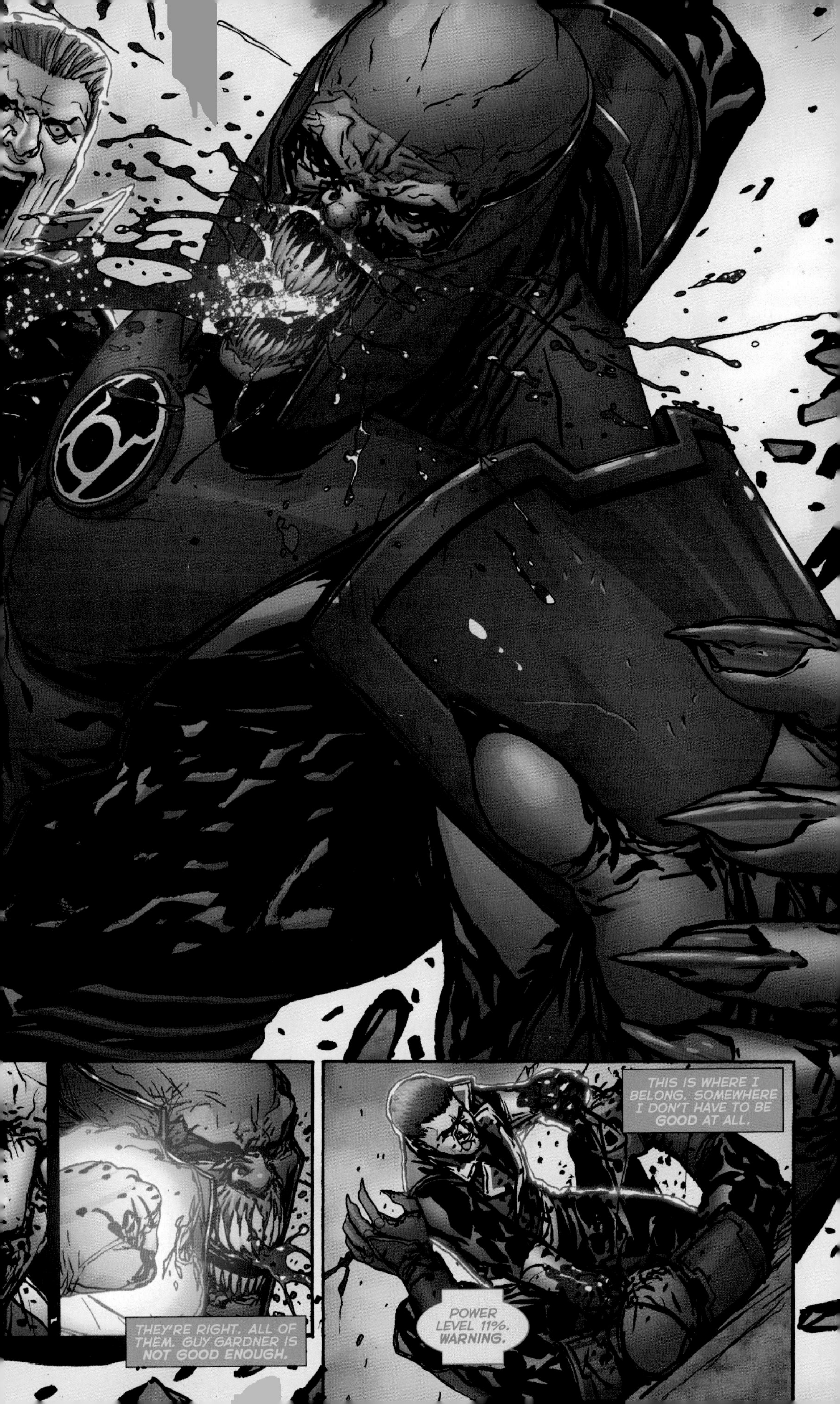
THEY'RE RIGHT. ALL OF THEM. GUY GARDNER IS NOT GOOD ENOUGH.
THIS IS WHERE I BELONG. SOMEWHERE I DON'T HAVE TO BE GOOD AT ALL.
POWER LEVEL 11%. WARNING.

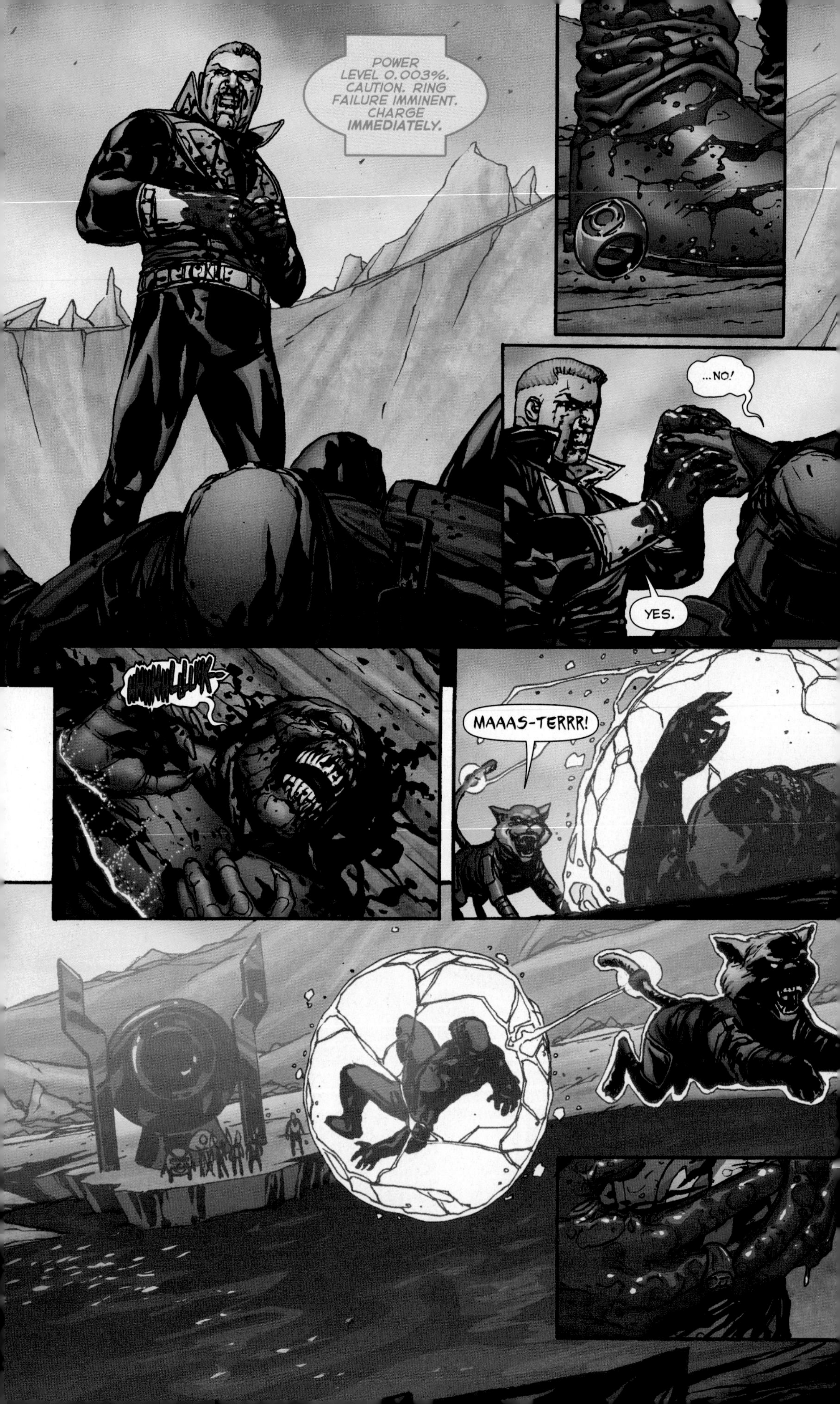
POWER LEVEL 0.003%. CAUTION. RING FAILURE IMMINENT. CHARGE IMMEDIATELY.
...NO!
YES.
MAAAS-TERRR!

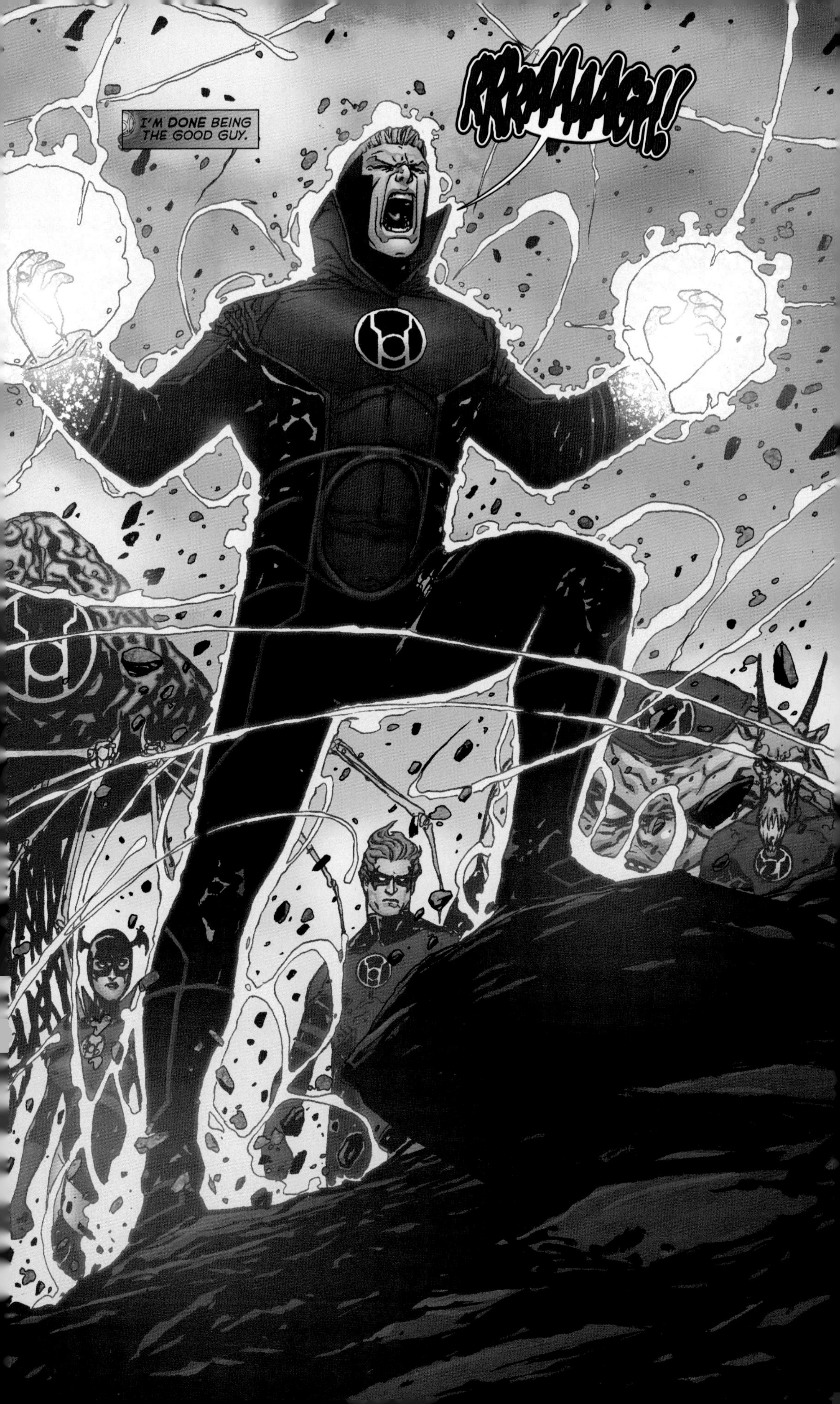

I'M DONE BEING THE GOOD GUY.
RRRAAAAAGH!!

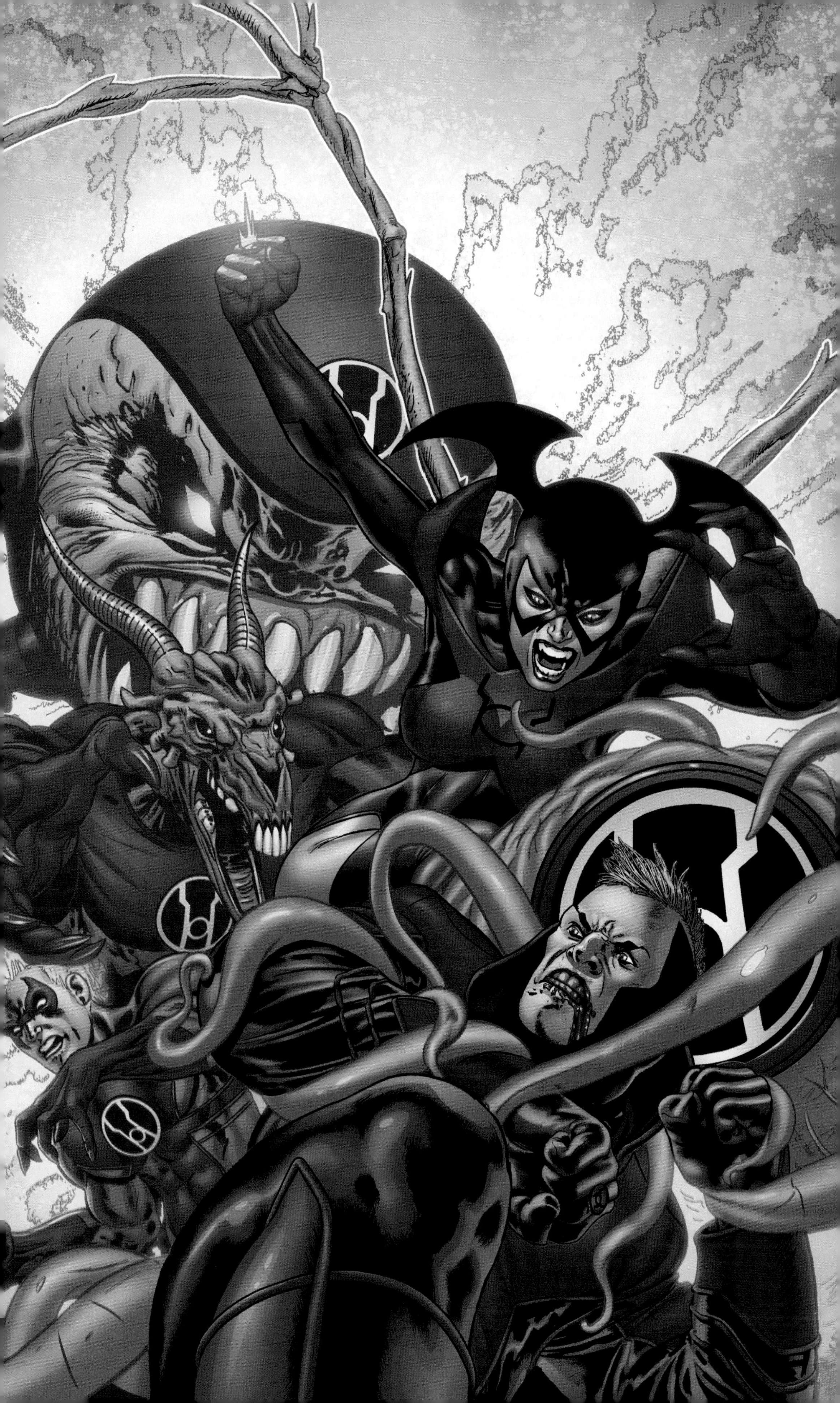

THE KING IS RED

CHARLES SOULE writer ALESSANDRO VITTI artist GABE ELTAEB colorist cover art by STEVE PUGH with GABE ELTAEB

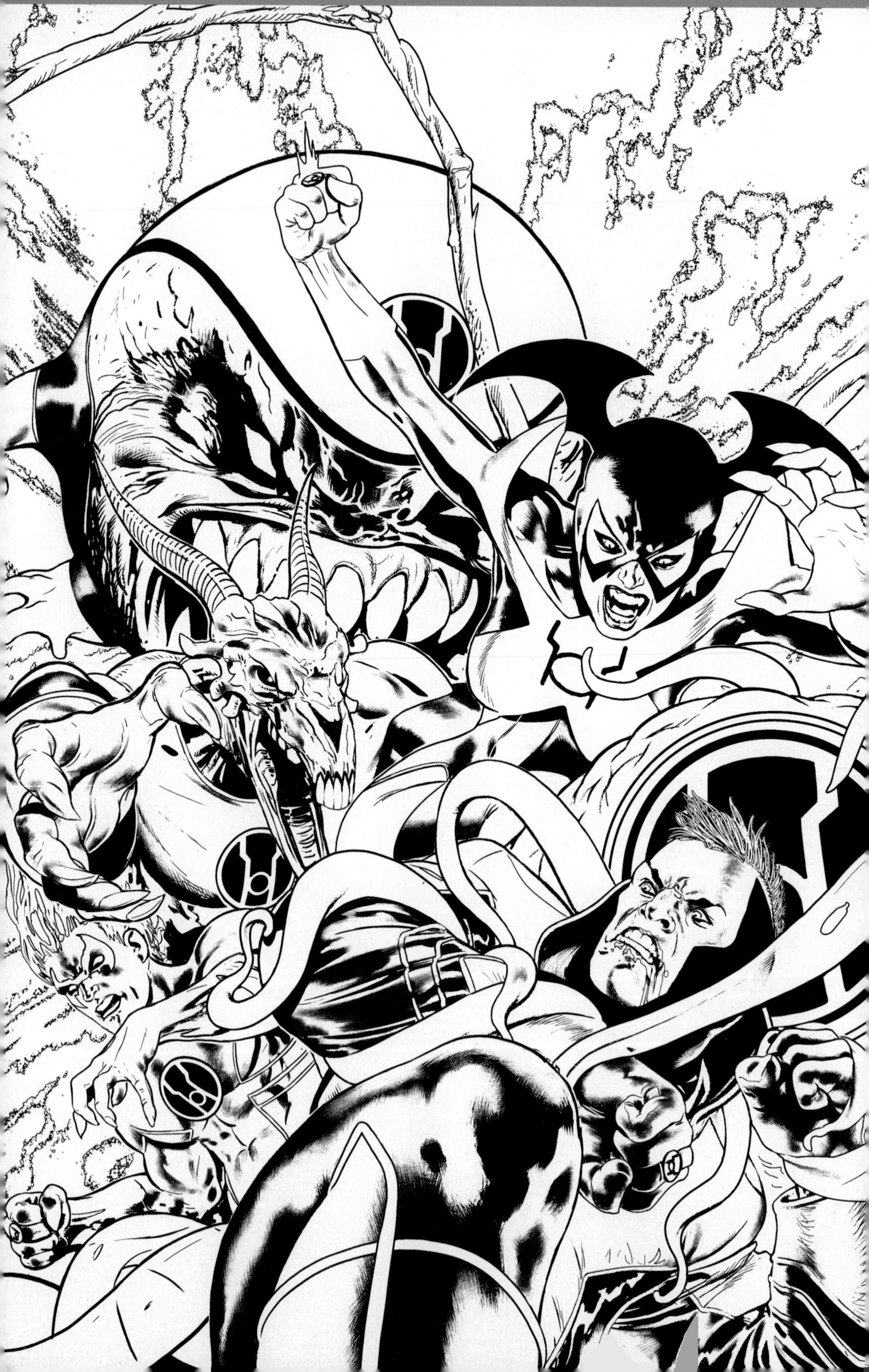

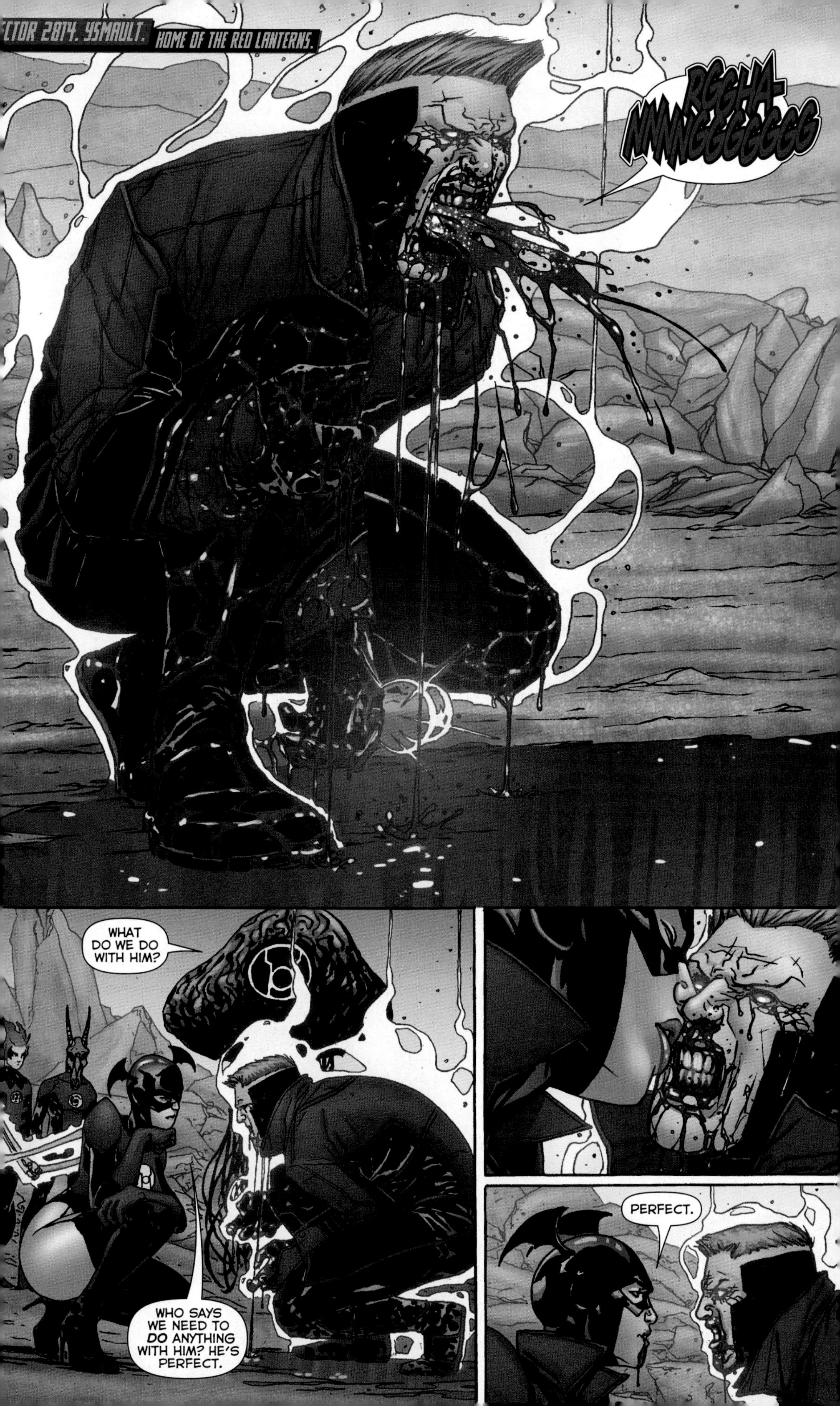

CTOR 2814. YSMAULT. HOME OF THE RED LANTERNS.
RGGHA NNNNGGGGGGG
WHAT DO WE DO WITH HIM?
WHO SAYS WE NEED TO DO ANYTHING WITH HIM? HE'S PERFECT.
PERFECT.

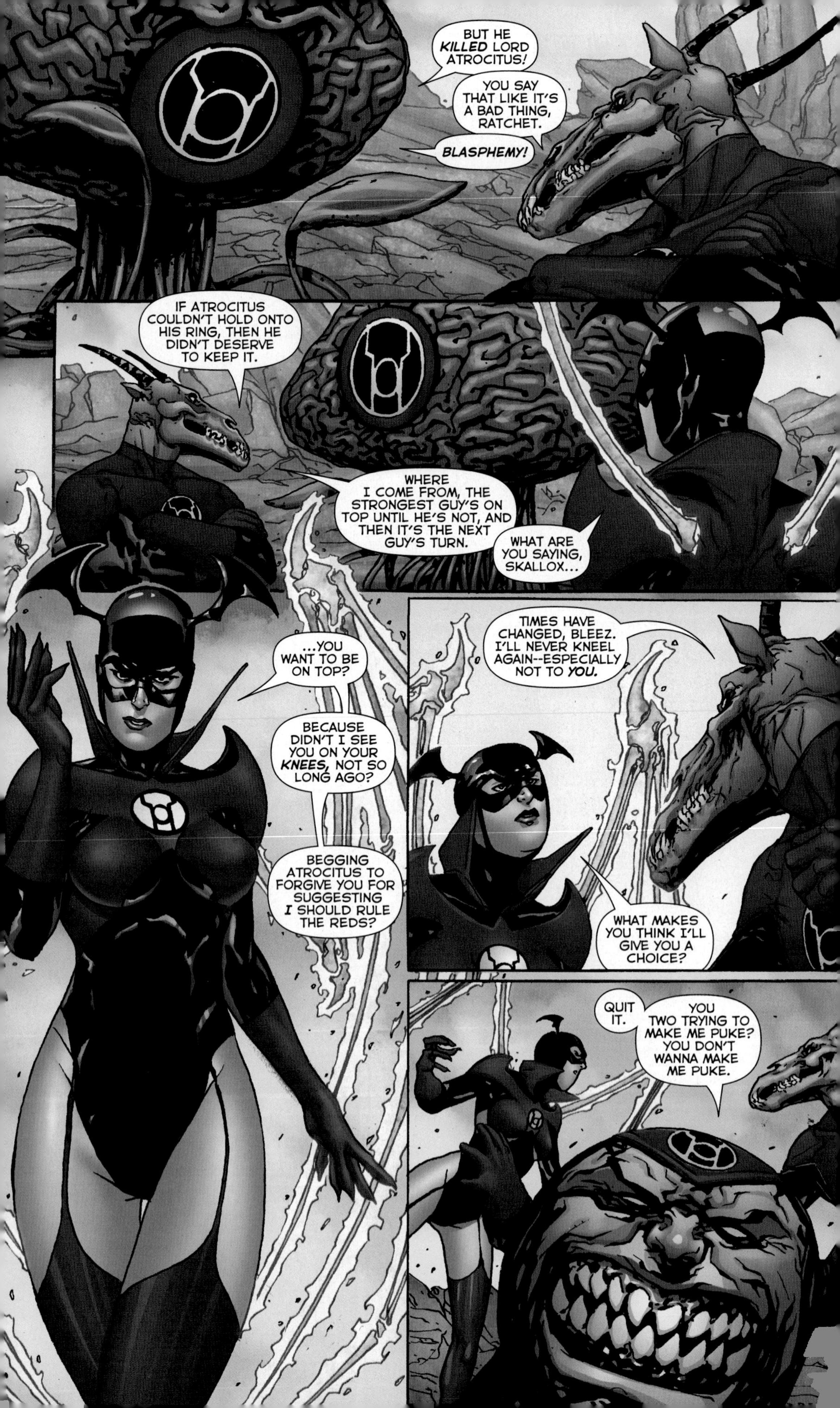
BUT HE *KILLED* LORD ATROCITUS!
YOU SAY THAT LIKE IT'S A BAD THING, RATCHET.
BLASPHEMY!
IF ATROCITUS COULDN'T HOLD ONTO HIS RING, THEN HE DIDN'T DESERVE TO KEEP IT.
WHERE I COME FROM, THE STRONGEST GUY'S ON TOP UNTIL HE'S NOT, AND THEN IT'S THE NEXT GUY'S TURN.
WHAT ARE YOU SAYING, SKALLOX...
...YOU WANT TO BE ON TOP?
BECAUSE DIDN'T I SEE YOU ON YOUR *KNEES,* NOT SO LONG AGO?
BEGGING ATROCITUS TO FORGIVE YOU FOR SUGGESTING *I* SHOULD RULE THE REDS?
TIMES HAVE CHANGED, BLEEZ. I'LL NEVER KNEEL AGAIN--ESPECIALLY NOT TO *YOU.*
WHAT MAKES YOU THINK I'LL GIVE YOU A CHOICE?
QUIT IT.
YOU TWO TRYING TO MAKE ME PUKE? YOU DON'T WANNA MAKE ME PUKE.

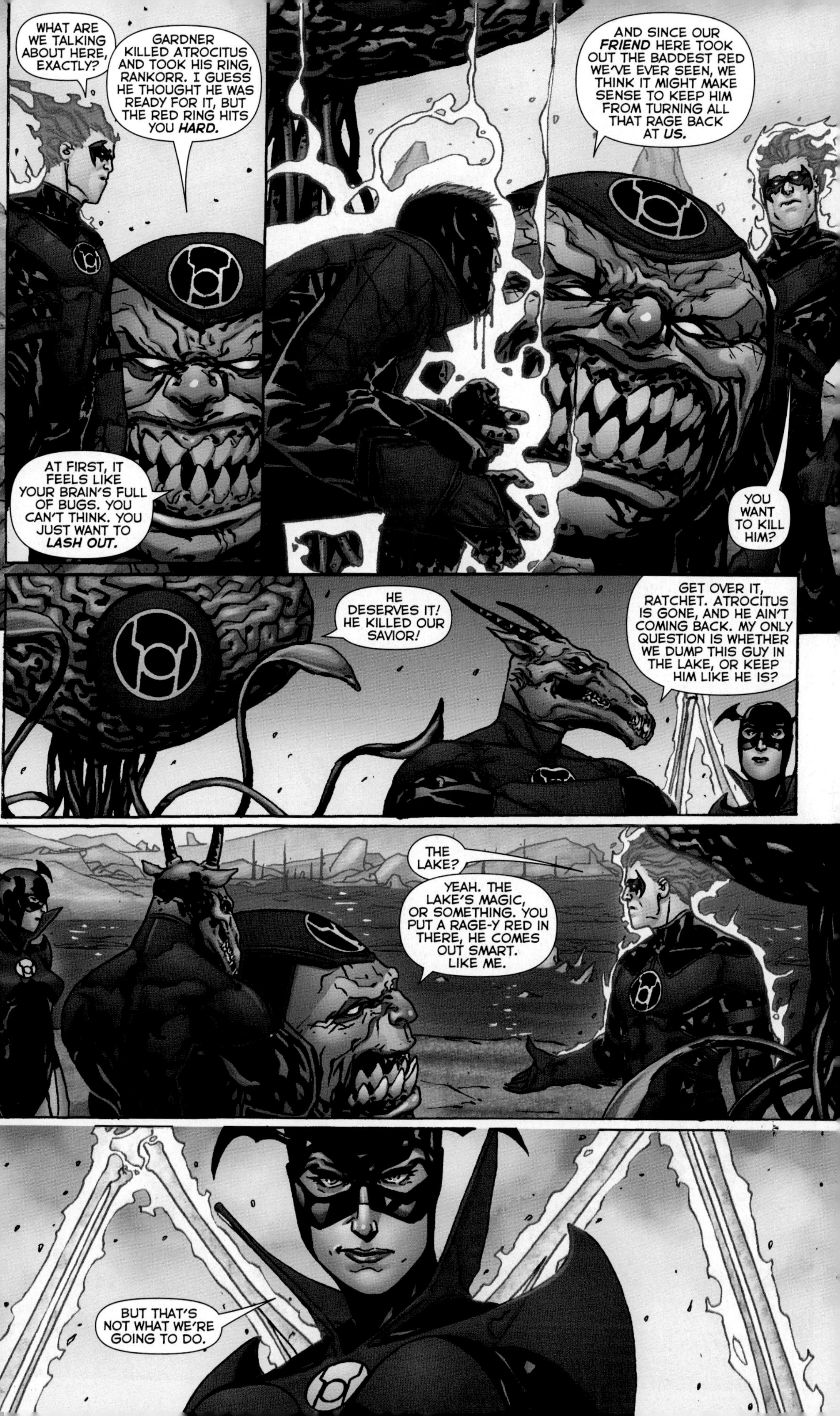
WHAT ARE WE TALKING ABOUT HERE, EXACTLY?
GARDNER KILLED ATROCITUS AND TOOK HIS RING, RANKORR. I GUESS HE THOUGHT HE WAS READY FOR IT, BUT THE RED RING HITS YOU *HARD.*
AT FIRST, IT FEELS LIKE YOUR BRAIN'S FULL OF BUGS. YOU CAN'T THINK. YOU JUST WANT TO *LASH OUT.*
AND SINCE OUR *FRIEND* HERE TOOK OUT THE BADDEST RED WE'VE EVER SEEN, WE THINK IT MIGHT MAKE SENSE TO KEEP HIM FROM TURNING ALL THAT RAGE BACK AT *US.*
YOU WANT TO KILL HIM?
HE DESERVES IT! HE KILLED OUR SAVIOR!
GET OVER IT, RATCHET. ATROCITUS IS GONE, AND HE AIN'T COMING BACK. MY ONLY QUESTION IS WHETHER WE DUMP THIS GUY IN THE LAKE, OR KEEP HIM LIKE HE IS?
THE LAKE?
YEAH. THE LAKE'S MAGIC, OR SOMETHING. YOU PUT A RAGE-Y RED IN THERE, HE COMES OUT SMART. LIKE ME.
BUT THAT'S NOT WHAT WE'RE GOING TO DO.

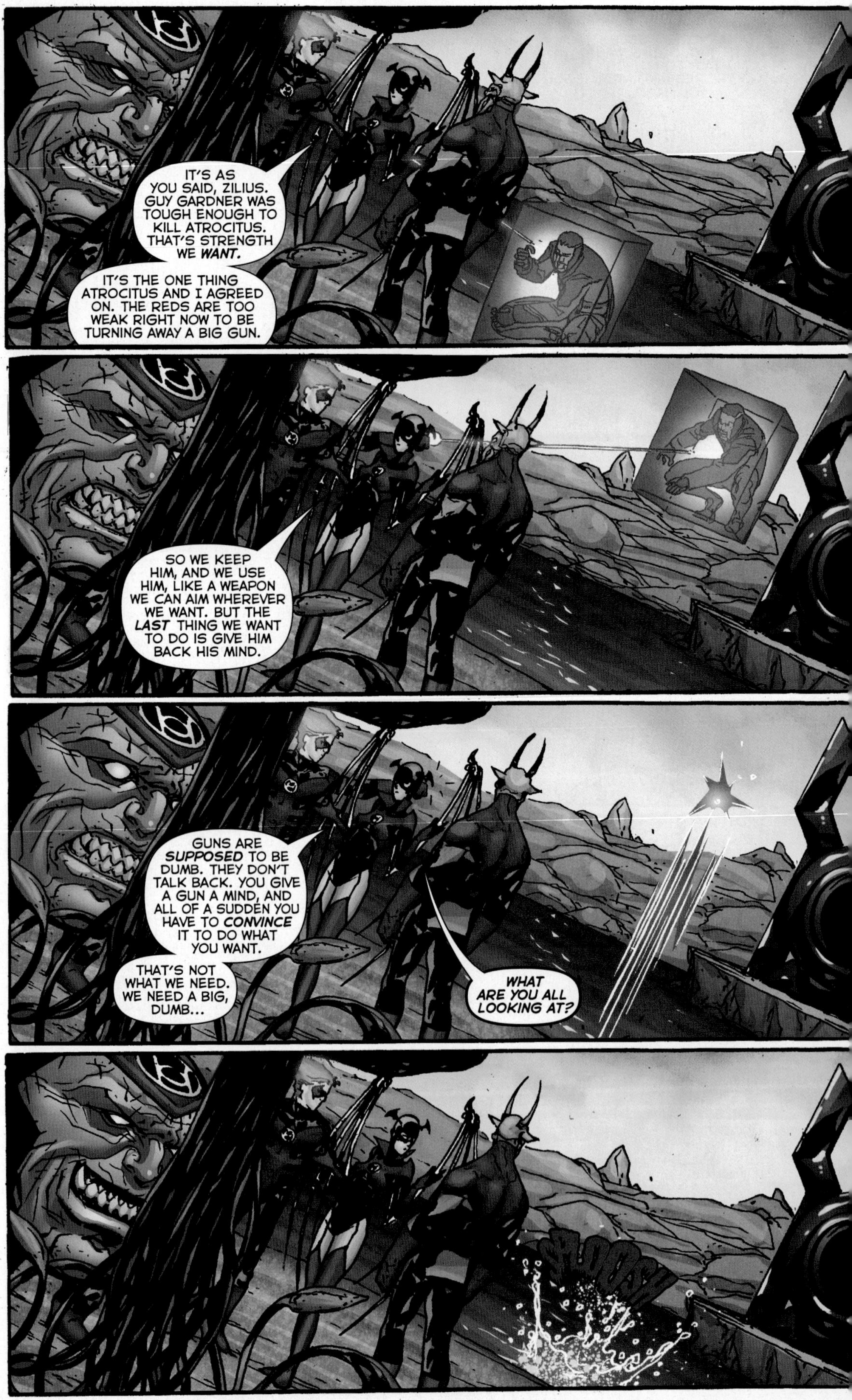

IT'S AS YOU SAID, ZILIUS. GUY GARDNER WAS TOUGH ENOUGH TO KILL ATROCITUS. THAT'S STRENGTH WE *WANT.*
IT'S THE ONE THING ATROCITUS AND I AGREED ON. THE REDS ARE TOO WEAK RIGHT NOW TO BE TURNING AWAY A BIG GUN.
SO WE KEEP HIM, AND WE USE HIM, LIKE A WEAPON WE CAN AIM WHEREVER WE WANT. BUT THE *LAST* THING WE WANT TO DO IS GIVE HIM BACK HIS MIND.
GUNS ARE *SUPPOSED* TO BE DUMB. THEY DON'T TALK BACK. YOU GIVE A GUN A MIND, AND ALL OF A SUDDEN YOU HAVE TO *CONVINCE* IT TO DO WHAT YOU WANT.
THAT'S NOT WHAT WE NEED. WE NEED A BIG, DUMB...
WHAT ARE YOU ALL LOOKING AT?

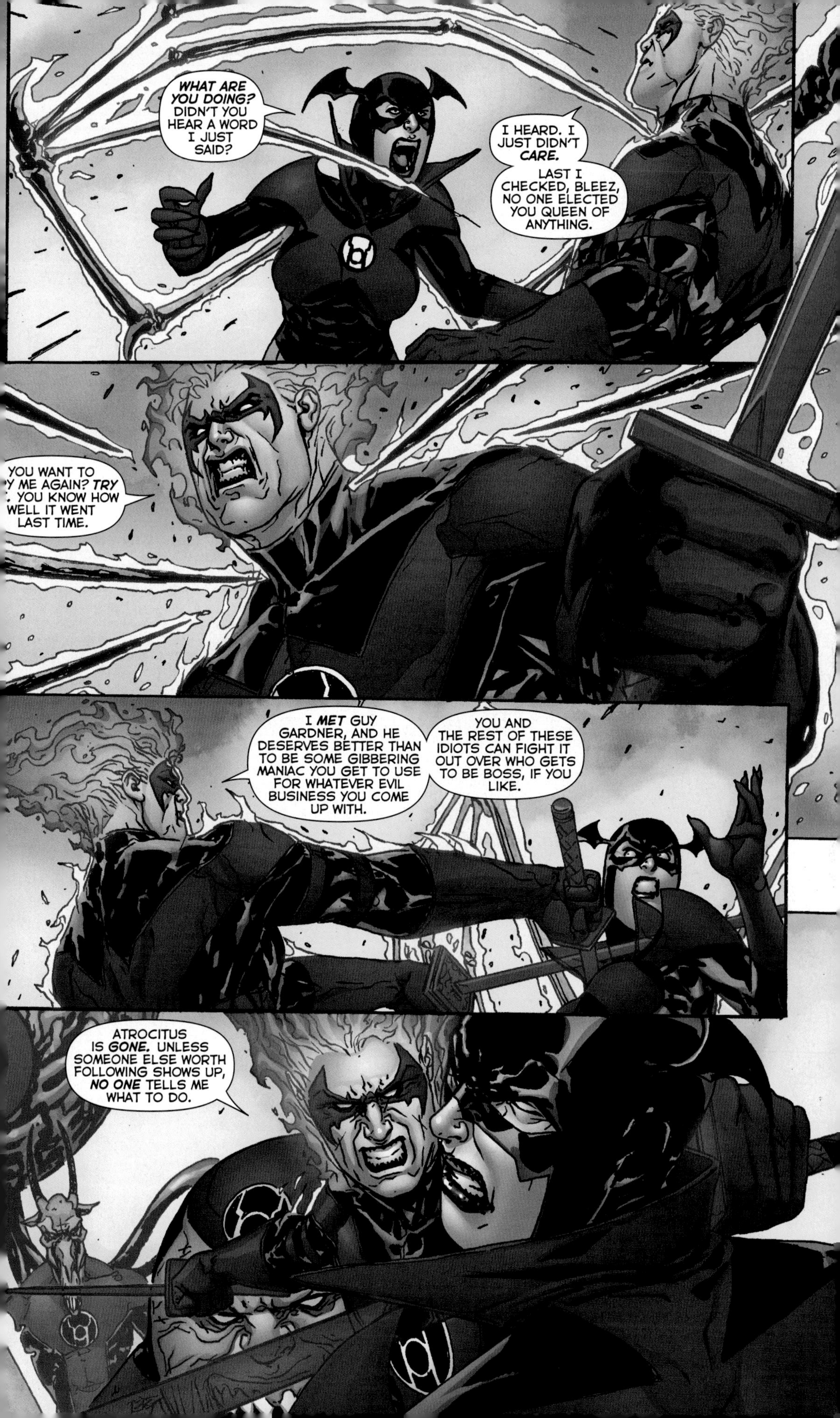
WHAT ARE YOU DOING? DIDN'T YOU HEAR A WORD I JUST SAID?
I HEARD. I JUST DIDN'T *CARE.*
LAST I CHECKED, BLEEZ, NO ONE ELECTED YOU QUEEN OF ANYTHING.
YOU WANT TO ME AGAIN? *TRY* YOU KNOW HOW WELL IT WENT LAST TIME.
I *MET* GUY GARDNER, AND HE DESERVES BETTER THAN TO BE SOME GIBBERING MANIAC YOU GET TO USE FOR WHATEVER EVIL BUSINESS YOU COME UP WITH.
YOU AND THE REST OF THESE IDIOTS CAN FIGHT IT OUT OVER WHO GETS TO BE BOSS, IF YOU LIKE.
ATROCITUS IS *GONE.* UNLESS SOMEONE ELSE WORTH FOLLOWING SHOWS UP, *NO ONE* TELLS ME WHAT TO DO.

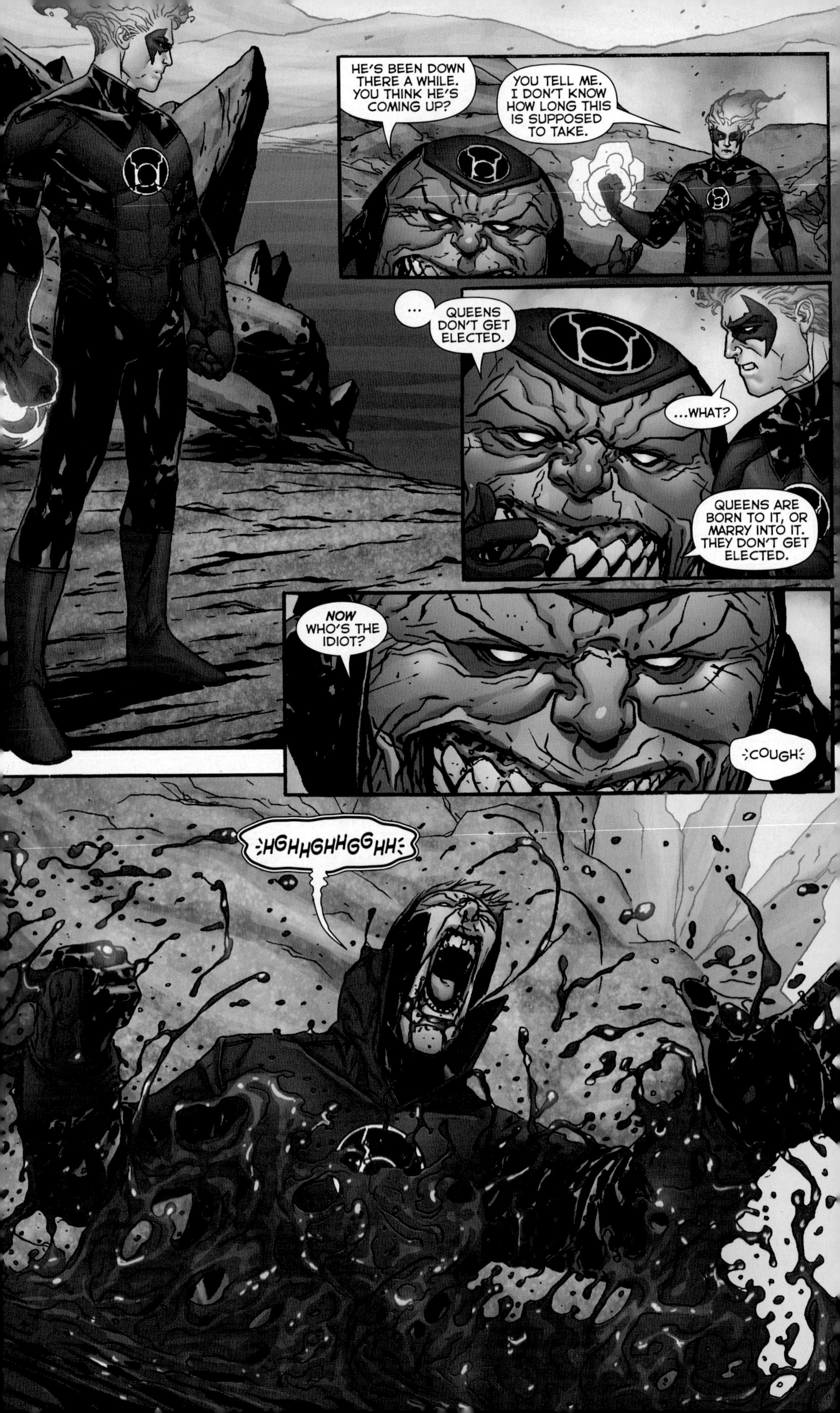
HE'S BEEN DOWN THERE A WHILE. YOU THINK HE'S COMING UP?
YOU TELL ME. I DON'T KNOW HOW LONG THIS IS SUPPOSED TO TAKE.
...
QUEENS DON'T GET ELECTED.
...WHAT?
QUEENS ARE BORN TO IT, OR MARRY INTO IT. THEY DON'T GET ELECTED.
NOW WHO'S THE IDIOT?
COUGH
HGHHGHHGGHH

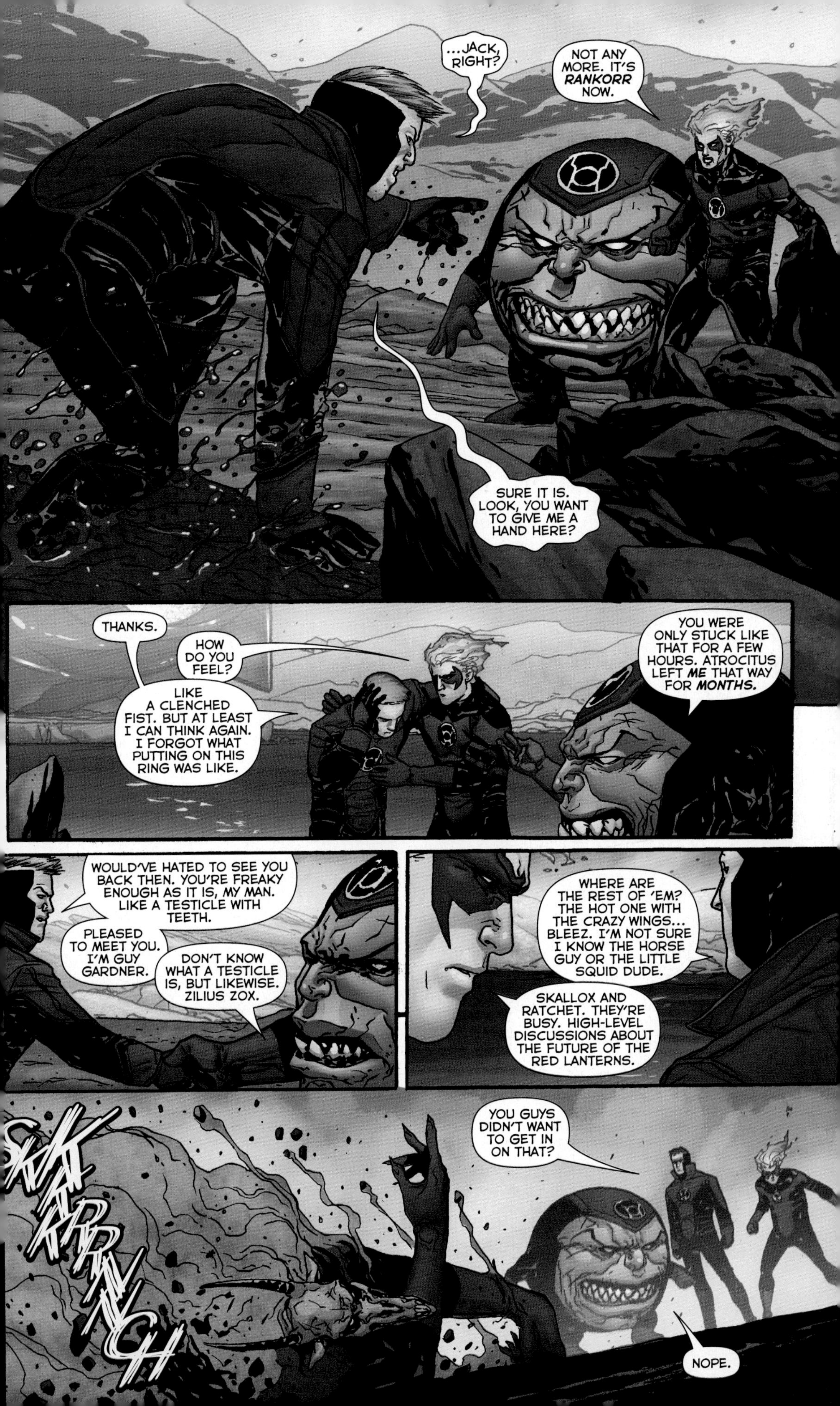

...JACK, RIGHT?
NOT ANY MORE. IT'S RANKORR NOW.
SURE IT IS. LOOK, YOU WANT TO GIVE ME A HAND HERE?
THANKS.
HOW DO YOU FEEL?
LIKE A CLENCHED FIST. BUT AT LEAST I CAN THINK AGAIN. I FORGOT WHAT PUTTING ON THIS RING WAS LIKE.
YOU WERE ONLY STUCK LIKE THAT FOR A FEW HOURS. ATROCITUS LEFT ME THAT WAY FOR MONTHS.
WOULD'VE HATED TO SEE YOU BACK THEN. YOU'RE FREAKY ENOUGH AS IT IS, MY MAN. LIKE A TESTICLE WITH TEETH.
PLEASED TO MEET YOU. I'M GUY GARDNER.
DON'T KNOW WHAT A TESTICLE IS, BUT LIKEWISE. ZILIUS ZOX.
WHERE ARE THE REST OF 'EM? THE HOT ONE WITH THE CRAZY WINGS... BLEEZ. I'M NOT SURE I KNOW THE HORSE GUY OR THE LITTLE SQUID DUDE.
SKALLOX AND RATCHET. THEY'RE BUSY. HIGH-LEVEL DISCUSSIONS ABOUT THE FUTURE OF THE RED LANTERNS.
YOU GUYS DIDN'T WANT TO GET IN ON THAT?
NOPE.

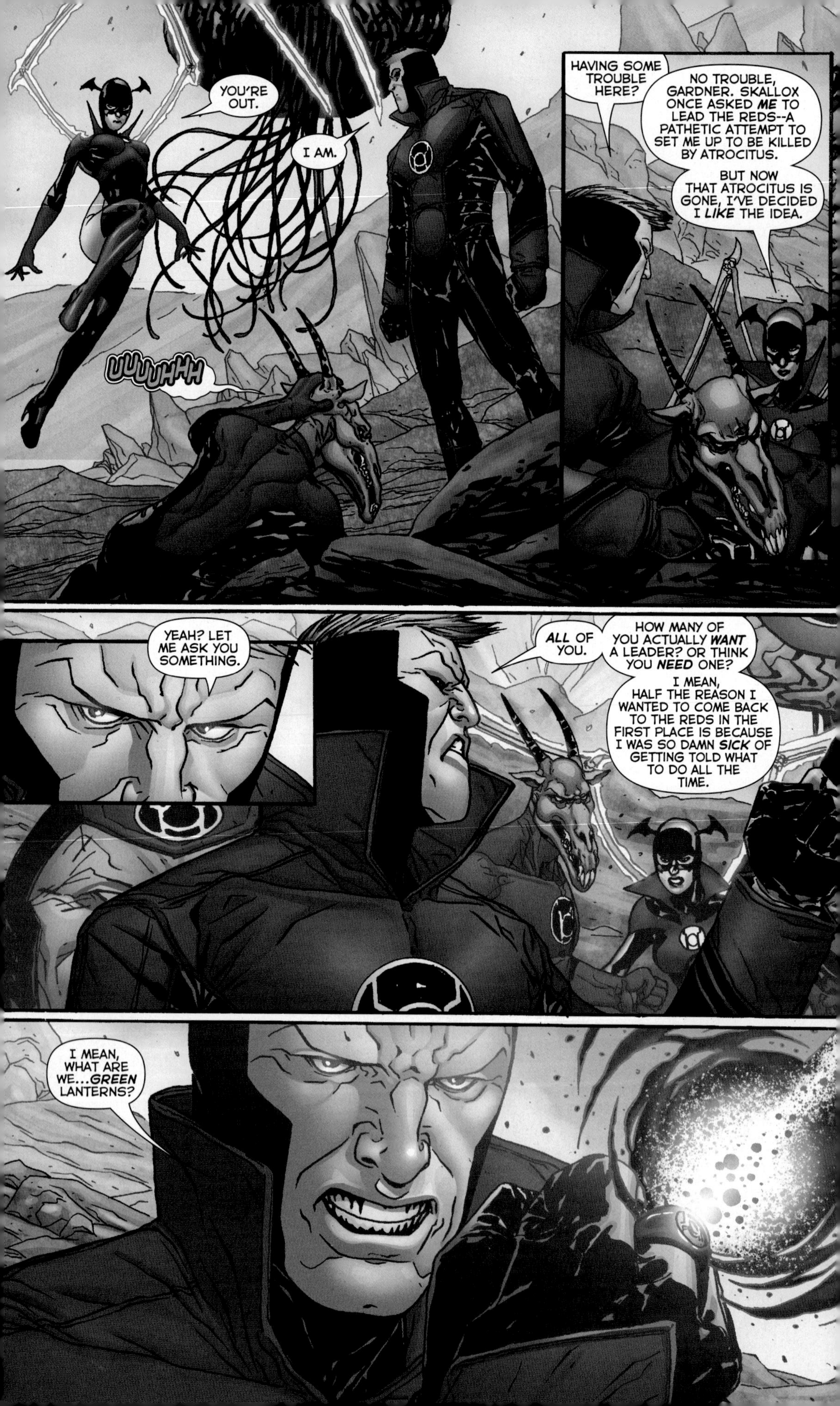
YOU'RE OUT.
I AM.
UUUUHHH
HAVING SOME TROUBLE HERE?
NO TROUBLE, GARDNER. SKALLOX ONCE ASKED ME TO LEAD THE REDS--A PATHETIC ATTEMPT TO SET ME UP TO BE KILLED BY ATROCITUS.
BUT NOW THAT ATROCITUS IS GONE, I'VE DECIDED I LIKE THE IDEA.
YEAH? LET ME ASK YOU SOMETHING.
ALL OF YOU.
HOW MANY OF YOU ACTUALLY WANT A LEADER? OR THINK YOU NEED ONE?
I MEAN, HALF THE REASON I WANTED TO COME BACK TO THE REDS IN THE FIRST PLACE IS BECAUSE I WAS SO DAMN SICK OF GETTING TOLD WHAT TO DO ALL THE TIME.
I MEAN, WHAT ARE WE...GREEN LANTERNS?

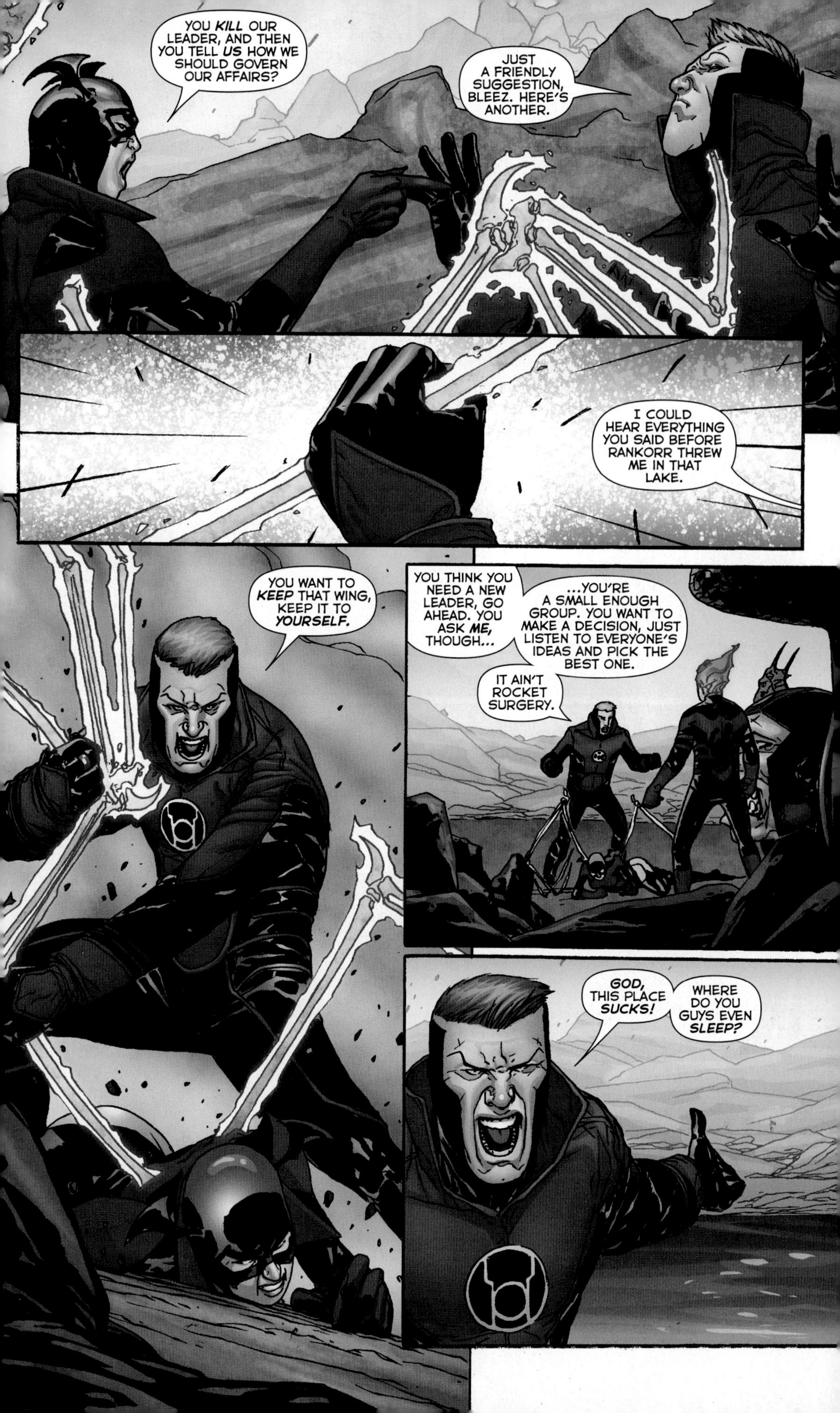
YOU KILL OUR LEADER, AND THEN YOU TELL US HOW WE SHOULD GOVERN OUR AFFAIRS?
JUST A FRIENDLY SUGGESTION, BLEEZ. HERE'S ANOTHER.
I COULD HEAR EVERYTHING YOU SAID BEFORE RANKORR THREW ME IN THAT LAKE.
YOU WANT TO KEEP THAT WING, KEEP IT TO YOURSELF.
YOU THINK YOU NEED A NEW LEADER, GO AHEAD. YOU ASK ME, THOUGH...
...YOU'RE A SMALL ENOUGH GROUP. YOU WANT TO MAKE A DECISION, JUST LISTEN TO EVERYONE'S IDEAS AND PICK THE BEST ONE.
IT AIN'T ROCKET SURGERY.
GOD, THIS PLACE SUCKS!
WHERE DO YOU GUYS EVEN SLEEP?

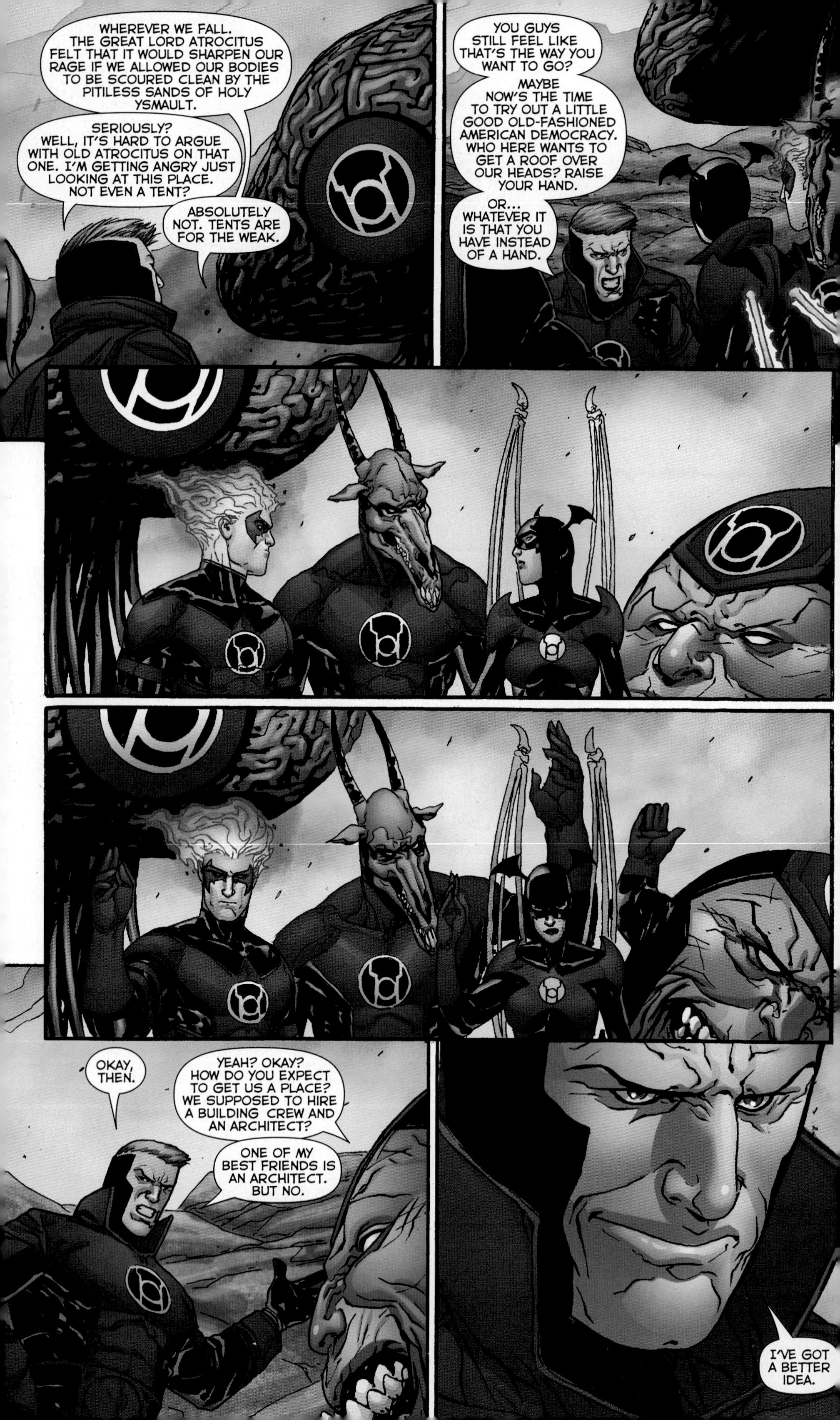
WHEREVER WE FALL. THE GREAT LORD ATROCITUS FELT THAT IT WOULD SHARPEN OUR RAGE IF WE ALLOWED OUR BODIES TO BE SCOURED CLEAN BY THE PITILESS SANDS OF HOLY YSMAULT.
SERIOUSLY? WELL, IT'S HARD TO ARGUE WITH OLD ATROCITUS ON THAT ONE. I'M GETTING ANGRY JUST LOOKING AT THIS PLACE. NOT EVEN A TENT?
ABSOLUTELY NOT. TENTS ARE FOR THE WEAK.
YOU GUYS STILL FEEL LIKE THAT'S THE WAY YOU WANT TO GO?
MAYBE NOW'S THE TIME TO TRY OUT A LITTLE GOOD OLD-FASHIONED AMERICAN DEMOCRACY. WHO HERE WANTS TO GET A ROOF OVER OUR HEADS? RAISE YOUR HAND.
OR... WHATEVER IT IS THAT YOU HAVE INSTEAD OF A HAND.
OKAY, THEN.
YEAH? OKAY? HOW DO YOU EXPECT TO GET US A PLACE? WE SUPPOSED TO HIRE A BUILDING CREW AND AN ARCHITECT?
ONE OF MY BEST FRIENDS IS AN ARCHITECT. BUT NO.
I'VE GOT A BETTER IDEA.

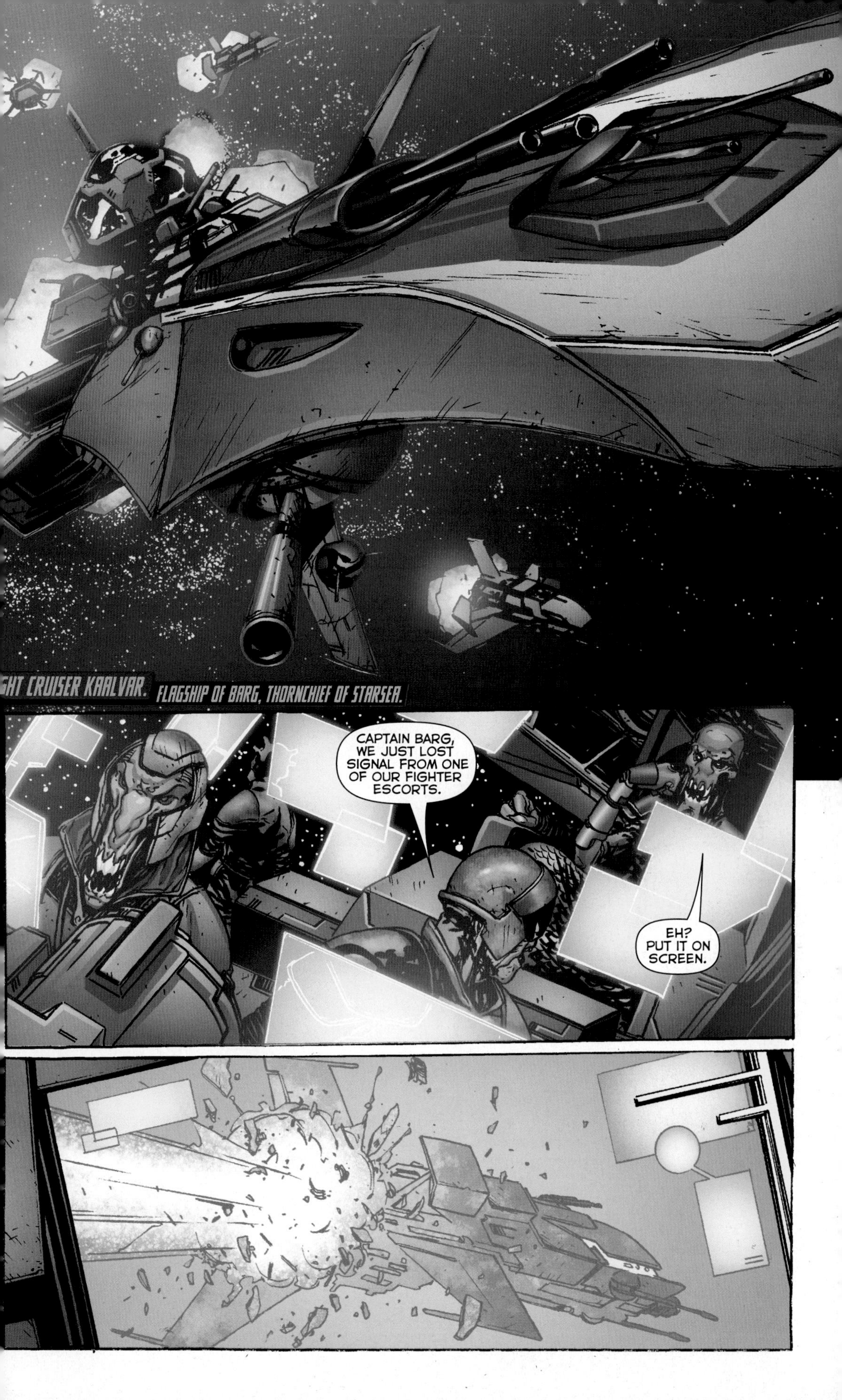
GHT CRUISER KAALVAR.
FLAGSHIP OF BARG, THORNCHIEF OF STARSEA.
CAPTAIN BARG, WE JUST LOST SIGNAL FROM ONE OF OUR FIGHTER ESCORTS.
EH? PUT IT ON SCREEN.

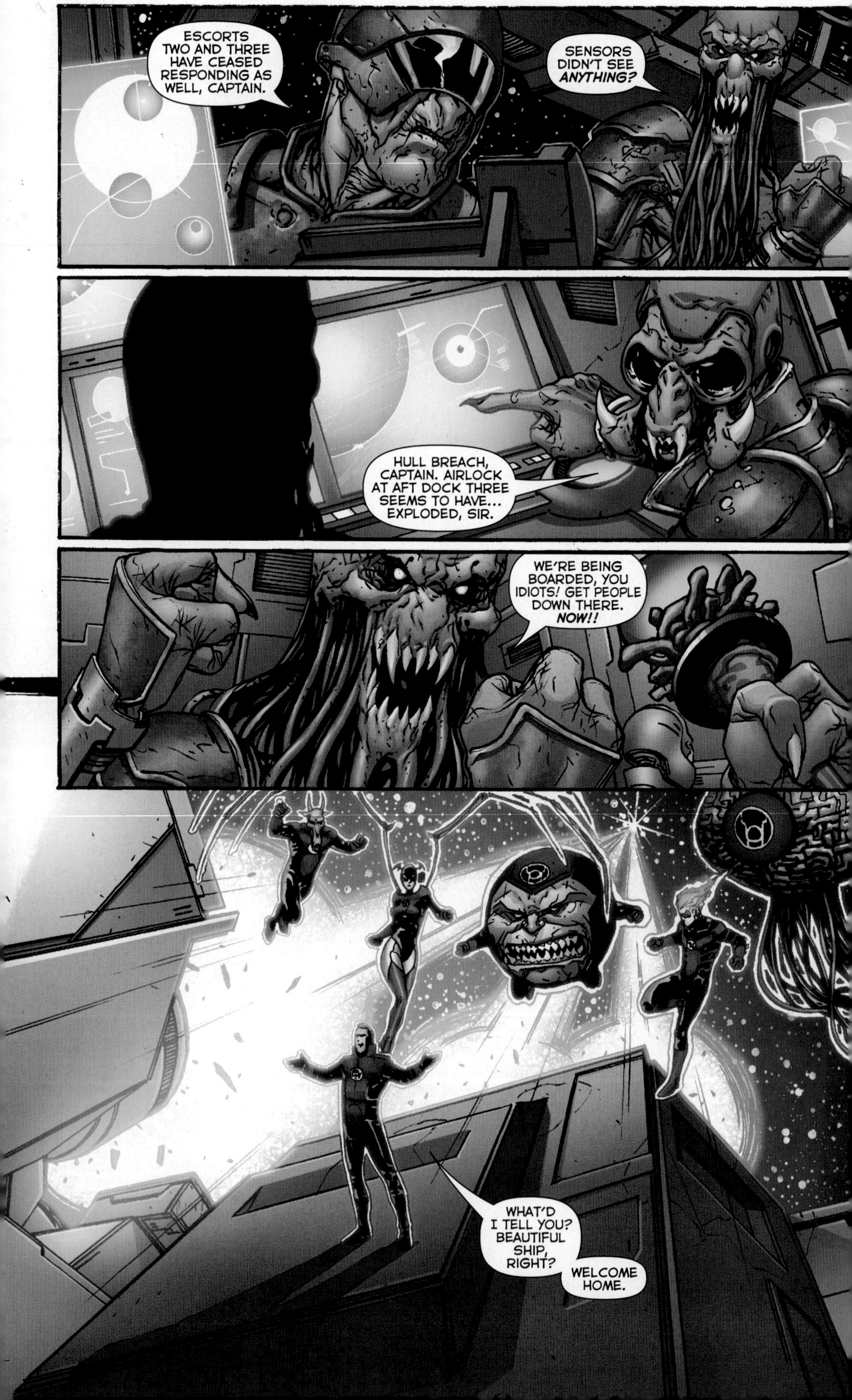
ESCORTS TWO AND THREE HAVE CEASED RESPONDING AS WELL, CAPTAIN.
SENSORS DIDN'T SEE *ANYTHING?*
HULL BREACH, CAPTAIN. AIRLOCK AT AFT DOCK THREE SEEMS TO HAVE... EXPLODED, SIR.
WE'RE BEING BOARDED, YOU IDIOTS! GET PEOPLE DOWN THERE. *NOW!!*
WHAT'D I TELL YOU? BEAUTIFUL SHIP, RIGHT?
WELCOME HOME.

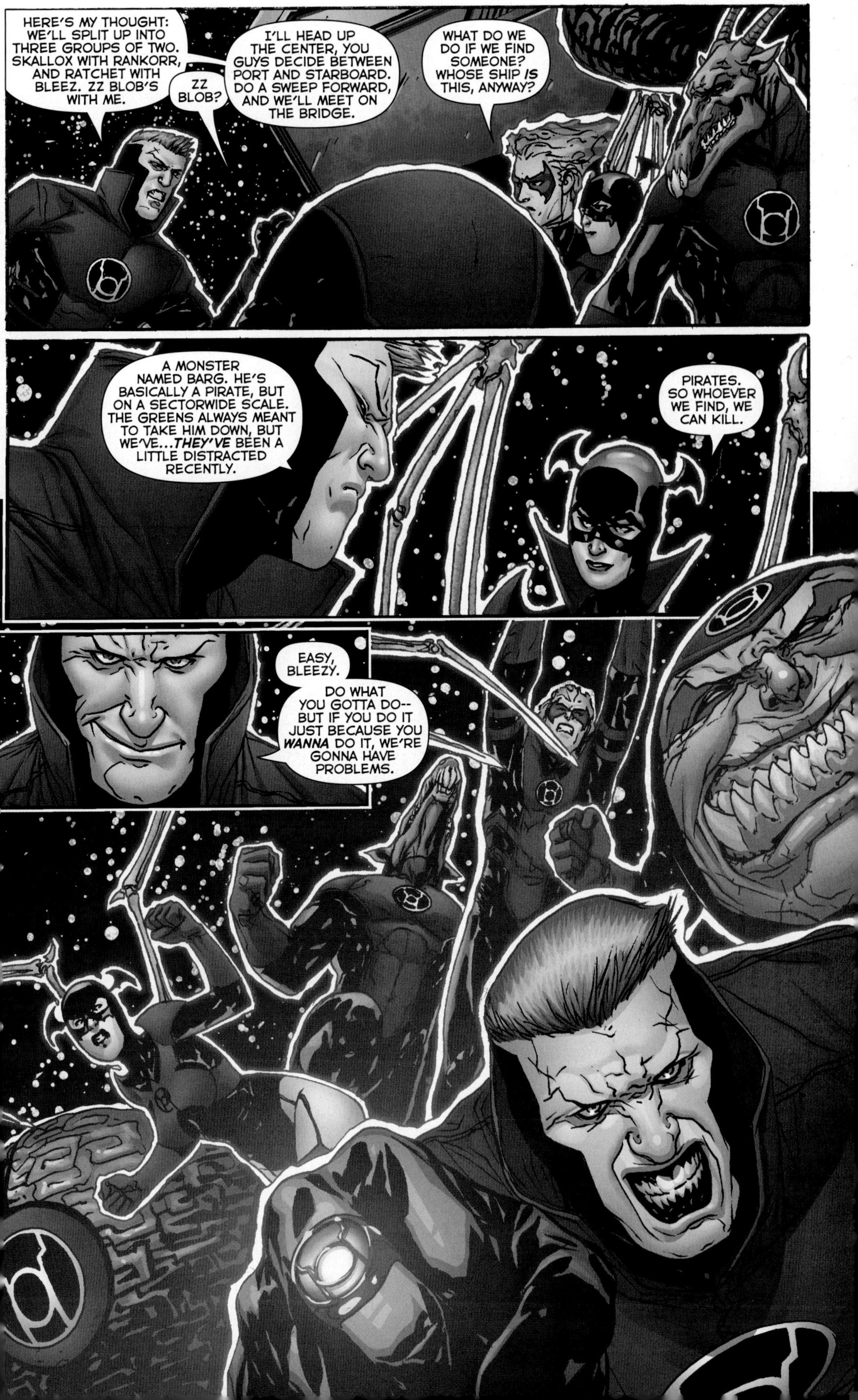
HERE'S MY THOUGHT: WE'LL SPLIT UP INTO THREE GROUPS OF TWO. SKALLOX WITH RANKORR, AND RATCHET WITH BLEEZ. ZZ BLOB'S WITH ME.
ZZ BLOB?
I'LL HEAD UP THE CENTER, YOU GUYS DECIDE BETWEEN PORT AND STARBOARD. DO A SWEEP FORWARD, AND WE'LL MEET ON THE BRIDGE.
WHAT DO WE DO IF WE FIND SOMEONE? WHOSE SHIP *IS* THIS, ANYWAY?
A MONSTER NAMED BARG. HE'S BASICALLY A PIRATE, BUT ON A SECTORWIDE SCALE. THE GREENS ALWAYS MEANT TO TAKE HIM DOWN, BUT WE'VE...*THEY'VE* BEEN A LITTLE DISTRACTED RECENTLY.
PIRATES. SO WHOEVER WE FIND, WE CAN KILL.
EASY, BLEEZY.
DO WHAT YOU GOTTA DO-- BUT IF YOU DO IT JUST BECAUSE YOU *WANNA* DO IT, WE'RE GONNA HAVE PROBLEMS.

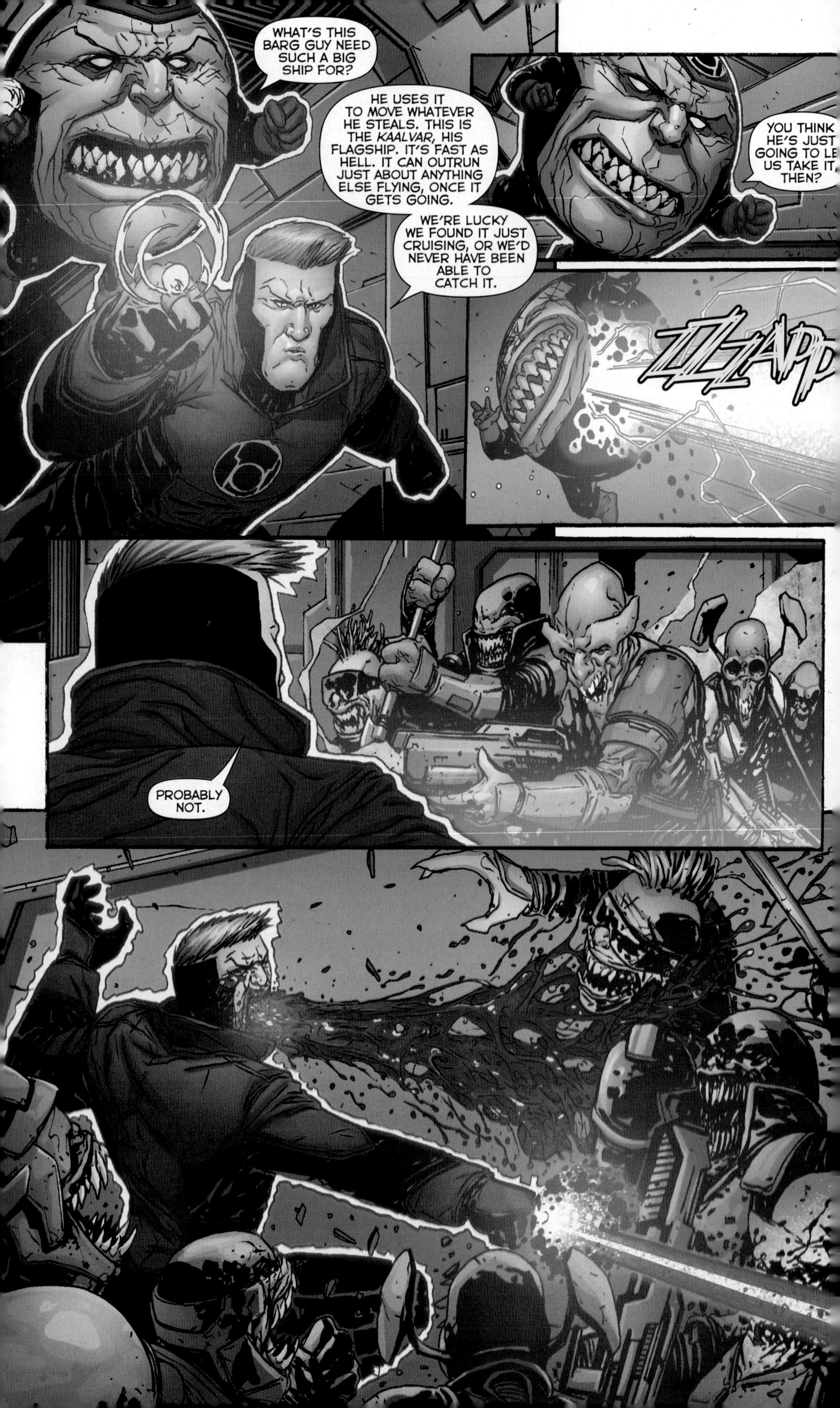
WHAT'S THIS BARG GUY NEED SUCH A BIG SHIP FOR?
HE USES IT TO MOVE WHATEVER HE STEALS. THIS IS THE *KAALVAR,* HIS FLAGSHIP. IT'S FAST AS HELL. IT CAN OUTRUN JUST ABOUT ANYTHING ELSE FLYING, ONCE IT GETS GOING.
WE'RE LUCKY WE FOUND IT JUST CRUISING, OR WE'D NEVER HAVE BEEN ABLE TO CATCH IT.
YOU THINK HE'S JUST GOING TO LE US TAKE IT, THEN?
ZZZAPP
PROBABLY NOT.

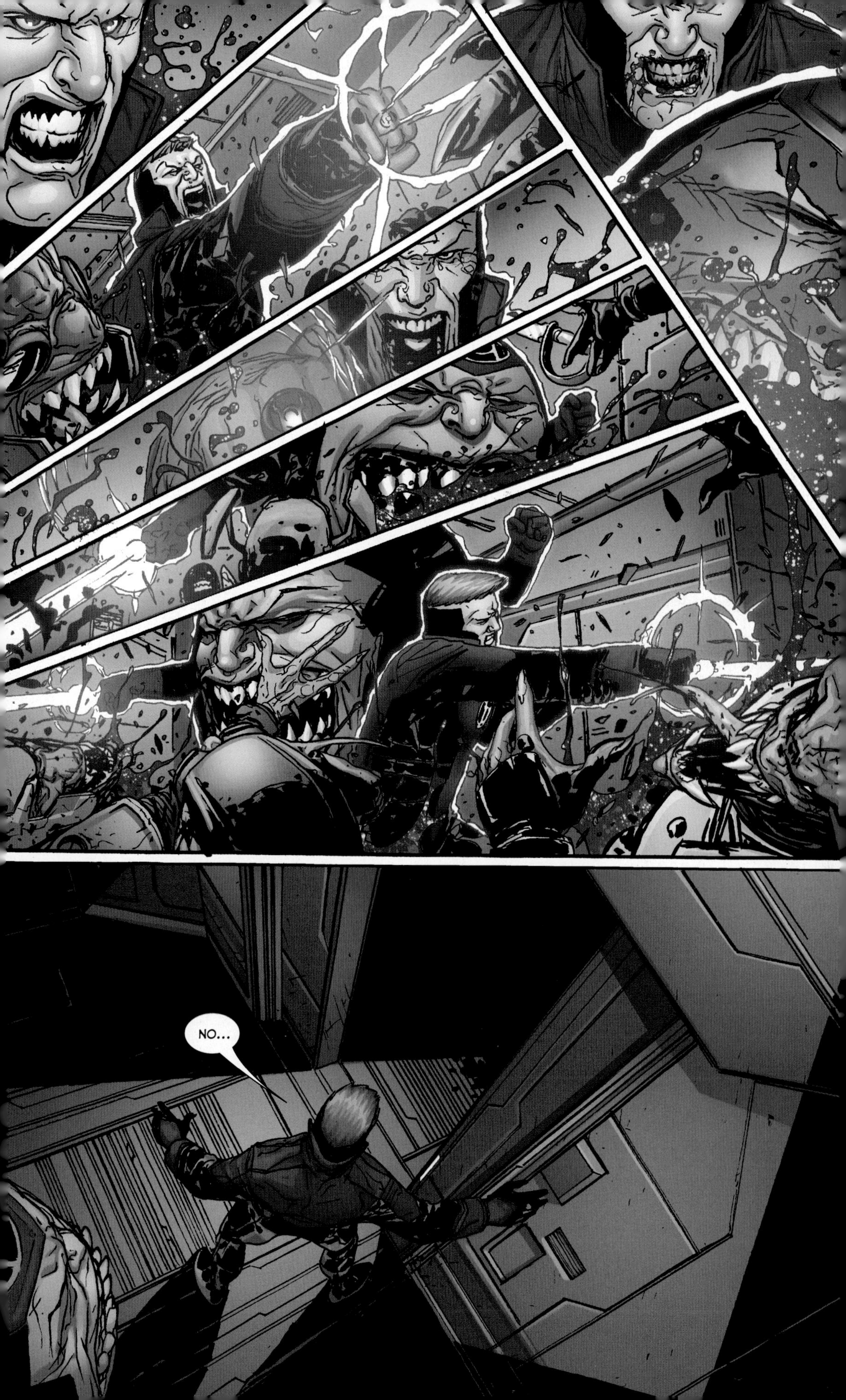
NO...

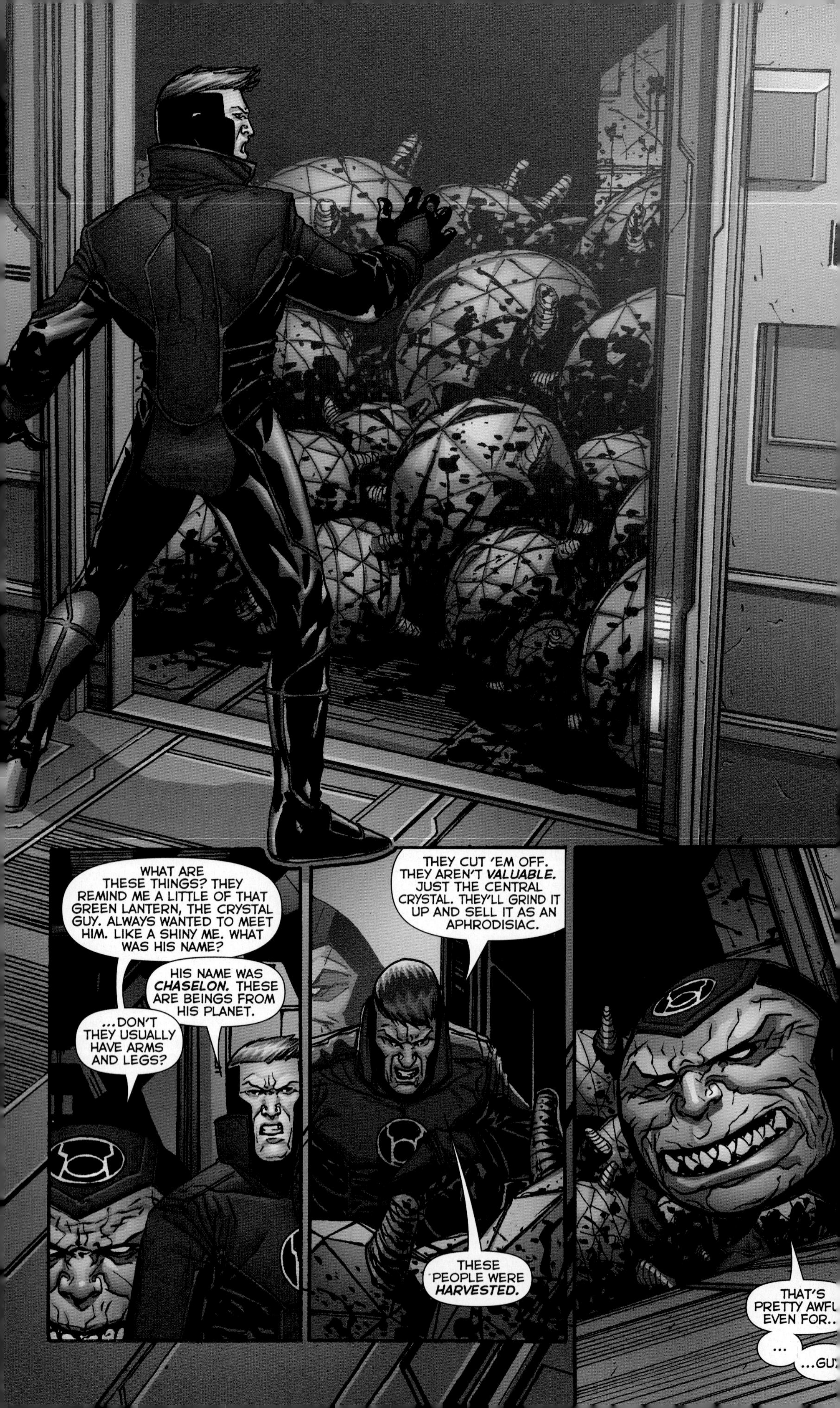

WHAT ARE THESE THINGS? THEY REMIND ME A LITTLE OF THAT GREEN LANTERN, THE CRYSTAL GUY. ALWAYS WANTED TO MEET HIM. LIKE A SHINY ME. WHAT WAS HIS NAME?
HIS NAME WAS CHASELON. THESE ARE BEINGS FROM HIS PLANET.
...DON'T THEY USUALLY HAVE ARMS AND LEGS?
THEY CUT 'EM OFF. THEY AREN'T VALUABLE. JUST THE CENTRAL CRYSTAL. THEY'LL GRIND IT UP AND SELL IT AS AN APHRODISIAC.
THESE PEOPLE WERE HARVESTED.
THAT'S PRETTY AWFU EVEN FOR...
...
...GU

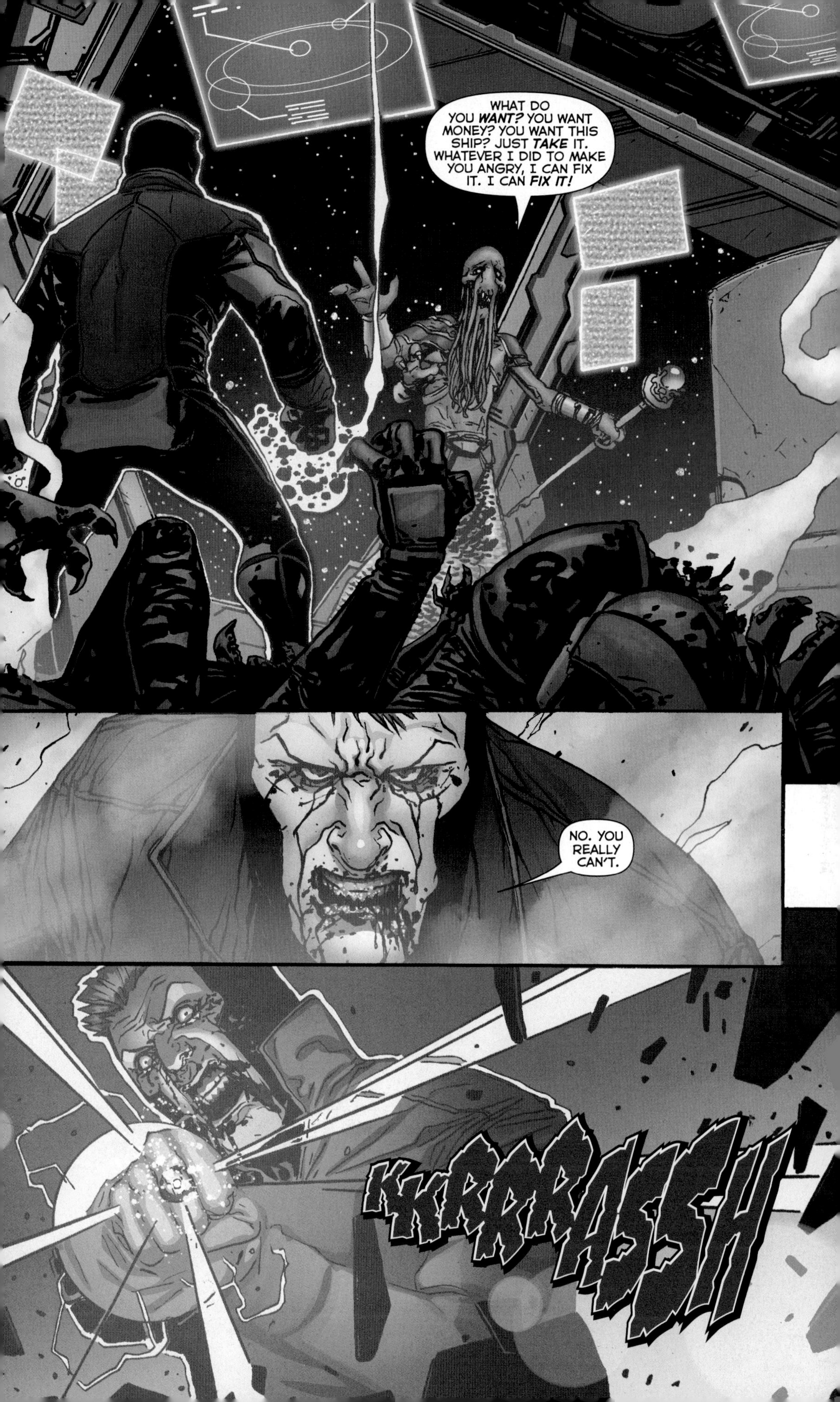
WHAT DO YOU *WANT?* YOU WANT MONEY? YOU WANT THIS SHIP? JUST *TAKE* IT. WHATEVER I DID TO MAKE YOU ANGRY, I CAN FIX IT. I CAN *FIX IT!*
NO. YOU REALLY CAN'T.
KKRRRRASSH

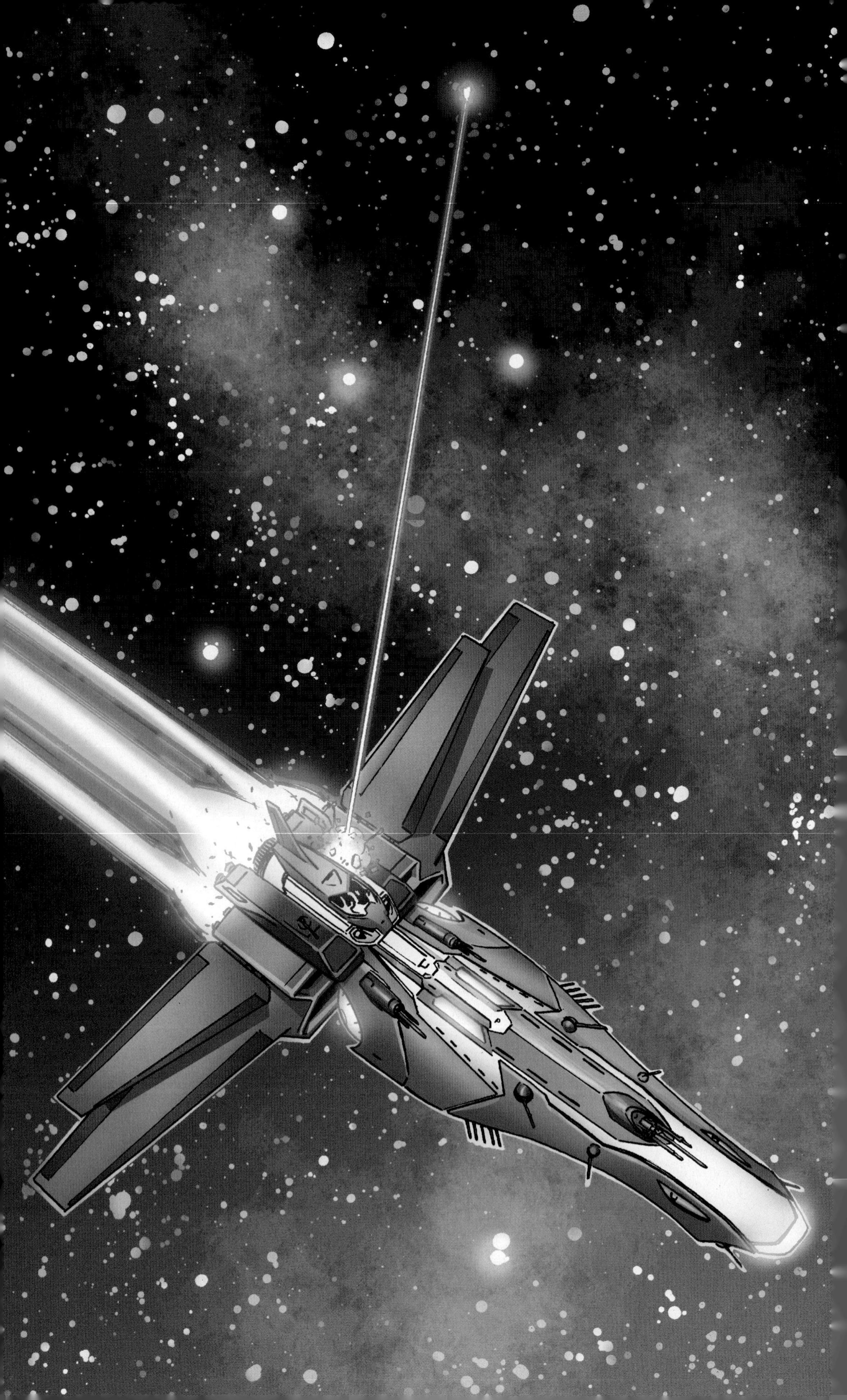

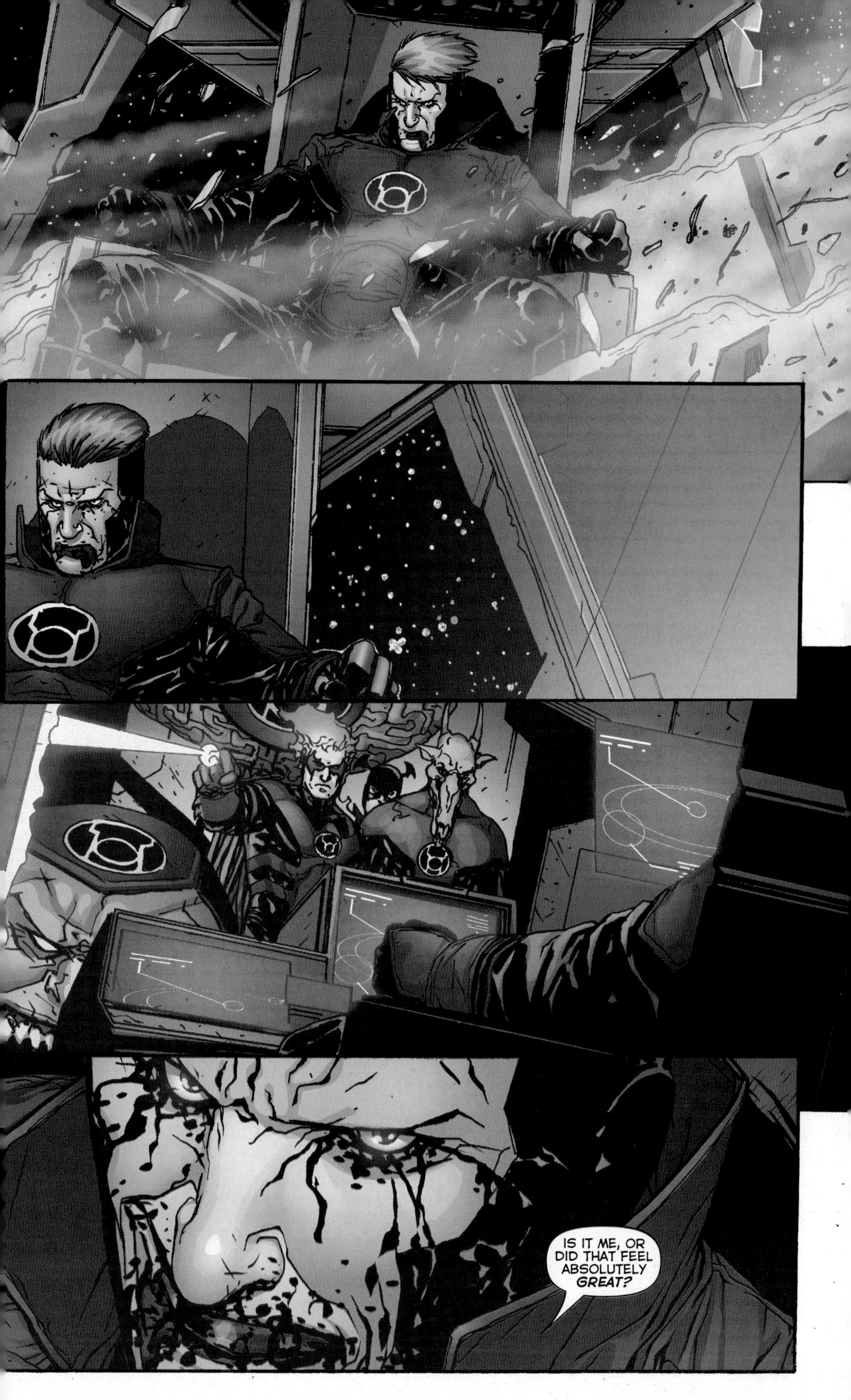
IS IT ME, OR DID THAT FEEL ABSOLUTELY *GREAT?*

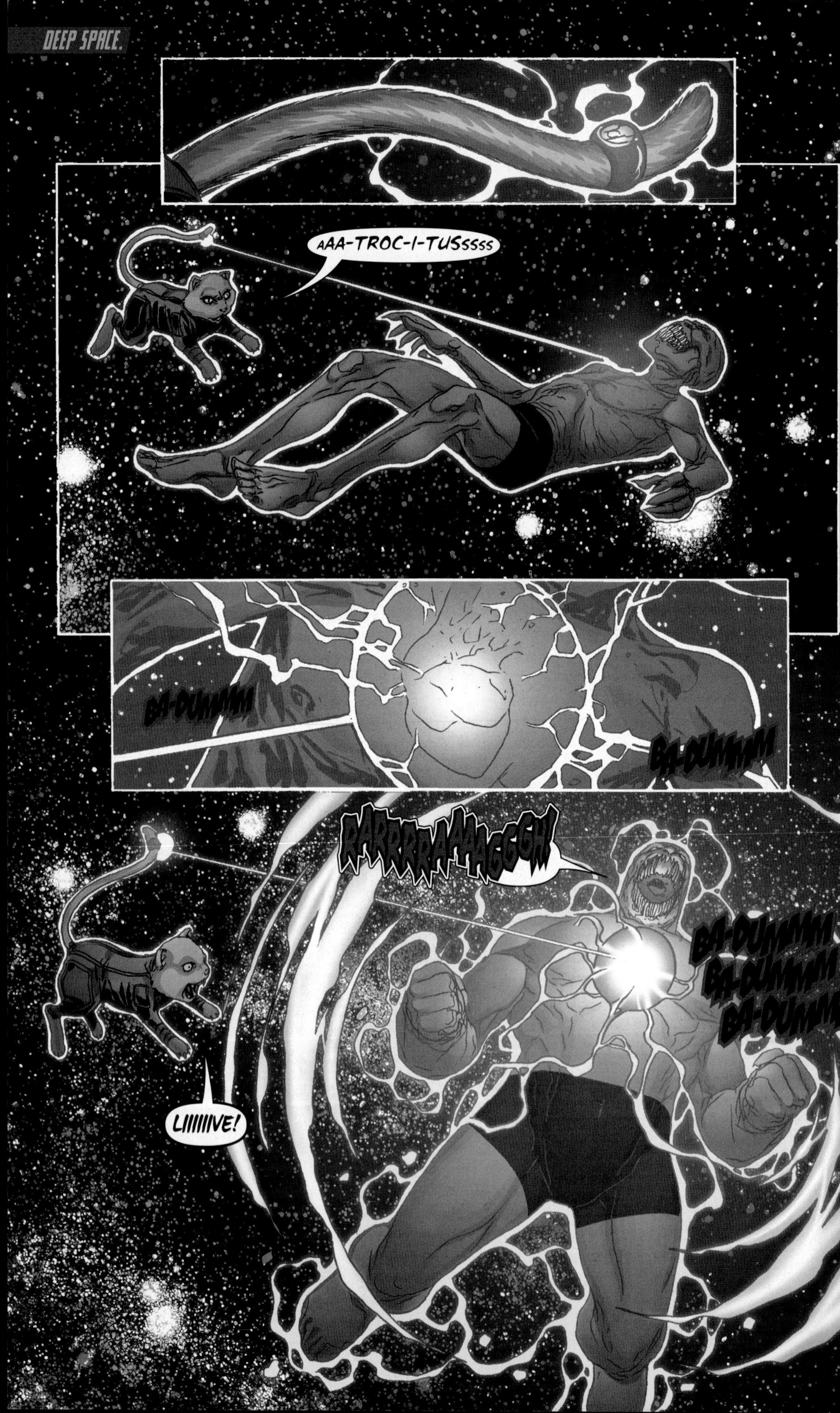
DEEP SPACE.
AAA-TROC-I-TUSSSSS
BA-DUMMM
BA-DUMMM
RARRRRAAAAGGGH!
LIIIIIIVE!
BA-DUMMM
BA-DUMMM
BA-DUMM

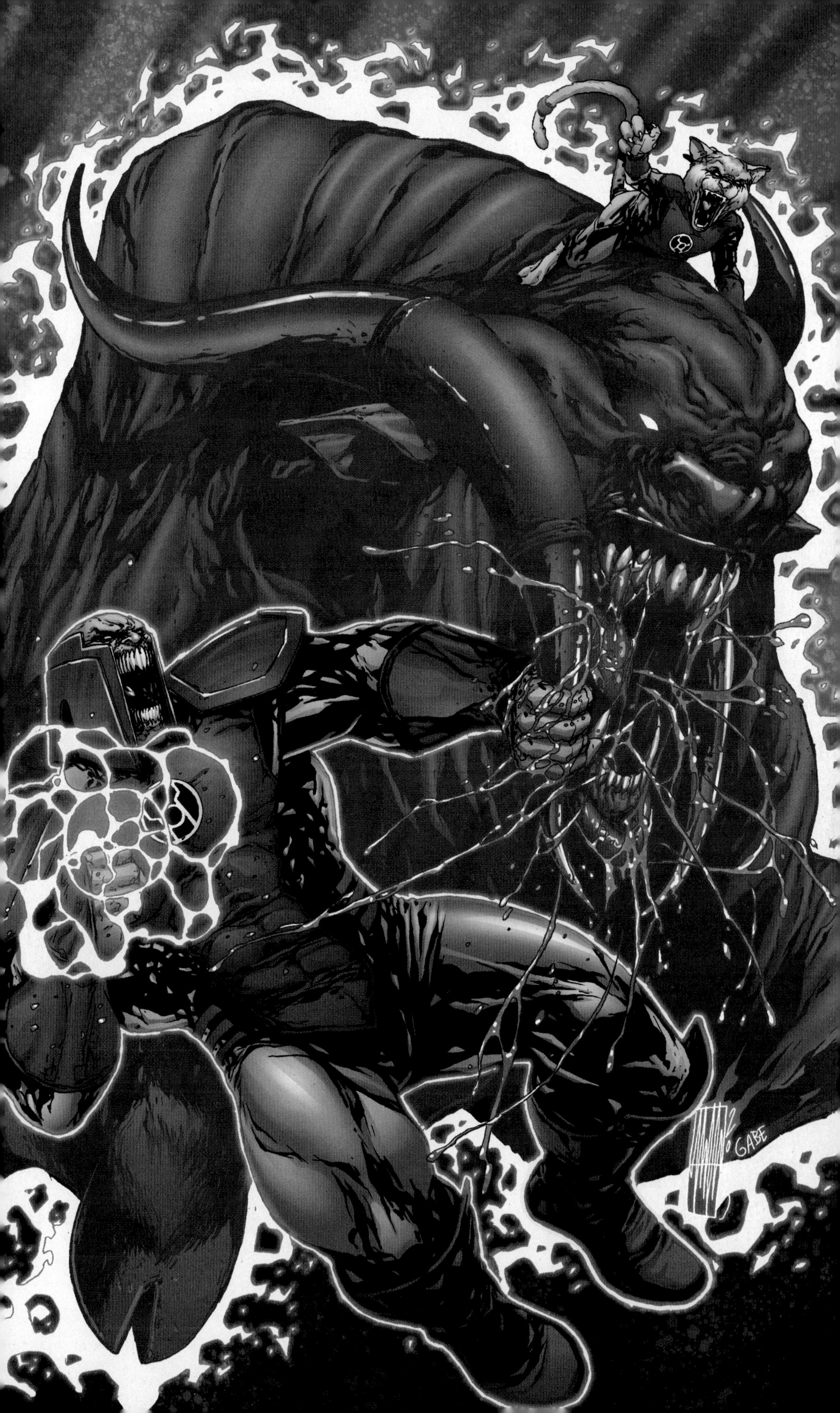
GABE

THE BUTCHER'S BILL

CHARLES SOULE writer **ALESSANDRO VITTI J. CALAFIORE** artists **GABE ELTAEB** colorist cover art by **ALESSANDRO VITTI** with **GABE ELTAE**

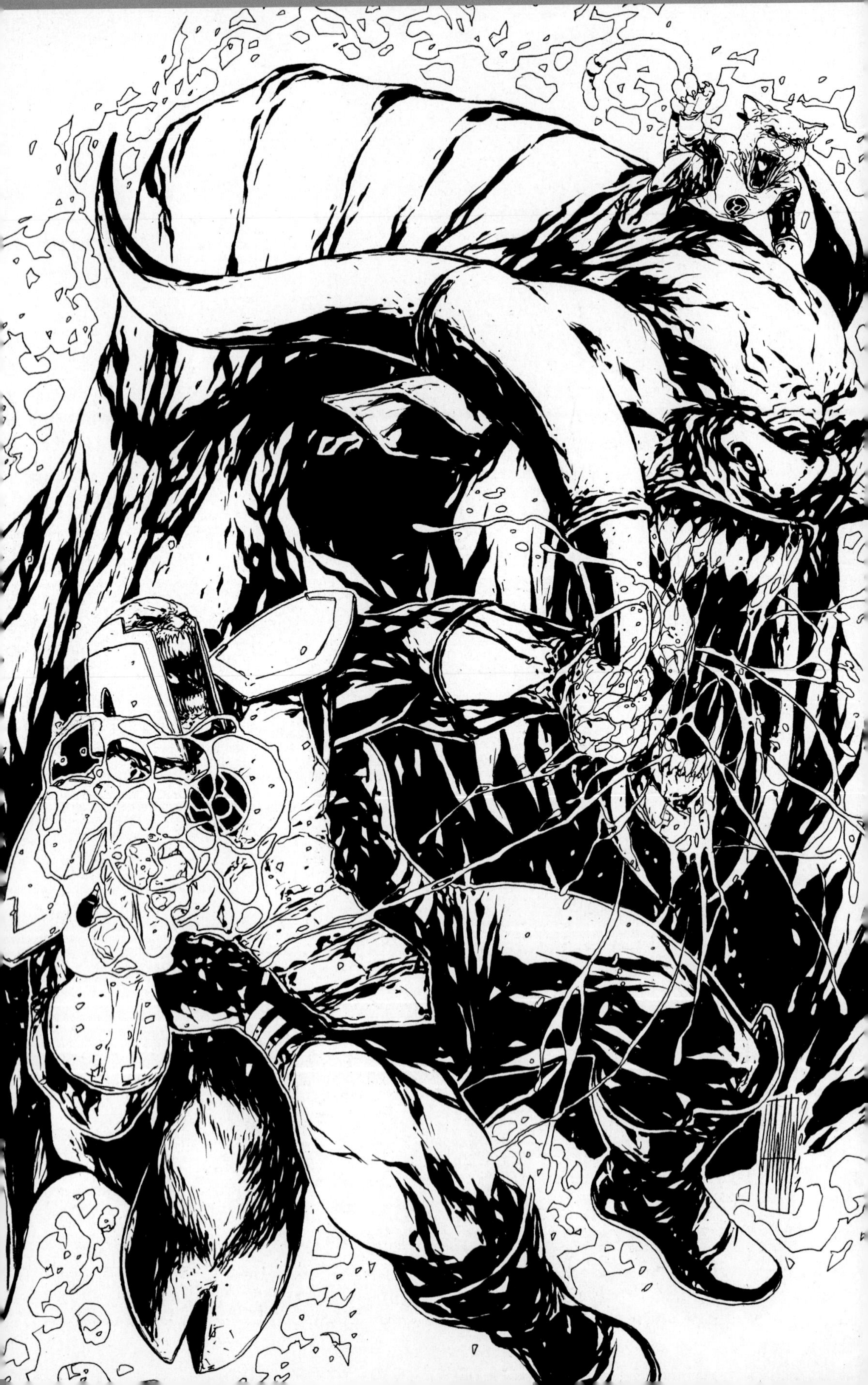

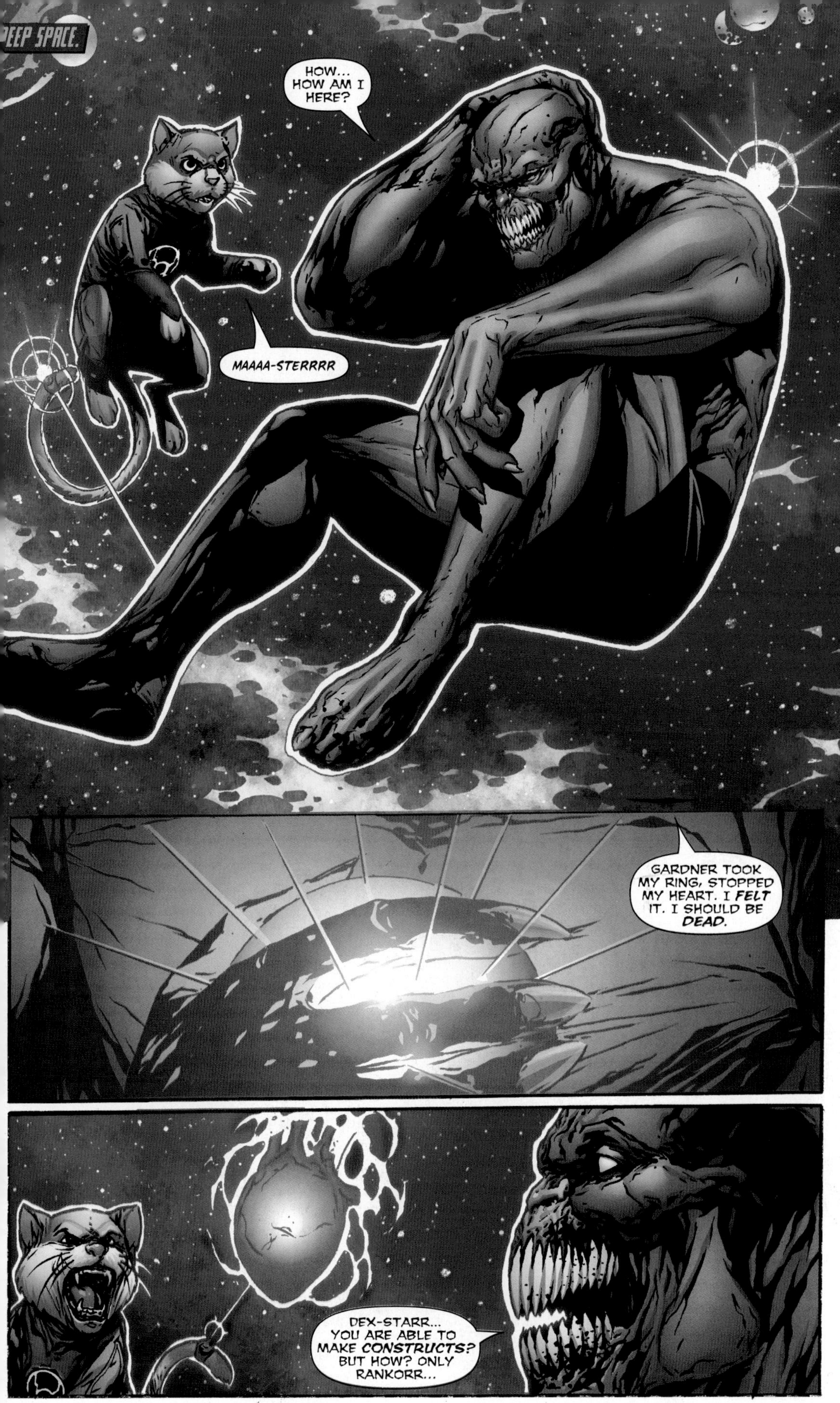
EEP SPACE.
HOW... HOW AM I HERE?
MAAAA-STERRRR
GARDNER TOOK MY RING, STOPPED MY HEART. I FELT IT. I SHOULD BE DEAD.
DEX-STARR... YOU ARE ABLE TO MAKE CONSTRUCTS? BUT HOW? ONLY RANKORR...

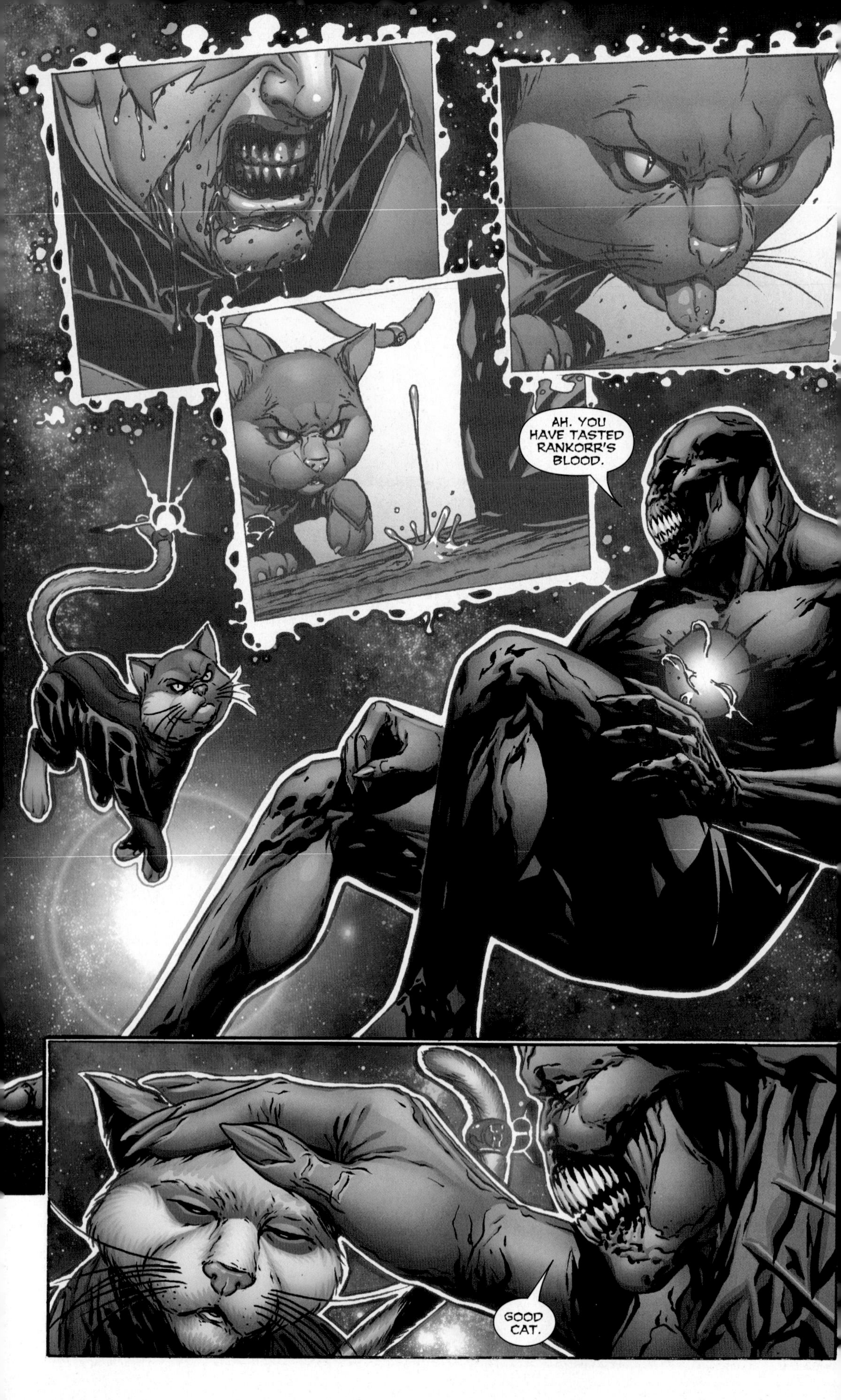
AH. YOU HAVE TASTED RANKORR'S BLOOD.
GOOD CAT.

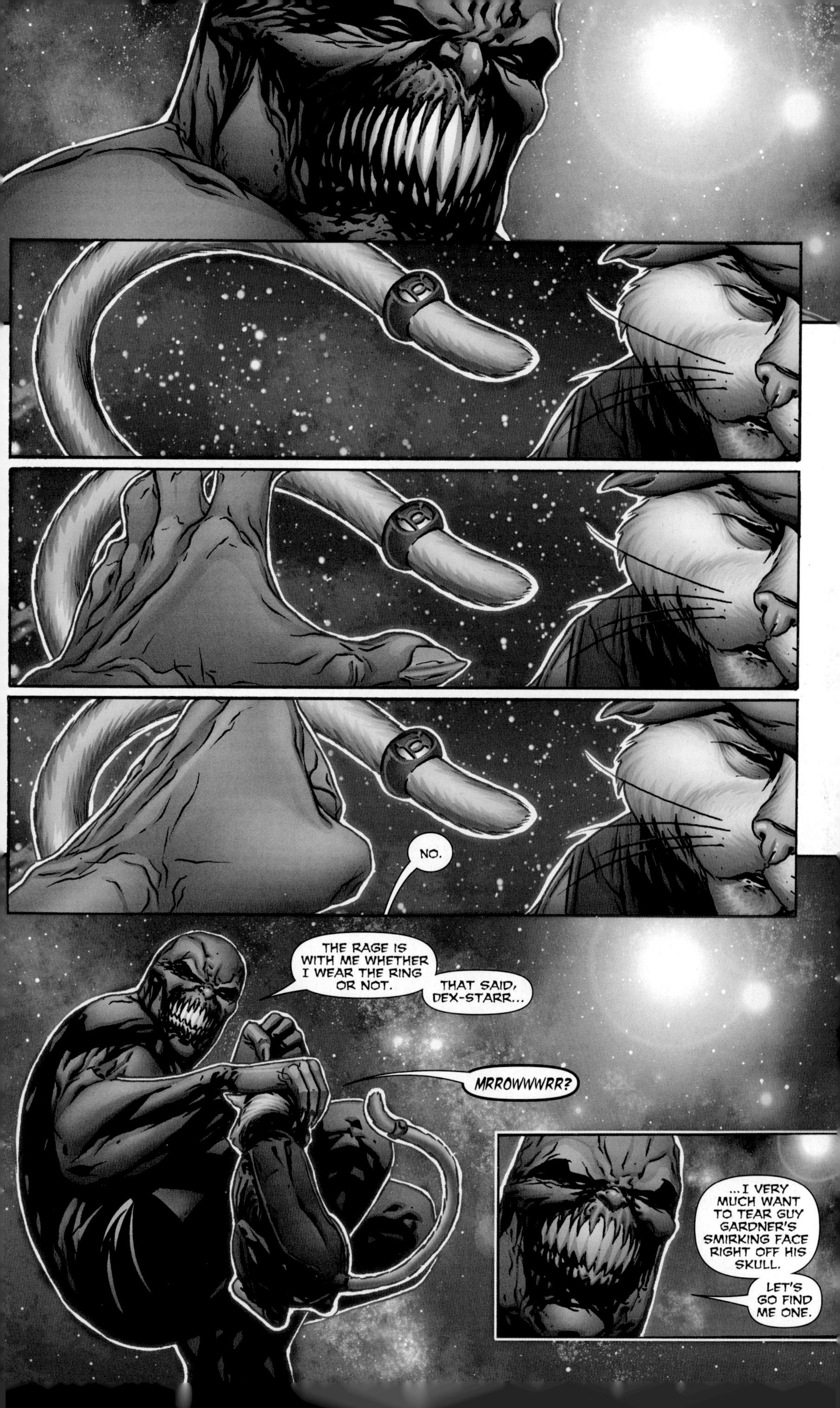
NO.
THE RAGE IS WITH ME WHETHER I WEAR THE RING OR NOT.
THAT SAID, DEX-STARR...
MRROWWWRR?
...I VERY MUCH WANT TO TEAR GUY GARDNER'S SMIRKING FACE RIGHT OFF HIS SKULL.
LET'S GO FIND ME ONE.

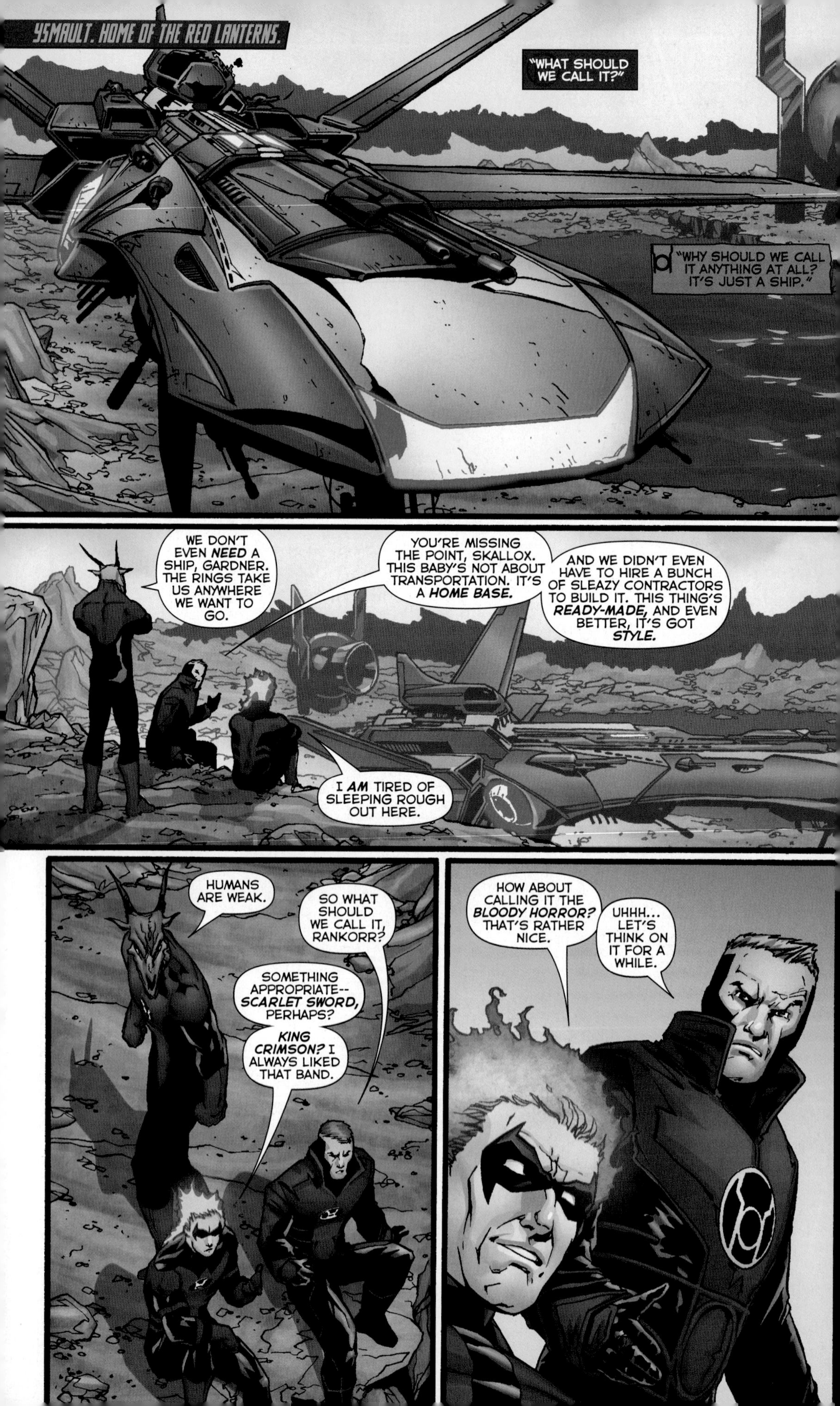
YSMAULT. HOME OF THE RED LANTERNS.
"WHAT SHOULD WE CALL IT?"
"WHY SHOULD WE CALL IT ANYTHING AT ALL? IT'S JUST A SHIP."
WE DON'T EVEN NEED A SHIP, GARDNER. THE RINGS TAKE US ANYWHERE WE WANT TO GO.
YOU'RE MISSING THE POINT, SKALLOX. THIS BABY'S NOT ABOUT TRANSPORTATION. IT'S A HOME BASE.
AND WE DIDN'T EVEN HAVE TO HIRE A BUNCH OF SLEAZY CONTRACTORS TO BUILD IT. THIS THING'S READY-MADE, AND EVEN BETTER, IT'S GOT STYLE.
I AM TIRED OF SLEEPING ROUGH OUT HERE.
HUMANS ARE WEAK.
SO WHAT SHOULD WE CALL IT, RANKORR?
SOMETHING APPROPRIATE-- SCARLET SWORD, PERHAPS?
KING CRIMSON? I ALWAYS LIKED THAT BAND.
HOW ABOUT CALLING IT THE BLOODY HORROR? THAT'S RATHER NICE.
UHHH... LET'S THINK ON IT FOR A WHILE.

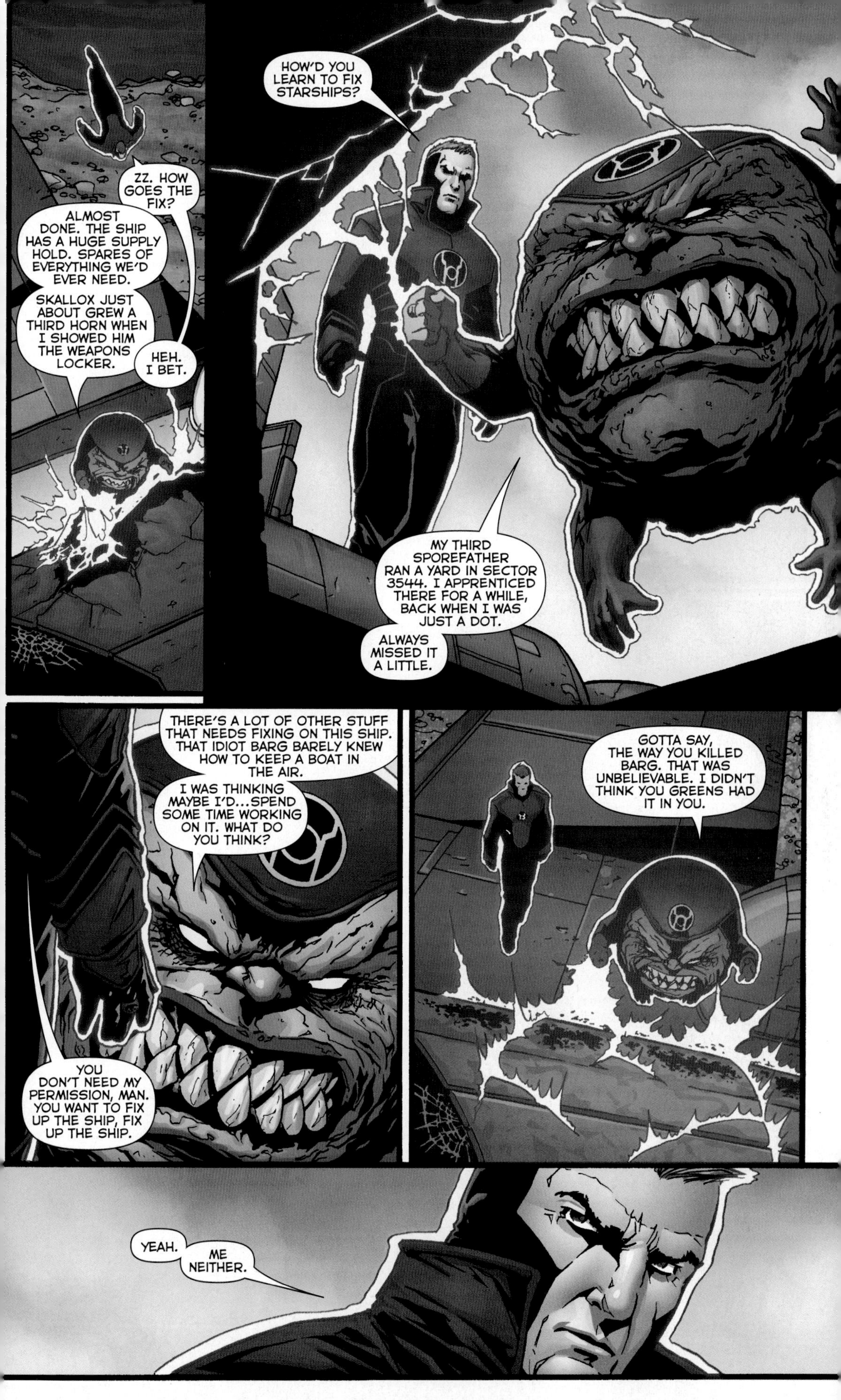

HOW'D YOU LEARN TO FIX STARSHIPS?
ZZ. HOW GOES THE FIX?
ALMOST DONE. THE SHIP HAS A HUGE SUPPLY HOLD. SPARES OF EVERYTHING WE'D EVER NEED.
SKALLOX JUST ABOUT GREW A THIRD HORN WHEN I SHOWED HIM THE WEAPONS LOCKER.
HEH. I BET.
MY THIRD SPOREFATHER RAN A YARD IN SECTOR 3544. I APPRENTICED THERE FOR A WHILE, BACK WHEN I WAS JUST A DOT.
ALWAYS MISSED IT A LITTLE.
THERE'S A LOT OF OTHER STUFF THAT NEEDS FIXING ON THIS SHIP. THAT IDIOT BARG BARELY KNEW HOW TO KEEP A BOAT IN THE AIR.
I WAS THINKING MAYBE I'D...SPEND SOME TIME WORKING ON IT. WHAT DO YOU THINK?
YOU DON'T NEED MY PERMISSION, MAN. YOU WANT TO FIX UP THE SHIP, FIX UP THE SHIP.
GOTTA SAY, THE WAY YOU KILLED BARG. THAT WAS UNBELIEVABLE. I DIDN'T THINK YOU GREENS HAD IT IN YOU.
YEAH.
ME NEITHER.

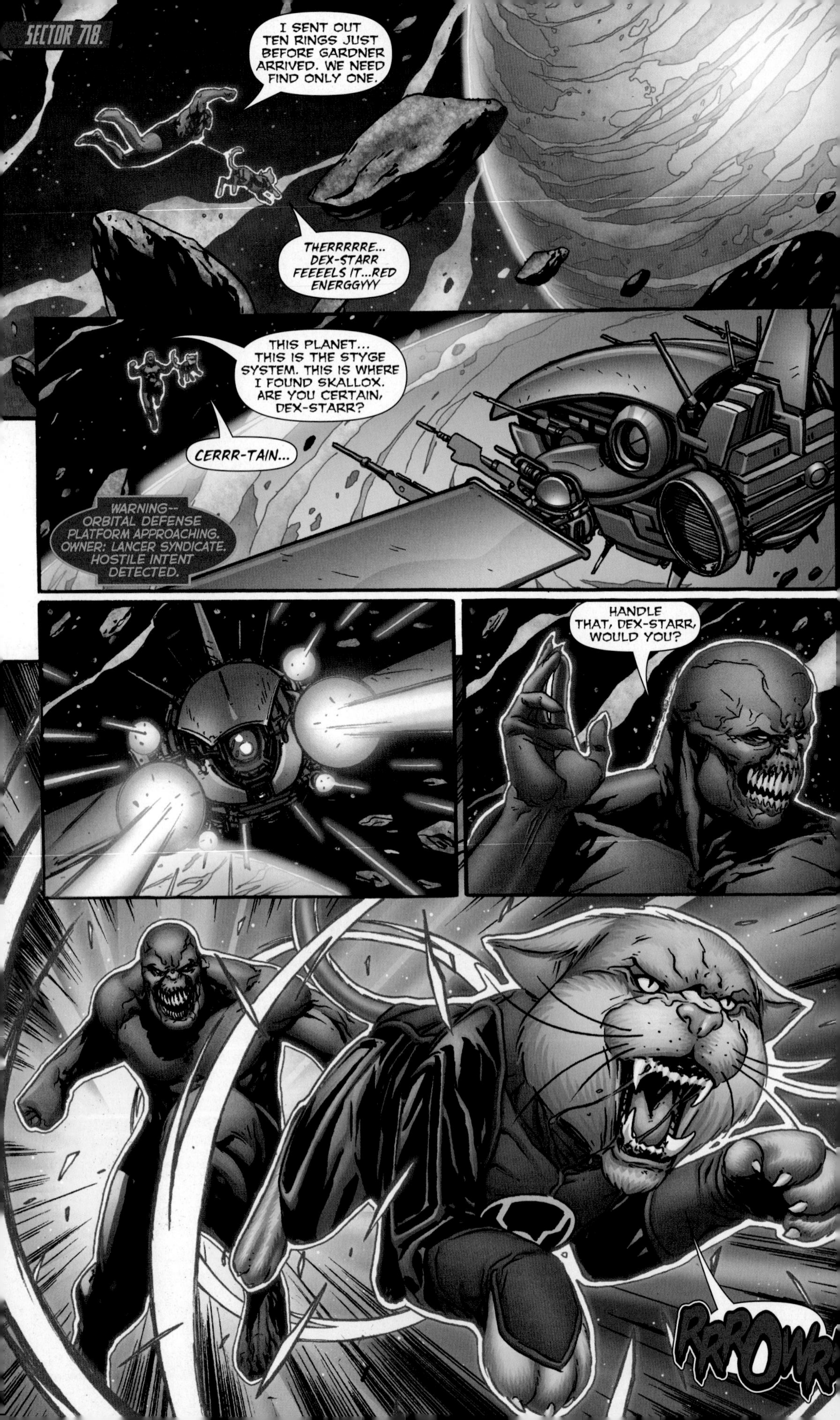
SECTOR 718.
I SENT OUT TEN RINGS JUST BEFORE GARDNER ARRIVED. WE NEED FIND ONLY ONE.
THERRRRRE... DEX-STARR FEEEELS IT...RED ENERGGYYY
THIS PLANET... THIS IS THE STYGE SYSTEM. THIS IS WHERE I FOUND SKALLOX. ARE YOU CERTAIN, DEX-STARR?
CERRR-TAIN...
WARNING-- ORBITAL DEFENSE PLATFORM APPROACHING. OWNER: LANCER SYNDICATE. HOSTILE INTENT DETECTED.
HANDLE THAT, DEX-STARR, WOULD YOU?
RRROWR

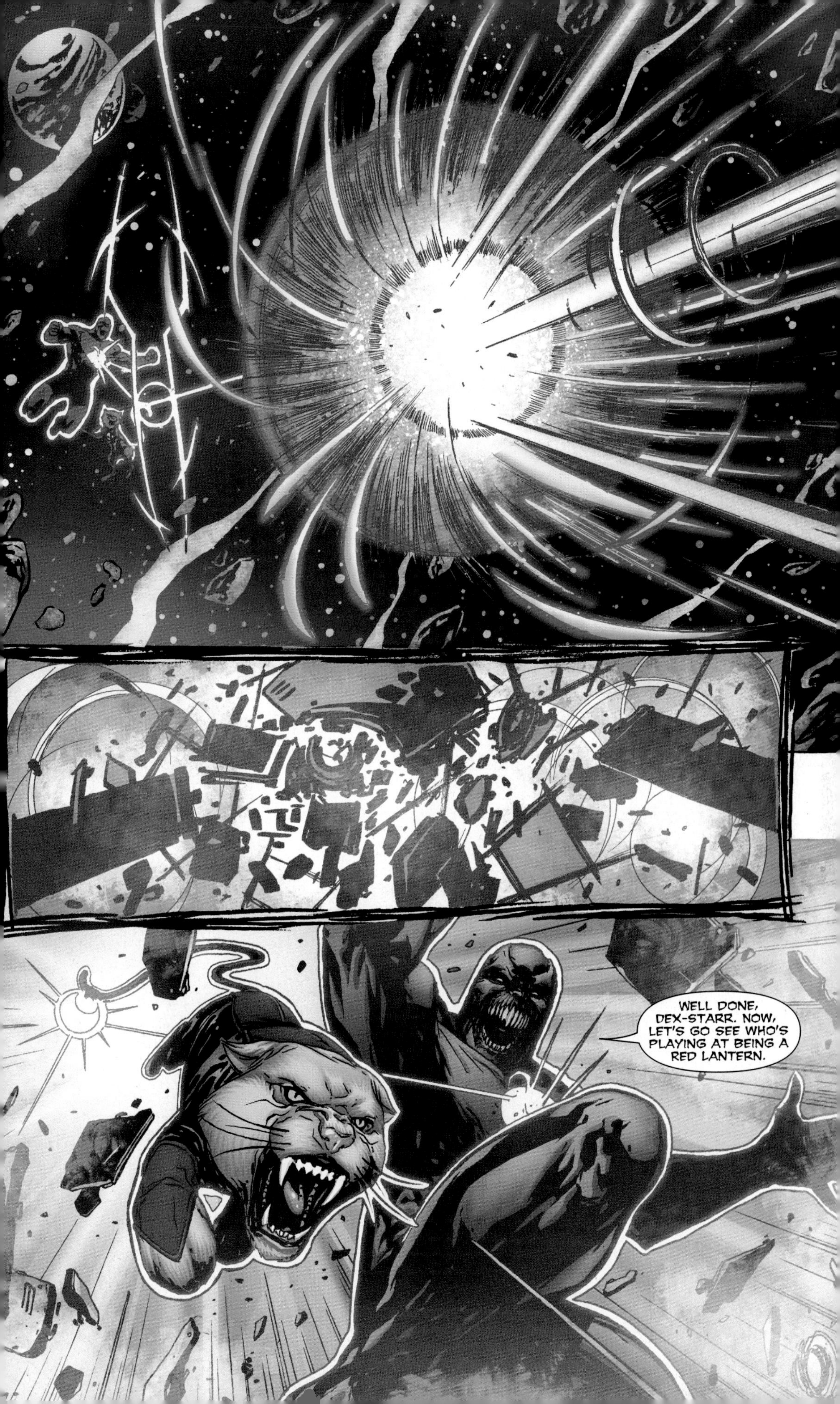
WELL DONE, DEX-STARR. NOW, LET'S GO SEE WHO'S PLAYING AT BEING A RED LANTERN.

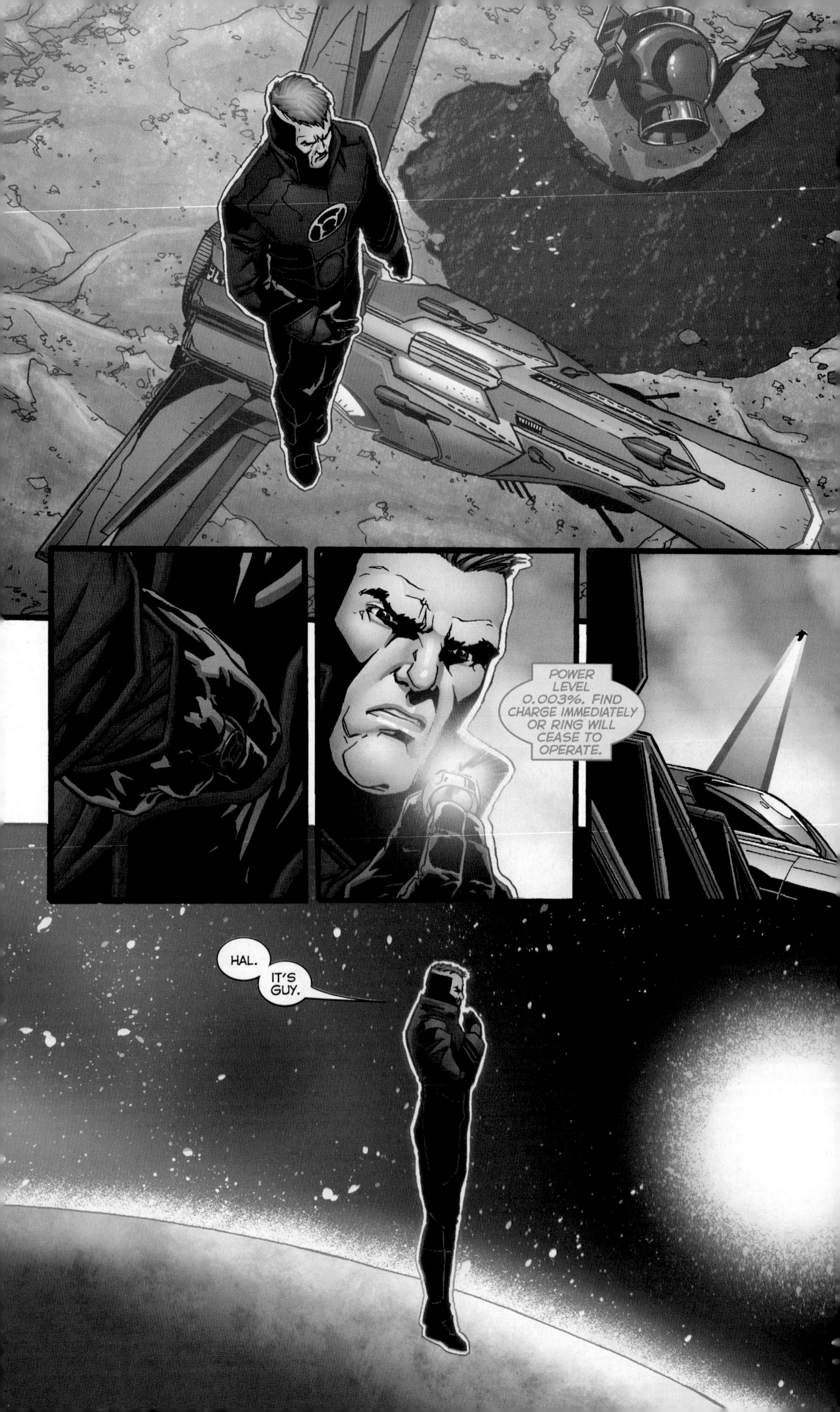
POWER LEVEL 0.003%. FIND CHARGE IMMEDIATELY OR RING WILL CEASE TO OPERATE.
HAL.
IT'S GUY.

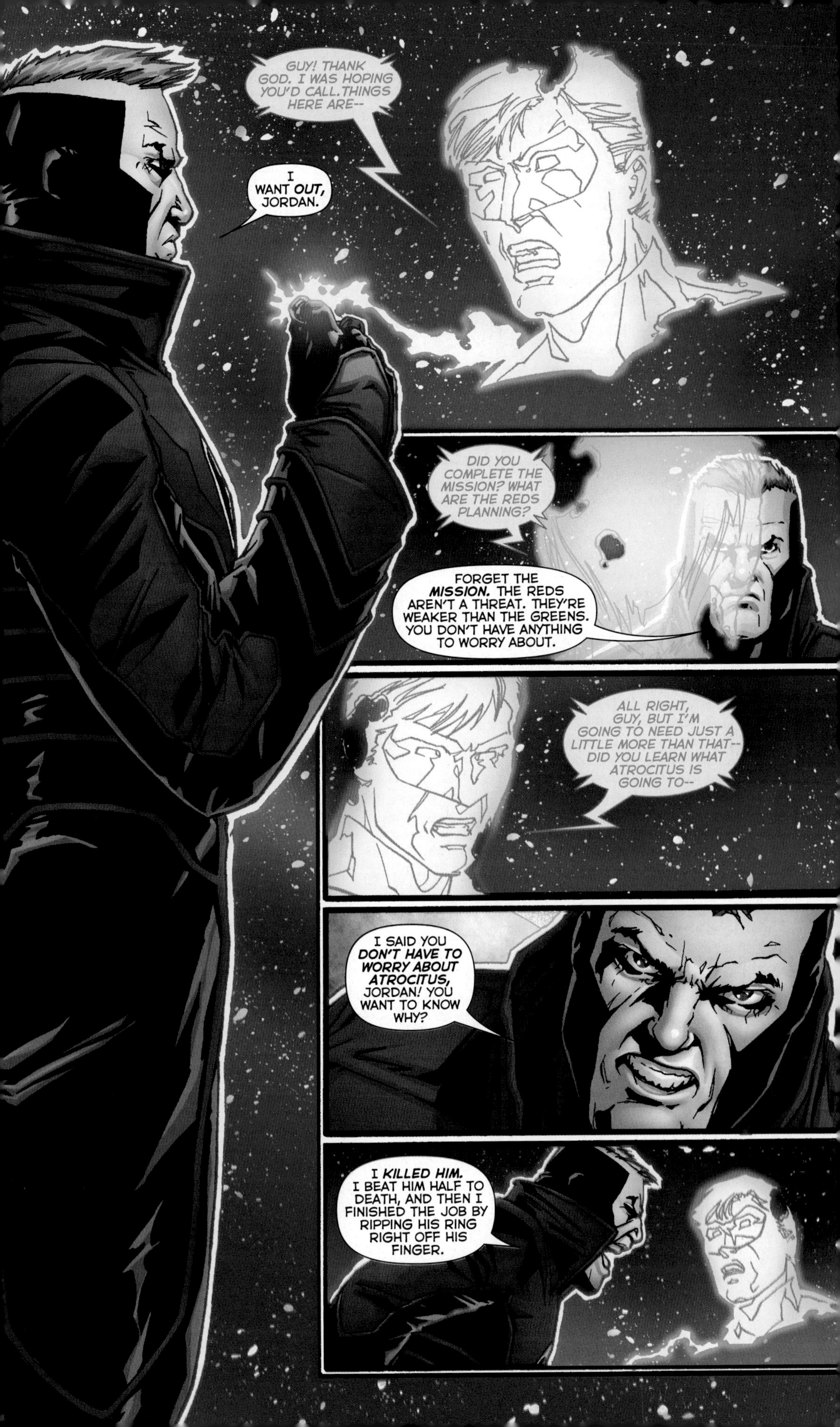
GUY! THANK GOD. I WAS HOPING YOU'D CALL. THINGS HERE ARE--
I WANT OUT, JORDAN.
DID YOU COMPLETE THE MISSION? WHAT ARE THE REDS PLANNING?
FORGET THE MISSION. THE REDS AREN'T A THREAT. THEY'RE WEAKER THAN THE GREENS. YOU DON'T HAVE ANYTHING TO WORRY ABOUT.
ALL RIGHT, GUY, BUT I'M GOING TO NEED JUST A LITTLE MORE THAN THAT-- DID YOU LEARN WHAT ATROCITUS IS GOING TO--
I SAID YOU DON'T HAVE TO WORRY ABOUT ATROCITUS, JORDAN! YOU WANT TO KNOW WHY?
I KILLED HIM. I BEAT HIM HALF TO DEATH, AND THEN I FINISHED THE JOB BY RIPPING HIS RING RIGHT OFF HIS FINGER.

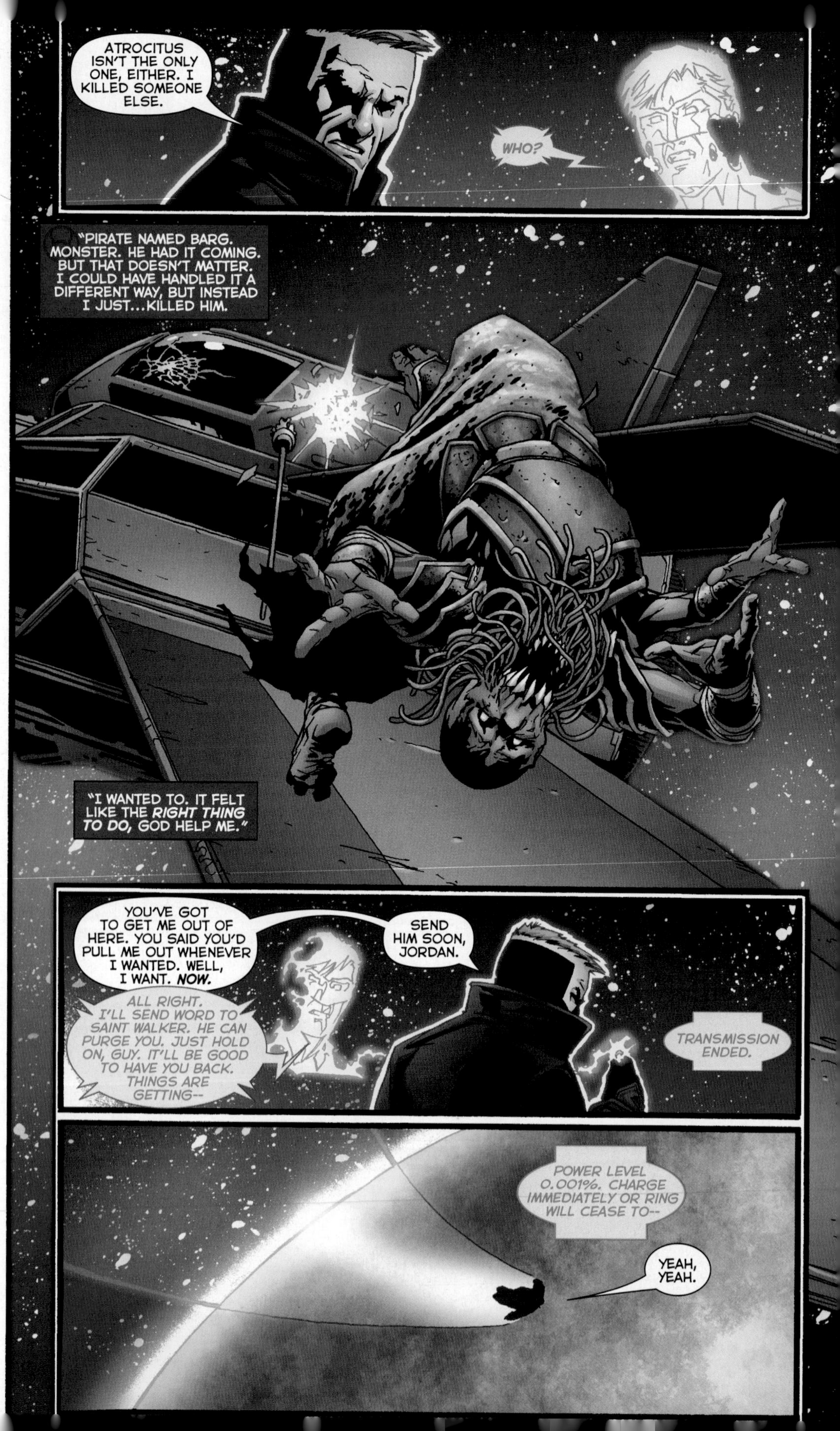
ATROCITUS ISN'T THE ONLY ONE, EITHER. I KILLED SOMEONE ELSE.
WHO?
"PIRATE NAMED BARG. MONSTER. HE HAD IT COMING. BUT THAT DOESN'T MATTER. I COULD HAVE HANDLED IT A DIFFERENT WAY, BUT INSTEAD I JUST...KILLED HIM.
"I WANTED TO. IT FELT LIKE THE *RIGHT THING TO DO,* GOD HELP ME."
YOU'VE GOT TO GET ME OUT OF HERE. YOU SAID YOU'D PULL ME OUT WHENEVER I WANTED. WELL, I WANT. ***NOW.***
ALL RIGHT. I'LL SEND WORD TO SAINT WALKER. HE CAN PURGE YOU. JUST HOLD ON, GUY. IT'LL BE GOOD TO HAVE YOU BACK. THINGS ARE GETTING--
SEND HIM SOON, JORDAN.
TRANSMISSION ENDED.
POWER LEVEL 0.001%. CHARGE IMMEDIATELY OR RING WILL CEASE TO--
YEAH, YEAH.

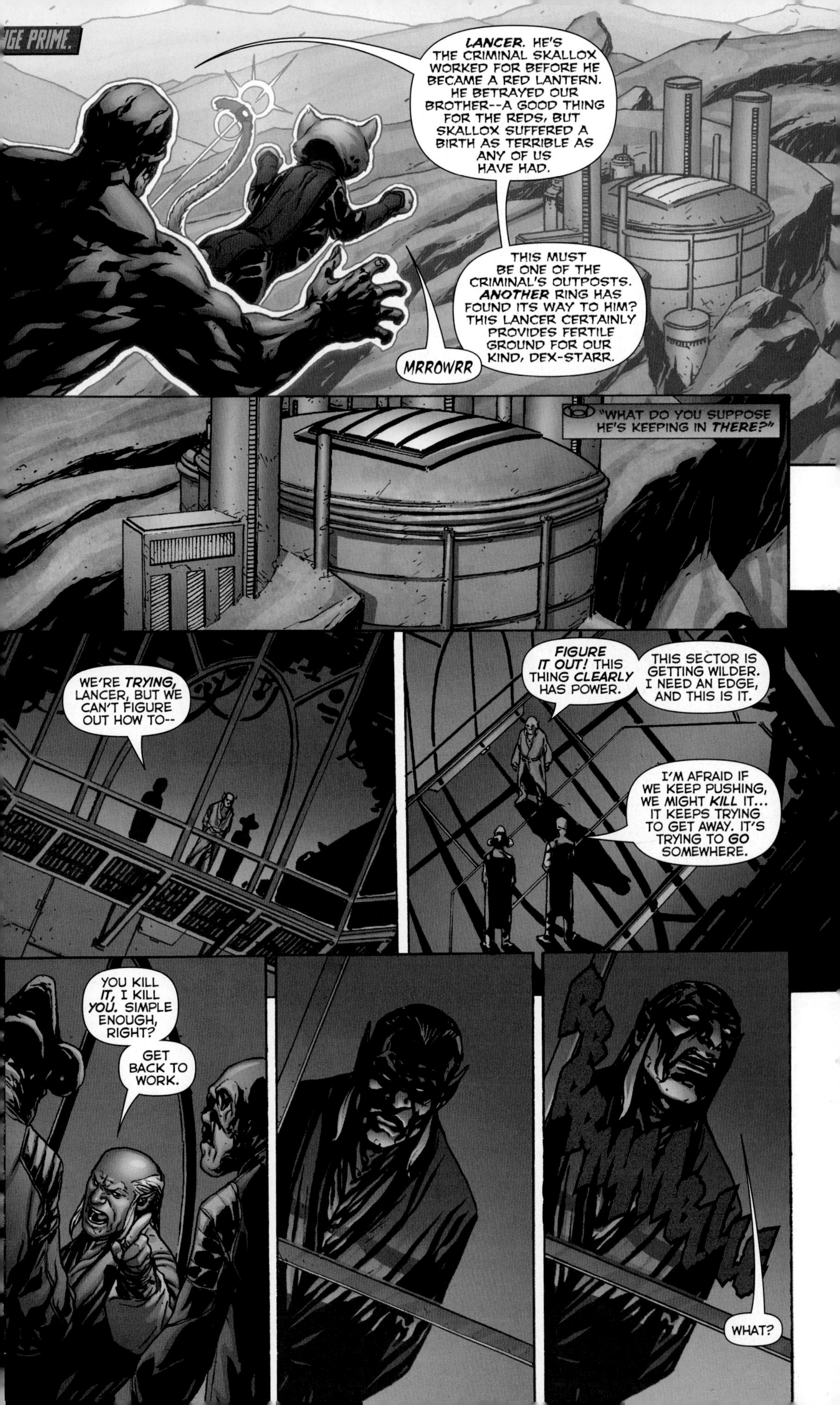

...GE PRIME.
LANCER. HE'S THE CRIMINAL SKALLOX WORKED FOR BEFORE HE BECAME A RED LANTERN. HE BETRAYED OUR BROTHER--A GOOD THING FOR THE REDS, BUT SKALLOX SUFFERED A BIRTH AS TERRIBLE AS ANY OF US HAVE HAD.
THIS MUST BE ONE OF THE CRIMINAL'S OUTPOSTS. ANOTHER RING HAS FOUND ITS WAY TO HIM? THIS LANCER CERTAINLY PROVIDES FERTILE GROUND FOR OUR KIND, DEX-STARR.
MRROWRR
"WHAT DO YOU SUPPOSE HE'S KEEPING IN THERE?"
WE'RE TRYING, LANCER, BUT WE CAN'T FIGURE OUT HOW TO--
FIGURE IT OUT! THIS THING CLEARLY HAS POWER.
THIS SECTOR IS GETTING WILDER. I NEED AN EDGE, AND THIS IS IT.
I'M AFRAID IF WE KEEP PUSHING, WE MIGHT KILL IT... IT KEEPS TRYING TO GET AWAY. IT'S TRYING TO GO SOMEWHERE.
YOU KILL IT, I KILL YOU. SIMPLE ENOUGH, RIGHT?
GET BACK TO WORK.
WHAT?

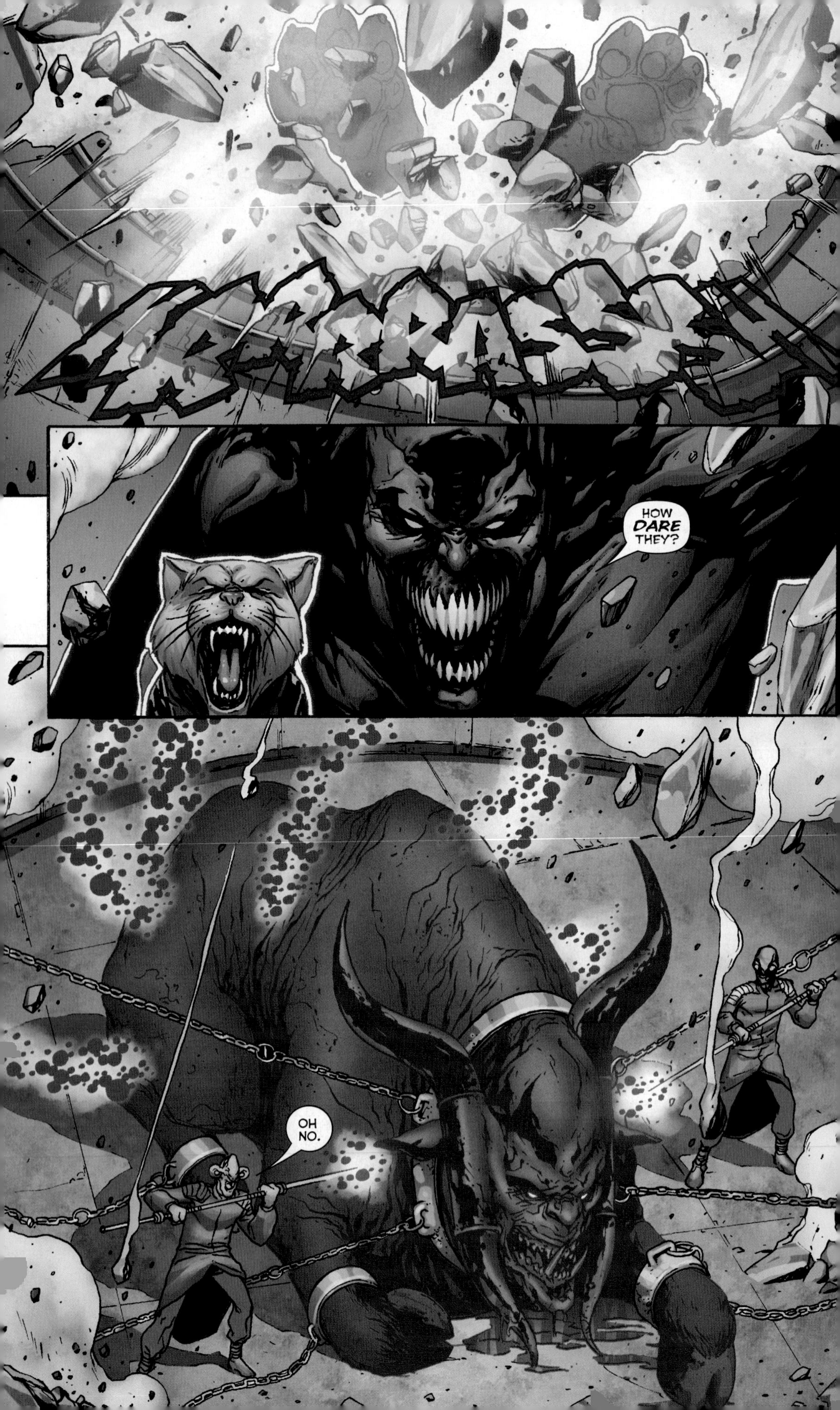
HOW DARE THEY?
OH NO.

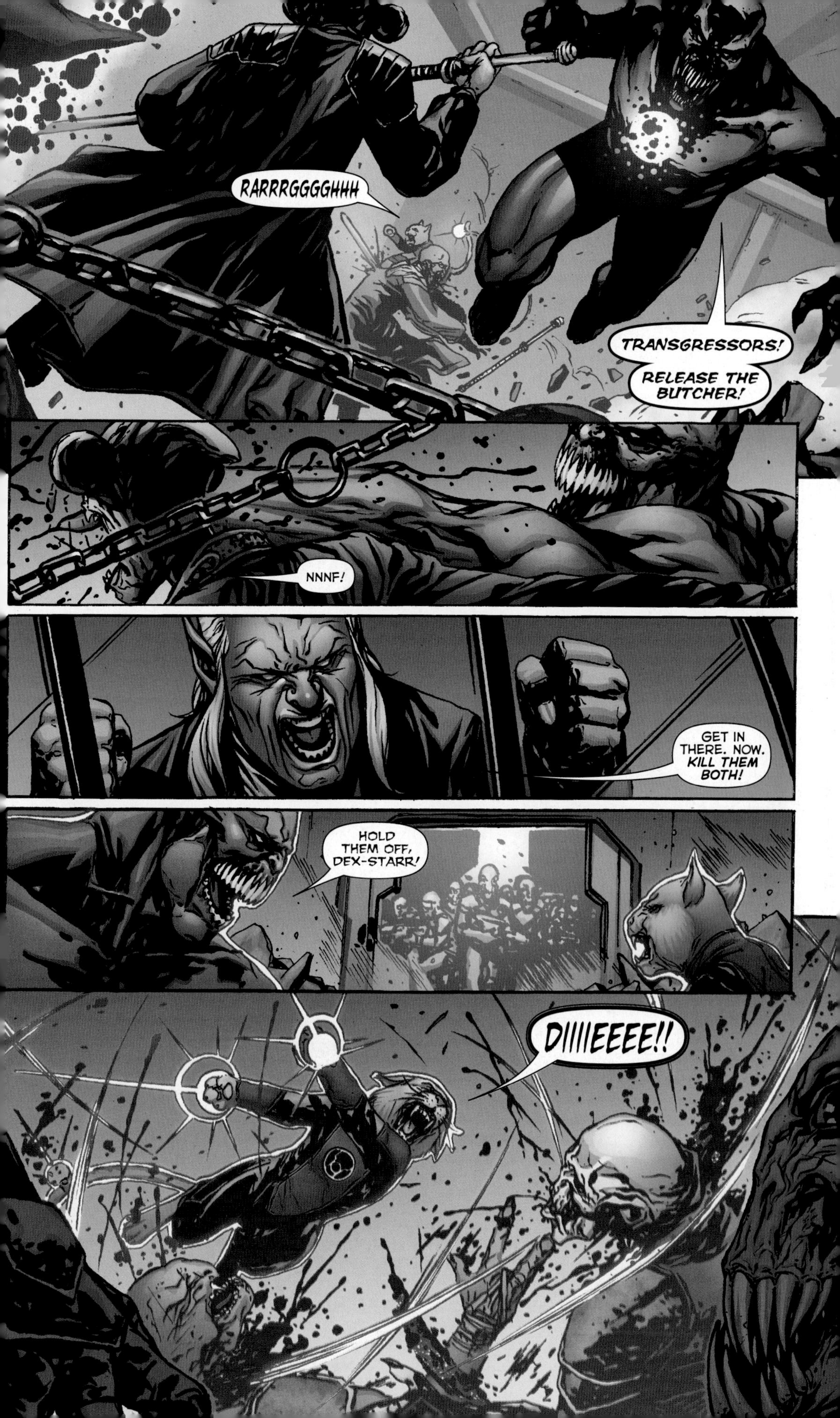
RARRRGGGGHHH
TRANSGRESSORS!
RELEASE THE BUTCHER!
NNNF!
GET IN THERE. NOW. KILL THEM BOTH!
HOLD THEM OFF, DEX-STARR!
DIIIIEEEE!!

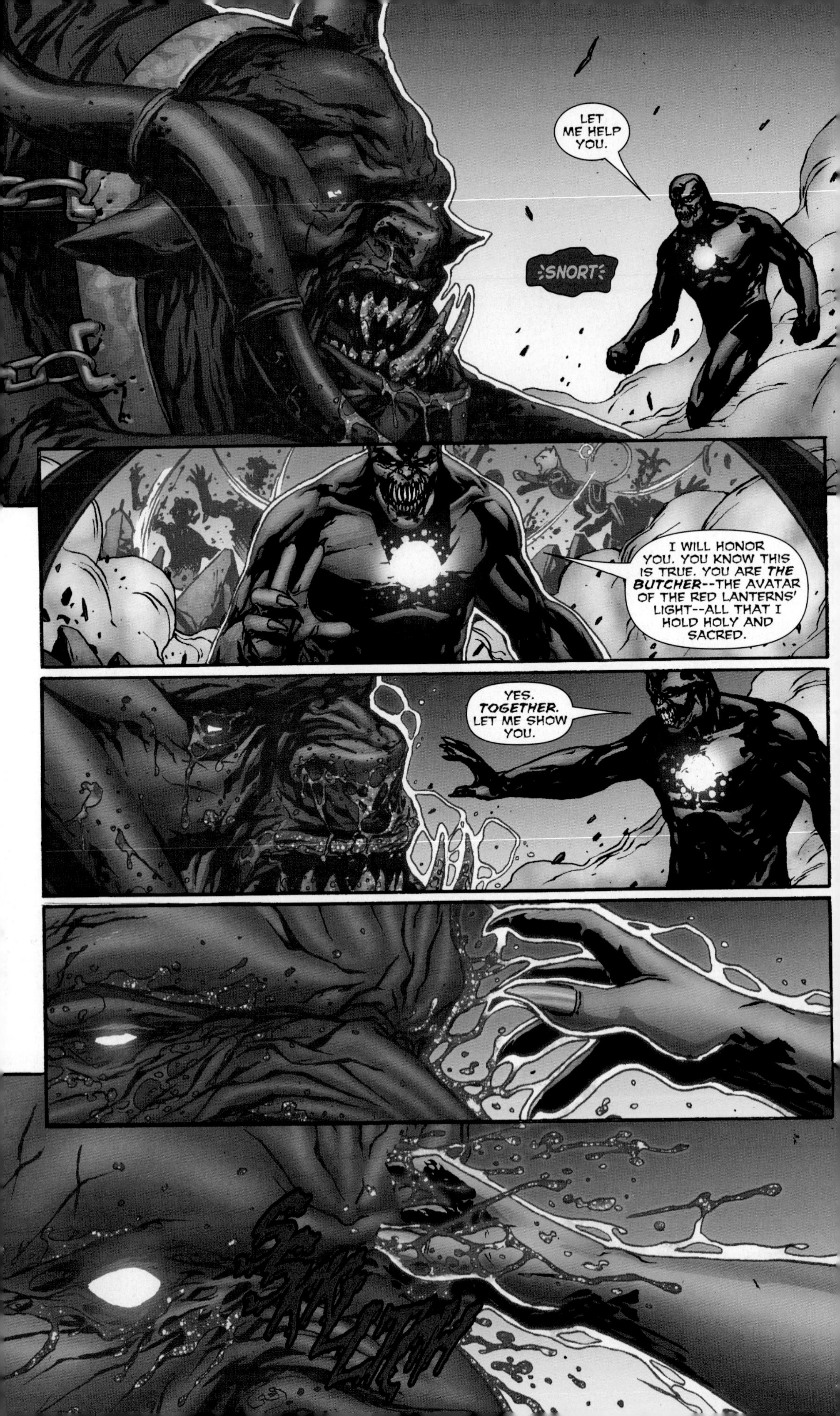
LET ME HELP YOU.
SNORT
I WILL HONOR YOU. YOU KNOW THIS IS TRUE. YOU ARE THE BUTCHER--THE AVATAR OF THE RED LANTERNS' LIGHT--ALL THAT I HOLD HOLY AND SACRED.
YES. TOGETHER. LET ME SHOW YOU.

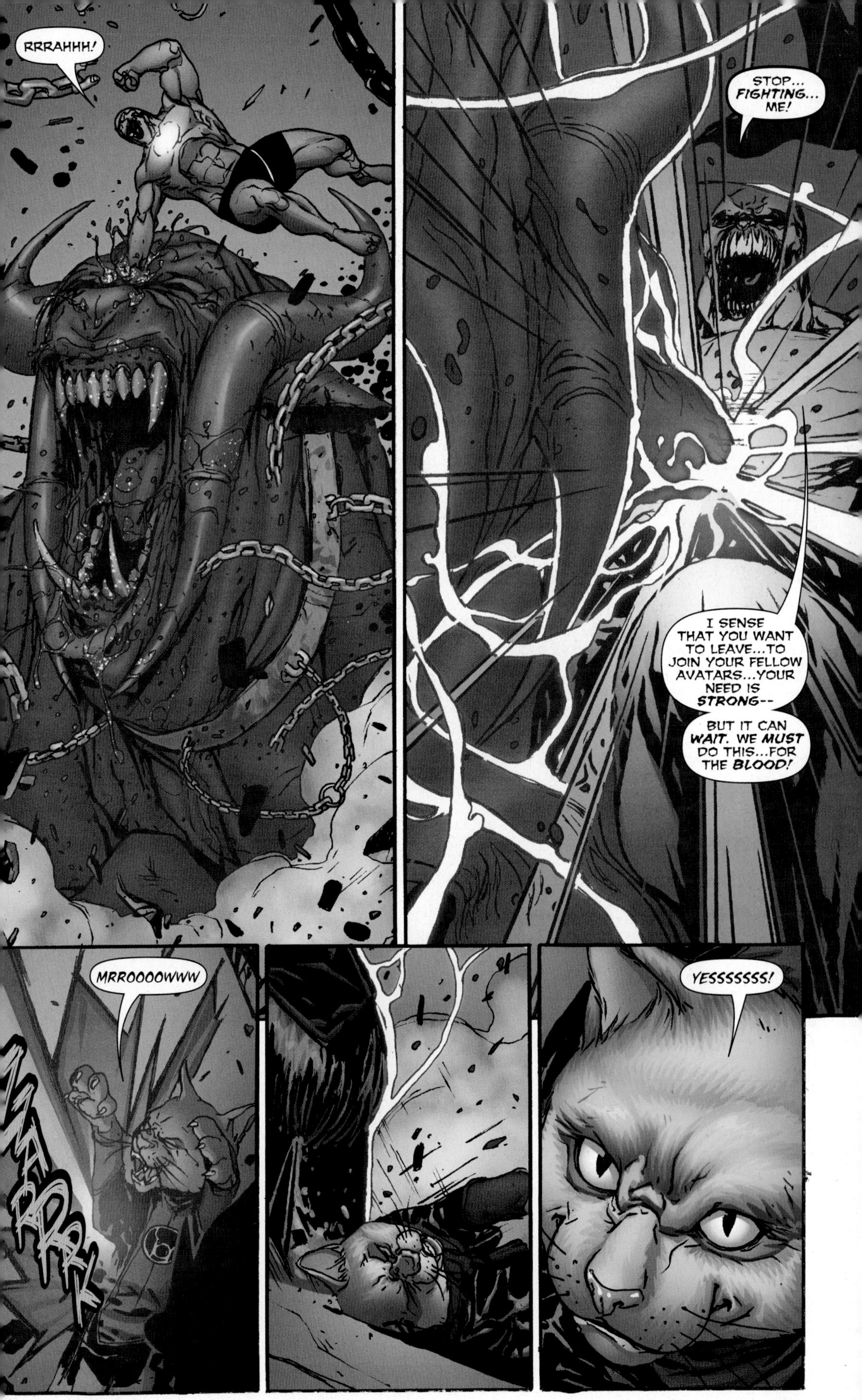
RRRAHHH!
STOP... FIGHTING... ME!
I SENSE THAT YOU WANT TO LEAVE...TO JOIN YOUR FELLOW AVATARS...YOUR NEED IS STRONG--
BUT IT CAN WAIT. WE MUST DO THIS...FOR THE BLOOD!
MRROOOOWWW
YESSSSSSS!

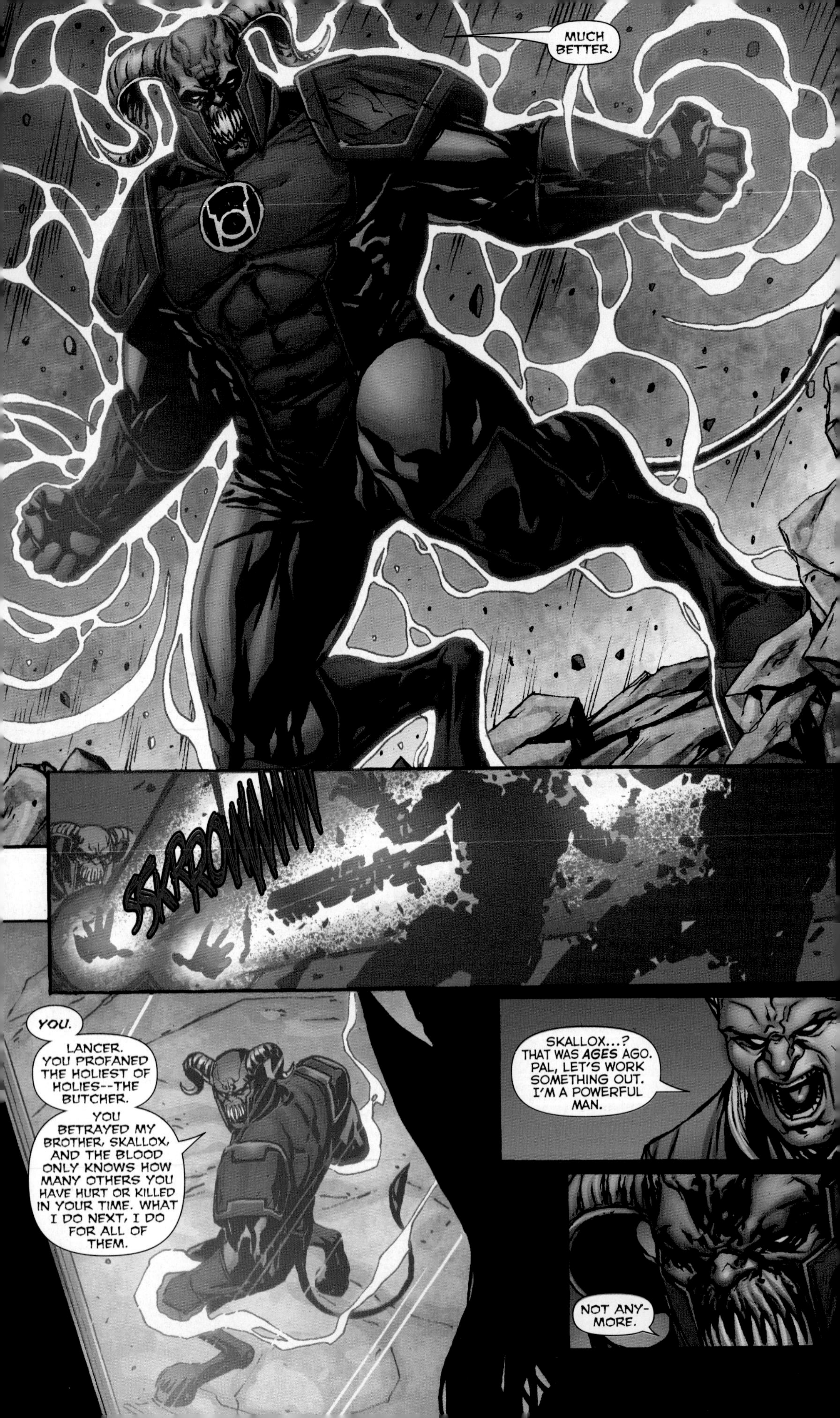
MUCH BETTER.
SKRROWMMMM
YOU.
LANCER. YOU PROFANED THE HOLIEST OF HOLIES--THE BUTCHER.
YOU BETRAYED MY BROTHER, SKALLOX, AND THE BLOOD ONLY KNOWS HOW MANY OTHERS YOU HAVE HURT OR KILLED IN YOUR TIME. WHAT I DO NEXT, I DO FOR ALL OF THEM.
SKALLOX...? THAT WAS AGES AGO. PAL, LET'S WORK SOMETHING OUT. I'M A POWERFUL MAN.
NOT ANY-MORE.

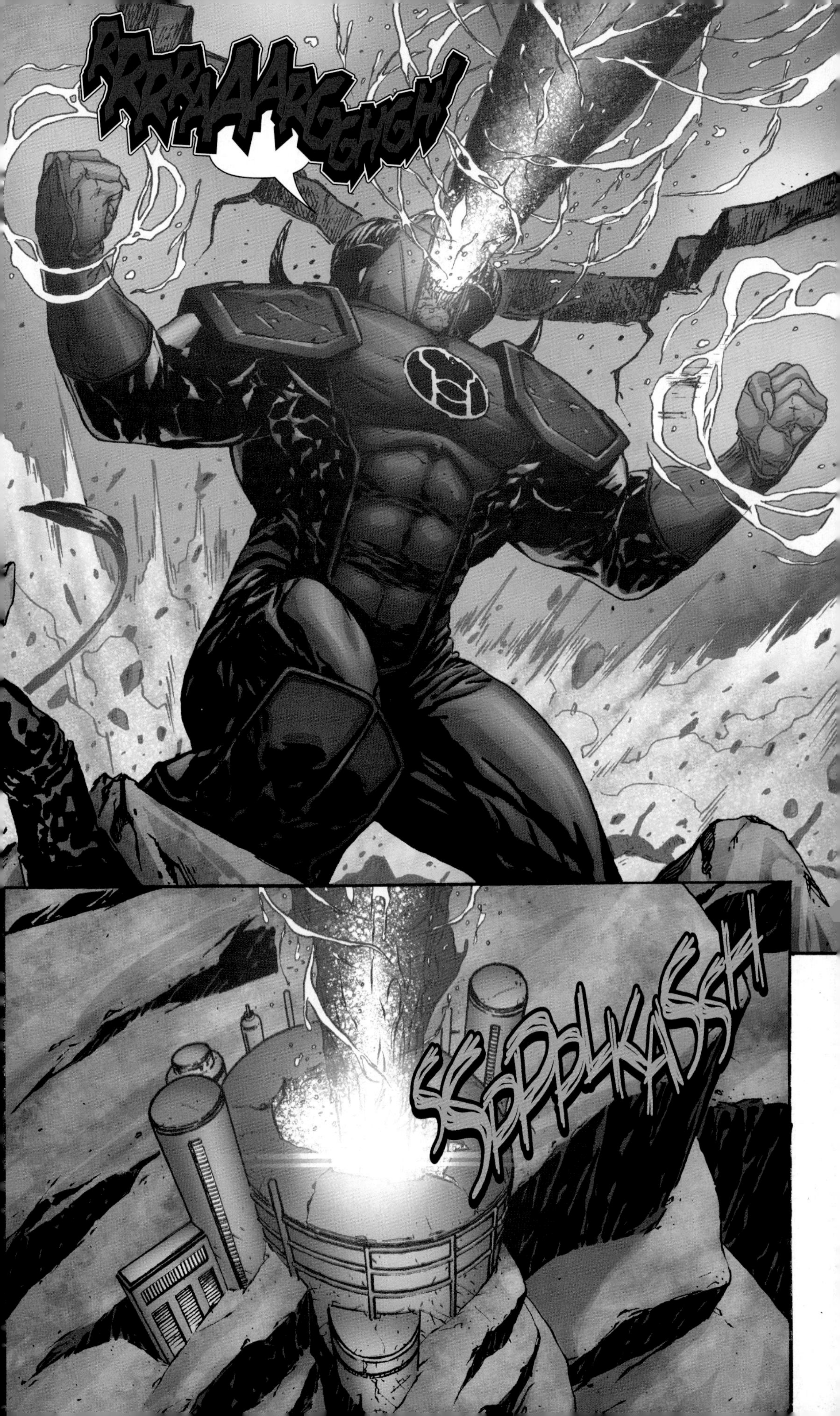
RRRRAAARGGHGH!
SPPPLKASSH

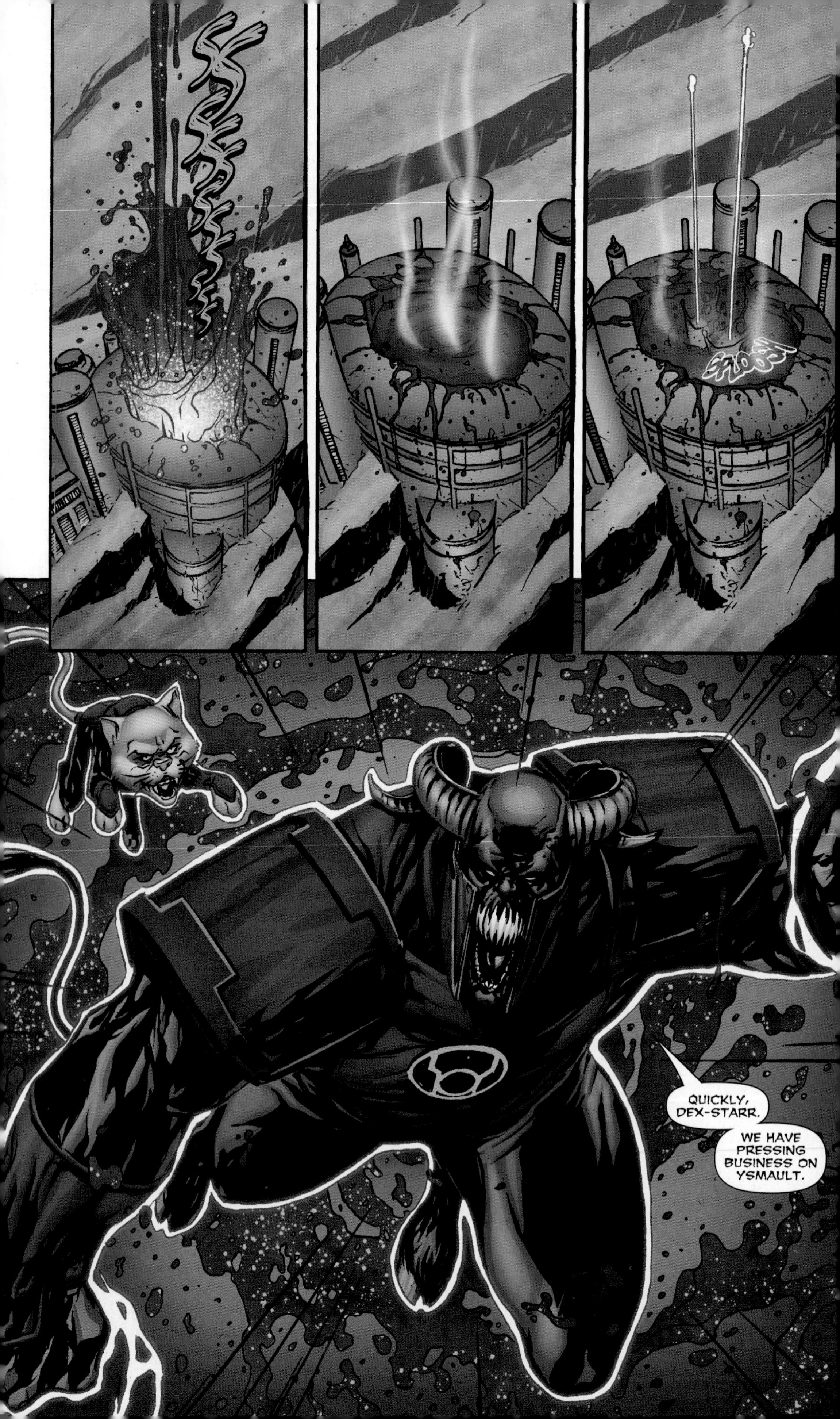
QUICKLY, DEX-STARR.
WE HAVE PRESSING BUSINESS ON YSMAULT.

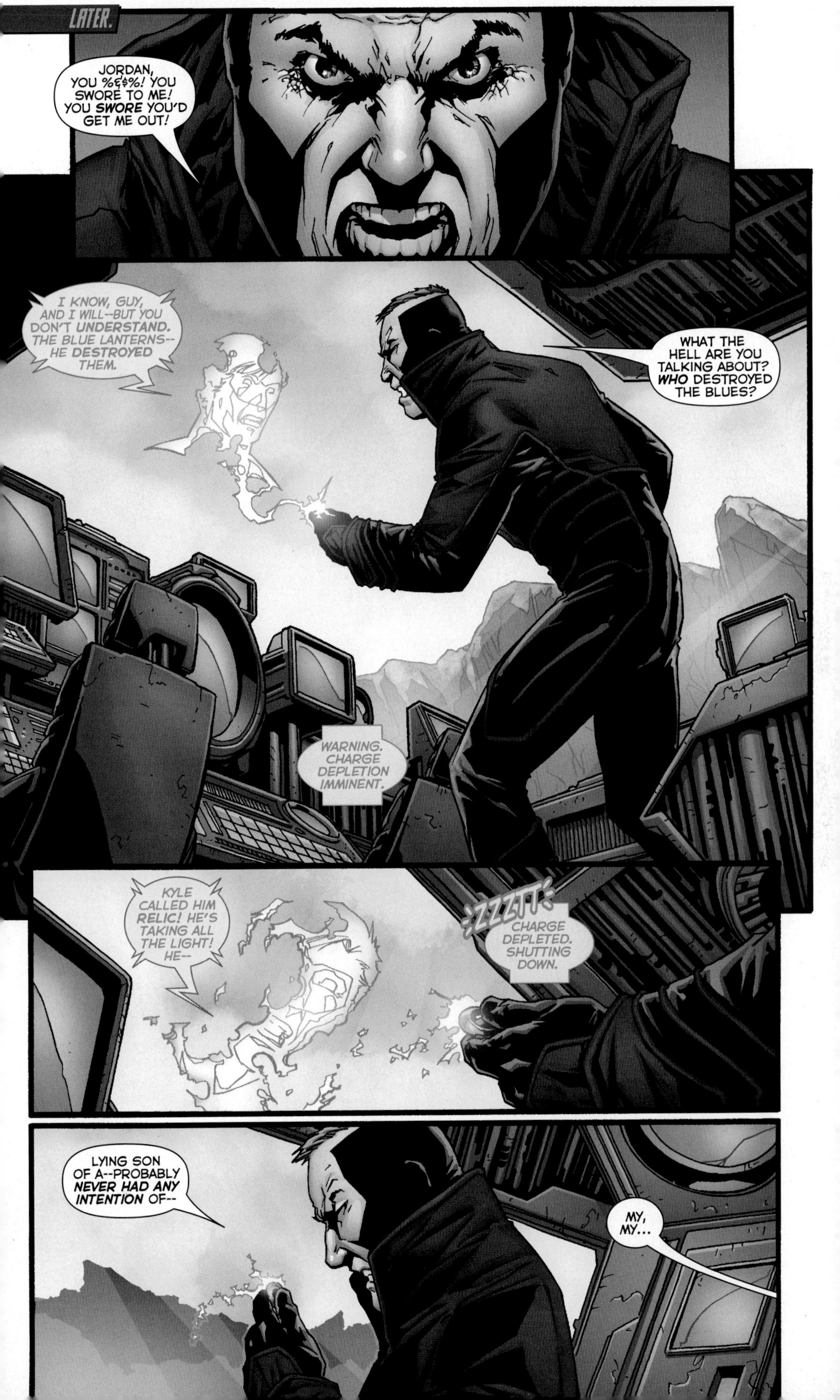
LATER.
JORDAN, YOU %&$%! YOU SWORE TO ME! YOU SWORE YOU'D GET ME OUT!
I KNOW, GUY, AND I WILL--BUT YOU DON'T UNDERSTAND. THE BLUE LANTERNS--HE DESTROYED THEM.
WHAT THE HELL ARE YOU TALKING ABOUT? WHO DESTROYED THE BLUES?
WARNING. CHARGE DEPLETION IMMINENT.
KYLE CALLED HIM RELIC! HE'S TAKING ALL THE LIGHT! HE--
ZZZZTT
CHARGE DEPLETED. SHUTTING DOWN.
LYING SON OF A--PROBABLY NEVER HAD ANY INTENTION OF--
MY, MY...

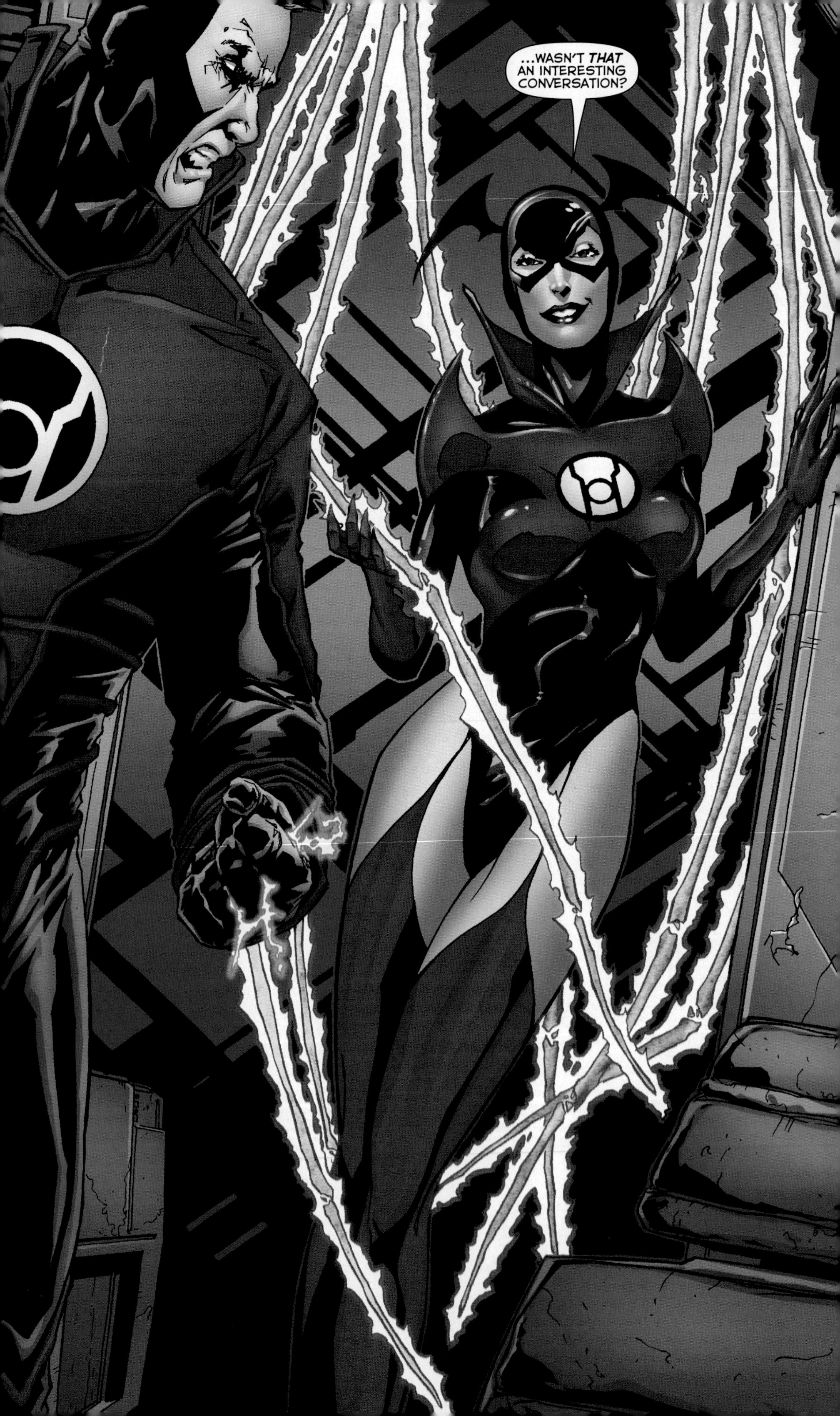
...WASN'T *THAT* AN INTERESTING CONVERSATION?

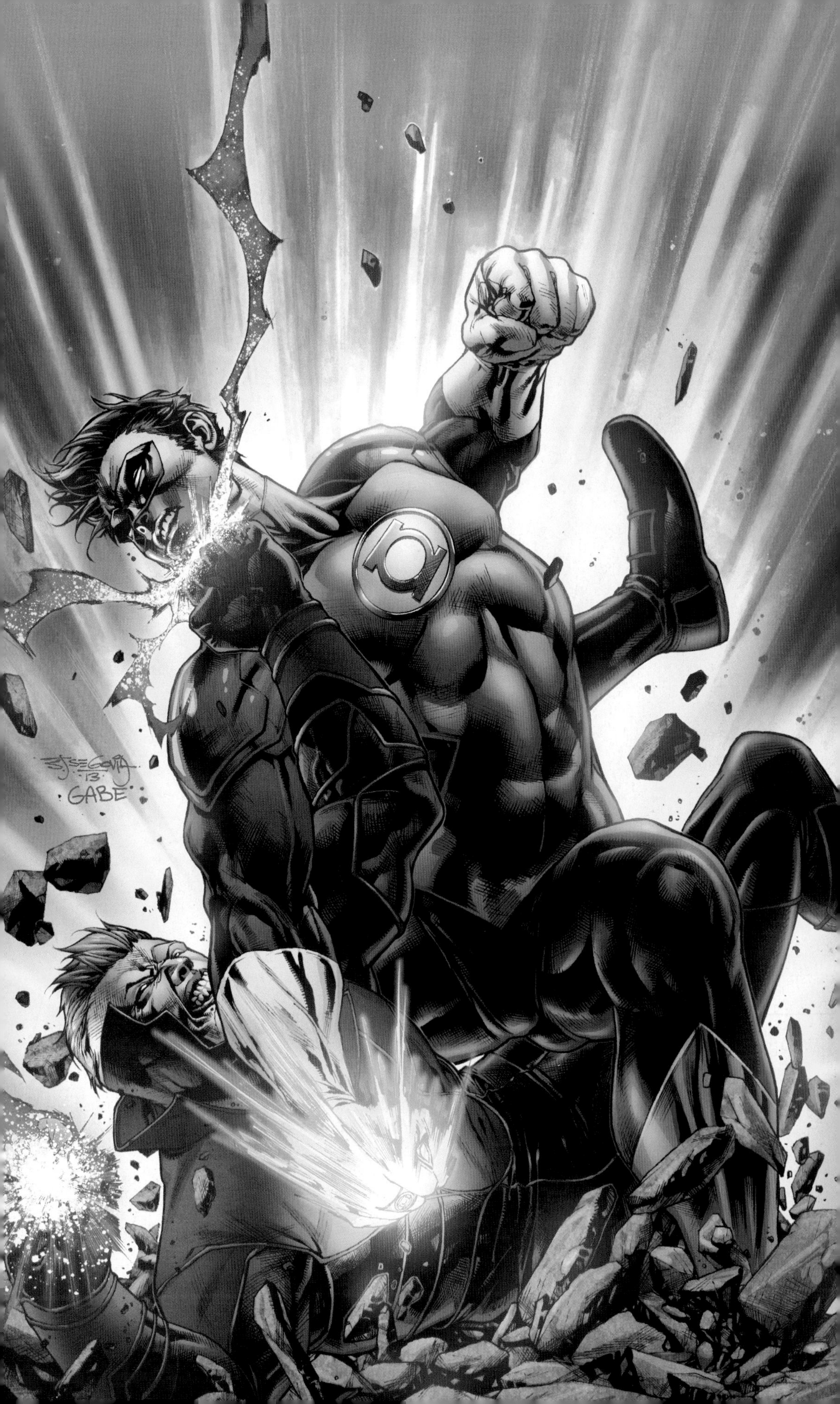

LIGHTS OUT part four: BLOOD BROTHERS

CHARLES SOULE writer **ALESSANDRO VITTI** artist **GABE ELTAEB** colorist cover art by **STEPHEN SEGOVIA** with **GABE ELTAEB**

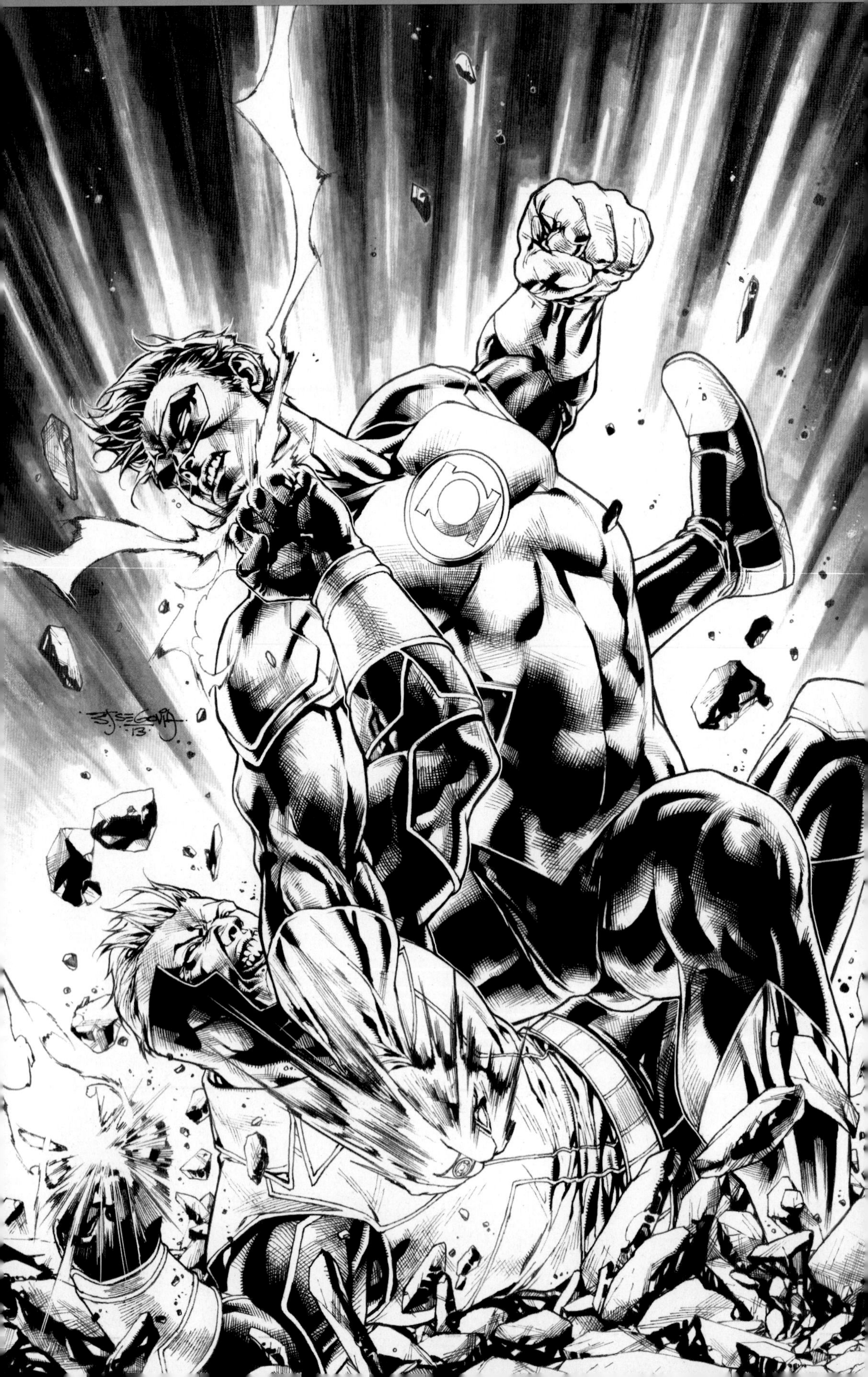

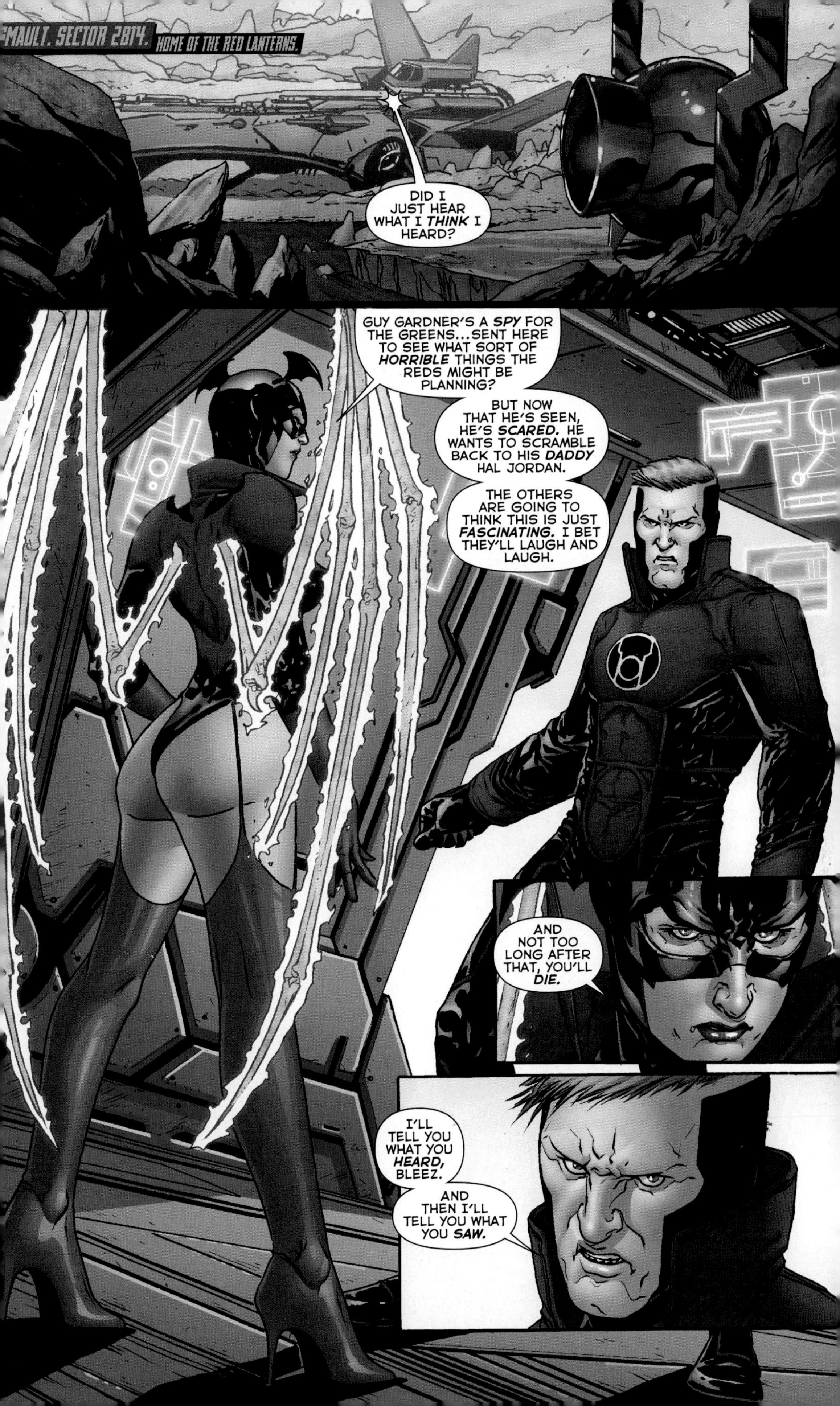
MAULT. SECTOR 2814.
HOME OF THE RED LANTERNS.
DID I JUST HEAR WHAT I *THINK* I HEARD?
GUY GARDNER'S A *SPY* FOR THE GREENS...SENT HERE TO SEE WHAT SORT OF *HORRIBLE* THINGS THE REDS MIGHT BE PLANNING?
BUT NOW THAT HE'S SEEN, HE'S *SCARED.* HE WANTS TO SCRAMBLE BACK TO HIS *DADDY* HAL JORDAN.
THE OTHERS ARE GOING TO THINK THIS IS JUST *FASCINATING.* I BET THEY'LL LAUGH AND LAUGH.
AND NOT TOO LONG AFTER THAT, YOU'LL *DIE.*
I'LL TELL YOU WHAT YOU *HEARD,* BLEEZ.
AND THEN I'LL TELL YOU WHAT YOU *SAW.*

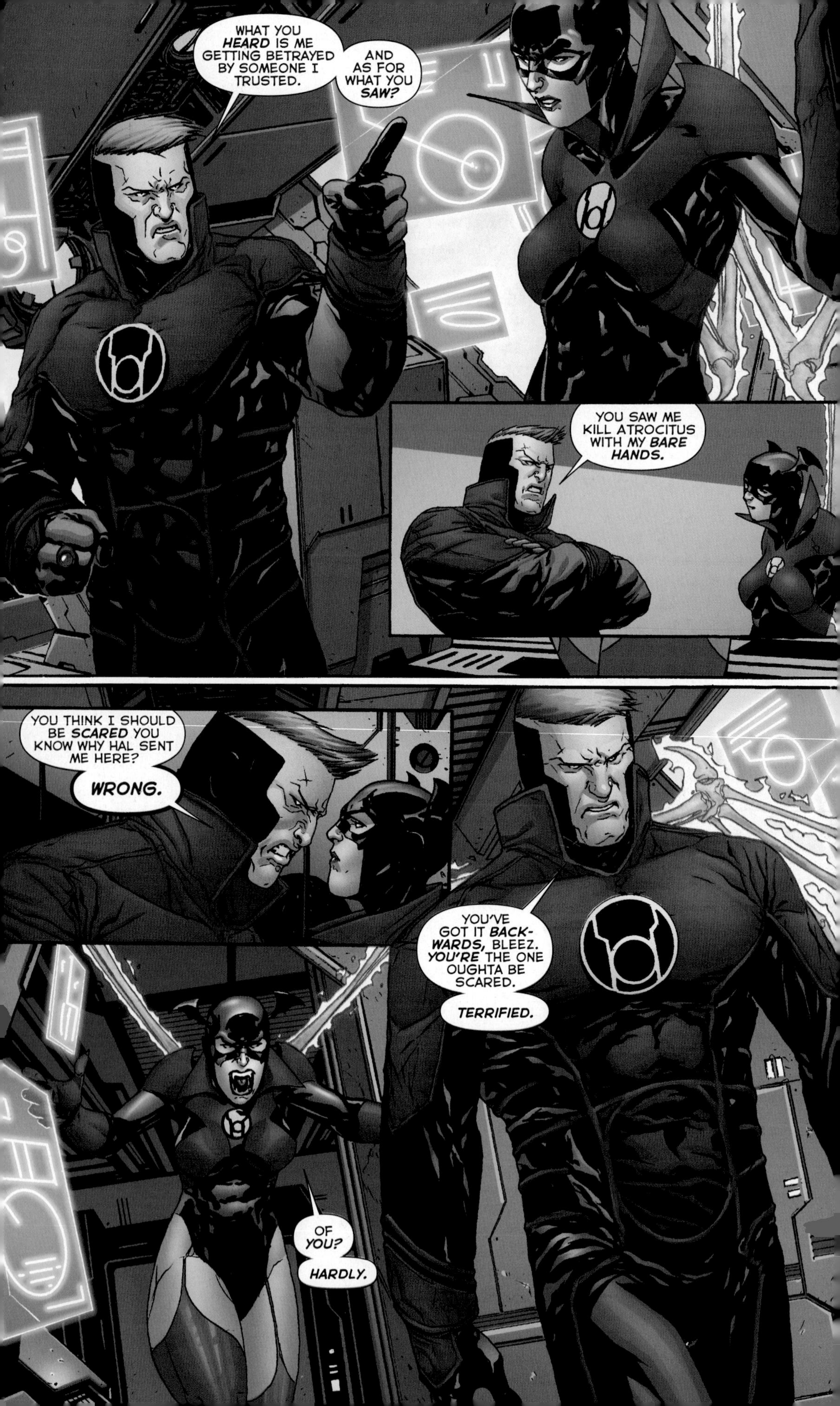
WHAT YOU HEARD IS ME GETTING BETRAYED BY SOMEONE I TRUSTED.
AND AS FOR WHAT YOU SAW?
YOU SAW ME KILL ATROCITUS WITH MY BARE HANDS.
YOU THINK I SHOULD BE SCARED YOU KNOW WHY HAL SENT ME HERE?
WRONG.
YOU'VE GOT IT BACK-WARDS, BLEEZ. YOU'RE THE ONE OUGHTA BE SCARED.
TERRIFIED.
OF YOU?
HARDLY.

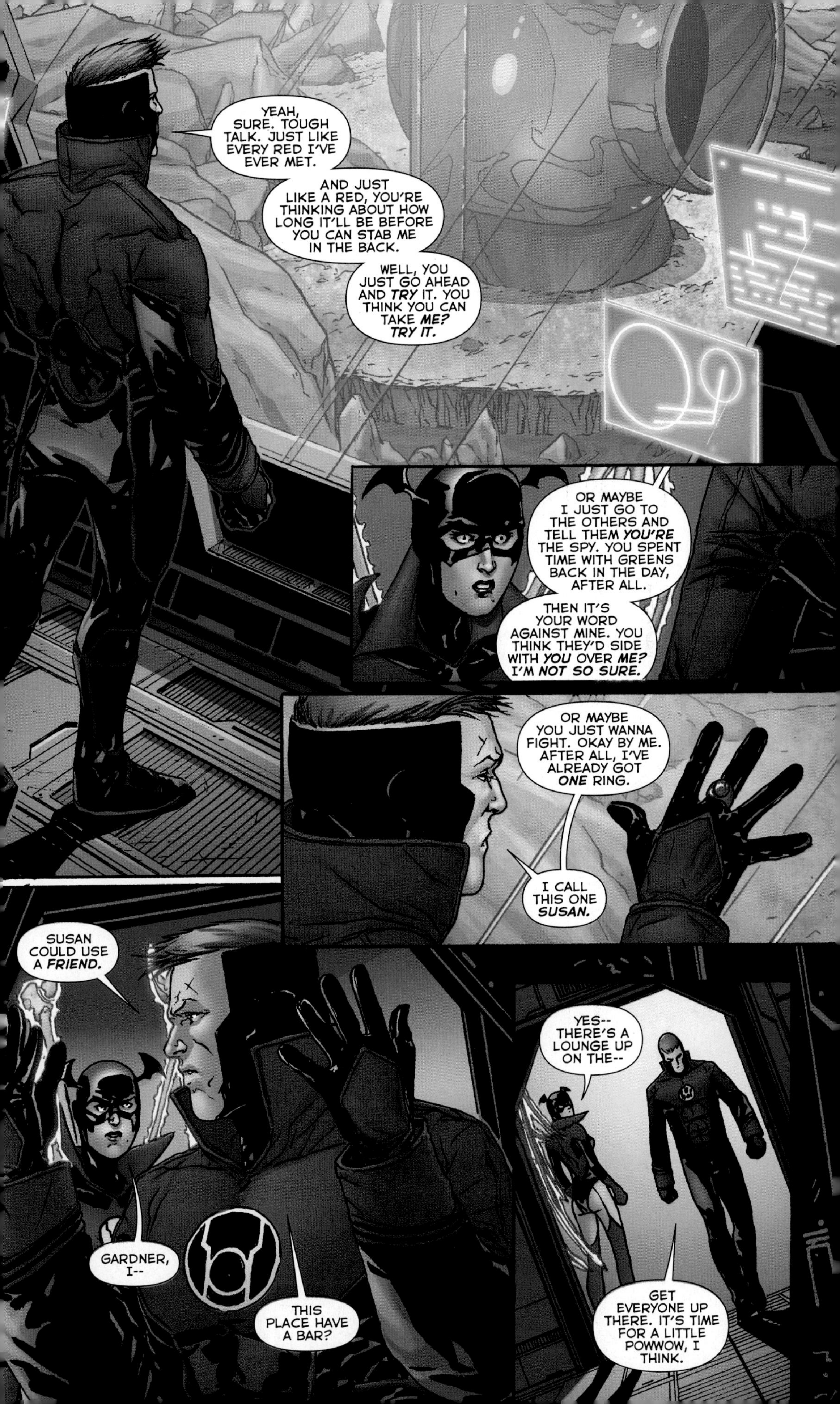
YEAH, SURE. TOUGH TALK. JUST LIKE EVERY RED I'VE EVER MET.
AND JUST LIKE A RED, YOU'RE THINKING ABOUT HOW LONG IT'LL BE BEFORE YOU CAN STAB ME IN THE BACK.
WELL, YOU JUST GO AHEAD AND *TRY* IT. YOU THINK YOU CAN TAKE *ME? TRY IT.*
OR MAYBE I JUST GO TO THE OTHERS AND TELL THEM *YOU'RE* THE SPY. YOU SPENT TIME WITH GREENS BACK IN THE DAY, AFTER ALL.
THEN IT'S YOUR WORD AGAINST MINE. YOU THINK THEY'D SIDE WITH *YOU* OVER *ME?* I'M *NOT SO SURE.*
OR MAYBE YOU JUST WANNA FIGHT. OKAY BY ME. AFTER ALL, I'VE ALREADY GOT *ONE* RING.
I CALL THIS ONE *SUSAN.*
SUSAN COULD USE A *FRIEND.*
GARDNER, I--
THIS PLACE HAVE A BAR?
YES-- THERE'S A LOUNGE UP ON THE--
GET EVERYONE UP THERE. IT'S TIME FOR A LITTLE POWWOW, I THINK.

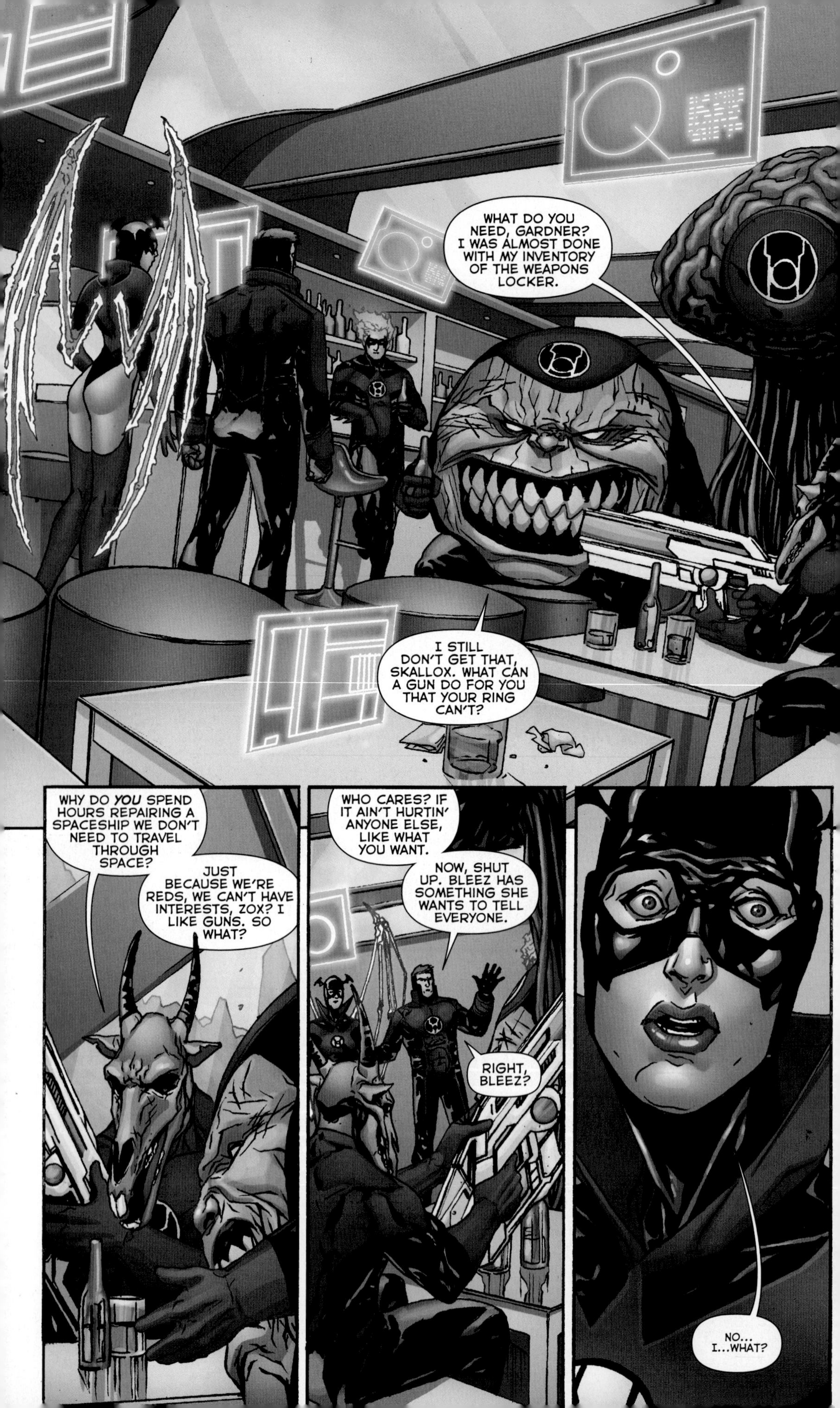
WHAT DO YOU NEED, GARDNER? I WAS ALMOST DONE WITH MY INVENTORY OF THE WEAPONS LOCKER.
I STILL DON'T GET THAT, SKALLOX. WHAT CAN A GUN DO FOR YOU THAT YOUR RING CAN'T?
WHY DO *YOU* SPEND HOURS REPAIRING A SPACESHIP WE DON'T NEED TO TRAVEL THROUGH SPACE?
JUST BECAUSE WE'RE REDS, WE CAN'T HAVE INTERESTS, ZOX? I LIKE GUNS. SO WHAT?
WHO CARES? IF IT AIN'T HURTIN' ANYONE ELSE, LIKE WHAT YOU WANT.
NOW, SHUT UP. BLEEZ HAS SOMETHING SHE WANTS TO TELL EVERYONE.
RIGHT, BLEEZ?
NO... I...WHAT?

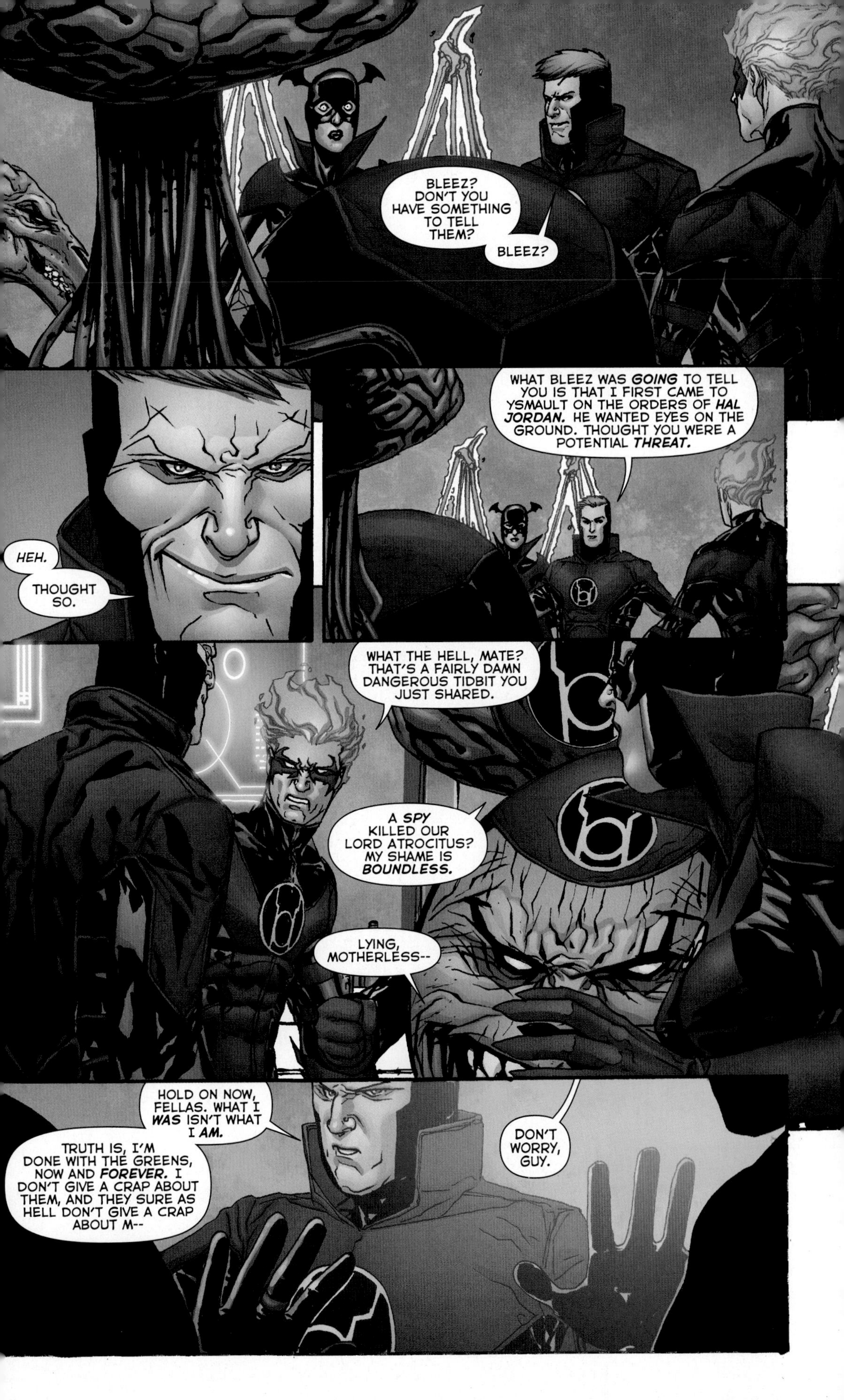
BLEEZ? DON'T YOU HAVE SOMETHING TO TELL THEM?
BLEEZ?
HEH.
THOUGHT SO.
WHAT BLEEZ WAS GOING TO TELL YOU IS THAT I FIRST CAME TO YSMAULT ON THE ORDERS OF HAL JORDAN. HE WANTED EYES ON THE GROUND. THOUGHT YOU WERE A POTENTIAL THREAT.
WHAT THE HELL, MATE? THAT'S A FAIRLY DAMN DANGEROUS TIDBIT YOU JUST SHARED.
A SPY KILLED OUR LORD ATROCITUS? MY SHAME IS BOUNDLESS.
LYING, MOTHERLESS--
HOLD ON NOW, FELLAS. WHAT I WAS ISN'T WHAT I AM.
TRUTH IS, I'M DONE WITH THE GREENS, NOW AND FOREVER. I DON'T GIVE A CRAP ABOUT THEM, AND THEY SURE AS HELL DON'T GIVE A CRAP ABOUT M--
DON'T WORRY, GUY.

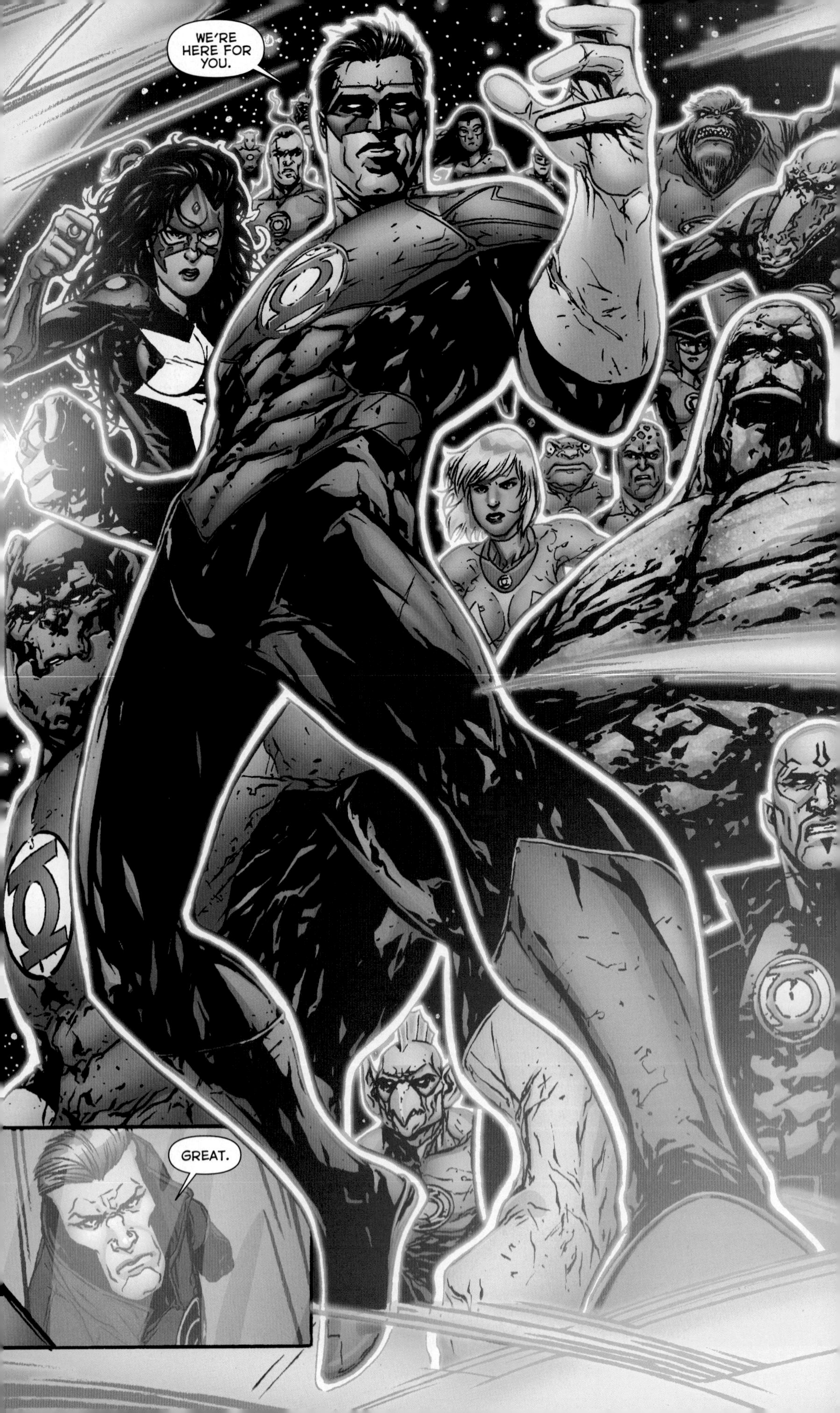
WE'RE HERE FOR YOU.
GREAT.

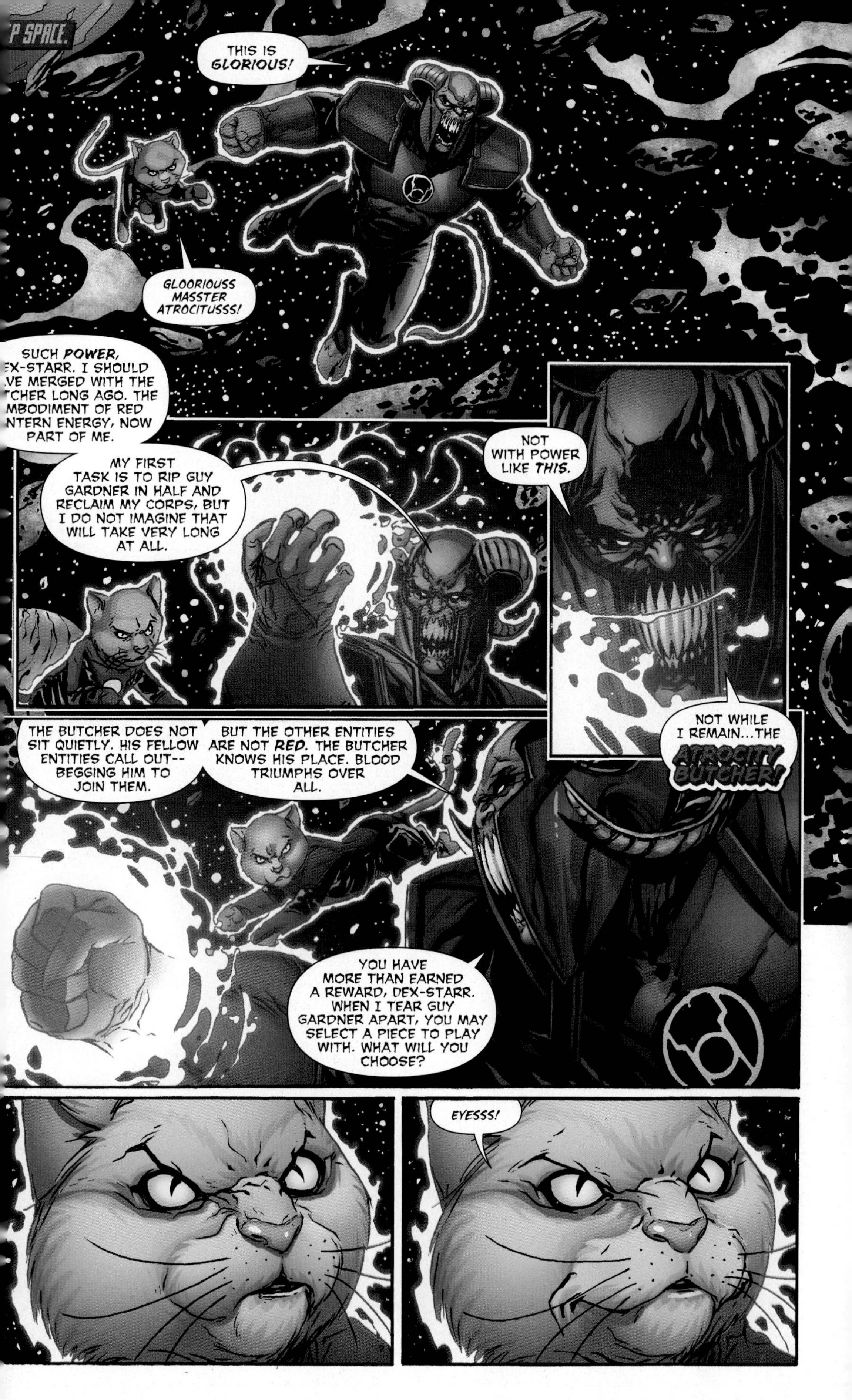
P SPACE.
THIS IS GLORIOUS!
GLOORIOUSS MASSTER ATROCITUSSS!
SUCH POWER, EX-STARR. I SHOULD VE MERGED WITH THE TCHER LONG AGO. THE MBODIMENT OF RED NTERN ENERGY, NOW PART OF ME.
MY FIRST TASK IS TO RIP GUY GARDNER IN HALF AND RECLAIM MY CORPS, BUT I DO NOT IMAGINE THAT WILL TAKE VERY LONG AT ALL.
NOT WITH POWER LIKE THIS.
NOT WHILE I REMAIN...THE ATROCITY BUTCHER!
THE BUTCHER DOES NOT SIT QUIETLY. HIS FELLOW ENTITIES CALL OUT-- BEGGING HIM TO JOIN THEM.
BUT THE OTHER ENTITIES ARE NOT RED. THE BUTCHER KNOWS HIS PLACE. BLOOD TRIUMPHS OVER ALL.
YOU HAVE MORE THAN EARNED A REWARD, DEX-STARR. WHEN I TEAR GUY GARDNER APART, YOU MAY SELECT A PIECE TO PLAY WITH. WHAT WILL YOU CHOOSE?
EYESSS!

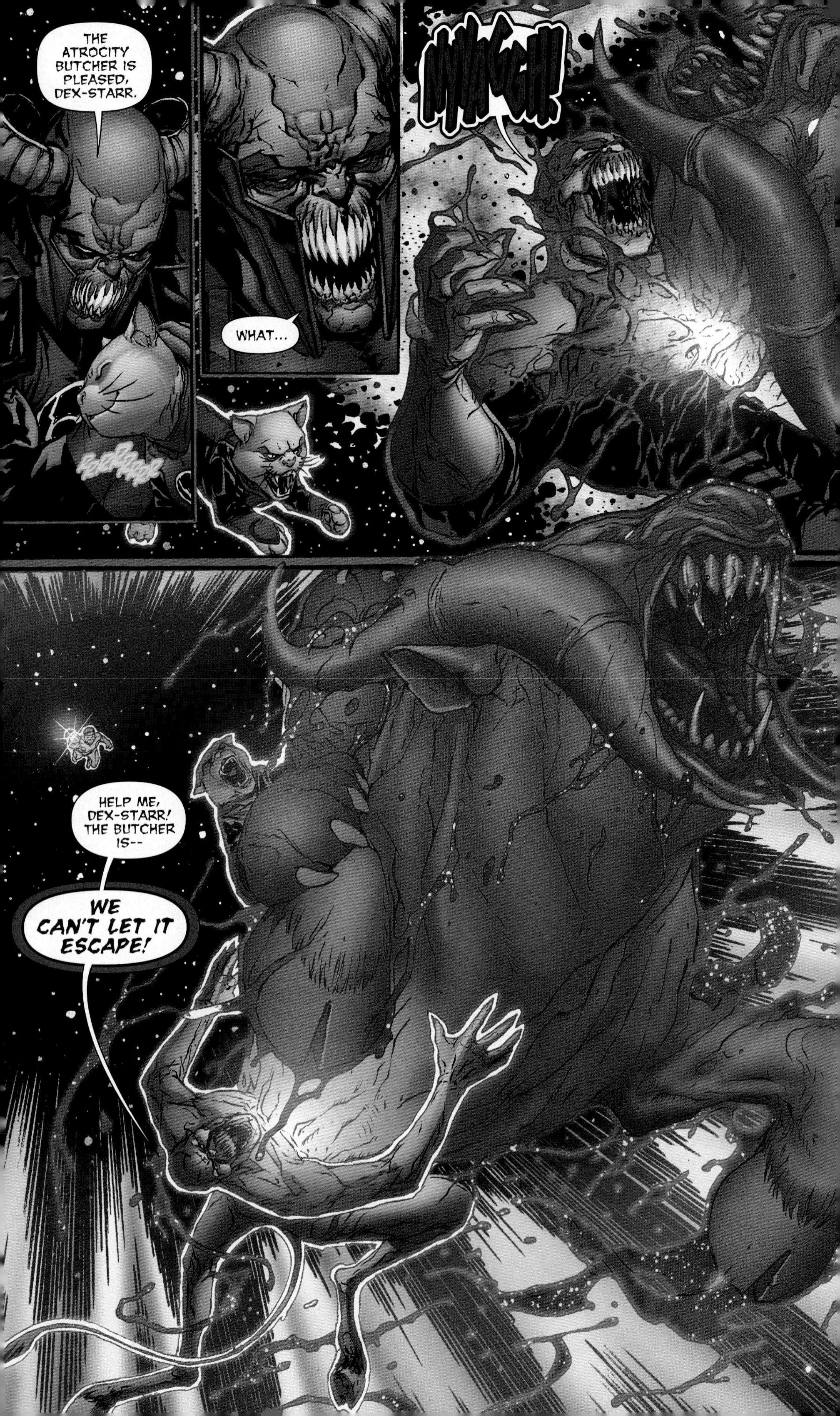
THE ATROCITY BUTCHER IS PLEASED, DEX-STARR.
RRRRRRRRR
WHAT...
HRWAAGH!!
HELP ME, DEX-STARR! THE BUTCHER IS--
WE CAN'T LET IT ESCAPE!

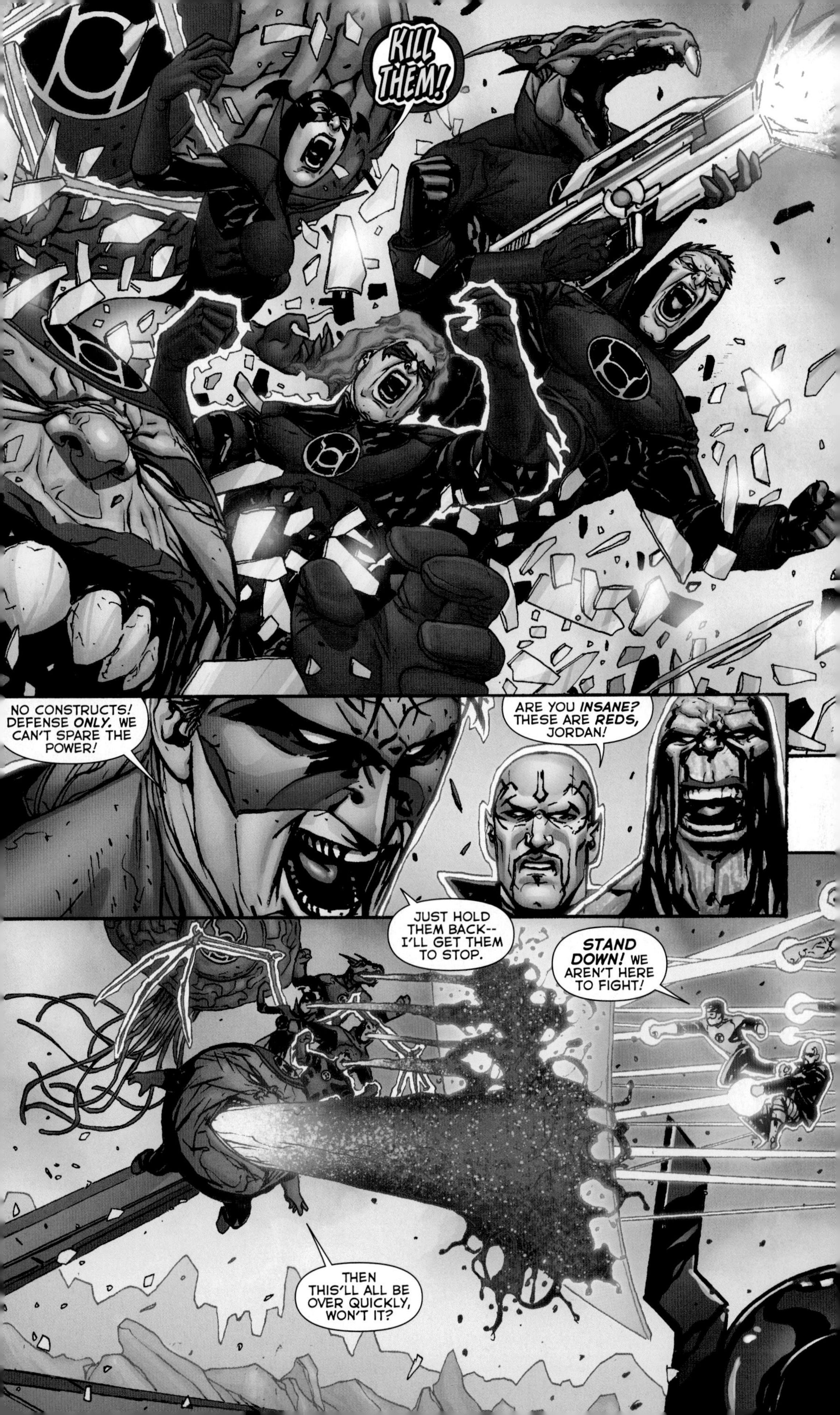
KILL THEM!
NO CONSTRUCTS! DEFENSE ONLY. WE CAN'T SPARE THE POWER!
ARE YOU INSANE? THESE ARE REDS, JORDAN!
JUST HOLD THEM BACK-- I'LL GET THEM TO STOP.
STAND DOWN! WE AREN'T HERE TO FIGHT!
THEN THIS'LL ALL BE OVER QUICKLY, WON'T IT?

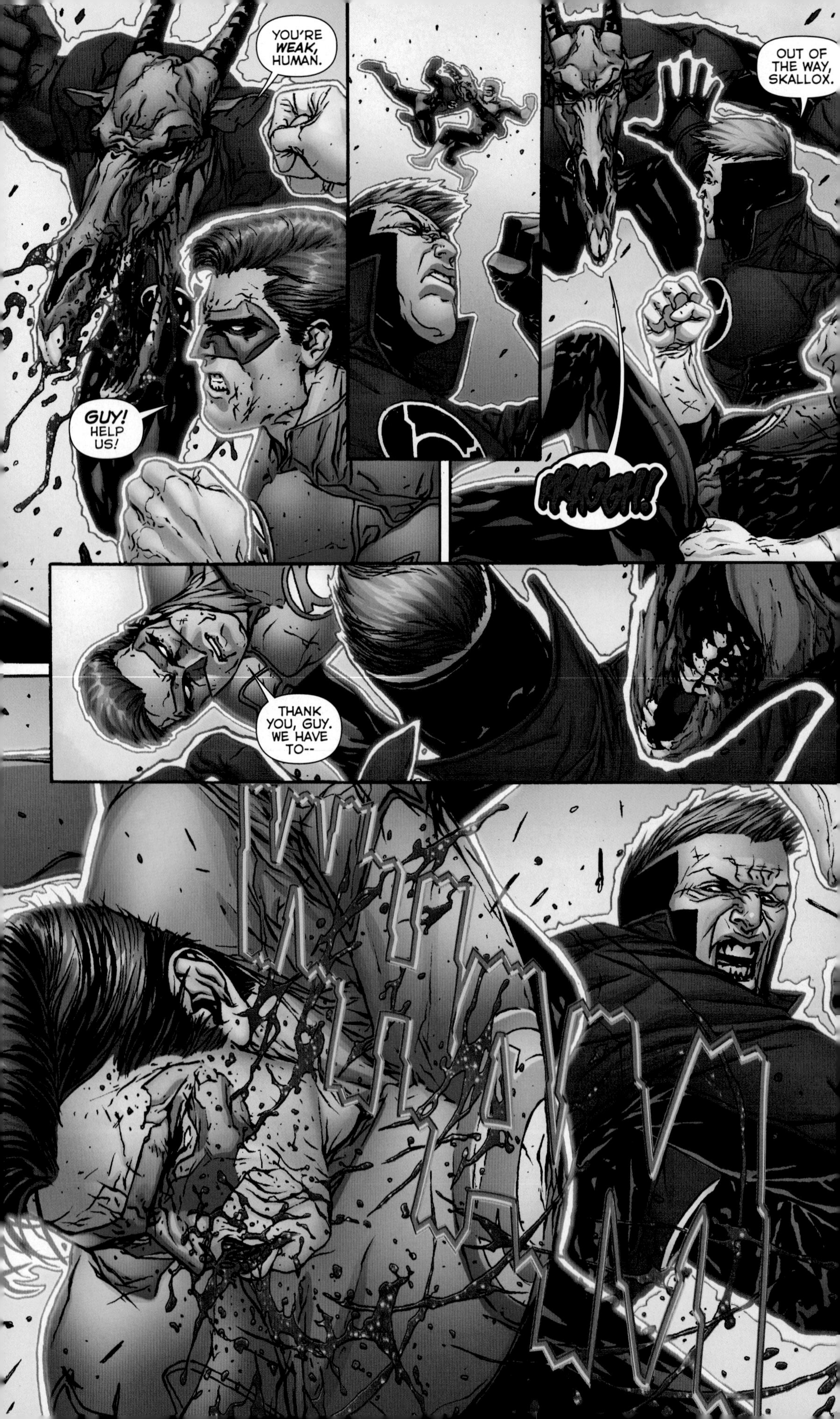
YOU'RE WEAK, HUMAN.
GUY! HELP US!
OUT OF THE WAY, SKALLOX.
ARAGGH!
THANK YOU, GUY. WE HAVE TO--
WHAM!

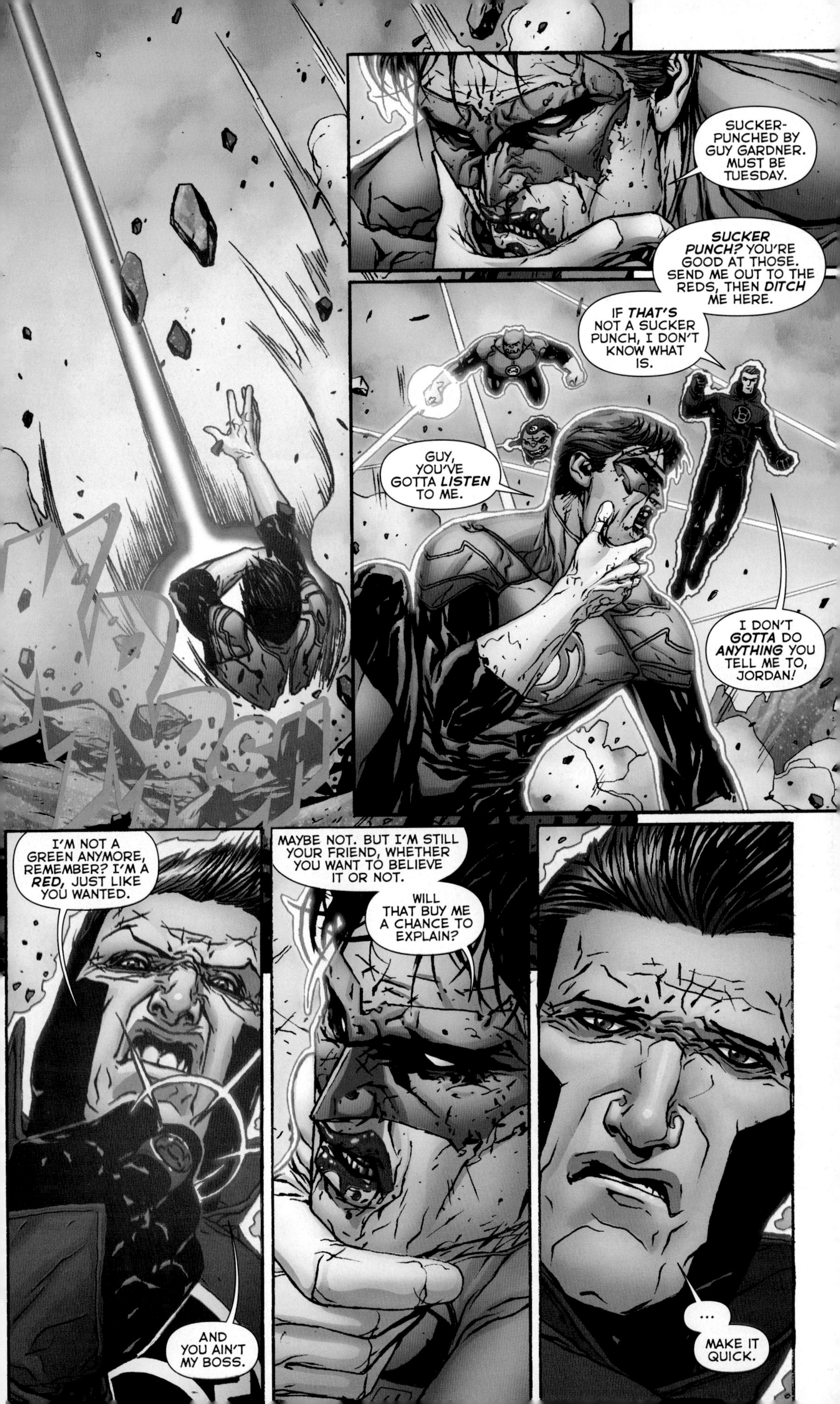
SUCKER-PUNCHED BY GUY GARDNER. MUST BE TUESDAY.
SUCKER PUNCH? YOU'RE GOOD AT THOSE. SEND ME OUT TO THE REDS, THEN DITCH ME HERE.
IF THAT'S NOT A SUCKER PUNCH, I DON'T KNOW WHAT IS.
GUY, YOU'VE GOTTA LISTEN TO ME.
I DON'T GOTTA DO ANYTHING YOU TELL ME TO, JORDAN!
I'M NOT A GREEN ANYMORE, REMEMBER? I'M A RED, JUST LIKE YOU WANTED.
AND YOU AIN'T MY BOSS.
MAYBE NOT. BUT I'M STILL YOUR FRIEND, WHETHER YOU WANT TO BELIEVE IT OR NOT.
WILL THAT BUY ME A CHANCE TO EXPLAIN?
...
MAKE IT QUICK.

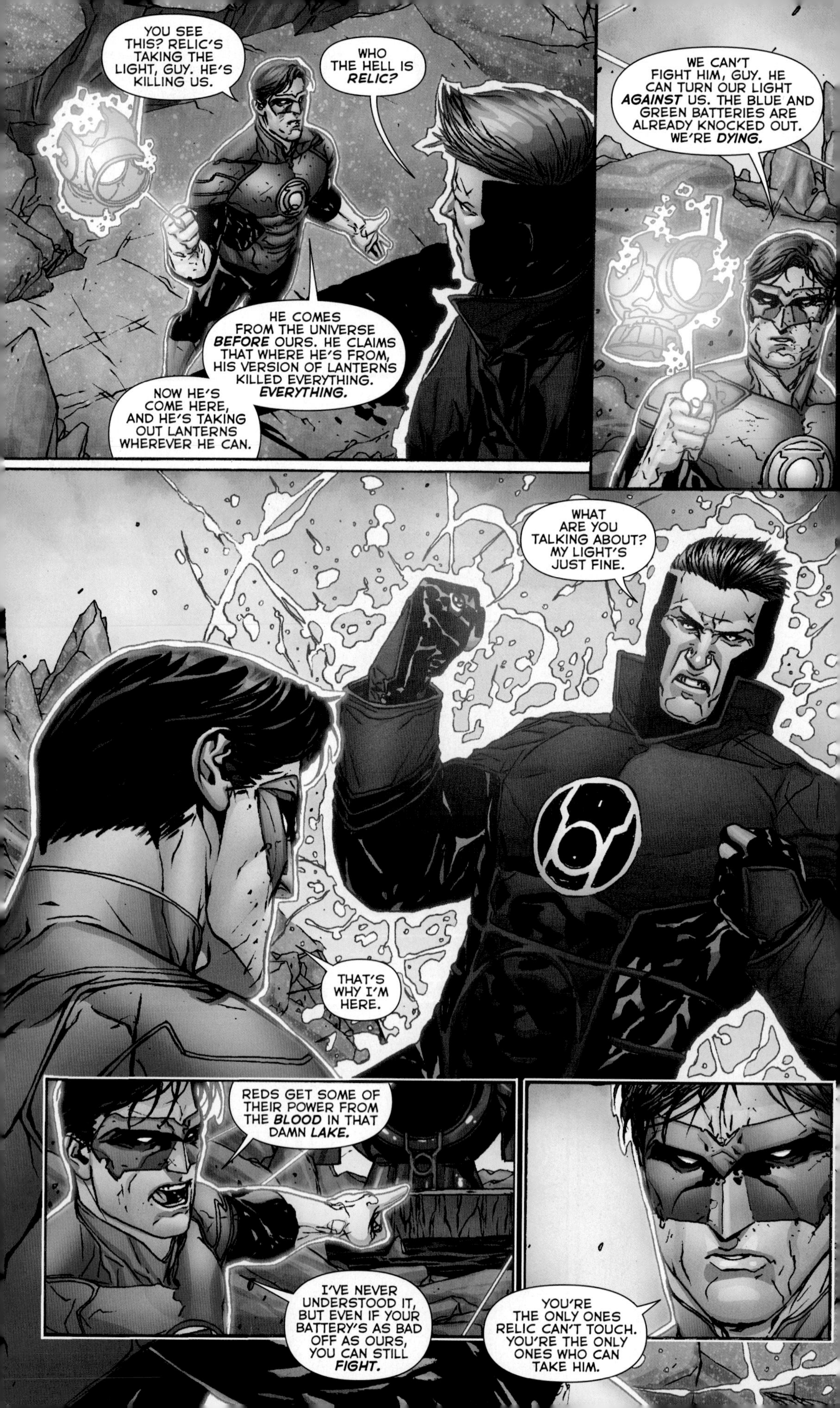

YOU SEE THIS? RELIC'S TAKING THE LIGHT, GUY. HE'S KILLING US.
WHO THE HELL IS *RELIC?*
HE COMES FROM THE UNIVERSE *BEFORE* OURS. HE CLAIMS THAT WHERE HE'S FROM, HIS VERSION OF LANTERNS KILLED EVERYTHING. *EVERYTHING.*
NOW HE'S COME HERE, AND HE'S TAKING OUT LANTERNS WHEREVER HE CAN.
WE CAN'T FIGHT HIM, GUY. HE CAN TURN OUR LIGHT *AGAINST* US. THE BLUE AND GREEN BATTERIES ARE ALREADY KNOCKED OUT. WE'RE *DYING.*
WHAT ARE YOU TALKING ABOUT? MY LIGHT'S JUST FINE.
THAT'S WHY I'M HERE.
REDS GET SOME OF THEIR POWER FROM THE *BLOOD* IN THAT DAMN *LAKE.*
I'VE NEVER UNDERSTOOD IT, BUT EVEN IF YOUR BATTERY'S AS BAD OFF AS OURS, YOU CAN STILL *FIGHT.*
YOU'RE THE ONLY ONES RELIC *CAN'T* TOUCH. YOU'RE THE ONLY ONES WHO CAN TAKE HIM.

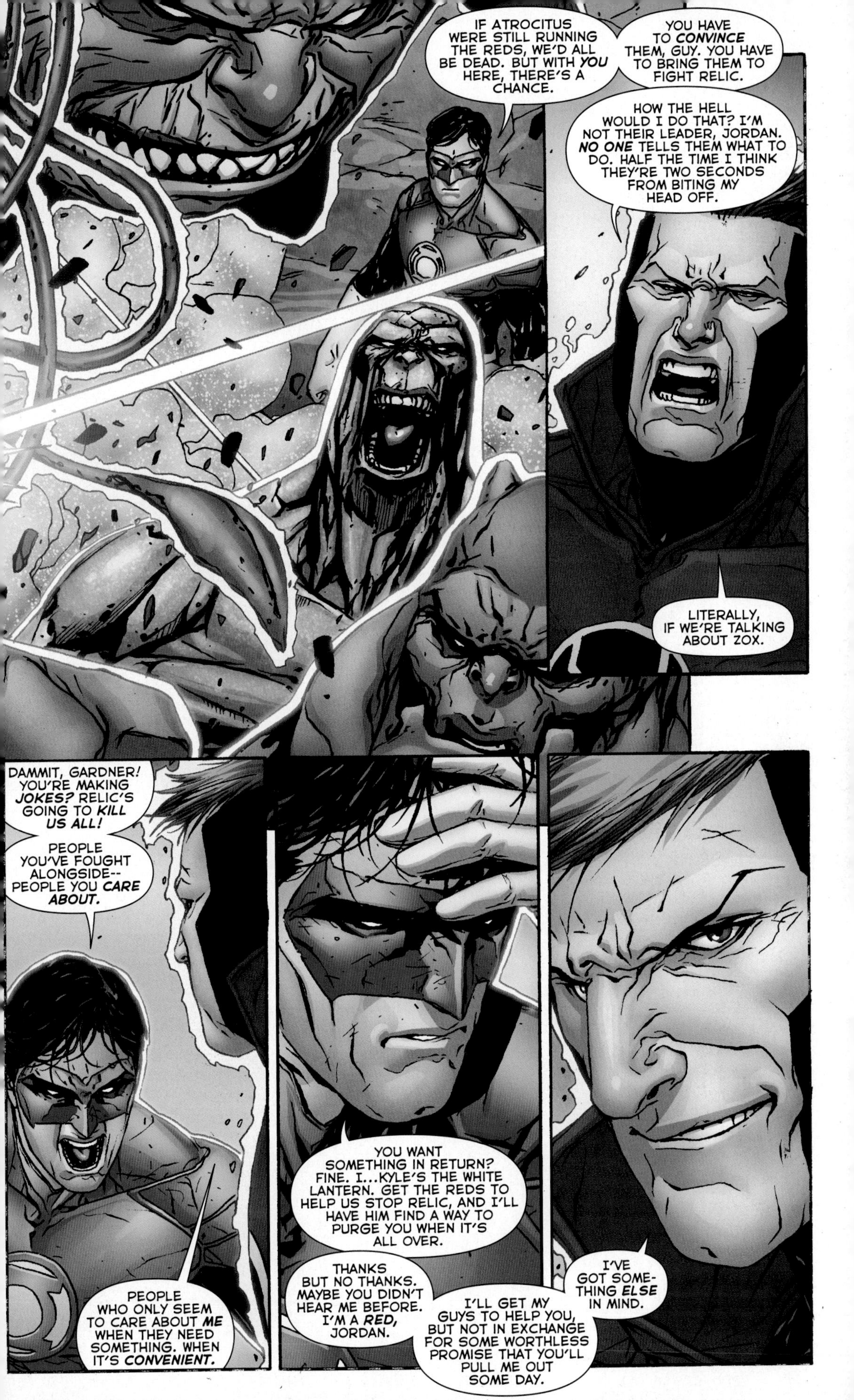
IF ATROCITUS WERE STILL RUNNING THE REDS, WE'D ALL BE DEAD. BUT WITH *YOU* HERE, THERE'S A CHANCE.
YOU HAVE TO *CONVINCE* THEM, GUY. YOU HAVE TO BRING THEM TO FIGHT RELIC.
HOW THE HELL WOULD I DO THAT? I'M NOT THEIR LEADER, JORDAN. *NO ONE* TELLS THEM WHAT TO DO. HALF THE TIME I THINK THEY'RE TWO SECONDS FROM BITING MY HEAD OFF.
LITERALLY, IF WE'RE TALKING ABOUT ZOX.
DAMMIT, GARDNER! YOU'RE MAKING *JOKES?* RELIC'S GOING TO *KILL US ALL!*
PEOPLE YOU'VE FOUGHT ALONGSIDE-- PEOPLE YOU *CARE ABOUT.*
PEOPLE WHO ONLY SEEM TO CARE ABOUT *ME* WHEN THEY NEED SOMETHING. WHEN IT'S *CONVENIENT.*
YOU WANT SOMETHING IN RETURN? FINE. I...KYLE'S THE WHITE LANTERN. GET THE REDS TO HELP US STOP RELIC, AND I'LL HAVE HIM FIND A WAY TO PURGE YOU WHEN IT'S ALL OVER.
THANKS BUT NO THANKS. MAYBE YOU DIDN'T HEAR ME BEFORE. I'M A *RED,* JORDAN.
I'LL GET MY GUYS TO HELP YOU, BUT NOT IN EXCHANGE FOR SOME WORTHLESS PROMISE THAT YOU'LL PULL ME OUT SOME DAY.
I'VE GOT SOME-THING *ELSE* IN MIND.

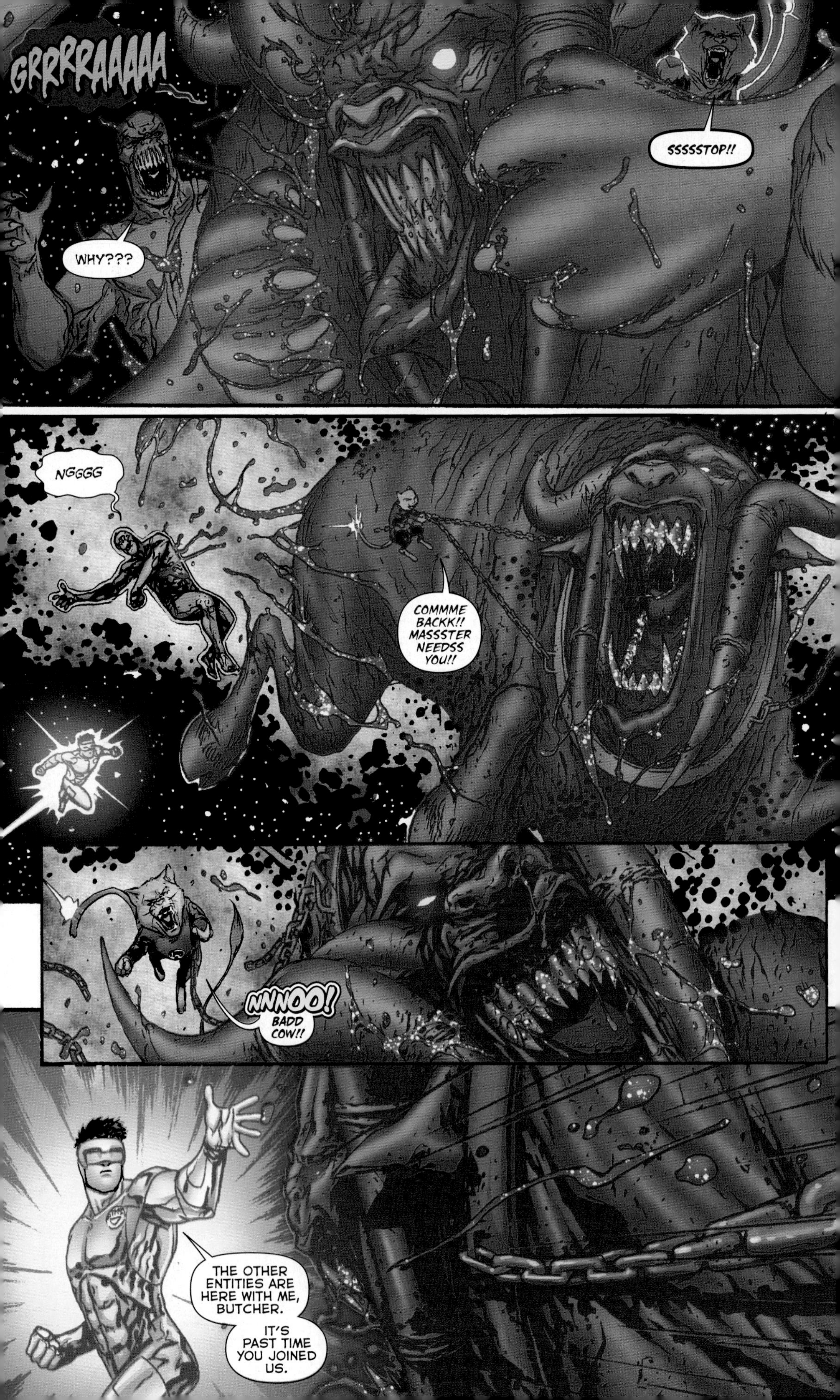
GRRRRAAAAAA
SSSSSTOP!!
WHY???
NGGGG
COMMME BACKK!! MASSSTER NEEDSS YOU!!
NNNOO! BADD COW!!
THE OTHER ENTITIES ARE HERE WITH ME, BUTCHER.
IT'S PAST TIME YOU JOINED US.

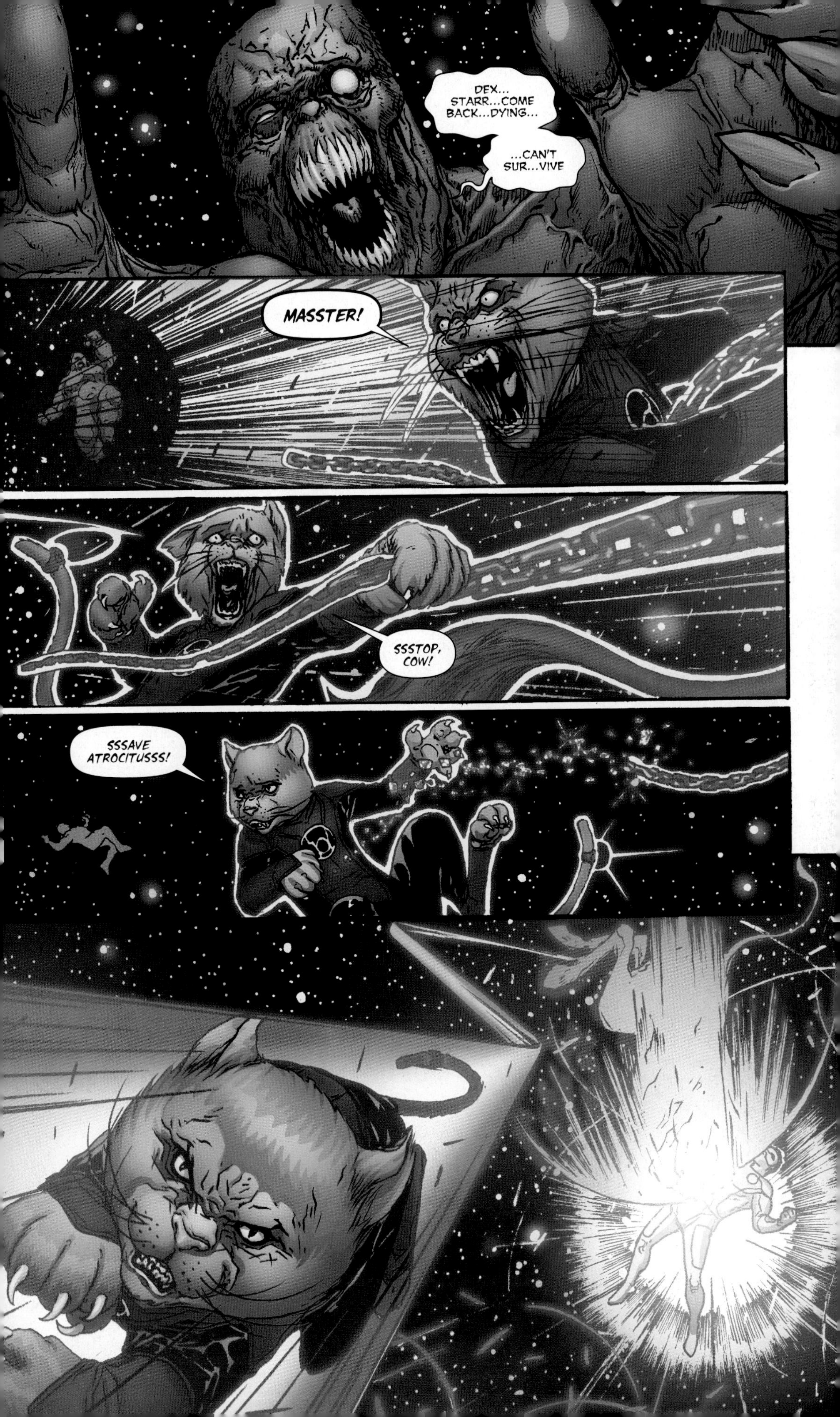
DEX... STARR...COME BACK...DYING...
...CAN'T SUR...VIVE
MASSTER!
SSSTOP, COW!
SSSAVE ATROCITUSSS!

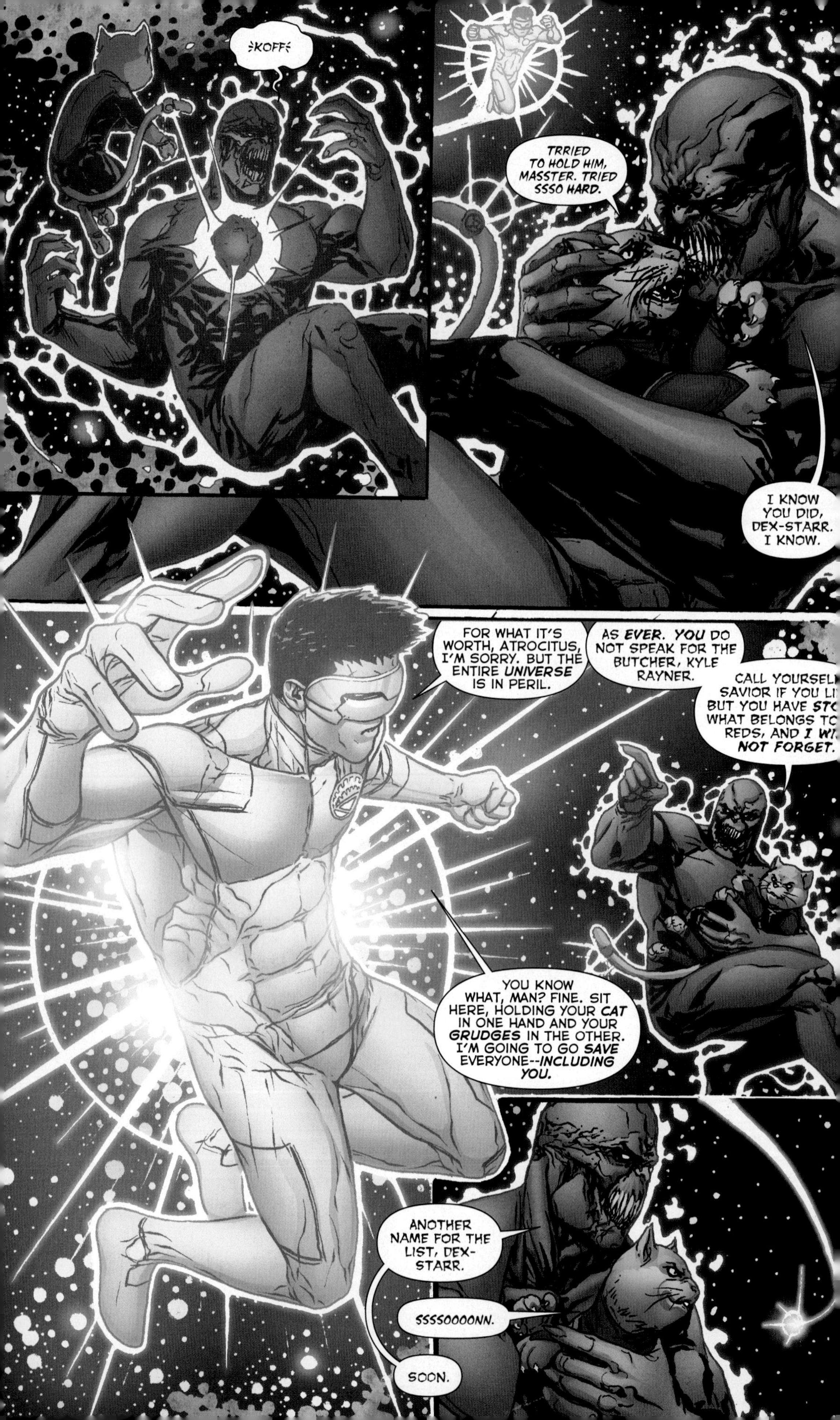

KOFF
TRRIED TO HOLD HIM, MASSTER. TRIED SSSO HARD.
I KNOW YOU DID, DEX-STARR. I KNOW.
FOR WHAT IT'S WORTH, ATROCITUS, I'M SORRY. BUT THE ENTIRE UNIVERSE IS IN PERIL.
AS EVER. YOU DO NOT SPEAK FOR THE BUTCHER, KYLE RAYNER.
CALL YOURSEL SAVIOR IF YOU LI BUT YOU HAVE STO WHAT BELONGS TO REDS, AND I WI NOT FORGET.
YOU KNOW WHAT, MAN? FINE. SIT HERE, HOLDING YOUR CAT IN ONE HAND AND YOUR GRUDGES IN THE OTHER. I'M GOING TO GO SAVE EVERYONE--INCLUDING YOU.
ANOTHER NAME FOR THE LIST, DEX-STARR.
SSSSOOOONN.
SOON.

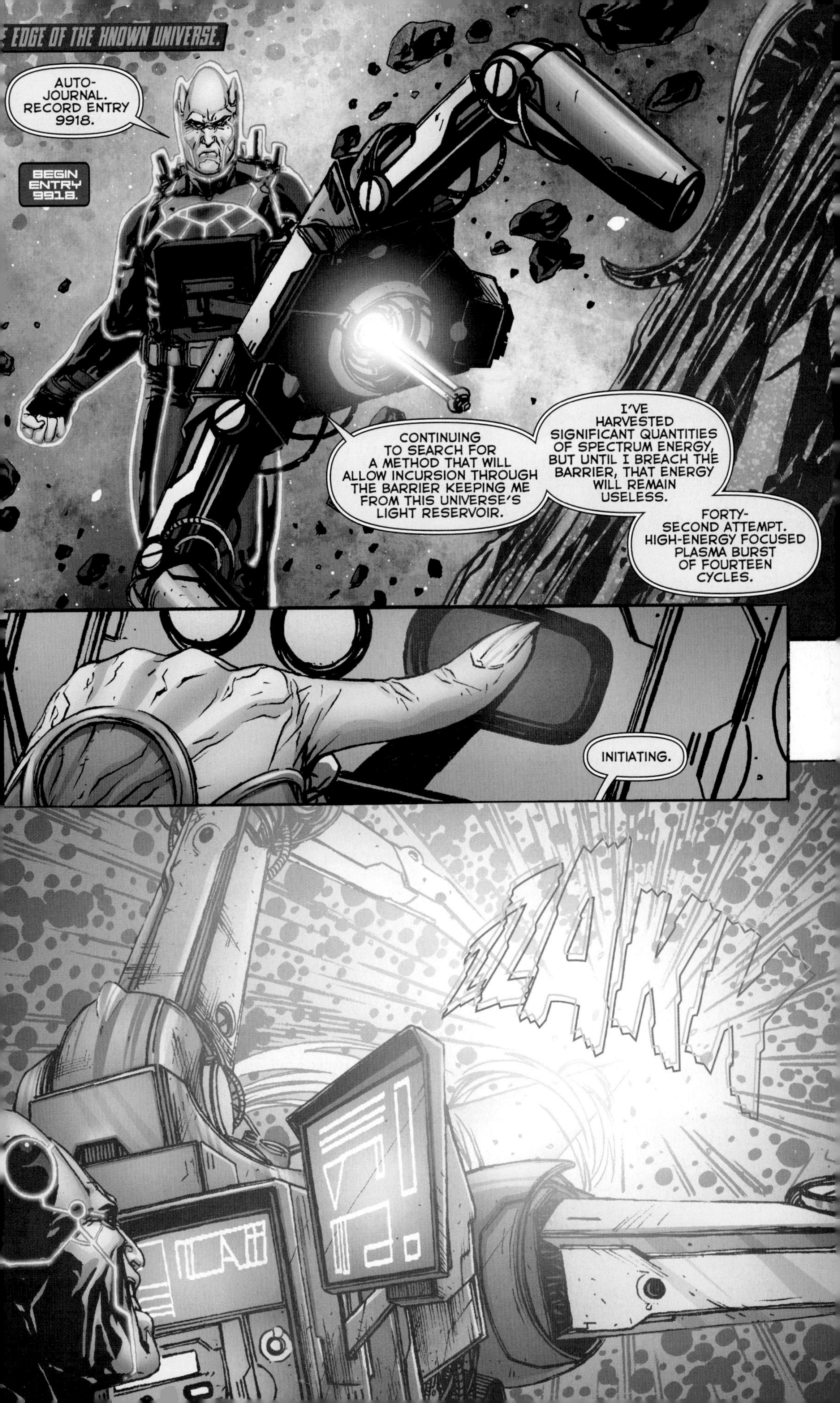
EDGE OF THE KNOWN UNIVERSE.
AUTO-JOURNAL. RECORD ENTRY 9918.
BEGIN ENTRY 9918.
CONTINUING TO SEARCH FOR A METHOD THAT WILL ALLOW INCURSION THROUGH THE BARRIER KEEPING ME FROM THIS UNIVERSE'S LIGHT RESERVOIR.
I'VE HARVESTED SIGNIFICANT QUANTITIES OF SPECTRUM ENERGY, BUT UNTIL I BREACH THE BARRIER, THAT ENERGY WILL REMAIN USELESS.
FORTY-SECOND ATTEMPT. HIGH-ENERGY FOCUSED PLASMA BURST OF FOURTEEN CYCLES.
INITIATING.
ZZAKK

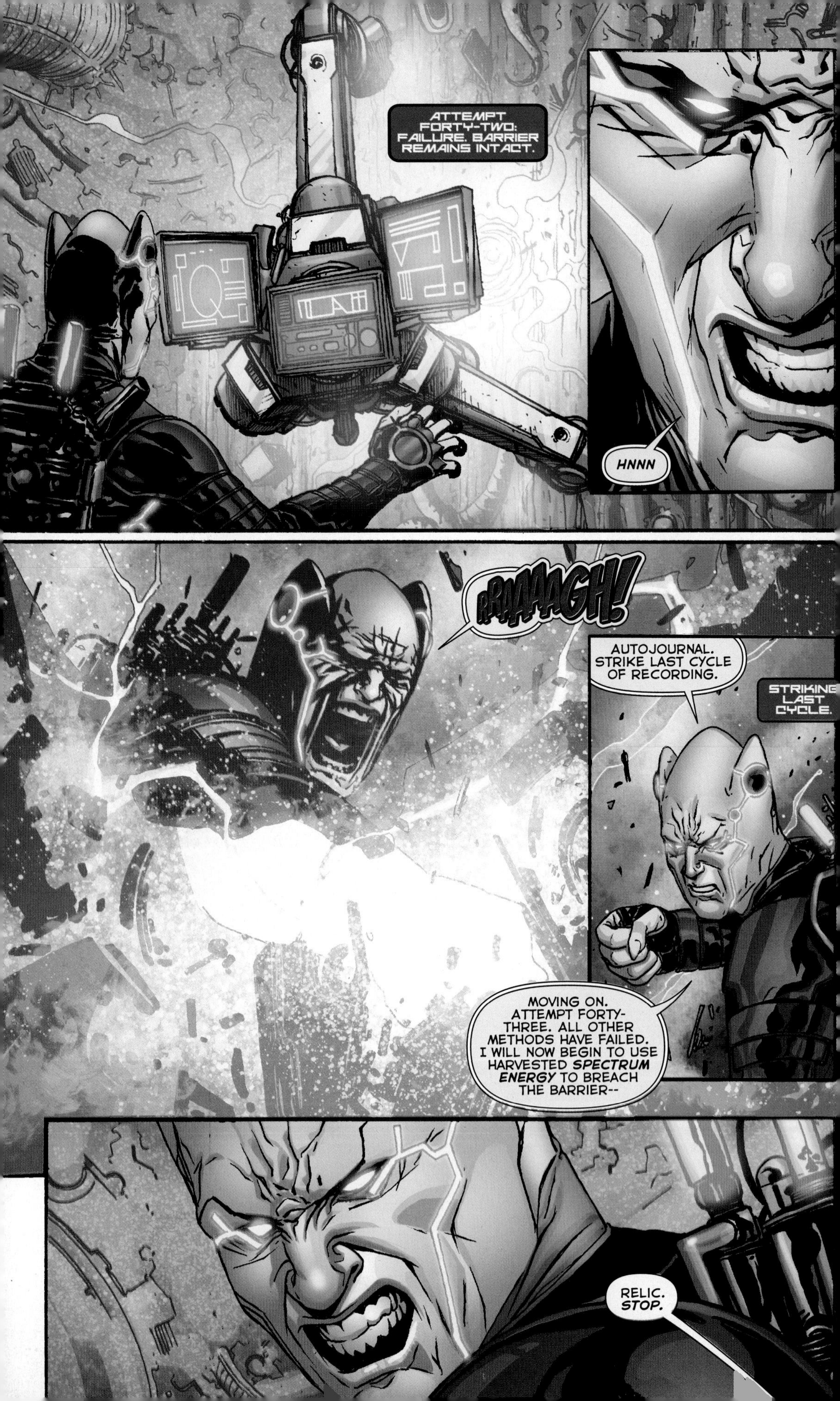
ATTEMPT FORTY-TWO: FAILURE. BARRIER REMAINS INTACT.
HNNN
RRAAAAAGH!
AUTOJOURNAL. STRIKE LAST CYCLE OF RECORDING.
STRIKING LAST CYCLE.
MOVING ON. ATTEMPT FORTY-THREE. ALL OTHER METHODS HAVE FAILED. I WILL NOW BEGIN TO USE HARVESTED SPECTRUM ENERGY TO BREACH THE BARRIER--
RELIC. STOP.

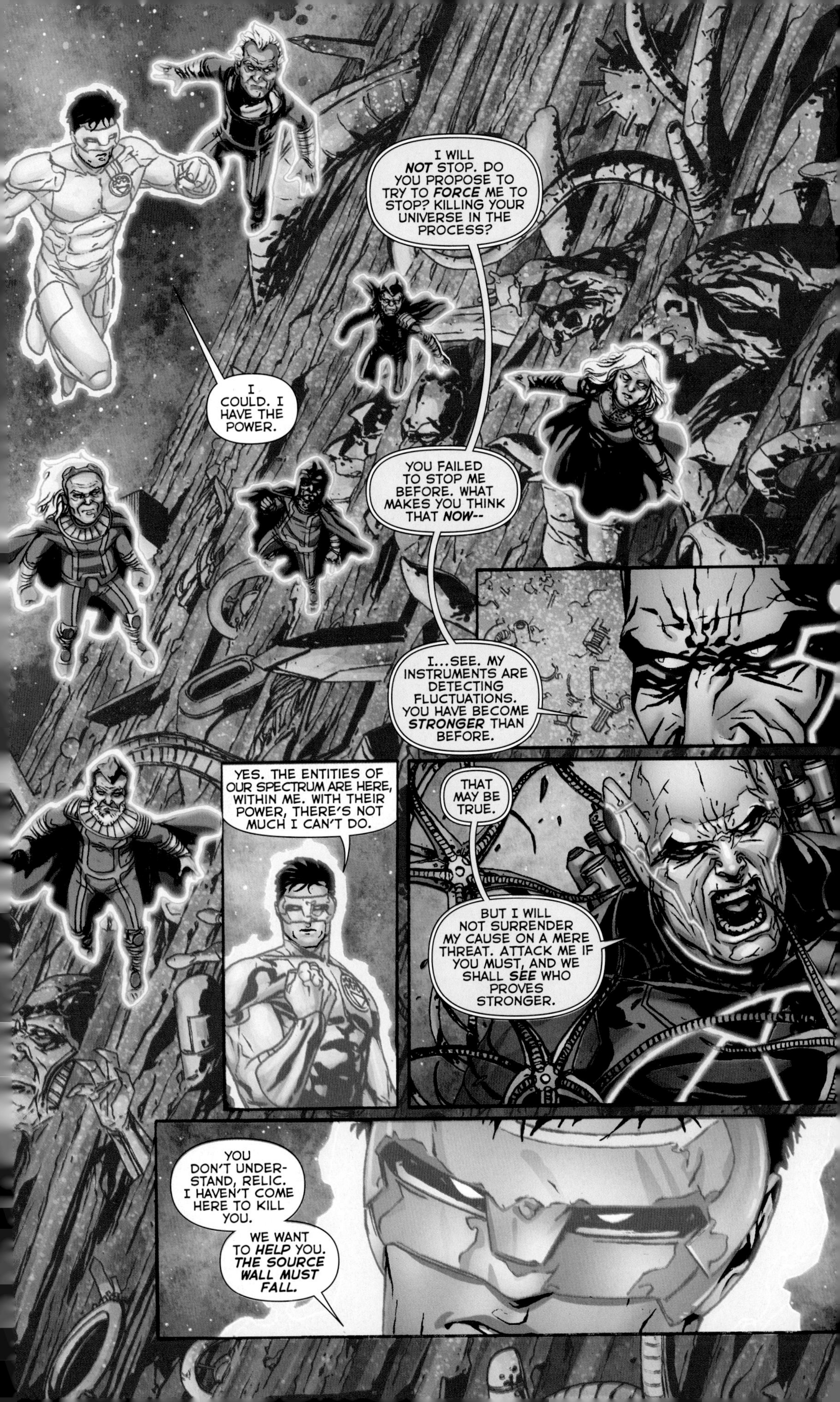
I WILL NOT STOP. DO YOU PROPOSE TO TRY TO FORCE ME TO STOP? KILLING YOUR UNIVERSE IN THE PROCESS?
I COULD. I HAVE THE POWER.
YOU FAILED TO STOP ME BEFORE. WHAT MAKES YOU THINK THAT NOW--
I...SEE. MY INSTRUMENTS ARE DETECTING FLUCTUATIONS. YOU HAVE BECOME STRONGER THAN BEFORE.
YES. THE ENTITIES OF OUR SPECTRUM ARE HERE, WITHIN ME. WITH THEIR POWER, THERE'S NOT MUCH I CAN'T DO.
THAT MAY BE TRUE.
BUT I WILL NOT SURRENDER MY CAUSE ON A MERE THREAT. ATTACK ME IF YOU MUST, AND WE SHALL SEE WHO PROVES STRONGER.
YOU DON'T UNDER-STAND, RELIC. I HAVEN'T COME HERE TO KILL YOU.
WE WANT TO HELP YOU. THE SOURCE WALL MUST FALL.

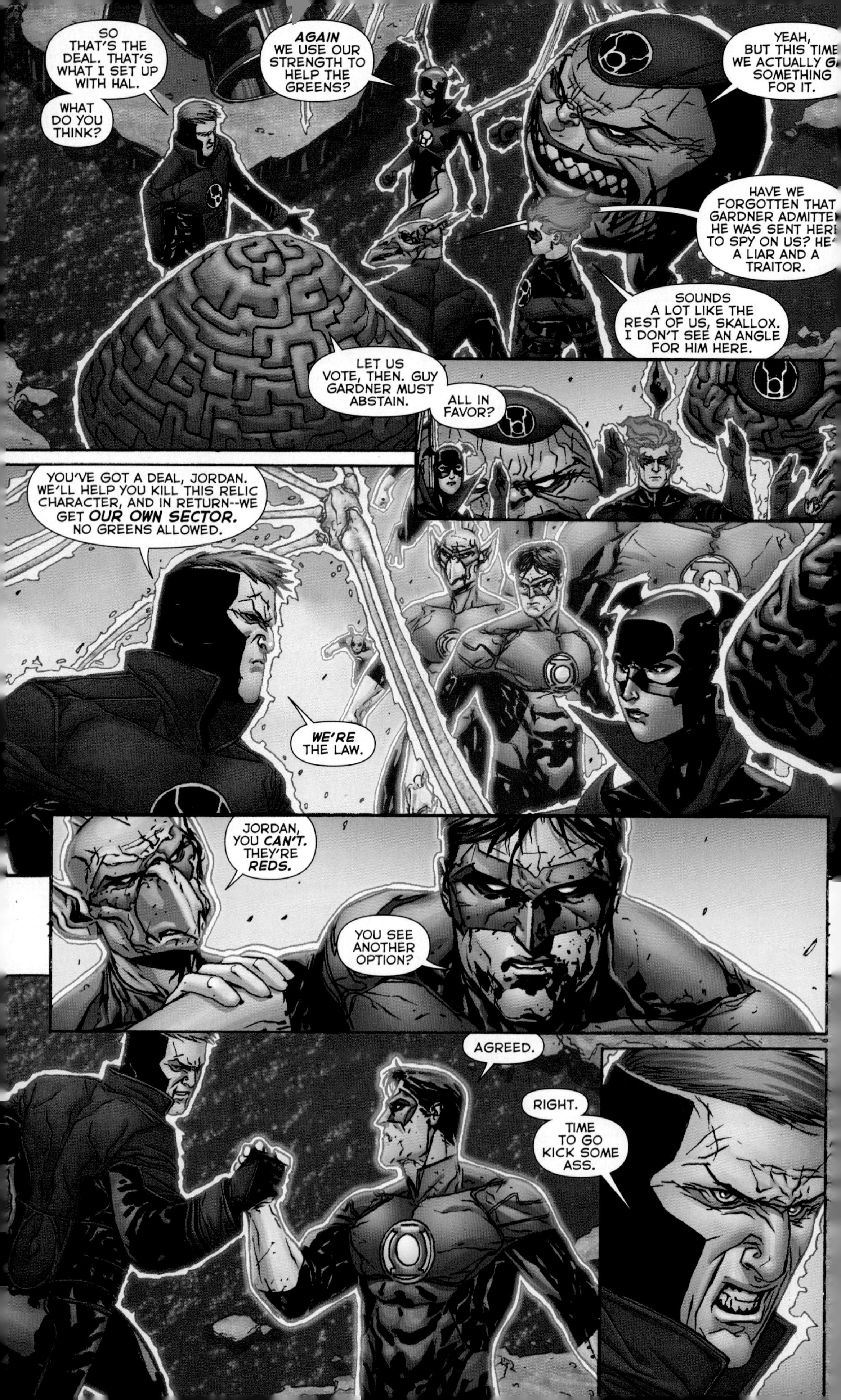

SO THAT'S THE DEAL. THAT'S WHAT I SET UP WITH HAL.
WHAT DO YOU THINK?
AGAIN WE USE OUR STRENGTH TO HELP THE GREENS?
YEAH, BUT THIS TIME WE ACTUALLY G SOMETHING FOR IT.
HAVE WE FORGOTTEN THAT GARDNER ADMITTE HE WAS SENT HER TO SPY ON US? HE A LIAR AND A TRAITOR.
SOUNDS A LOT LIKE THE REST OF US, SKALLOX. I DON'T SEE AN ANGLE FOR HIM HERE.
LET US VOTE, THEN. GUY GARDNER MUST ABSTAIN.
ALL IN FAVOR?
YOU'VE GOT A DEAL, JORDAN. WE'LL HELP YOU KILL THIS RELIC CHARACTER, AND IN RETURN--WE GET OUR OWN SECTOR. NO GREENS ALLOWED.
WE'RE THE LAW.
JORDAN, YOU CAN'T. THEY'RE REDS.
YOU SEE ANOTHER OPTION?
AGREED.
RIGHT.
TIME TO GO KICK SOME ASS.

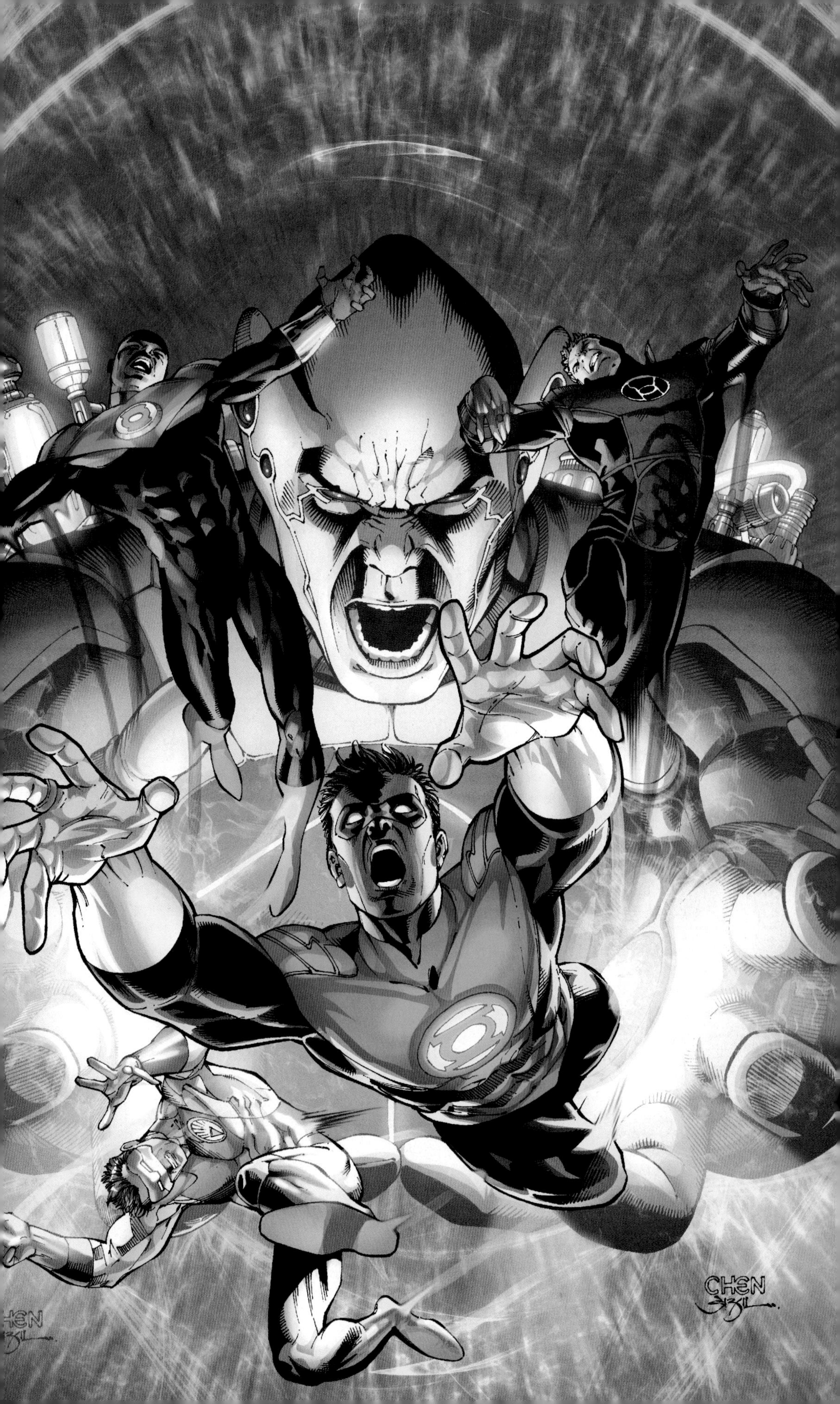
CHEN

LIGHTS OUT part five: THE SOURCE

ROBERT VENDITTI writer SEAN CHEN penciller JON SIBAL with WALDEN WONG inkers ANDREW DALHOUSE with WIL QUINTANA colori

cover art by SEAN CHEN with JON SIBAL & ALEX SINCLAIR

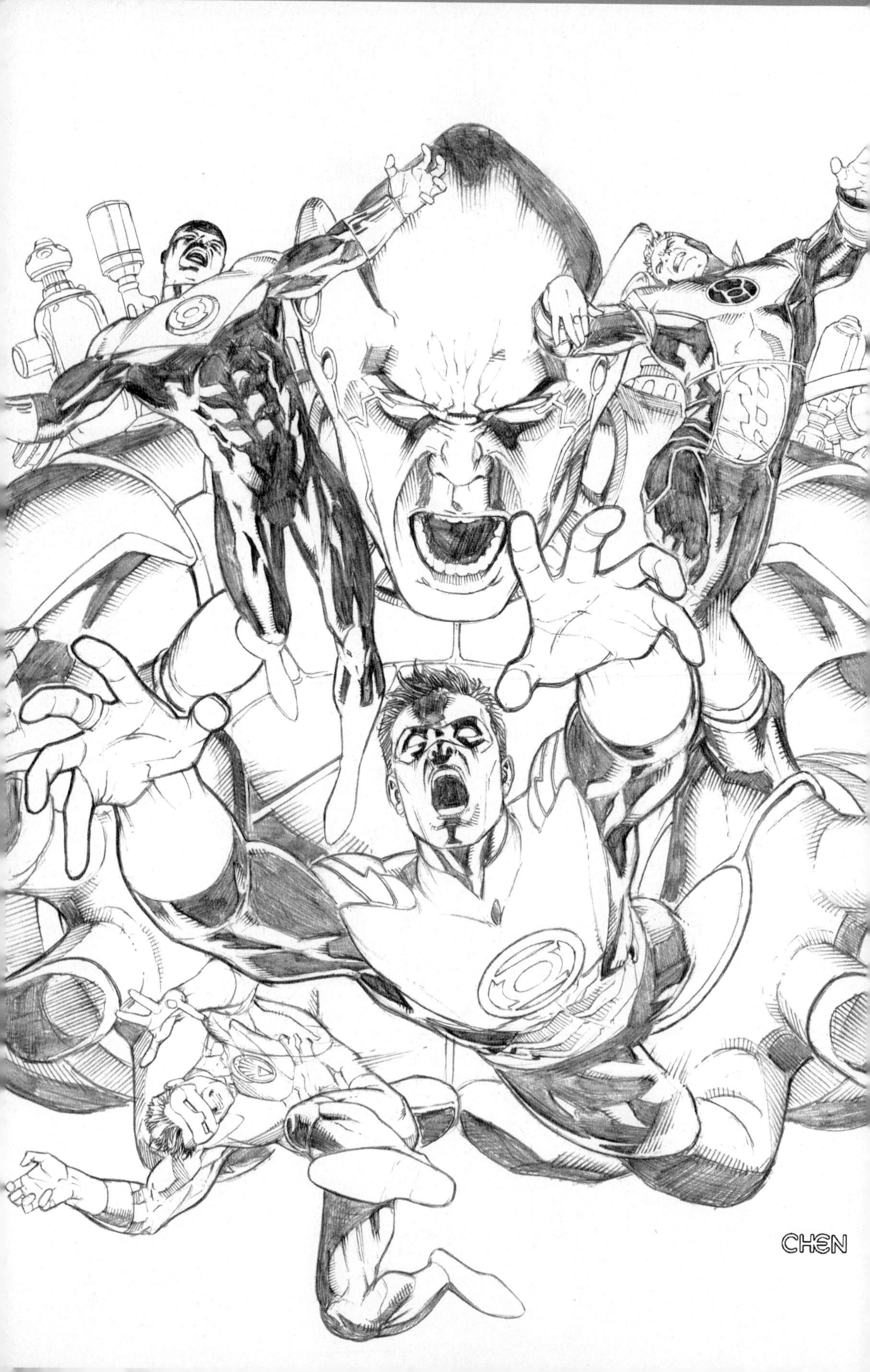
CHEN

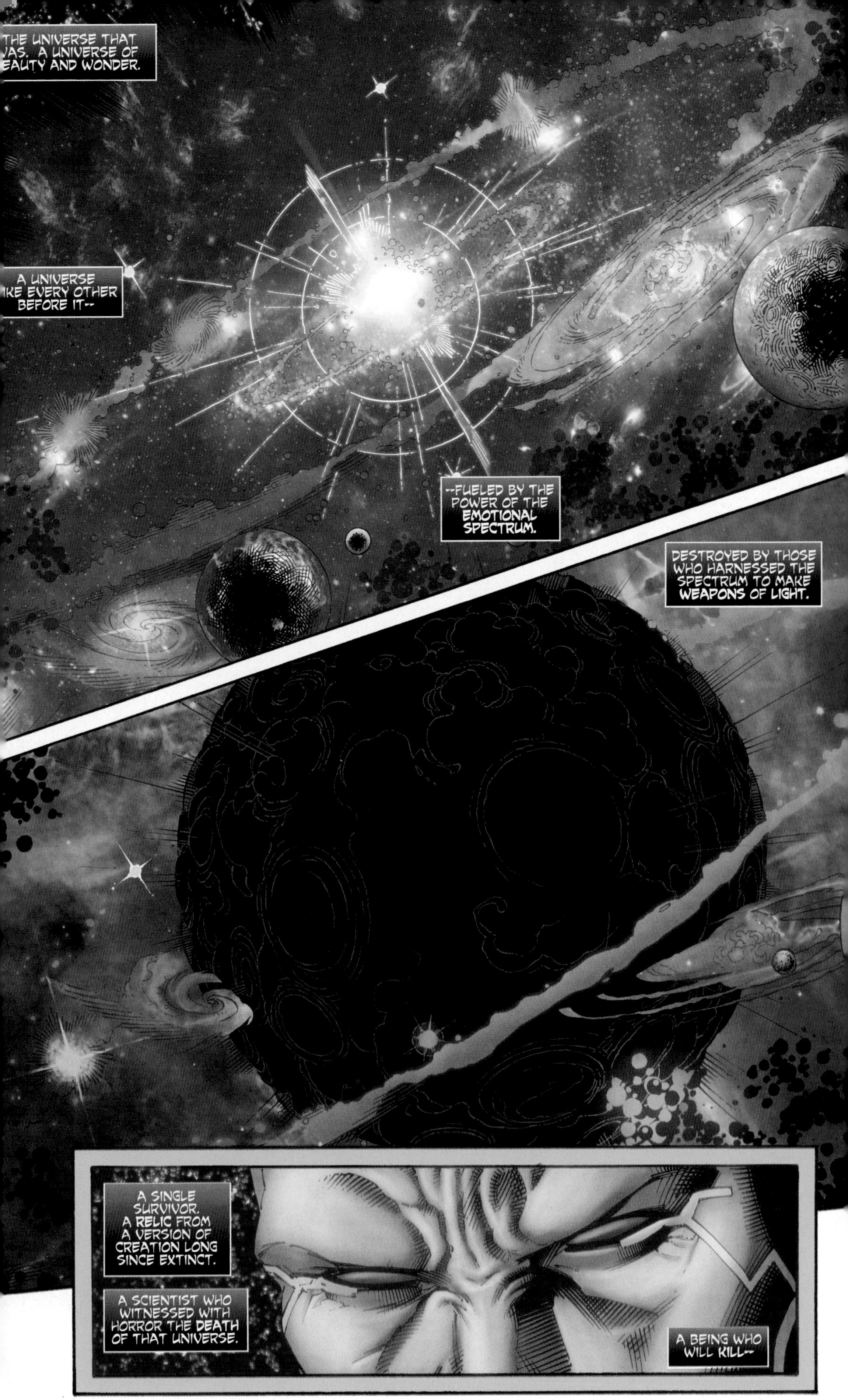
THE UNIVERSE THAT WAS. A UNIVERSE OF EAUTY AND WONDER.
A UNIVERSE IKE EVERY OTHER BEFORE IT--
--FUELED BY THE POWER OF THE EMOTIONAL SPECTRUM.
DESTROYED BY THOSE WHO HARNESSED THE SPECTRUM TO MAKE WEAPONS OF LIGHT.
A SINGLE SURVIVOR. A RELIC FROM A VERSION OF CREATION LONG SINCE EXTINCT.
A SCIENTIST WHO WITNESSED WITH HORROR THE DEATH OF THAT UNIVERSE.
A BEING WHO WILL KILL--

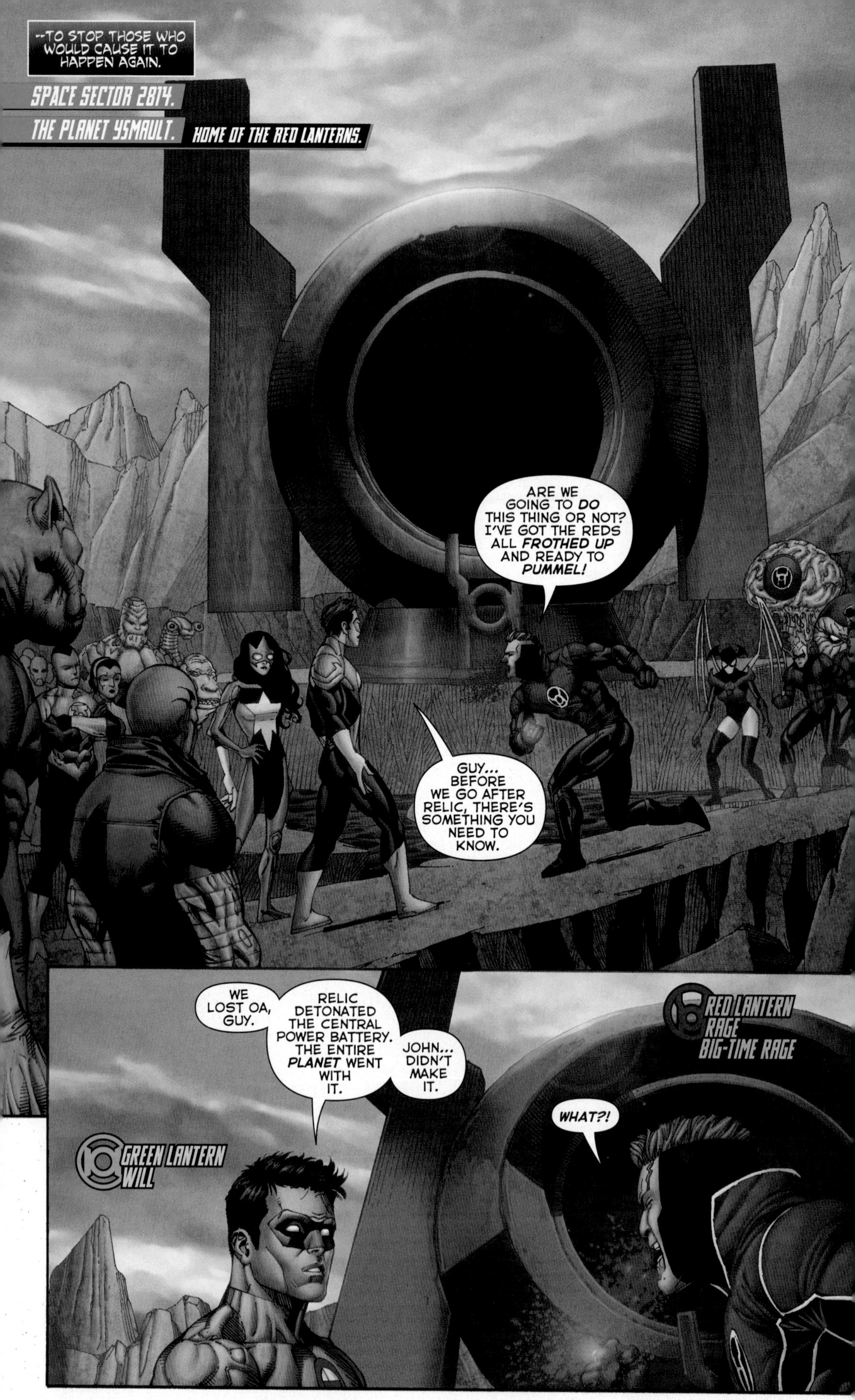
--TO STOP THOSE WHO WOULD CAUSE IT TO HAPPEN AGAIN.
SPACE SECTOR 2814.
THE PLANET YSMAULT.
HOME OF THE RED LANTERNS.
ARE WE GOING TO DO THIS THING OR NOT? I'VE GOT THE REDS ALL FROTHED UP AND READY TO PUMMEL!
GUY... BEFORE WE GO AFTER RELIC, THERE'S SOMETHING YOU NEED TO KNOW.
WE LOST OA, GUY.
RELIC DETONATED THE CENTRAL POWER BATTERY. THE ENTIRE PLANET WENT WITH IT.
JOHN... DIDN'T MAKE IT.
RED LANTERN RAGE BIG-TIME RAGE
WHAT?!
GREEN LANTERN WILL

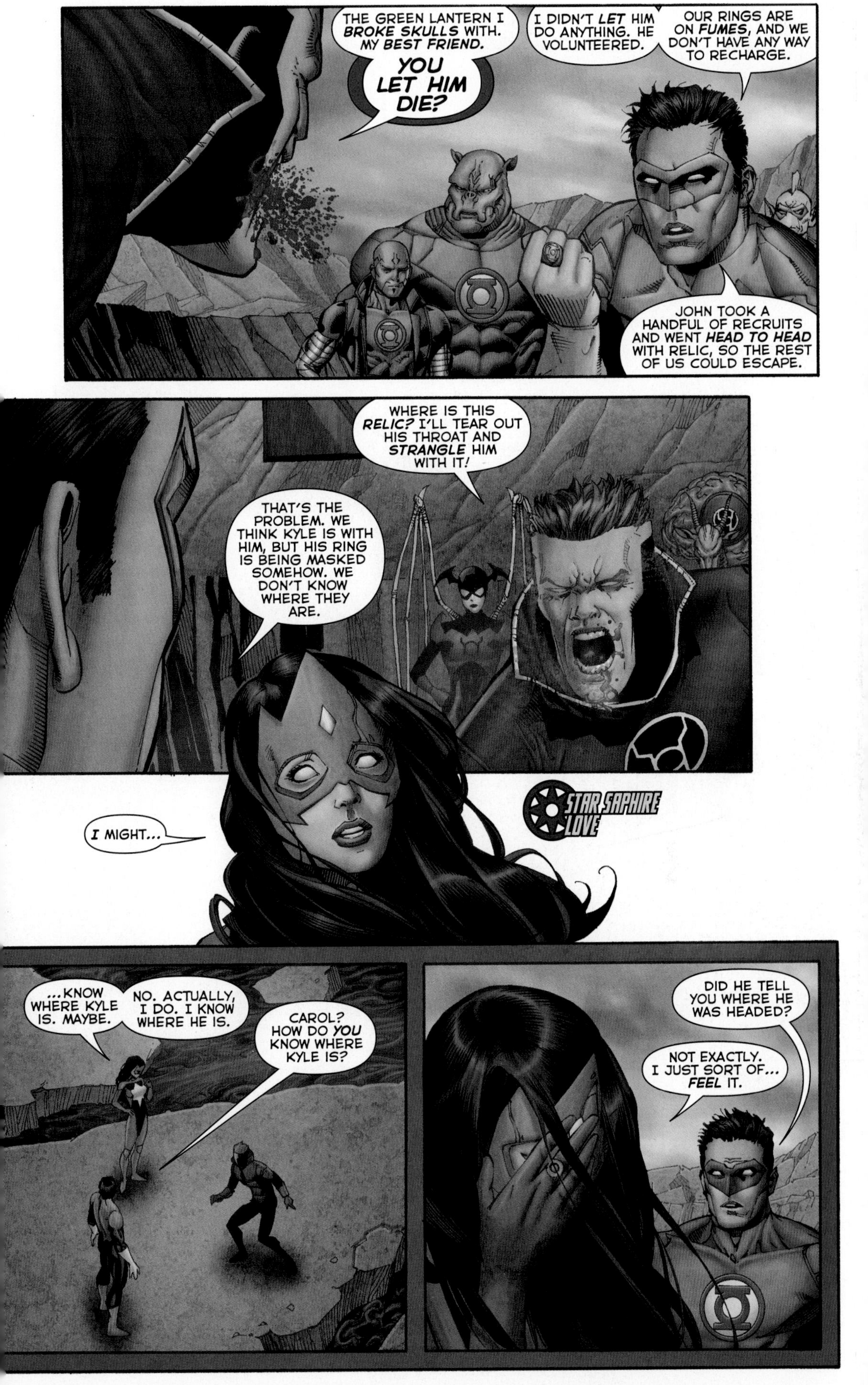
THE GREEN LANTERN I BROKE SKULLS WITH. MY BEST FRIEND.
YOU LET HIM DIE?
I DIDN'T LET HIM DO ANYTHING. HE VOLUNTEERED.
OUR RINGS ARE ON FUMES, AND WE DON'T HAVE ANY WAY TO RECHARGE.
JOHN TOOK A HANDFUL OF RECRUITS AND WENT HEAD TO HEAD WITH RELIC, SO THE REST OF US COULD ESCAPE.
WHERE IS THIS RELIC? I'LL TEAR OUT HIS THROAT AND STRANGLE HIM WITH IT!
THAT'S THE PROBLEM. WE THINK KYLE IS WITH HIM, BUT HIS RING IS BEING MASKED SOMEHOW. WE DON'T KNOW WHERE THEY ARE.
STAR SAPHIRE LOVE
I MIGHT...
...KNOW WHERE KYLE IS. MAYBE.
NO. ACTUALLY, I DO. I KNOW WHERE HE IS.
CAROL? HOW DO YOU KNOW WHERE KYLE IS?
DID HE TELL YOU WHERE HE WAS HEADED?
NOT EXACTLY. I JUST SORT OF... FEEL IT.

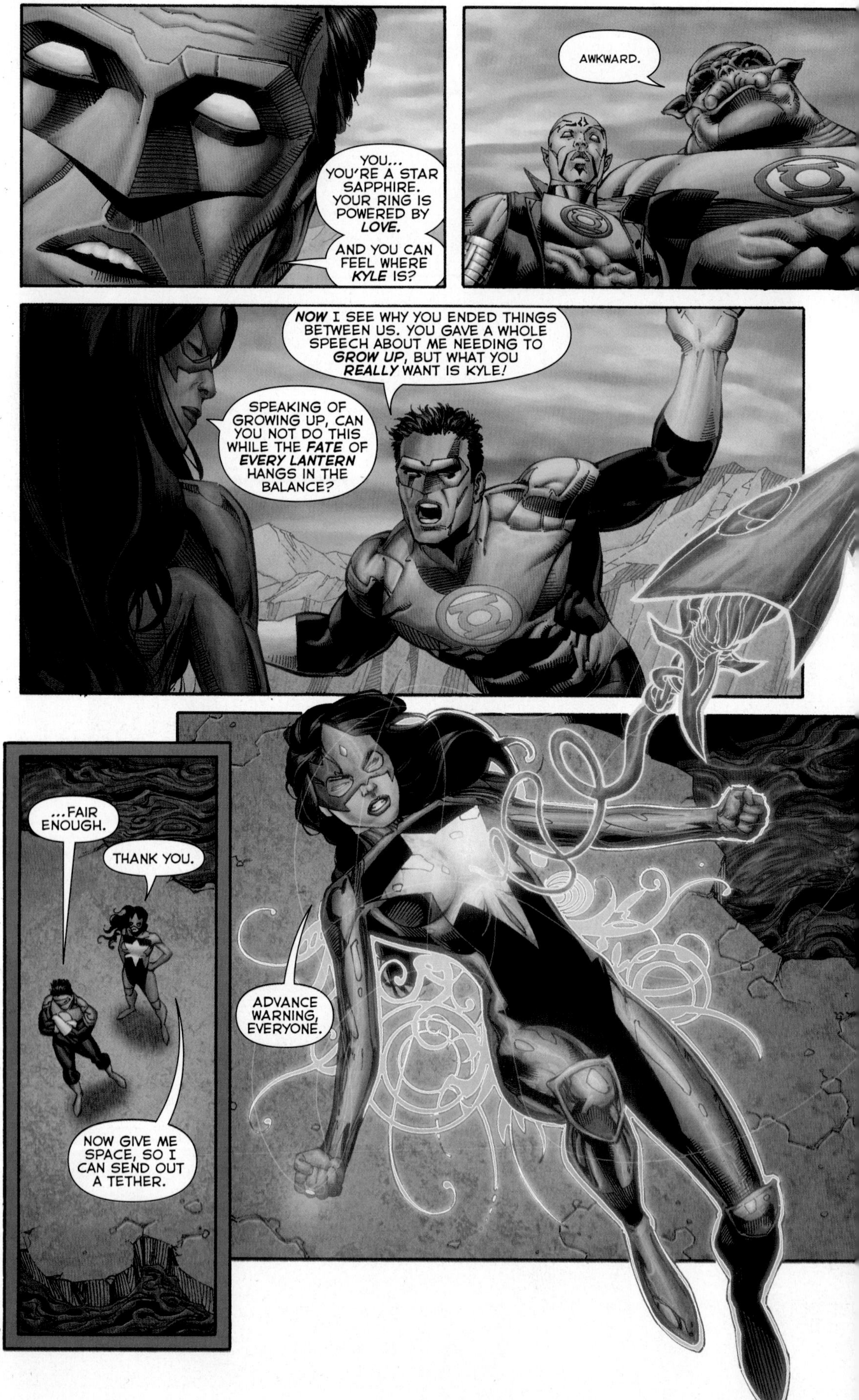

YOU... YOU'RE A STAR SAPPHIRE. YOUR RING IS POWERED BY LOVE.
AND YOU CAN FEEL WHERE KYLE IS?
AWKWARD.
NOW I SEE WHY YOU ENDED THINGS BETWEEN US. YOU GAVE A WHOLE SPEECH ABOUT ME NEEDING TO GROW UP, BUT WHAT YOU REALLY WANT IS KYLE!
SPEAKING OF GROWING UP, CAN YOU NOT DO THIS WHILE THE FATE OF EVERY LANTERN HANGS IN THE BALANCE?
...FAIR ENOUGH.
THANK YOU.
NOW GIVE ME SPACE, SO I CAN SEND OUT A TETHER.
ADVANCE WARNING, EVERYONE.

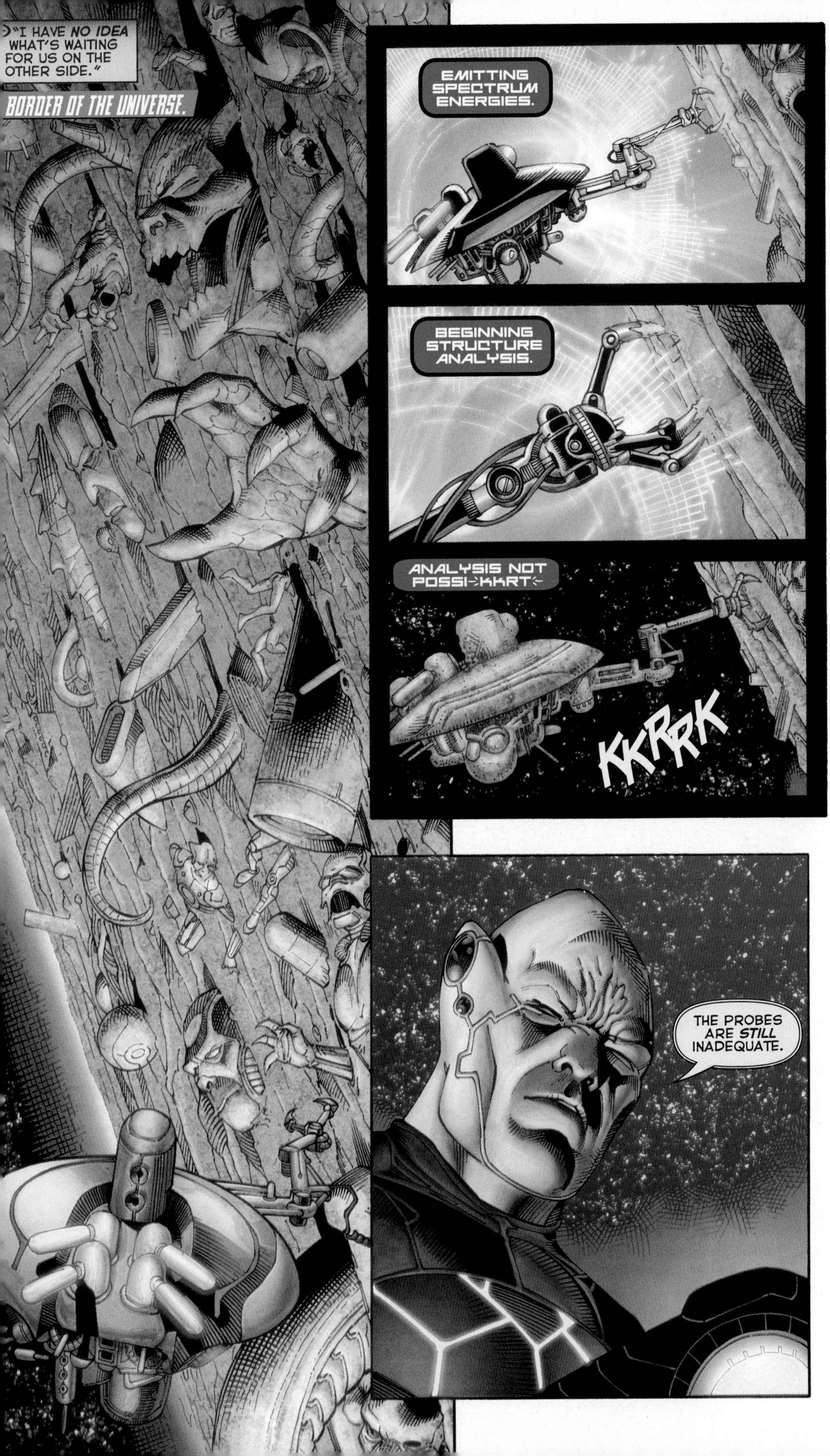
"I HAVE NO IDEA WHAT'S WAITING FOR US ON THE OTHER SIDE."
BORDER OF THE UNIVERSE.
EMITTING SPECTRUM ENERGIES.
BEGINNING STRUCTURE ANALYSIS.
ANALYSIS NOT POSSI-KKRT-
KKRRK
THE PROBES ARE STILL INADEQUATE.

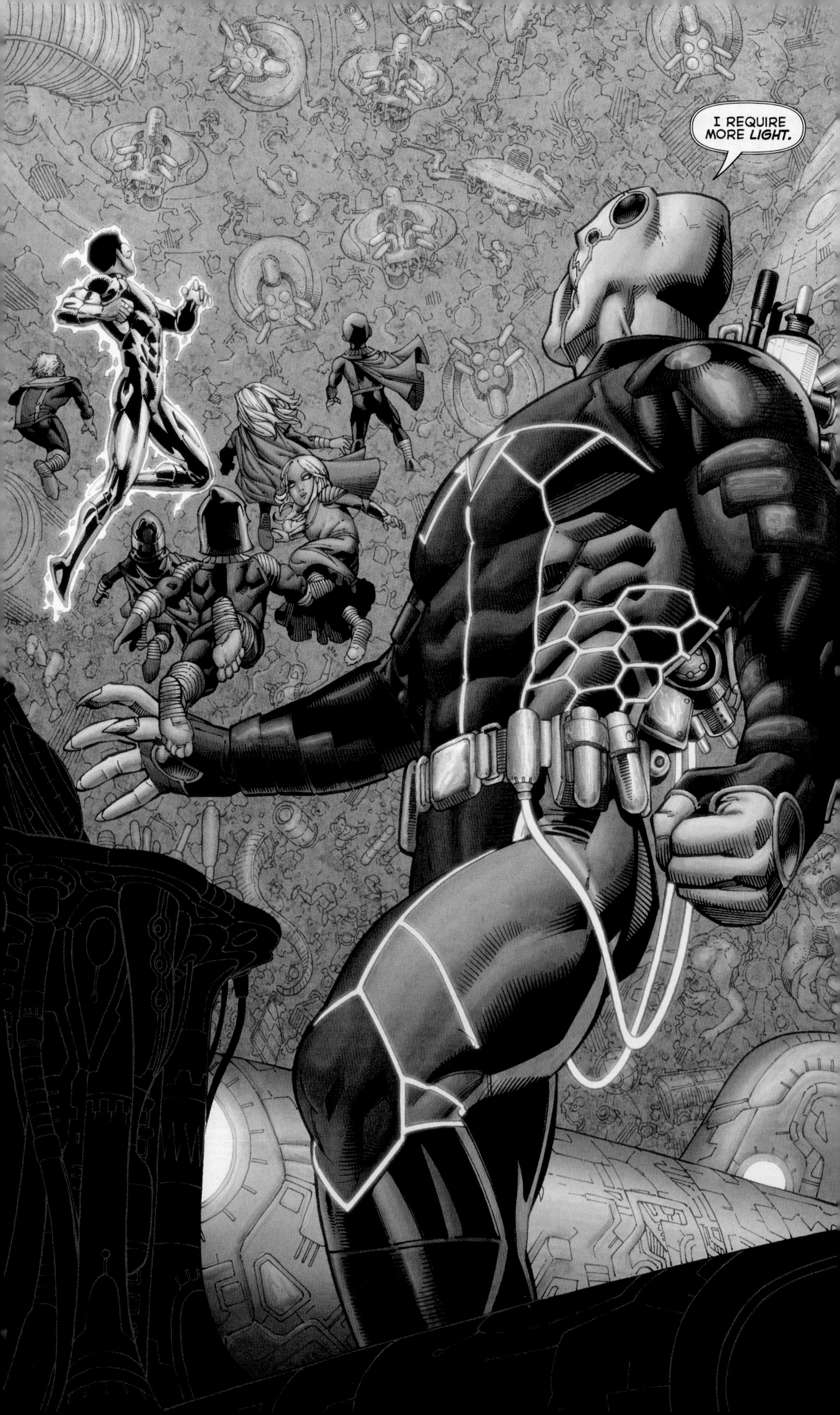
I REQUIRE MORE LIGHT.

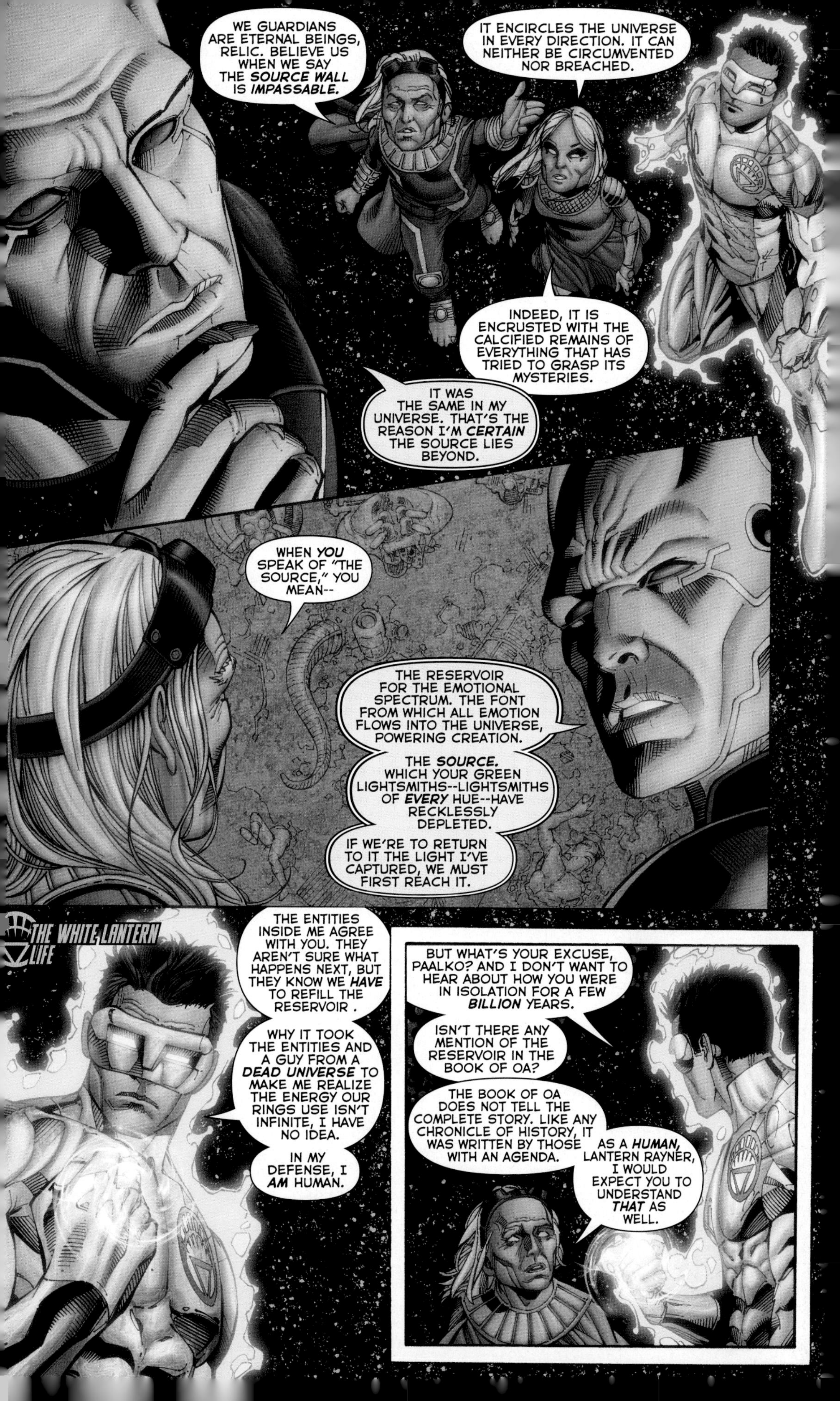

WE GUARDIANS ARE ETERNAL BEINGS, RELIC. BELIEVE US WHEN WE SAY THE SOURCE WALL IS IMPASSABLE.
IT ENCIRCLES THE UNIVERSE IN EVERY DIRECTION. IT CAN NEITHER BE CIRCUMVENTED NOR BREACHED.
INDEED, IT IS ENCRUSTED WITH THE CALCIFIED REMAINS OF EVERYTHING THAT HAS TRIED TO GRASP ITS MYSTERIES.
IT WAS THE SAME IN MY UNIVERSE. THAT'S THE REASON I'M CERTAIN THE SOURCE LIES BEYOND.
WHEN YOU SPEAK OF "THE SOURCE," YOU MEAN--
THE RESERVOIR FOR THE EMOTIONAL SPECTRUM. THE FONT FROM WHICH ALL EMOTION FLOWS INTO THE UNIVERSE, POWERING CREATION.
THE SOURCE. WHICH YOUR GREEN LIGHTSMITHS--LIGHTSMITHS OF EVERY HUE--HAVE RECKLESSLY DEPLETED.
IF WE'RE TO RETURN TO IT THE LIGHT I'VE CAPTURED, WE MUST FIRST REACH IT.
THE WHITE LANTERN
LIFE
THE ENTITIES INSIDE ME AGREE WITH YOU. THEY AREN'T SURE WHAT HAPPENS NEXT, BUT THEY KNOW WE HAVE TO REFILL THE RESERVOIR .
WHY IT TOOK THE ENTITIES AND A GUY FROM A DEAD UNIVERSE TO MAKE ME REALIZE THE ENERGY OUR RINGS USE ISN'T INFINITE, I HAVE NO IDEA.
IN MY DEFENSE, I AM HUMAN.
BUT WHAT'S YOUR EXCUSE, PAALKO? AND I DON'T WANT TO HEAR ABOUT HOW YOU WERE IN ISOLATION FOR A FEW BILLION YEARS.
ISN'T THERE ANY MENTION OF THE RESERVOIR IN THE BOOK OF OA?
THE BOOK OF OA DOES NOT TELL THE COMPLETE STORY. LIKE ANY CHRONICLE OF HISTORY, IT WAS WRITTEN BY THOSE WITH AN AGENDA.
AS A HUMAN, LANTERN RAYNER, I WOULD EXPECT YOU TO UNDERSTAND THAT AS WELL.

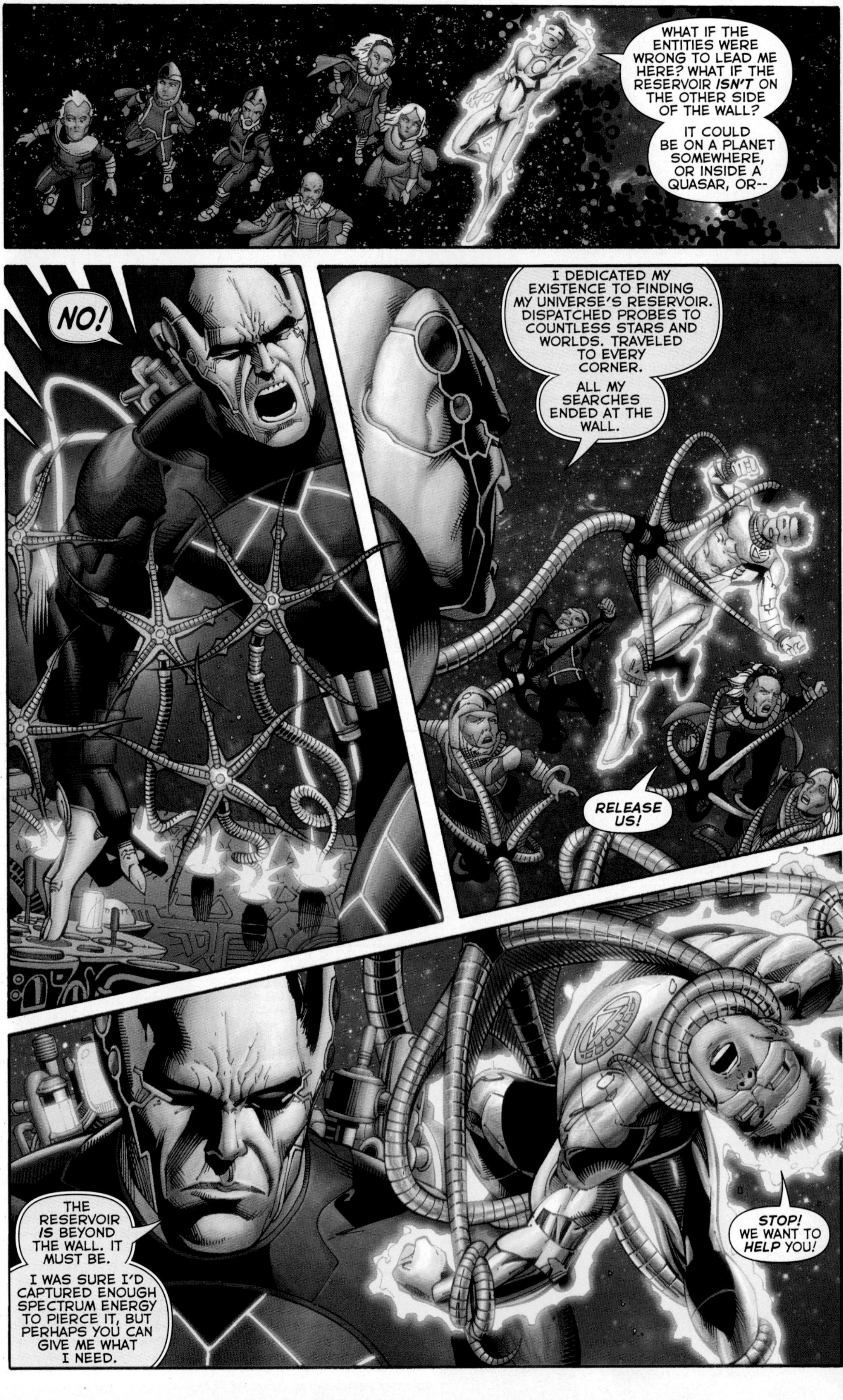

WHAT IF THE ENTITIES WERE WRONG TO LEAD ME HERE? WHAT IF THE RESERVOIR ISN'T ON THE OTHER SIDE OF THE WALL?
IT COULD BE ON A PLANET SOMEWHERE, OR INSIDE A QUASAR, OR--
NO!
I DEDICATED MY EXISTENCE TO FINDING MY UNIVERSE'S RESERVOIR. DISPATCHED PROBES TO COUNTLESS STARS AND WORLDS. TRAVELED TO EVERY CORNER.
ALL MY SEARCHES ENDED AT THE WALL.
RELEASE US!
THE RESERVOIR IS BEYOND THE WALL. IT MUST BE.
I WAS SURE I'D CAPTURED ENOUGH SPECTRUM ENERGY TO PIERCE IT, BUT PERHAPS YOU CAN GIVE ME WHAT I NEED.
STOP! WE WANT TO HELP YOU!

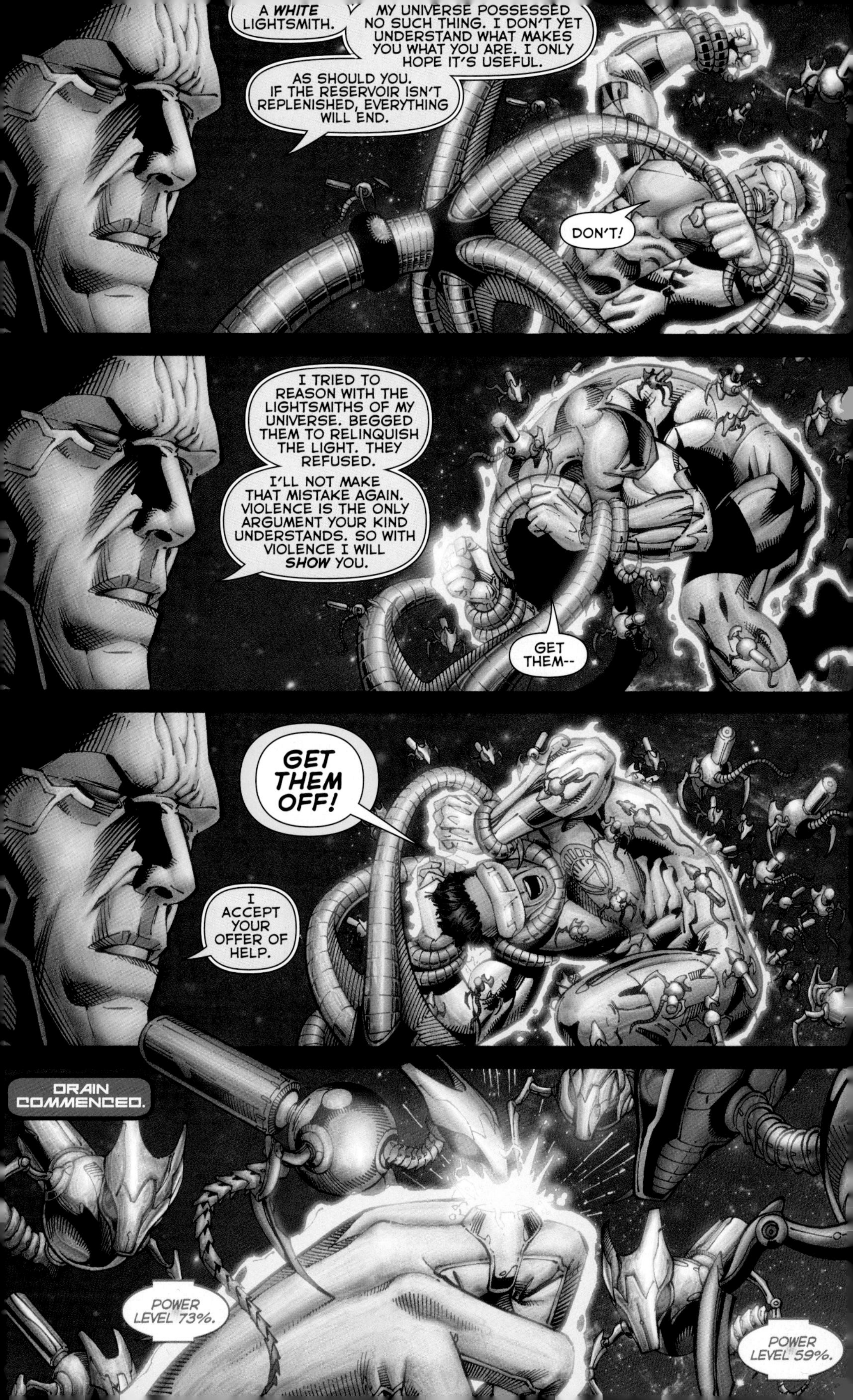
A WHITE LIGHTSMITH.
MY UNIVERSE POSSESSED NO SUCH THING. I DON'T YET UNDERSTAND WHAT MAKES YOU WHAT YOU ARE. I ONLY HOPE IT'S USEFUL.
AS SHOULD YOU. IF THE RESERVOIR ISN'T REPLENISHED, EVERYTHING WILL END.
DON'T!
I TRIED TO REASON WITH THE LIGHTSMITHS OF MY UNIVERSE. BEGGED THEM TO RELINQUISH THE LIGHT. THEY REFUSED.
I'LL NOT MAKE THAT MISTAKE AGAIN. VIOLENCE IS THE ONLY ARGUMENT YOUR KIND UNDERSTANDS. SO WITH VIOLENCE I WILL SHOW YOU.
GET THEM--
GET THEM OFF!
I ACCEPT YOUR OFFER OF HELP.
DRAIN COMMENCED.
POWER LEVEL 73%.
POWER LEVEL 59%.

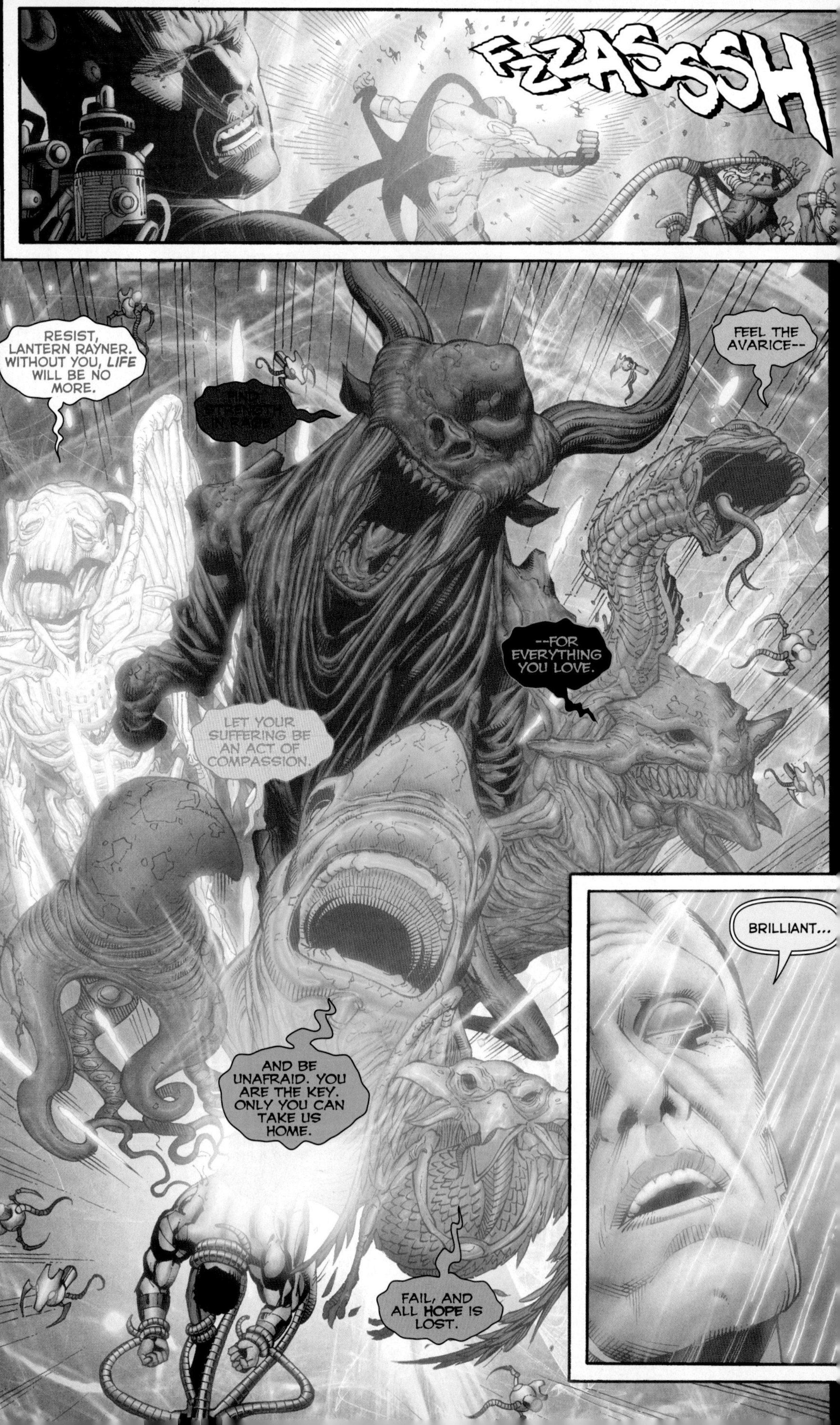
FZZASSSH
RESIST, LANTERN RAYNER. WITHOUT YOU, *LIFE* WILL BE NO MORE.
FIND STRENGTH IN RAGE.
FEEL THE AVARICE--
--FOR EVERYTHING YOU LOVE.
LET YOUR SUFFERING BE AN ACT OF COMPASSION.
AND BE UNAFRAID. YOU ARE THE KEY. ONLY YOU CAN TAKE US HOME.
FAIL, AND ALL **HOPE** IS LOST.
BRILLIANT...

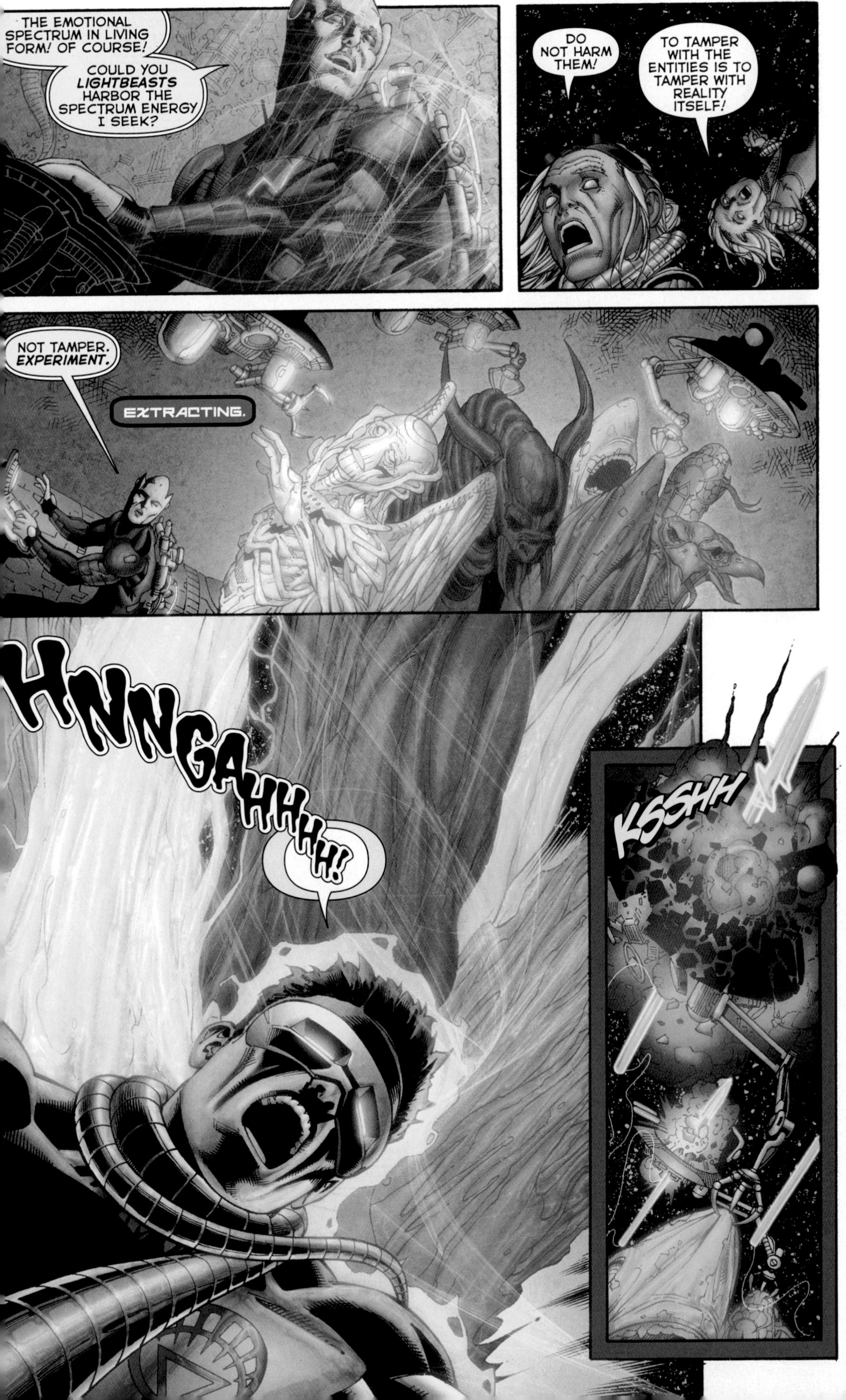
THE EMOTIONAL SPECTRUM IN LIVING FORM! OF COURSE!
COULD YOU *LIGHTBEASTS* HARBOR THE SPECTRUM ENERGY I SEEK?
DO NOT HARM THEM!
TO TAMPER WITH THE ENTITIES IS TO TAMPER WITH REALITY ITSELF!
NOT TAMPER. *EXPERIMENT.*
EXTRACTING.
HNNGAHHHHH!
KSSHH

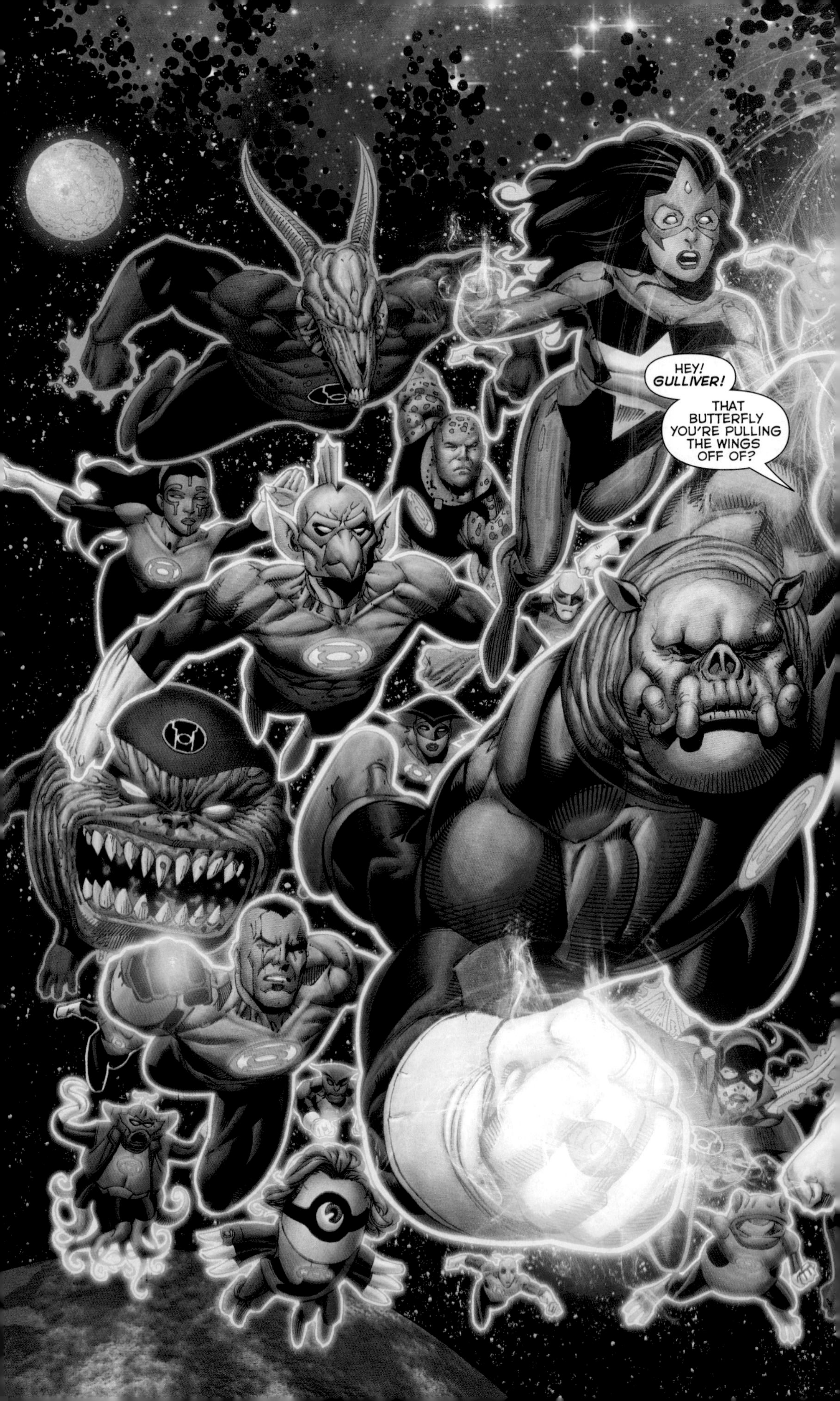
HEY! GULLIVER!
THAT BUTTERFLY YOU'RE PULLING THE WINGS OFF OF?

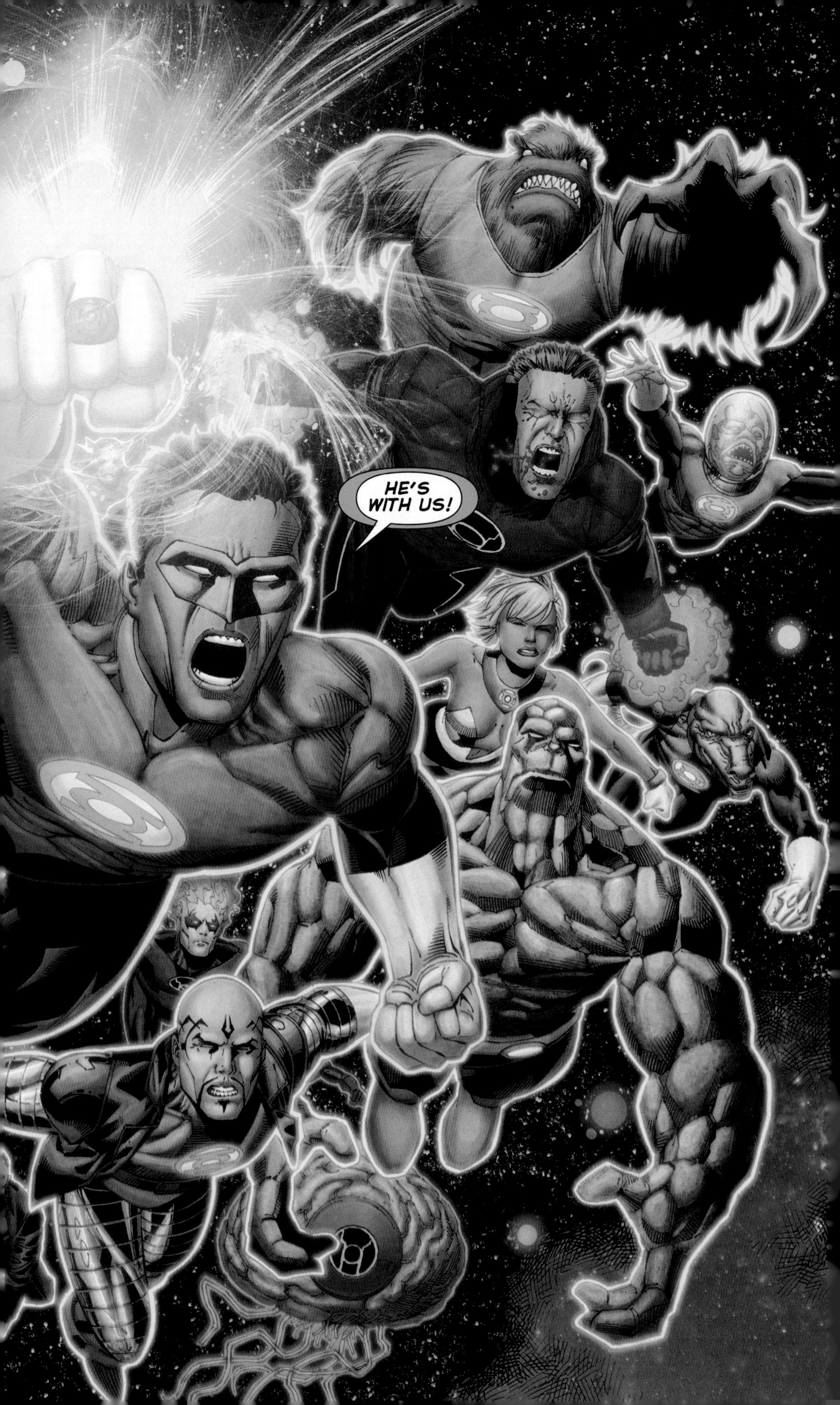
HE'S WITH US!

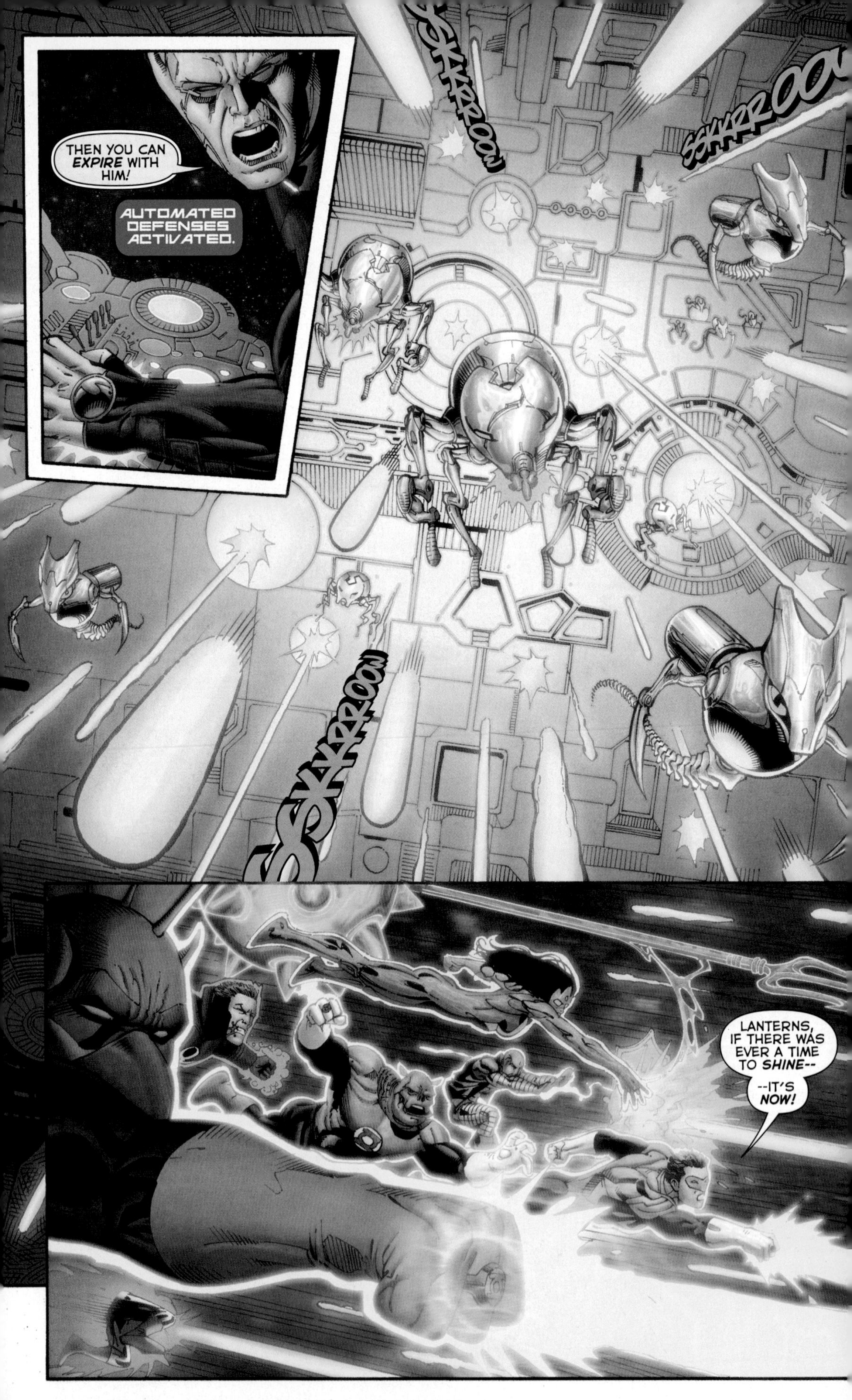
THEN YOU CAN EXPIRE WITH HIM!
AUTOMATED DEFENSES ACTIVATED.
SSKRROOW
SSKRROOW
SSKRROOW
LANTERNS, IF THERE WAS EVER A TIME TO SHINE--
--IT'S NOW!

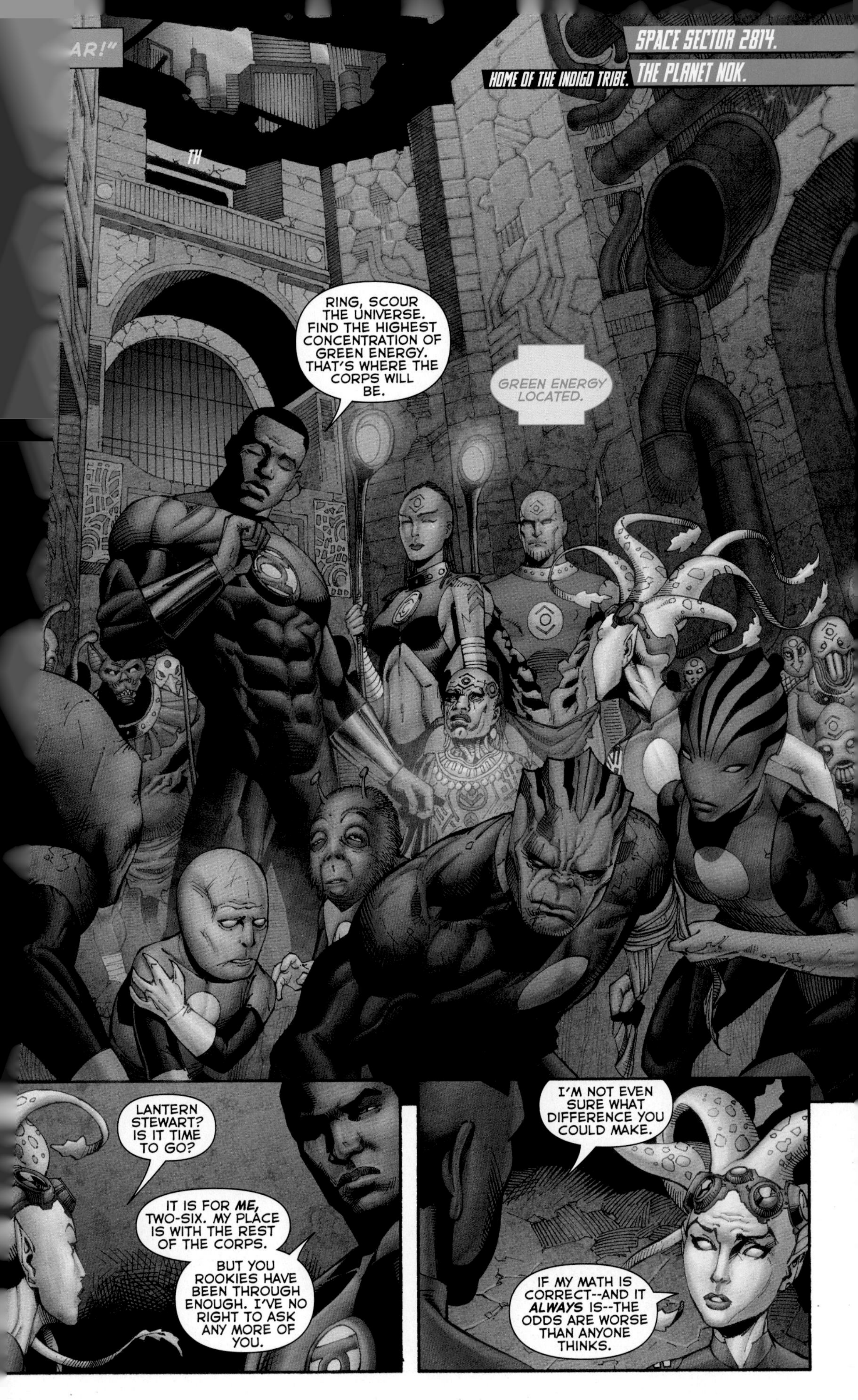
AR!"
SPACE SECTOR 2814.
HOME OF THE INDIGO TRIBE. THE PLANET NOK.
TH
RING, SCOUR THE UNIVERSE. FIND THE HIGHEST CONCENTRATION OF GREEN ENERGY. THAT'S WHERE THE CORPS WILL BE.
GREEN ENERGY LOCATED.
LANTERN STEWART? IS IT TIME TO GO?
IT IS FOR ME, TWO-SIX. MY PLACE IS WITH THE REST OF THE CORPS.
BUT YOU ROOKIES HAVE BEEN THROUGH ENOUGH. I'VE NO RIGHT TO ASK ANY MORE OF YOU.
I'M NOT EVEN SURE WHAT DIFFERENCE YOU COULD MAKE.
IF MY MATH IS CORRECT--AND IT ALWAYS IS--THE ODDS ARE WORSE THAN ANYONE THINKS.

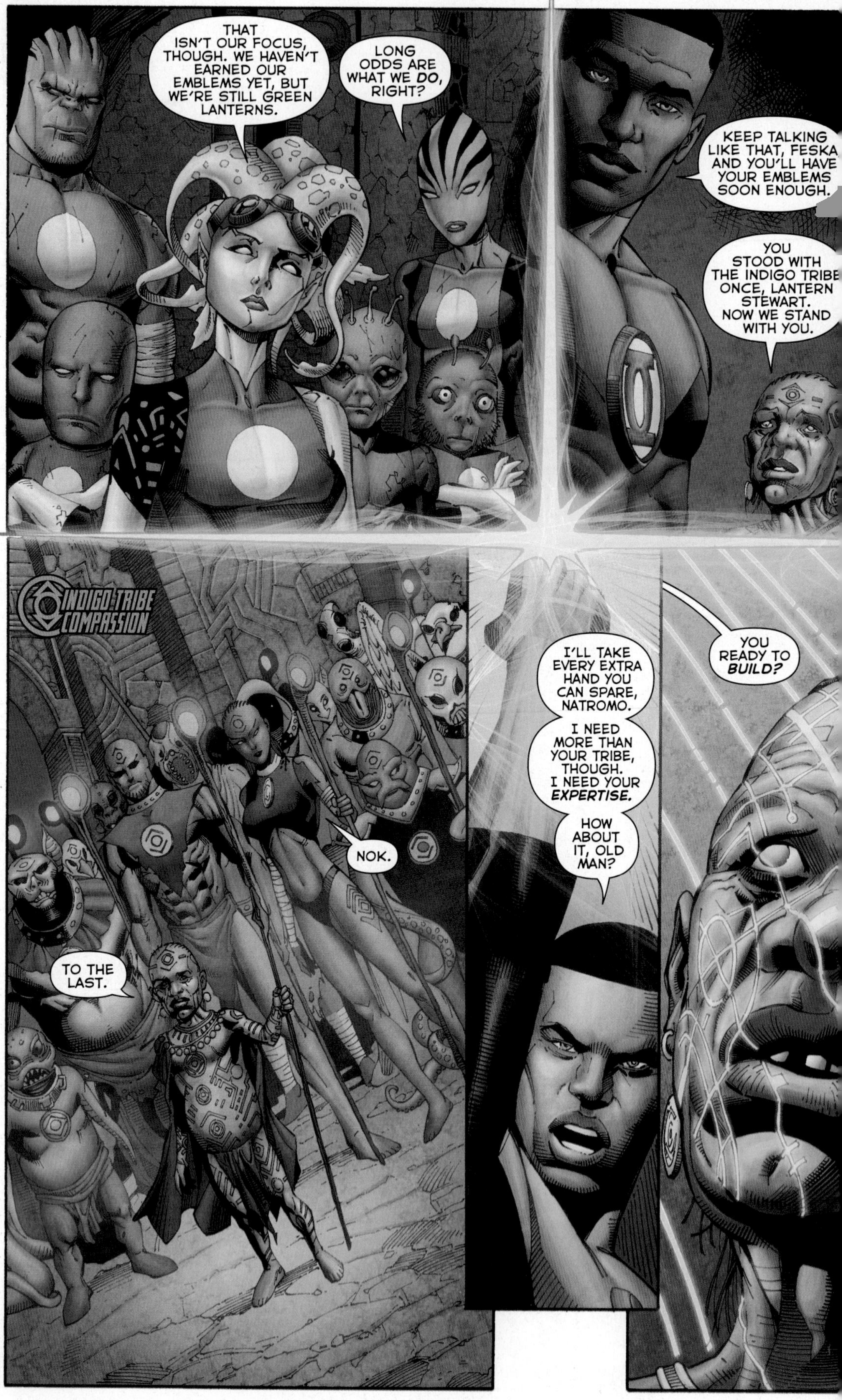

THAT ISN'T OUR FOCUS, THOUGH. WE HAVEN'T EARNED OUR EMBLEMS YET, BUT WE'RE STILL GREEN LANTERNS.
LONG ODDS ARE WHAT WE *DO*, RIGHT?
KEEP TALKING LIKE THAT, FESKA AND YOU'LL HAVE YOUR EMBLEMS SOON ENOUGH.
YOU STOOD WITH THE INDIGO TRIBE ONCE, LANTERN STEWART. NOW WE STAND WITH YOU.
INDIGO TRIBE COMPASSION
NOK.
TO THE LAST.
I'LL TAKE EVERY EXTRA HAND YOU CAN SPARE, NATROMO.
I NEED MORE THAN YOUR TRIBE, THOUGH. I NEED YOUR *EXPERTISE.*
HOW ABOUT IT, OLD MAN?
YOU READY TO *BUILD?*

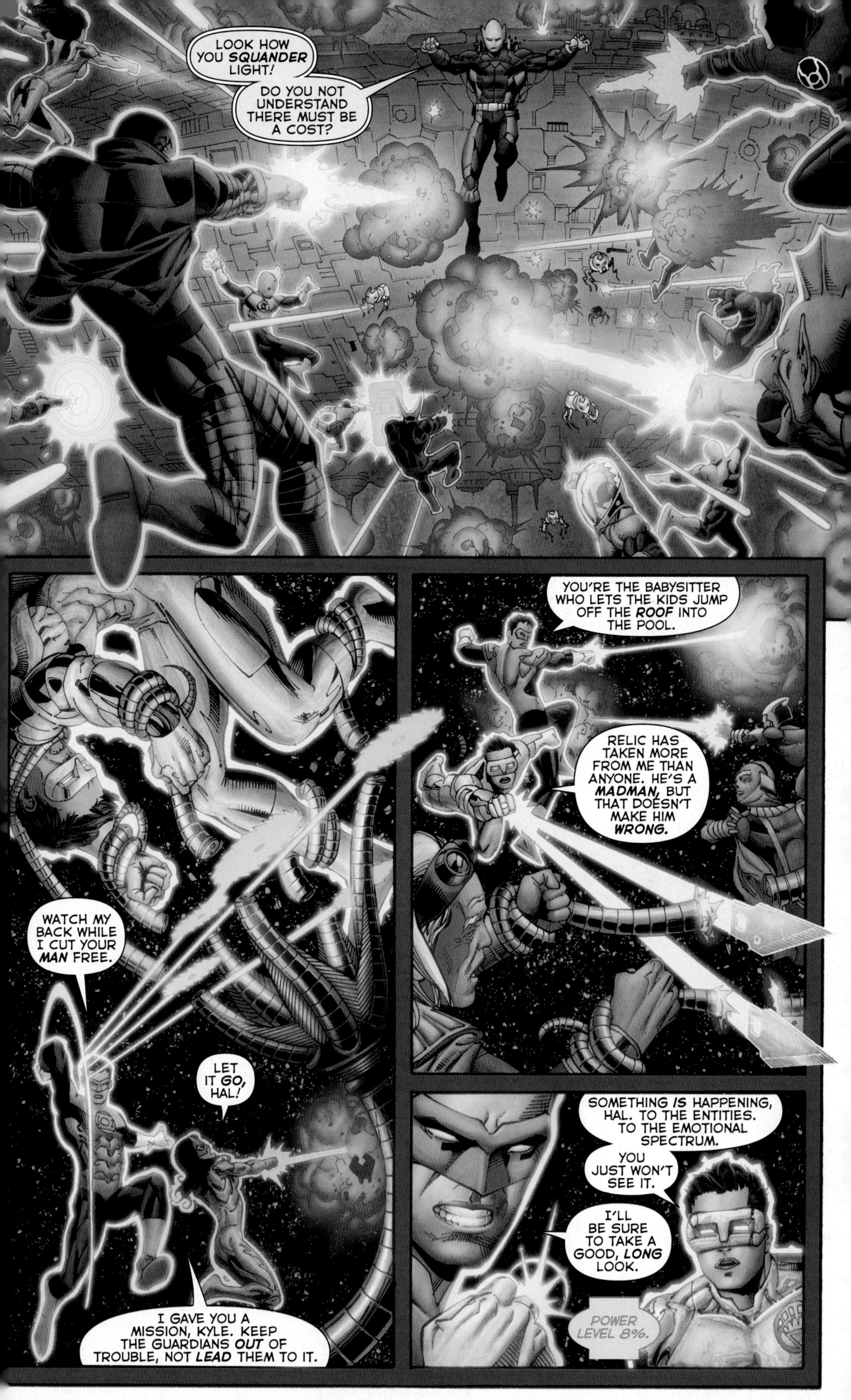
LOOK HOW YOU SQUANDER LIGHT!
DO YOU NOT UNDERSTAND THERE MUST BE A COST?
WATCH MY BACK WHILE I CUT YOUR MAN FREE.
LET IT GO, HAL!
I GAVE YOU A MISSION, KYLE. KEEP THE GUARDIANS OUT OF TROUBLE, NOT LEAD THEM TO IT.
YOU'RE THE BABYSITTER WHO LETS THE KIDS JUMP OFF THE ROOF INTO THE POOL.
RELIC HAS TAKEN MORE FROM ME THAN ANYONE. HE'S A MADMAN, BUT THAT DOESN'T MAKE HIM WRONG.
SOMETHING IS HAPPENING, HAL. TO THE ENTITIES. TO THE EMOTIONAL SPECTRUM.
YOU JUST WON'T SEE IT.
I'LL BE SURE TO TAKE A GOOD, LONG LOOK.
POWER LEVEL 8%.

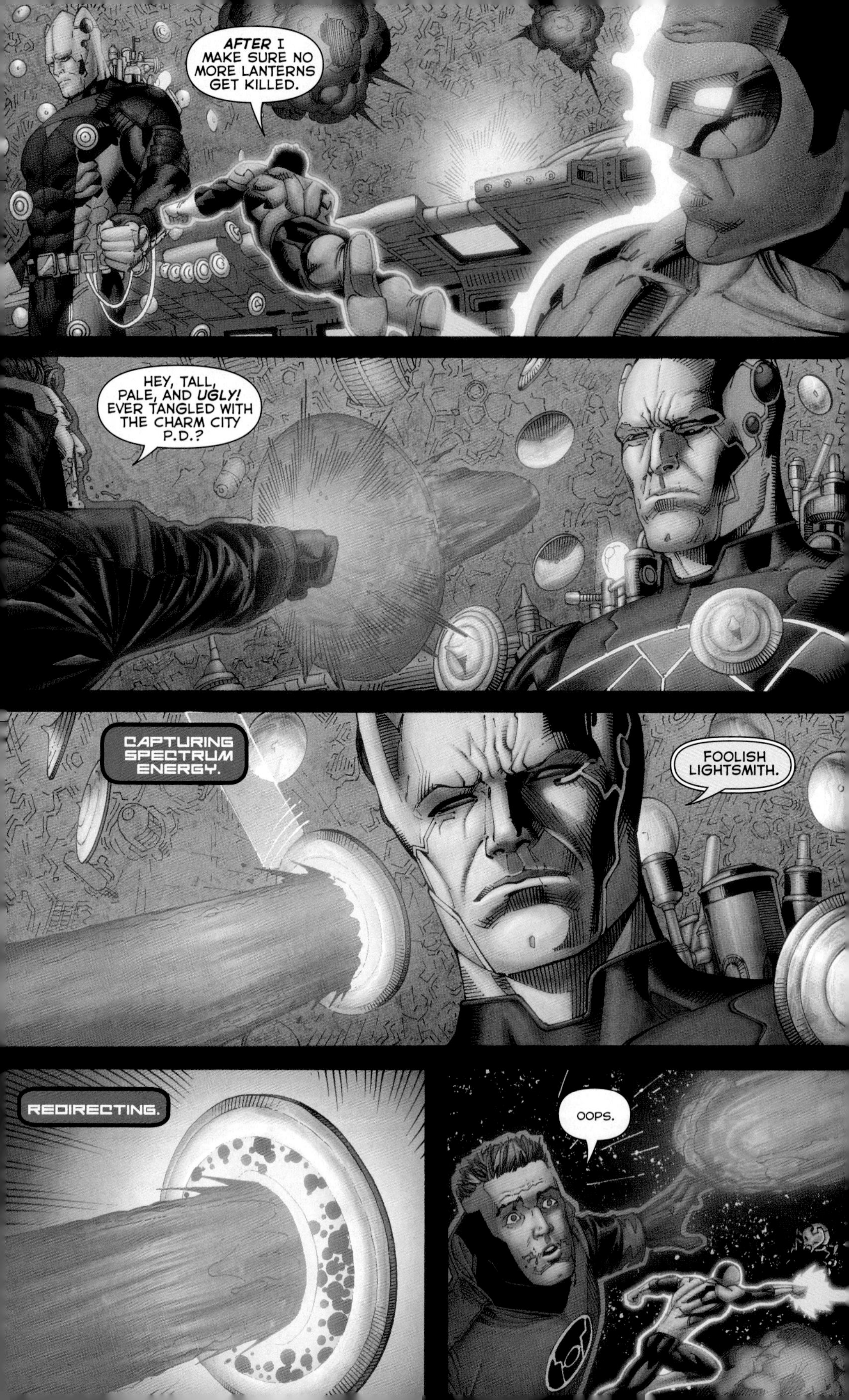
AFTER I MAKE SURE NO MORE LANTERNS GET KILLED.
HEY, TALL, PALE, AND UGLY! EVER TANGLED WITH THE CHARM CITY P.D.?
CAPTURING SPECTRUM ENERGY.
FOOLISH LIGHTSMITH.
REDIRECTING.
OOPS.

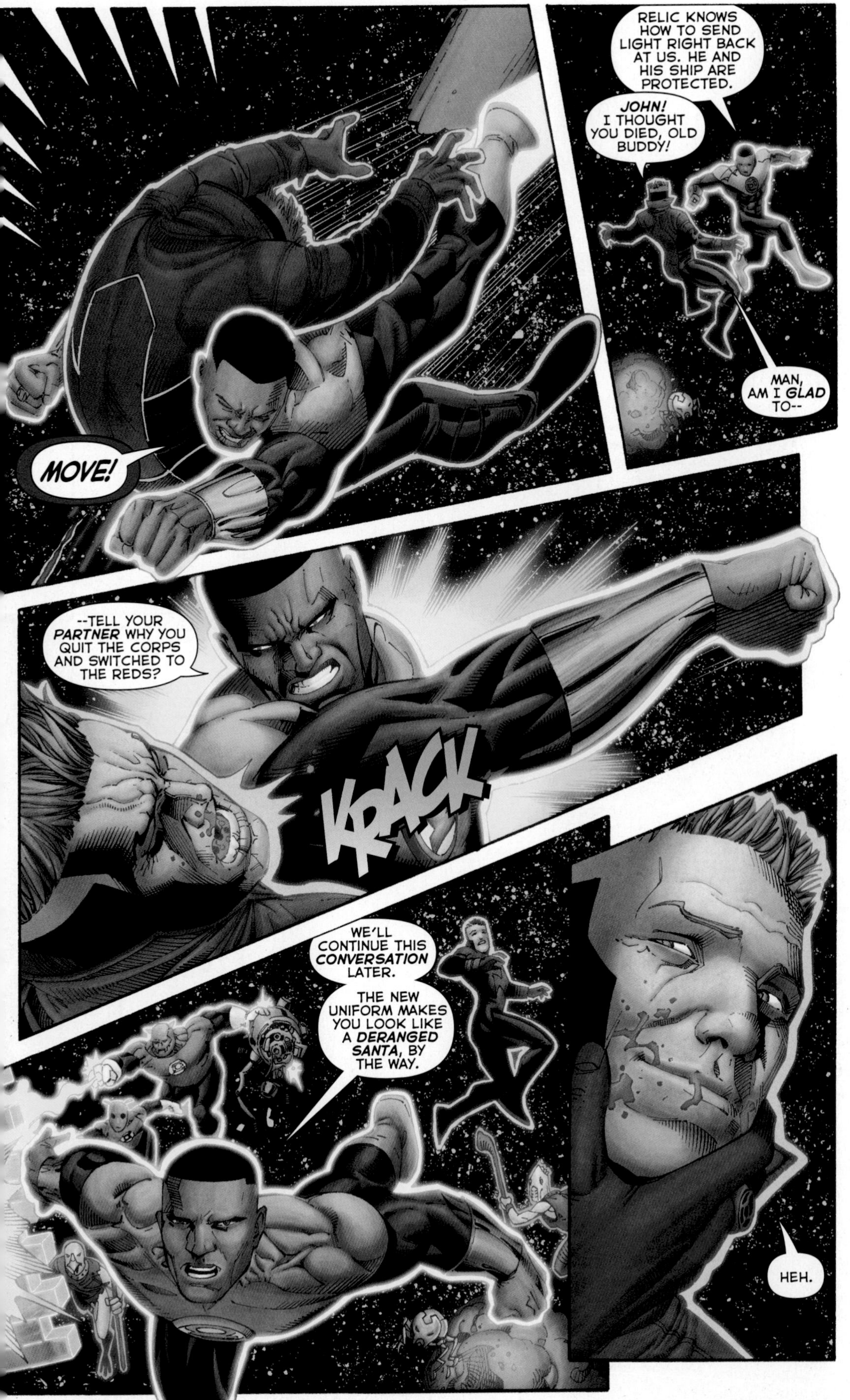
MOVE!
RELIC KNOWS HOW TO SEND LIGHT RIGHT BACK AT US. HE AND HIS SHIP ARE PROTECTED.
JOHN! I THOUGHT YOU DIED, OLD BUDDY!
MAN, AM I GLAD TO--
--TELL YOUR PARTNER WHY YOU QUIT THE CORPS AND SWITCHED TO THE REDS?
KRACK
WE'LL CONTINUE THIS CONVERSATION LATER.
THE NEW UNIFORM MAKES YOU LOOK LIKE A DERANGED SANTA, BY THE WAY.
HEH.

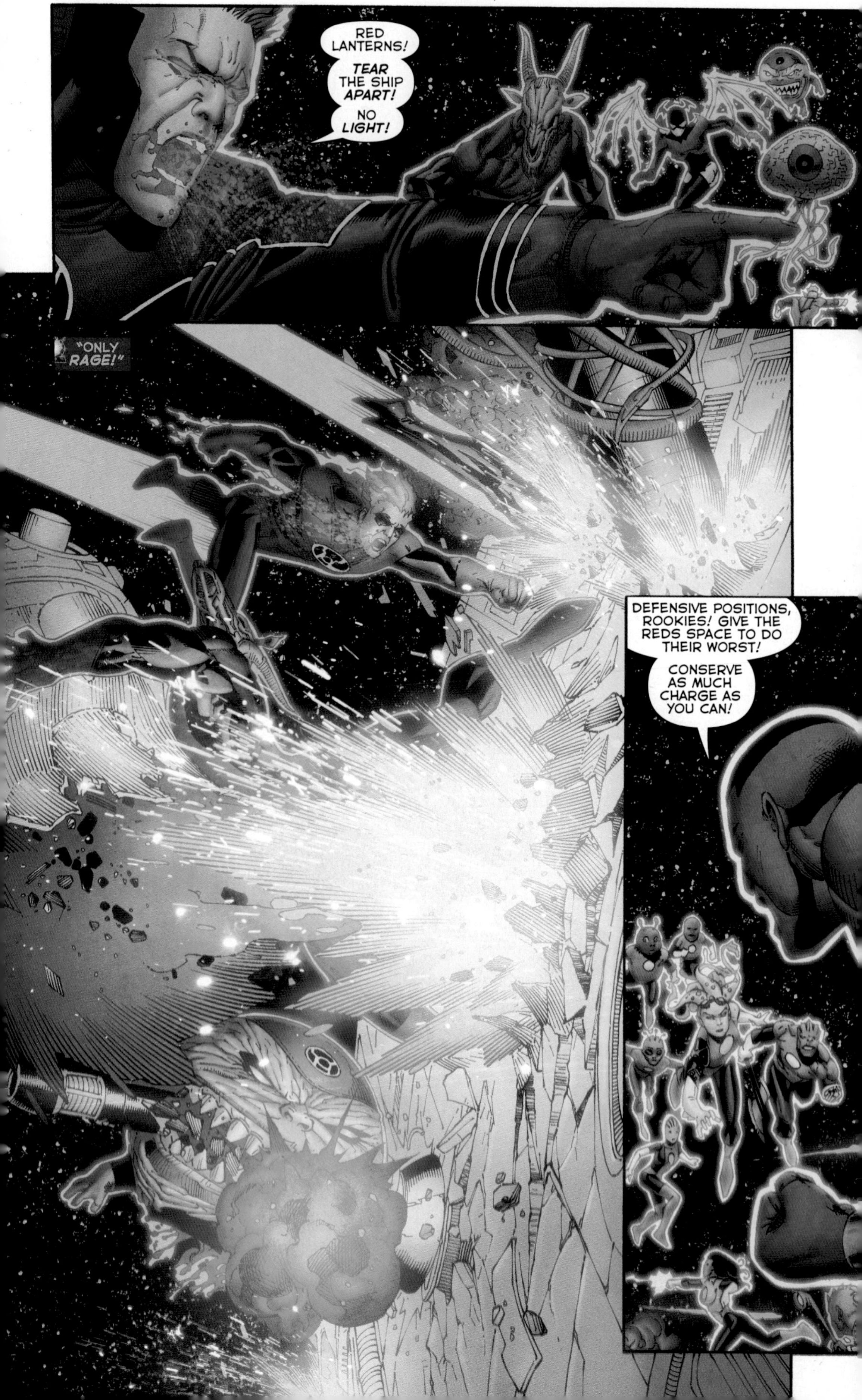
RED LANTERNS! TEAR THE SHIP APART! NO LIGHT!
"ONLY RAGE!"
DEFENSIVE POSITIONS, ROOKIES! GIVE THE REDS SPACE TO DO THEIR WORST!
CONSERVE AS MUCH CHARGE AS YOU CAN!

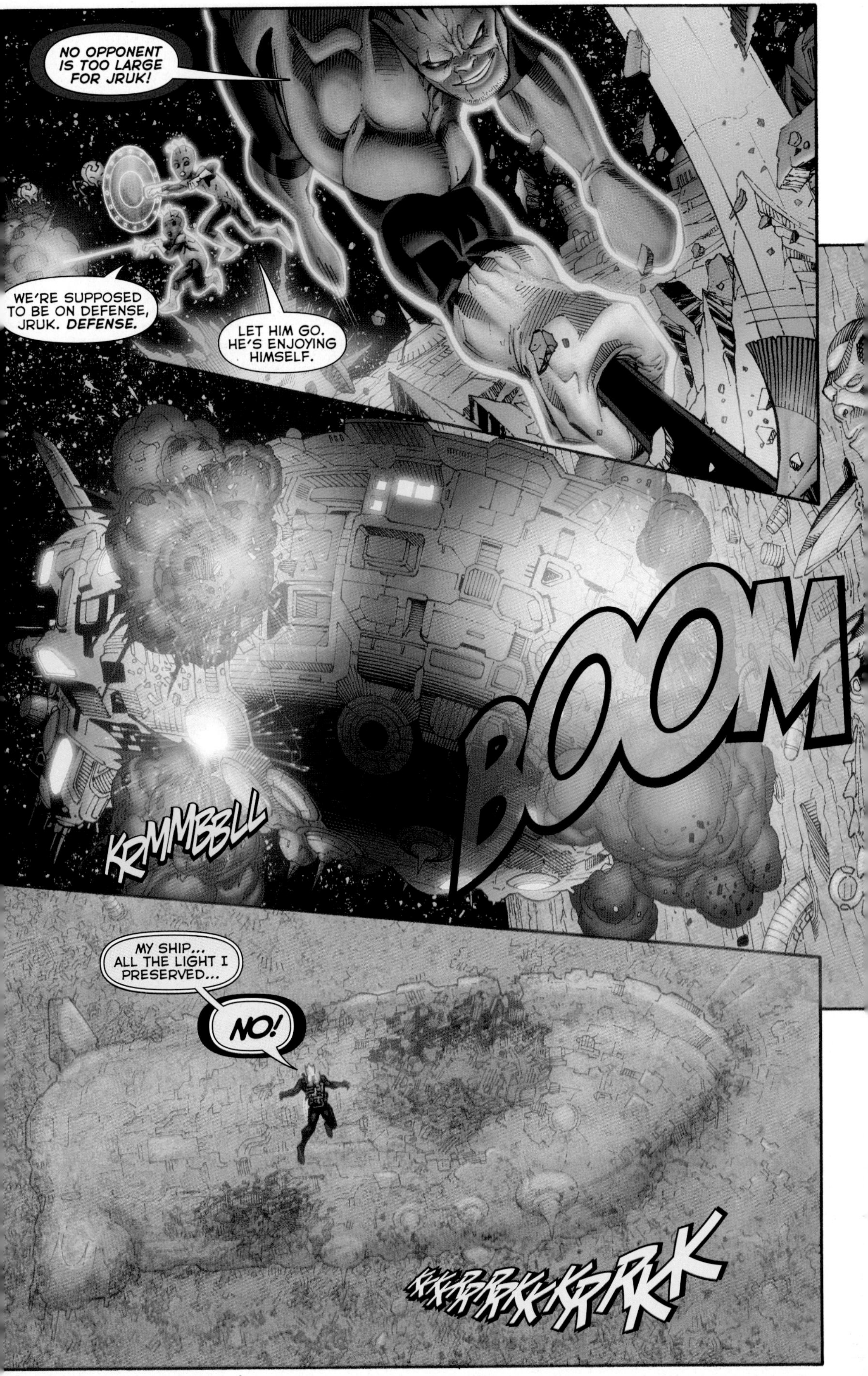
NO OPPONENT IS TOO LARGE FOR JRUK!
WE'RE SUPPOSED TO BE ON DEFENSE, JRUK. *DEFENSE.*
LET HIM GO. HE'S ENJOYING HIMSELF.
BOOM
KRMMBBLL
MY SHIP... ALL THE LIGHT I PRESERVED...
NO!

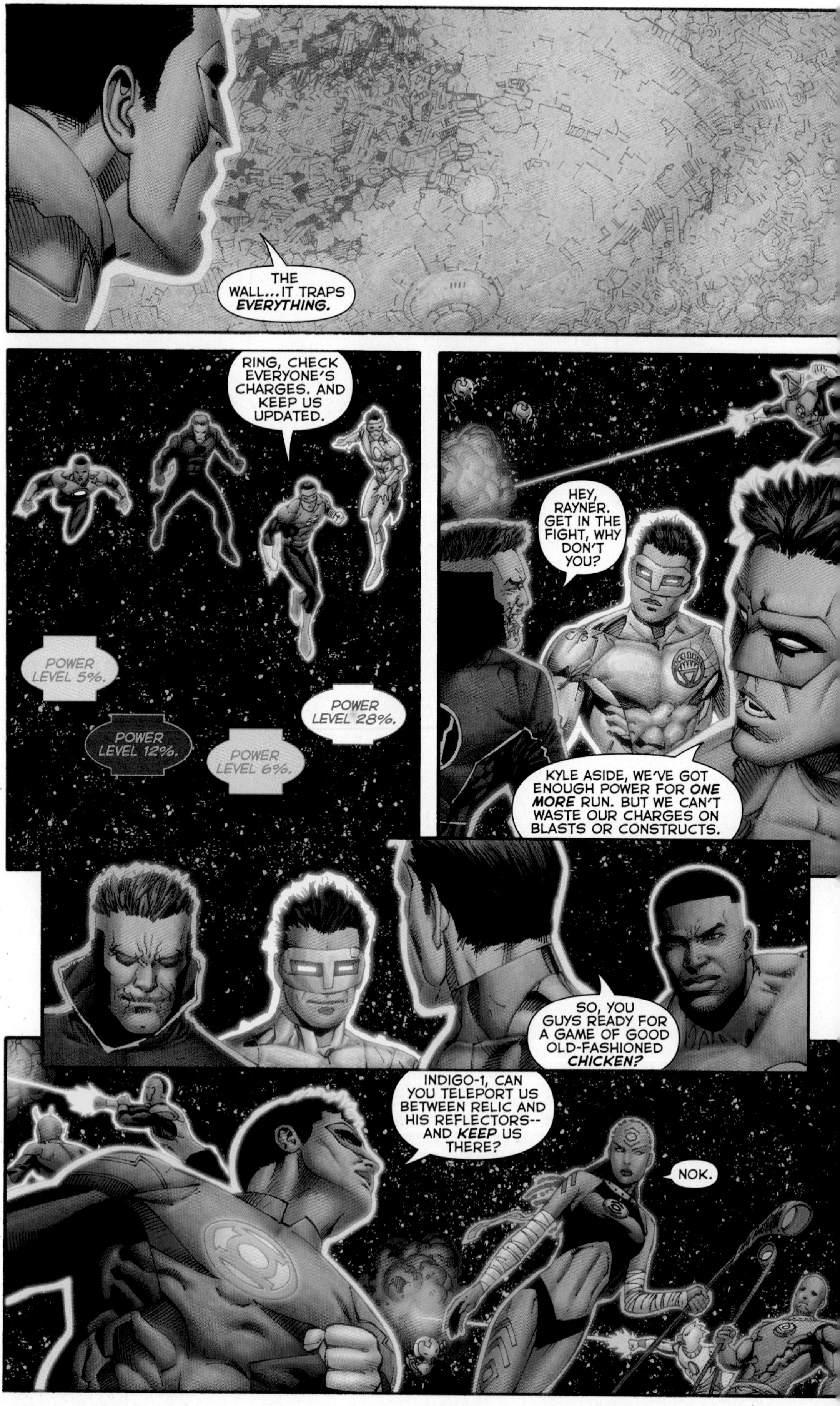
THE WALL...IT TRAPS EVERYTHING.
RING, CHECK EVERYONE'S CHARGES. AND KEEP US UPDATED.
POWER LEVEL 5%.
POWER LEVEL 12%.
POWER LEVEL 6%.
POWER LEVEL 28%.
HEY, RAYNER. GET IN THE FIGHT, WHY DON'T YOU?
KYLE ASIDE, WE'VE GOT ENOUGH POWER FOR ONE MORE RUN. BUT WE CAN'T WASTE OUR CHARGES ON BLASTS OR CONSTRUCTS.
SO, YOU GUYS READY FOR A GAME OF GOOD OLD-FASHIONED CHICKEN?
INDIGO-1, CAN YOU TELEPORT US BETWEEN RELIC AND HIS REFLECTORS-- AND KEEP US THERE?
NOK.

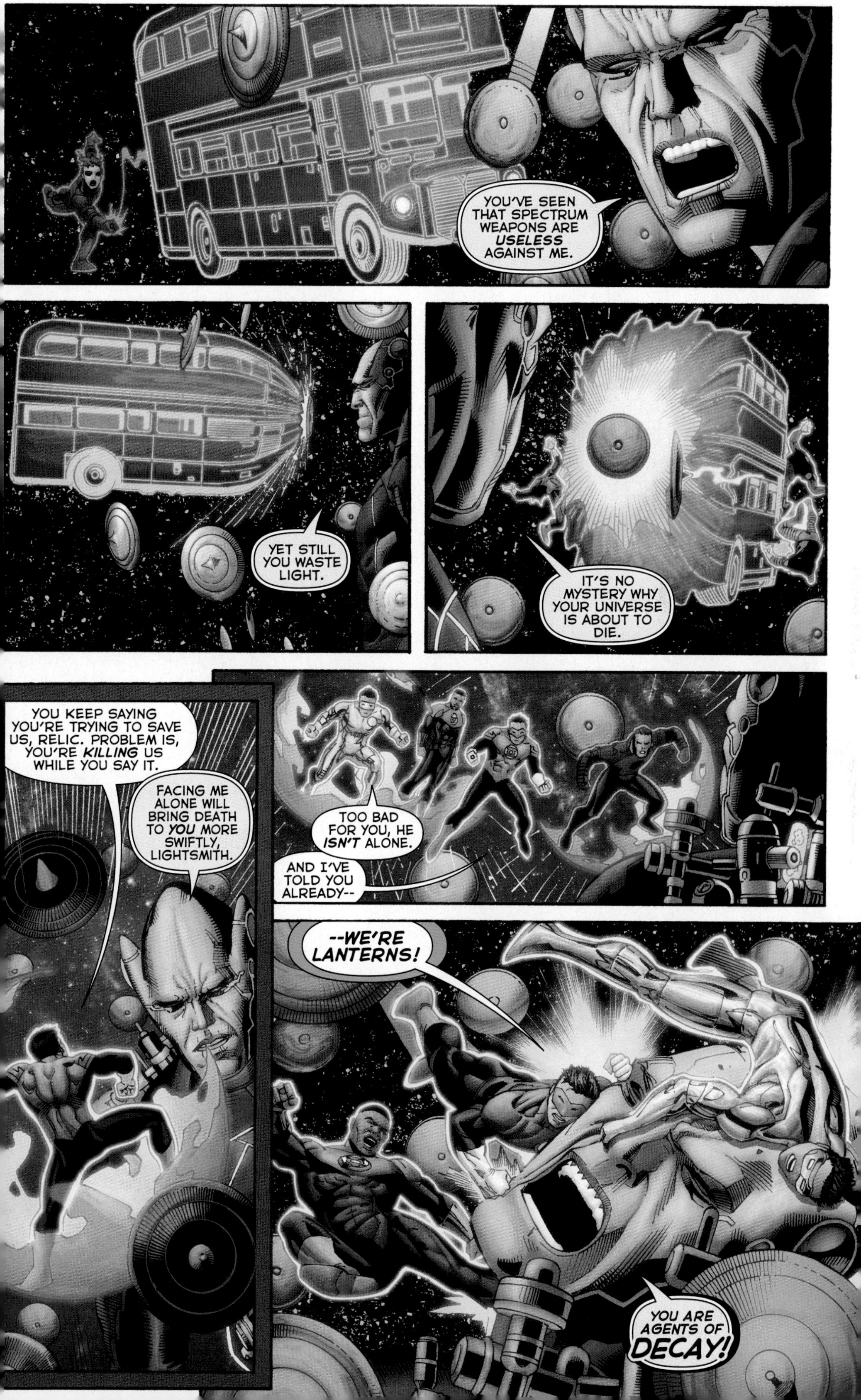

YOU'VE SEEN THAT SPECTRUM WEAPONS ARE *USELESS* AGAINST ME.
YET STILL YOU WASTE LIGHT.
IT'S NO MYSTERY WHY YOUR UNIVERSE IS ABOUT TO DIE.
YOU KEEP SAYING YOU'RE TRYING TO SAVE US, RELIC. PROBLEM IS, YOU'RE *KILLING* US WHILE YOU SAY IT.
FACING ME ALONE WILL BRING DEATH TO *YOU* MORE SWIFTLY, LIGHTSMITH.
TOO BAD FOR YOU, HE *ISN'T* ALONE.
AND I'VE TOLD YOU ALREADY--
--WE'RE LANTERNS!
YOU ARE AGENTS OF DECAY!

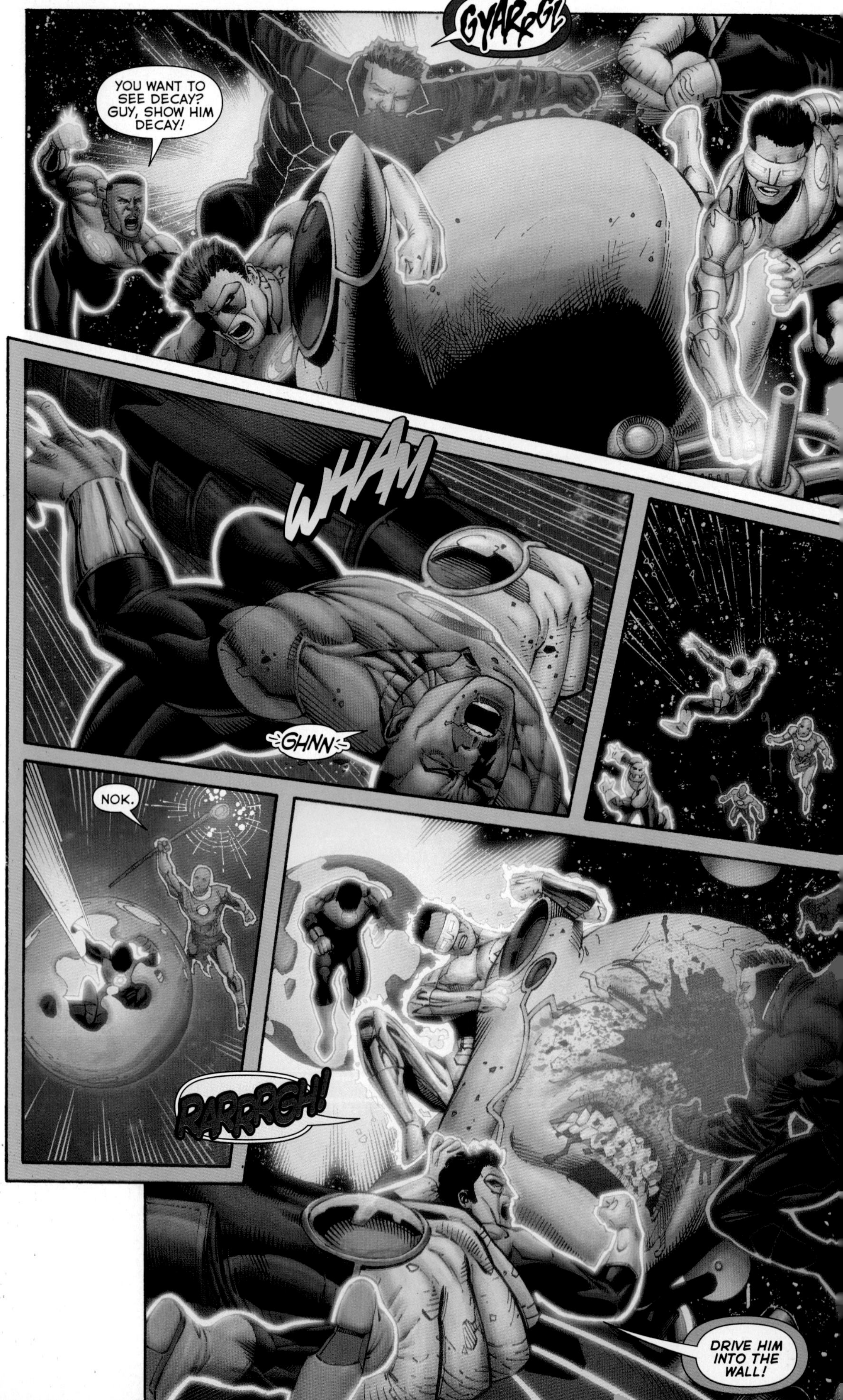
GYARRGL
YOU WANT TO SEE DECAY? GUY, SHOW HIM DECAY!
WHAM
GHNN
NOK.
RARRRGH!
DRIVE HIM INTO THE WALL!

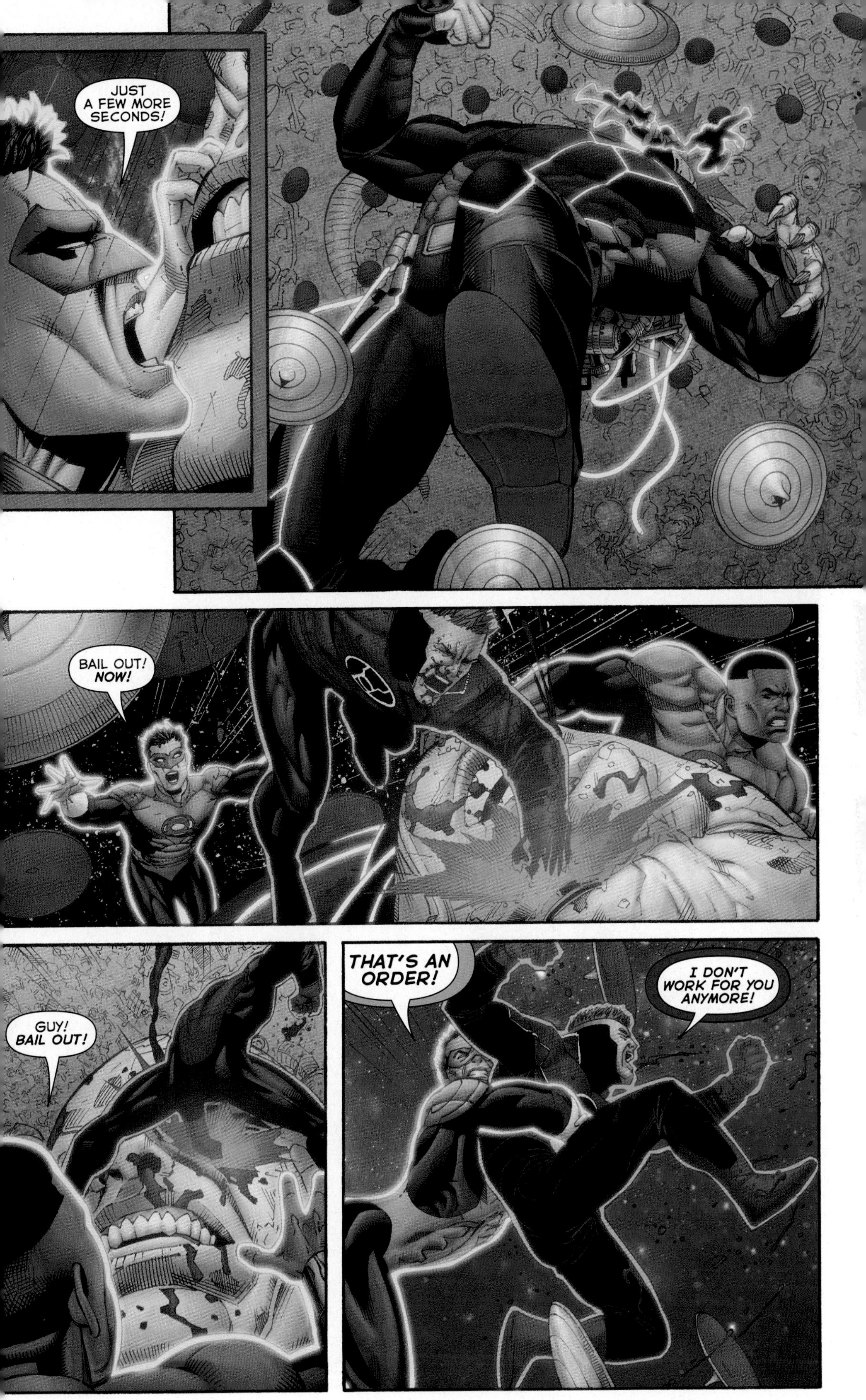

JUST A FEW MORE SECONDS!
BAIL OUT! NOW!
GUY! BAIL OUT!
THAT'S AN ORDER!
I DON'T WORK FOR YOU ANYMORE!

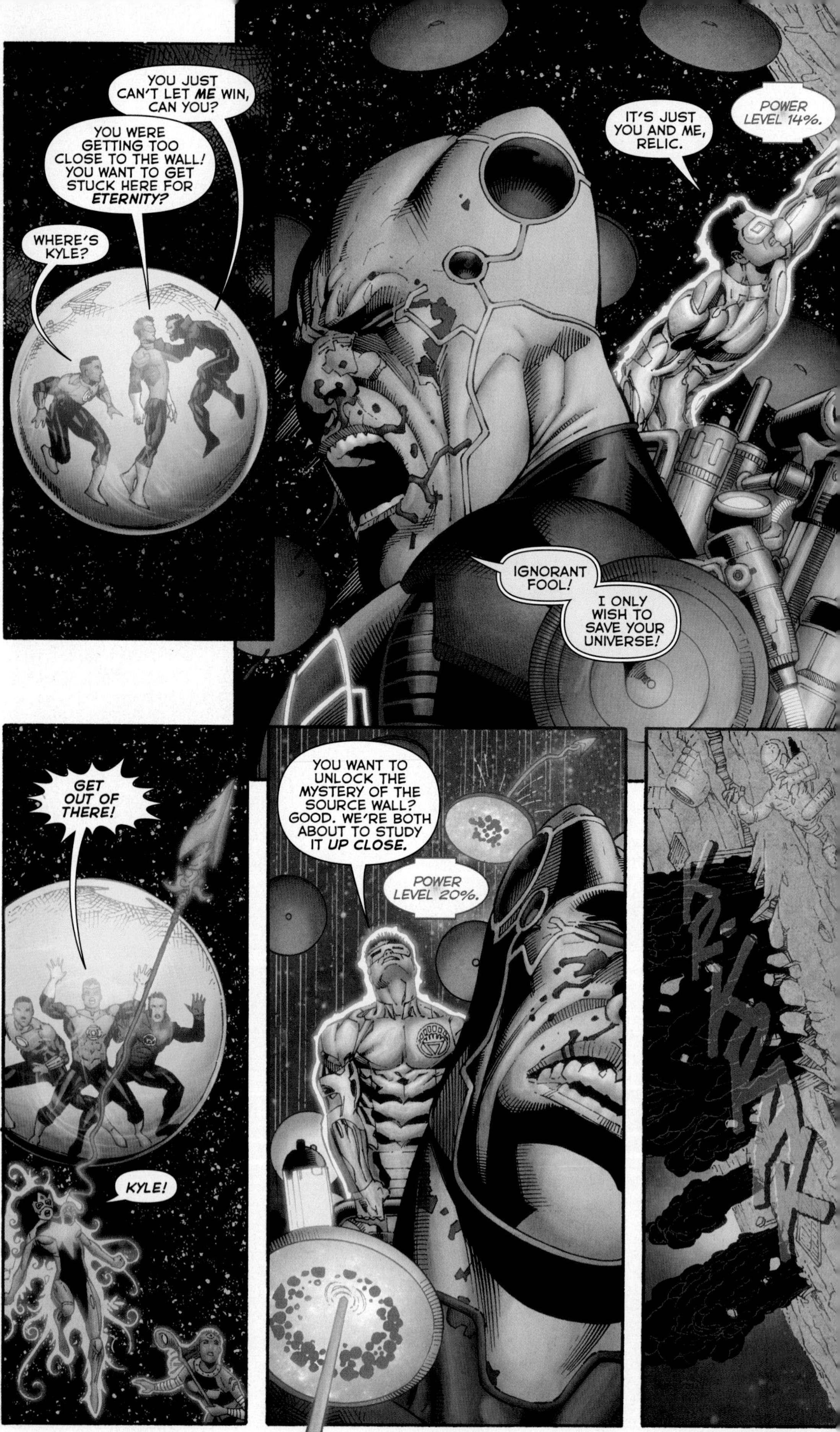

WHERE'S KYLE?
YOU WERE GETTING TOO CLOSE TO THE WALL! YOU WANT TO GET STUCK HERE FOR *ETERNITY?*
YOU JUST CAN'T LET *ME* WIN, CAN YOU?
POWER LEVEL 14%.
IT'S JUST YOU AND ME, RELIC.
IGNORANT FOOL!
I ONLY WISH TO SAVE YOUR UNIVERSE!
GET OUT OF THERE!
KYLE!
YOU WANT TO UNLOCK THE MYSTERY OF THE SOURCE WALL? GOOD. WE'RE BOTH ABOUT TO STUDY IT *UP CLOSE.*
POWER LEVEL 20%.

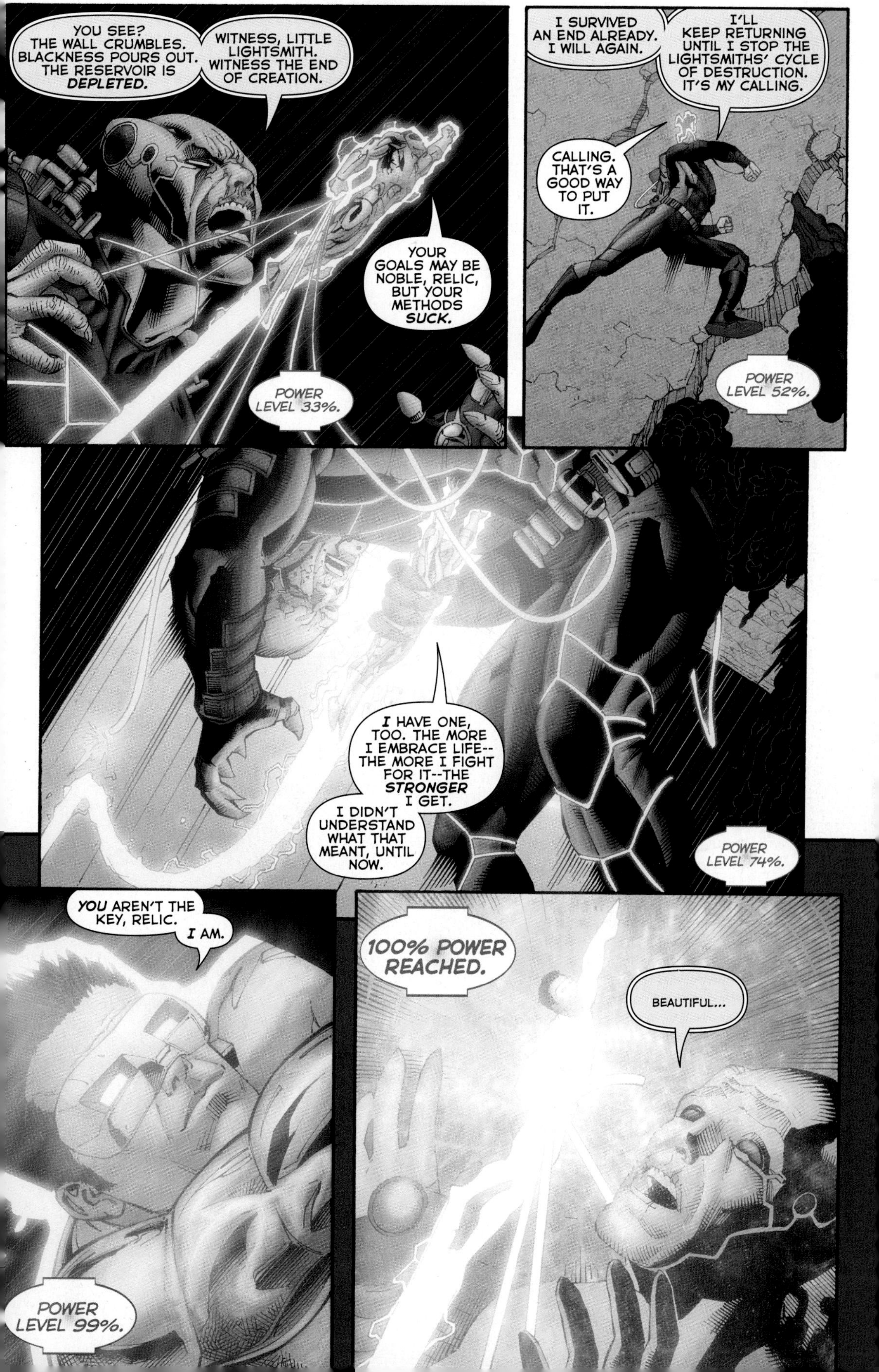

YOU SEE? THE WALL CRUMBLES. BLACKNESS POURS OUT. THE RESERVOIR IS *DEPLETED.*
WITNESS, LITTLE LIGHTSMITH. WITNESS THE END OF CREATION.
YOUR GOALS MAY BE NOBLE, RELIC, BUT YOUR METHODS *SUCK.*
POWER LEVEL 33%.
I SURVIVED AN END ALREADY. I WILL AGAIN.
I'LL KEEP RETURNING UNTIL I STOP THE LIGHTSMITHS' CYCLE OF DESTRUCTION. IT'S MY CALLING.
CALLING. THAT'S A GOOD WAY TO PUT IT.
POWER LEVEL 52%.
I HAVE ONE, TOO. THE MORE I EMBRACE LIFE-- THE MORE I FIGHT FOR IT--THE *STRONGER* I GET.
I DIDN'T UNDERSTAND WHAT THAT MEANT, UNTIL NOW.
POWER LEVEL 74%.
YOU AREN'T THE KEY, RELIC.
I AM.
POWER LEVEL 99%.
100% POWER REACHED.
BEAUTIFUL...

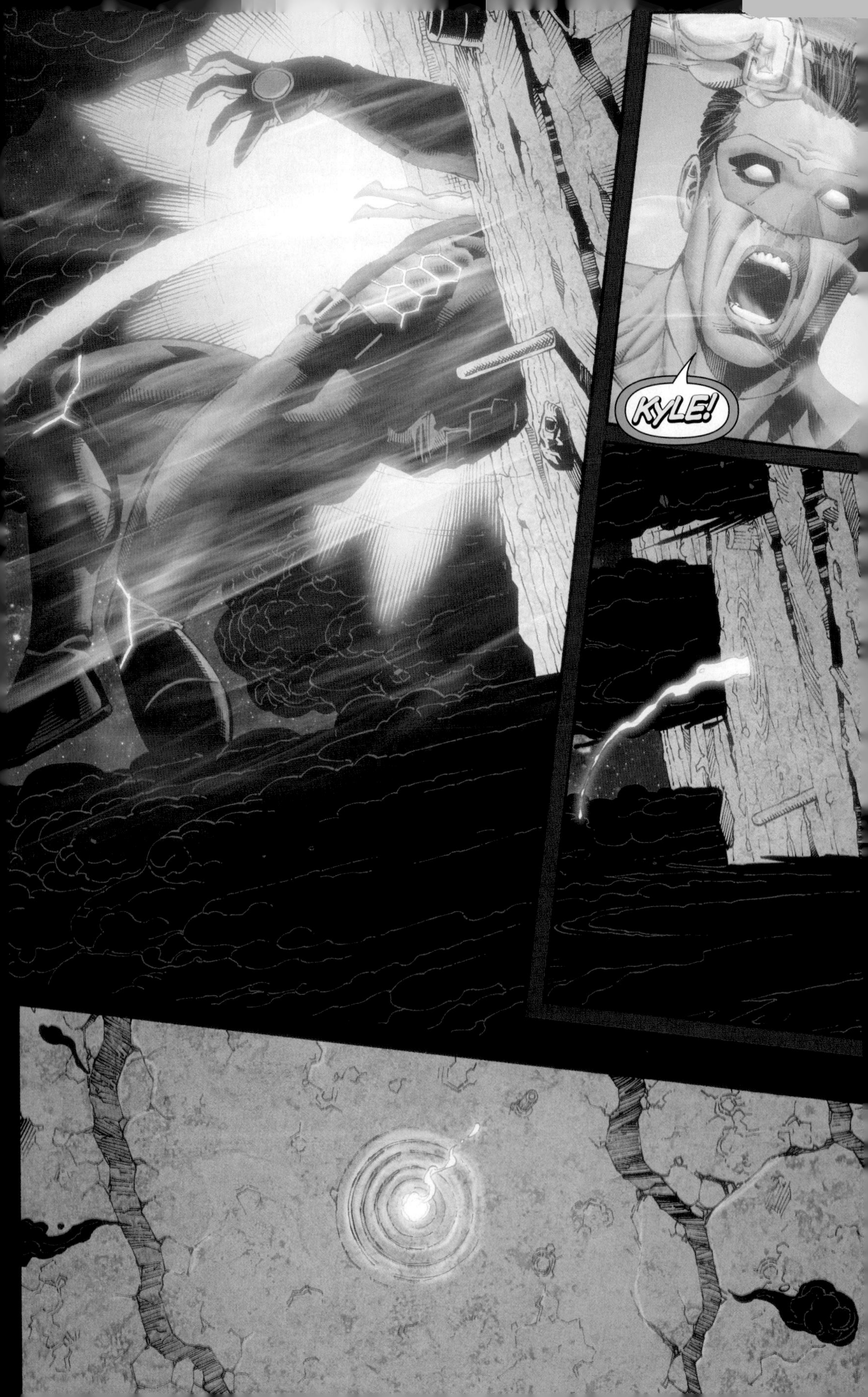
KYLE!

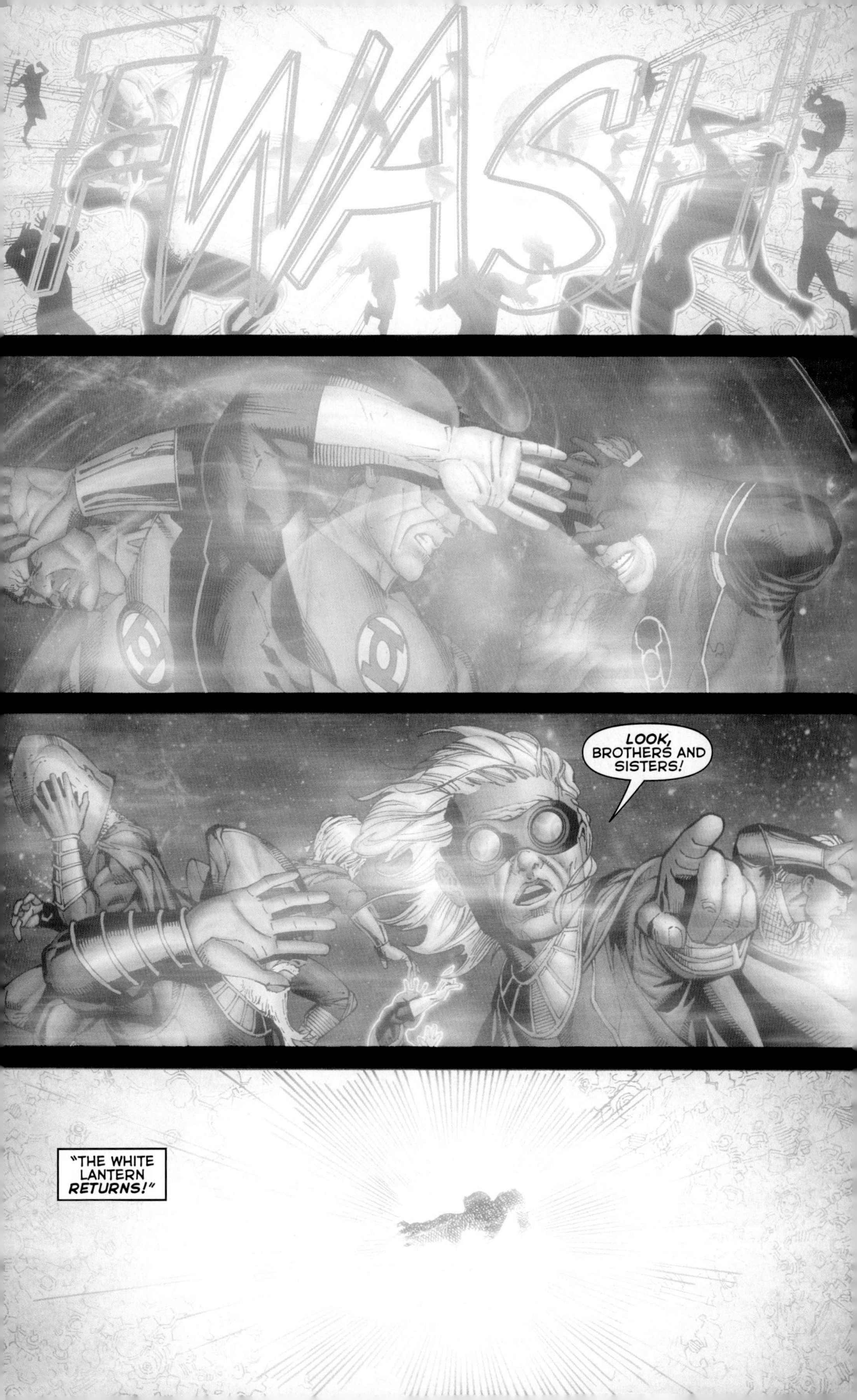
FWASH
LOOK, BROTHERS AND SISTERS!
"THE WHITE LANTERN RETURNS!"

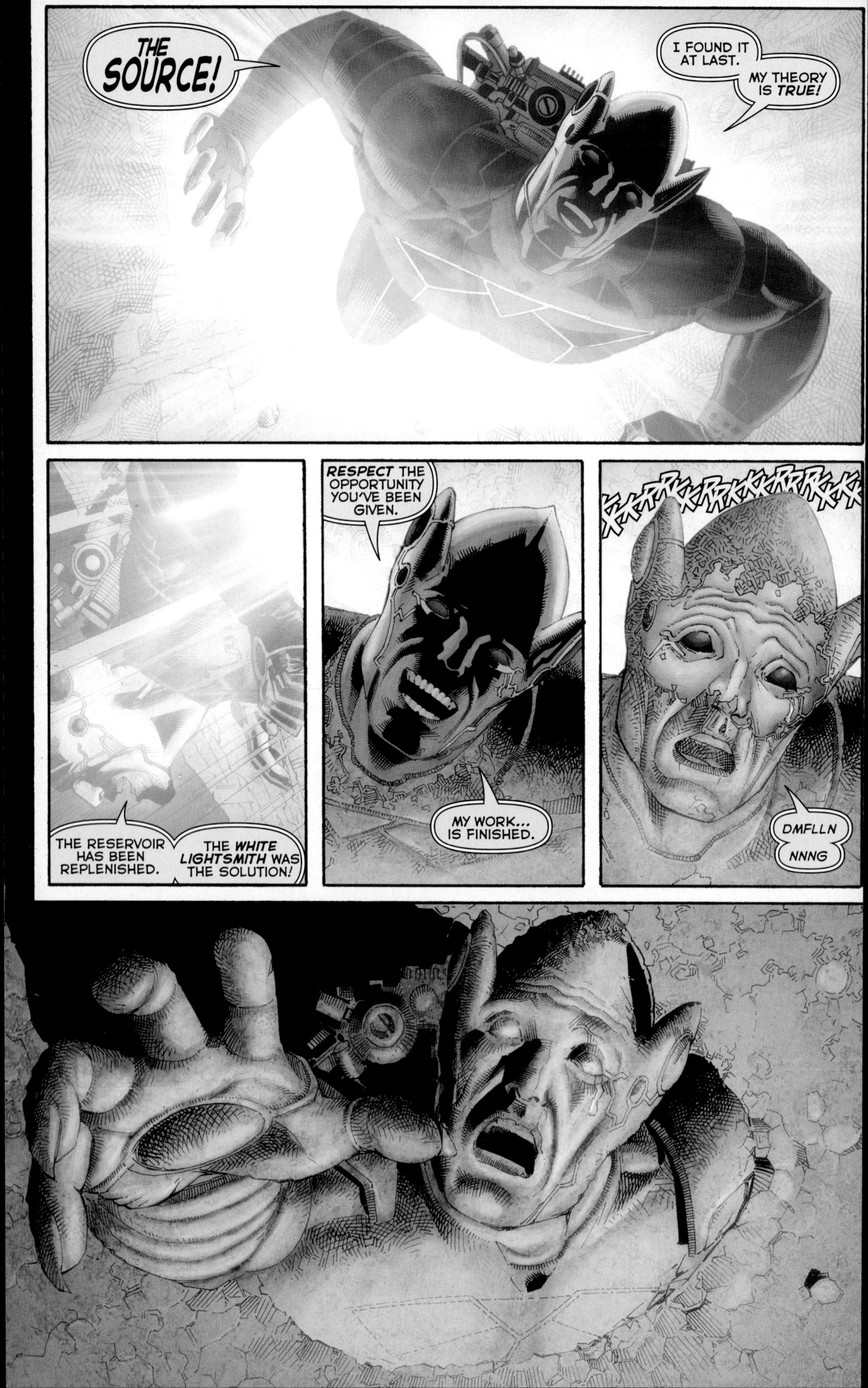
THE SOURCE!
I FOUND IT AT LAST.
MY THEORY IS TRUE!
THE RESERVOIR HAS BEEN REPLENISHED.
THE WHITE LIGHTSMITH WAS THE SOLUTION!
RESPECT THE OPPORTUNITY YOU'VE BEEN GIVEN.
MY WORK... IS FINISHED.
KKRRKKRRKKKRRRKKK
DMFLLN
NNNG

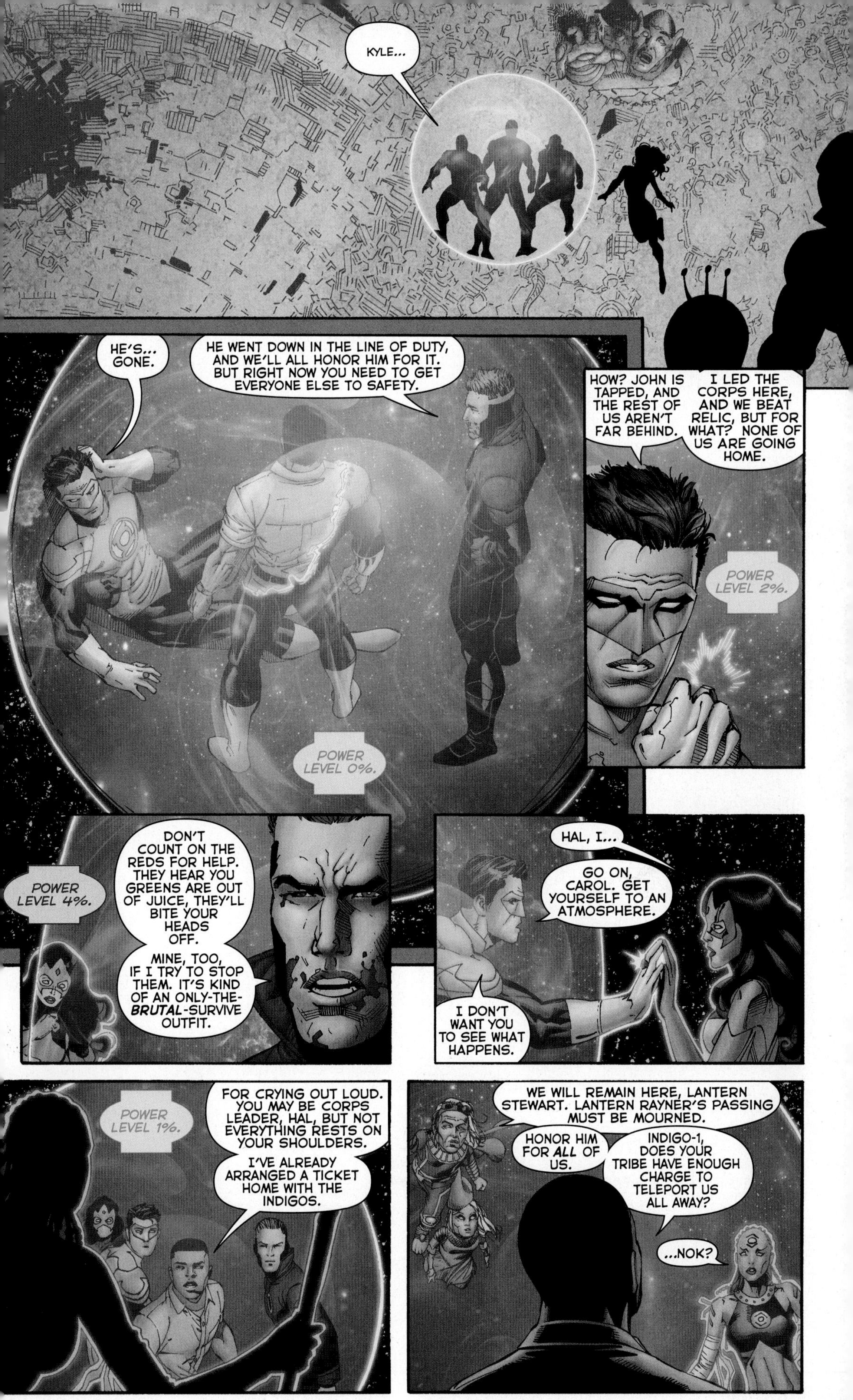
KYLE...
HE'S... GONE.
HE WENT DOWN IN THE LINE OF DUTY, AND WE'LL ALL HONOR HIM FOR IT. BUT RIGHT NOW YOU NEED TO GET EVERYONE ELSE TO SAFETY.
POWER LEVEL 0%.
HOW? JOHN IS TAPPED, AND THE REST OF US AREN'T FAR BEHIND.
I LED THE CORPS HERE, AND WE BEAT RELIC, BUT FOR WHAT? NONE OF US ARE GOING HOME.
POWER LEVEL 2%.
POWER LEVEL 4%.
DON'T COUNT ON THE REDS FOR HELP. THEY HEAR YOU GREENS ARE OUT OF JUICE, THEY'LL BITE YOUR HEADS OFF.
MINE, TOO, IF I TRY TO STOP THEM. IT'S KIND OF AN ONLY-THE-*BRUTAL*-SURVIVE OUTFIT.
HAL, I...
GO ON, CAROL. GET YOURSELF TO AN ATMOSPHERE.
I DON'T WANT YOU TO SEE WHAT HAPPENS.
POWER LEVEL 1%.
FOR CRYING OUT LOUD. YOU MAY BE CORPS LEADER, HAL, BUT NOT EVERYTHING RESTS ON YOUR SHOULDERS.
I'VE ALREADY ARRANGED A TICKET HOME WITH THE INDIGOS.
WE WILL REMAIN HERE, LANTERN STEWART. LANTERN RAYNER'S PASSING MUST BE MOURNED.
HONOR HIM FOR *ALL* OF US.
INDIGO-1, DOES YOUR TRIBE HAVE ENOUGH CHARGE TO TELEPORT US ALL AWAY?
...NOK?

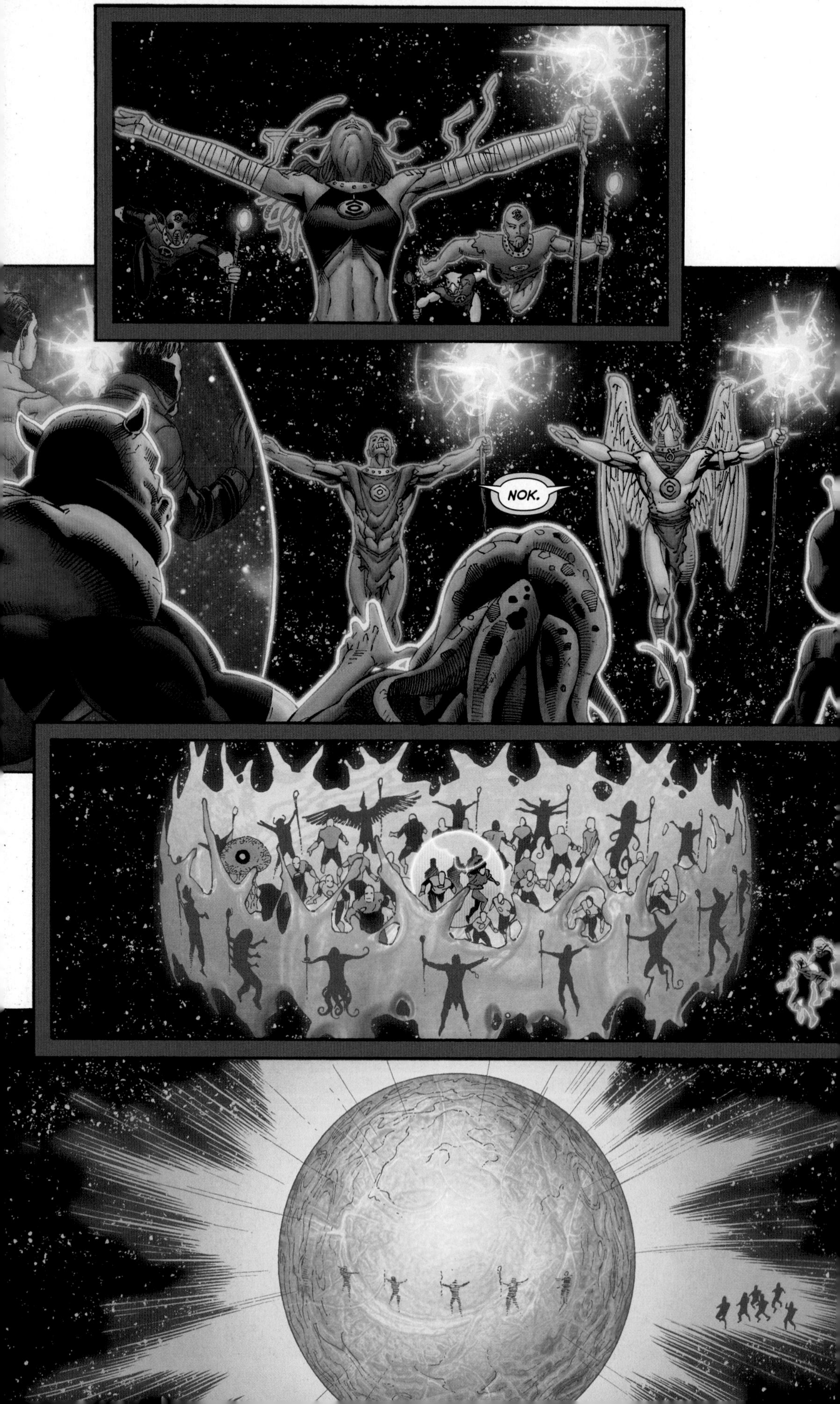
NOK.

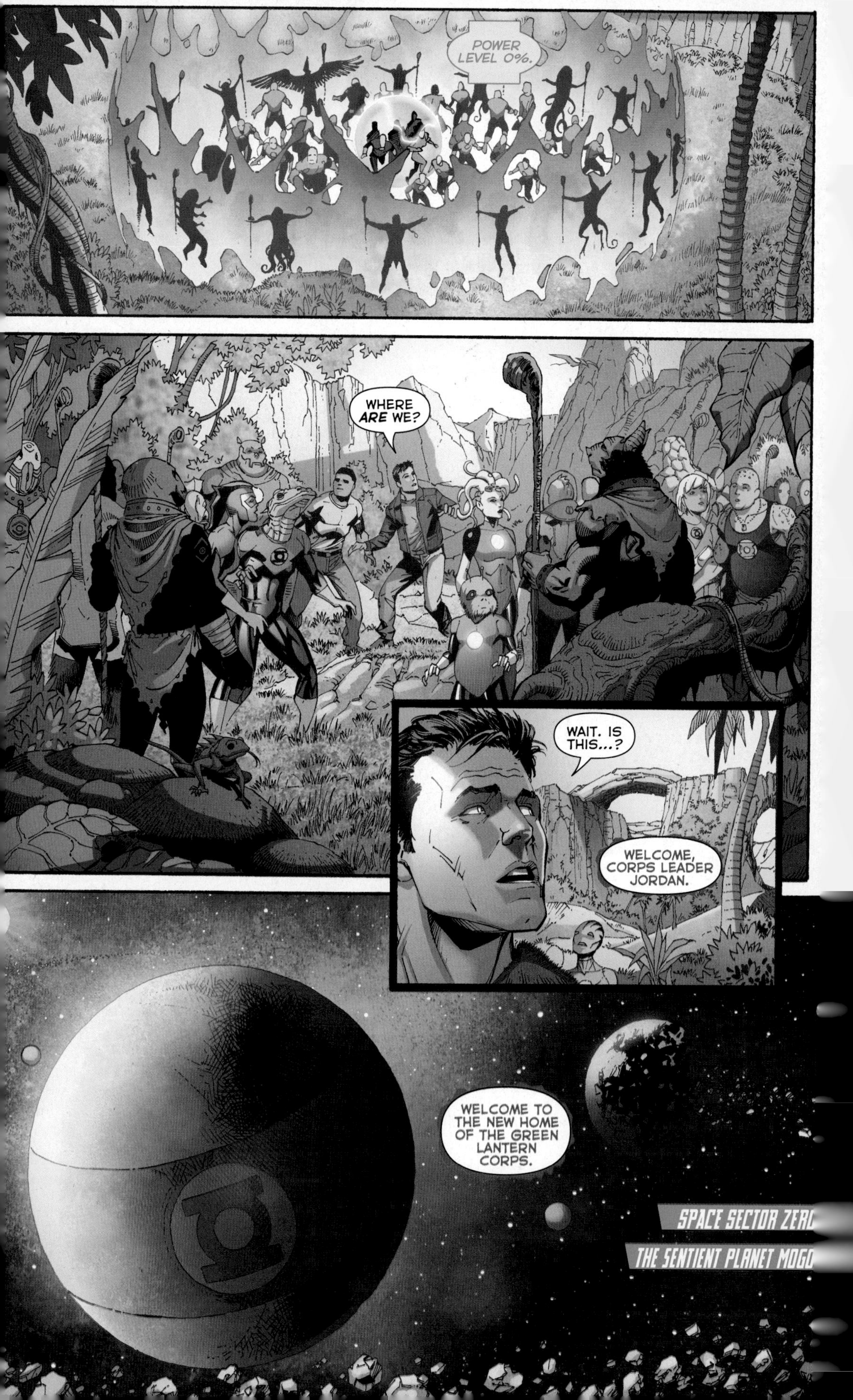
POWER LEVEL 0%.
WHERE ARE WE?
WAIT. IS THIS...?
WELCOME, CORPS LEADER JORDAN.
WELCOME TO THE NEW HOME OF THE GREEN LANTERN CORPS.
SPACE SECTOR ZERO
THE SENTIENT PLANET MOGO

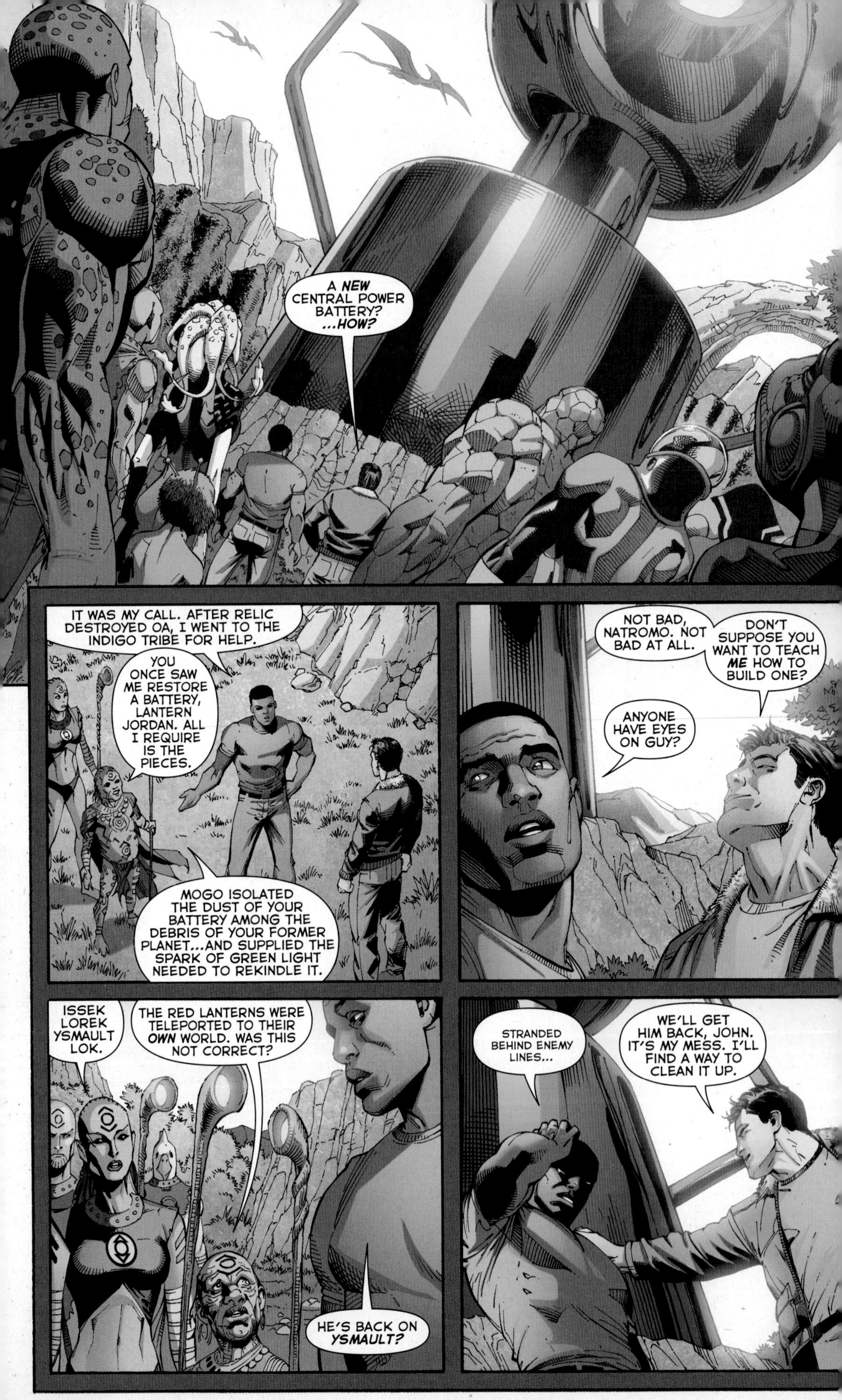
A NEW CENTRAL POWER BATTERY? ...HOW?
IT WAS MY CALL. AFTER RELIC DESTROYED OA, I WENT TO THE INDIGO TRIBE FOR HELP.
YOU ONCE SAW ME RESTORE A BATTERY, LANTERN JORDAN. ALL I REQUIRE IS THE PIECES.
MOGO ISOLATED THE DUST OF YOUR BATTERY AMONG THE DEBRIS OF YOUR FORMER PLANET...AND SUPPLIED THE SPARK OF GREEN LIGHT NEEDED TO REKINDLE IT.
NOT BAD, NATROMO. NOT BAD AT ALL.
DON'T SUPPOSE YOU WANT TO TEACH ME HOW TO BUILD ONE?
ANYONE HAVE EYES ON GUY?
ISSEK LOREK YSMAULT LOK.
THE RED LANTERNS WERE TELEPORTED TO THEIR OWN WORLD. WAS THIS NOT CORRECT?
HE'S BACK ON YSMAULT?
STRANDED BEHIND ENEMY LINES...
WE'LL GET HIM BACK, JOHN. IT'S MY MESS. I'LL FIND A WAY TO CLEAN IT UP.

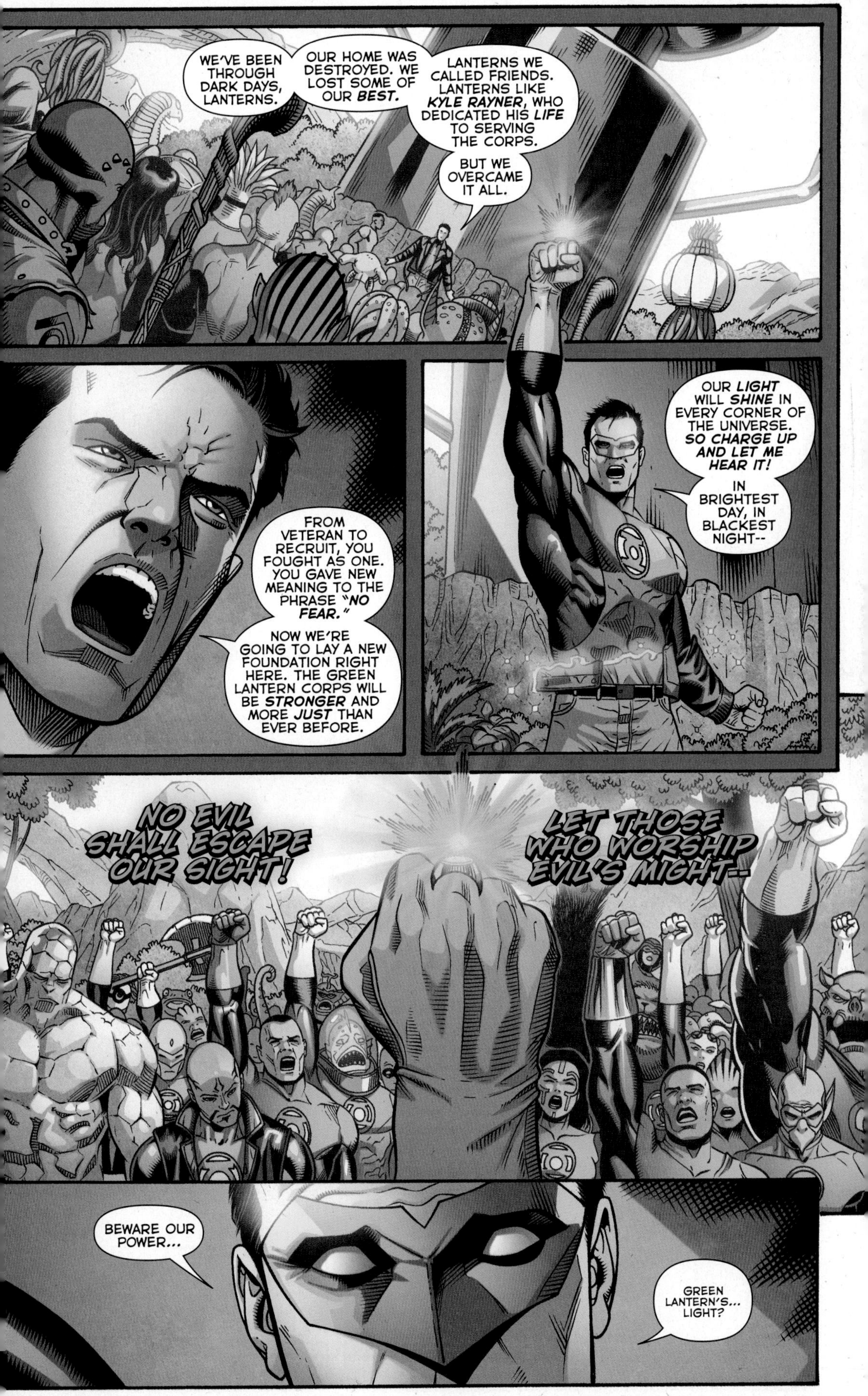

WE'VE BEEN THROUGH DARK DAYS, LANTERNS.
OUR HOME WAS DESTROYED. WE LOST SOME OF OUR BEST.
LANTERNS WE CALLED FRIENDS. LANTERNS LIKE KYLE RAYNER, WHO DEDICATED HIS LIFE TO SERVING THE CORPS.
BUT WE OVERCAME IT ALL.
FROM VETERAN TO RECRUIT, YOU FOUGHT AS ONE. YOU GAVE NEW MEANING TO THE PHRASE "NO FEAR."
NOW WE'RE GOING TO LAY A NEW FOUNDATION RIGHT HERE. THE GREEN LANTERN CORPS WILL BE STRONGER AND MORE JUST THAN EVER BEFORE.
OUR LIGHT WILL SHINE IN EVERY CORNER OF THE UNIVERSE. SO CHARGE UP AND LET ME HEAR IT!
IN BRIGHTEST DAY, IN BLACKEST NIGHT--
NO EVIL SHALL ESCAPE OUR SIGHT!
LET THOSE WHO WORSHIP EVIL'S MIGHT--
BEWARE OUR POWER...
GREEN LANTERN'S... LIGHT?

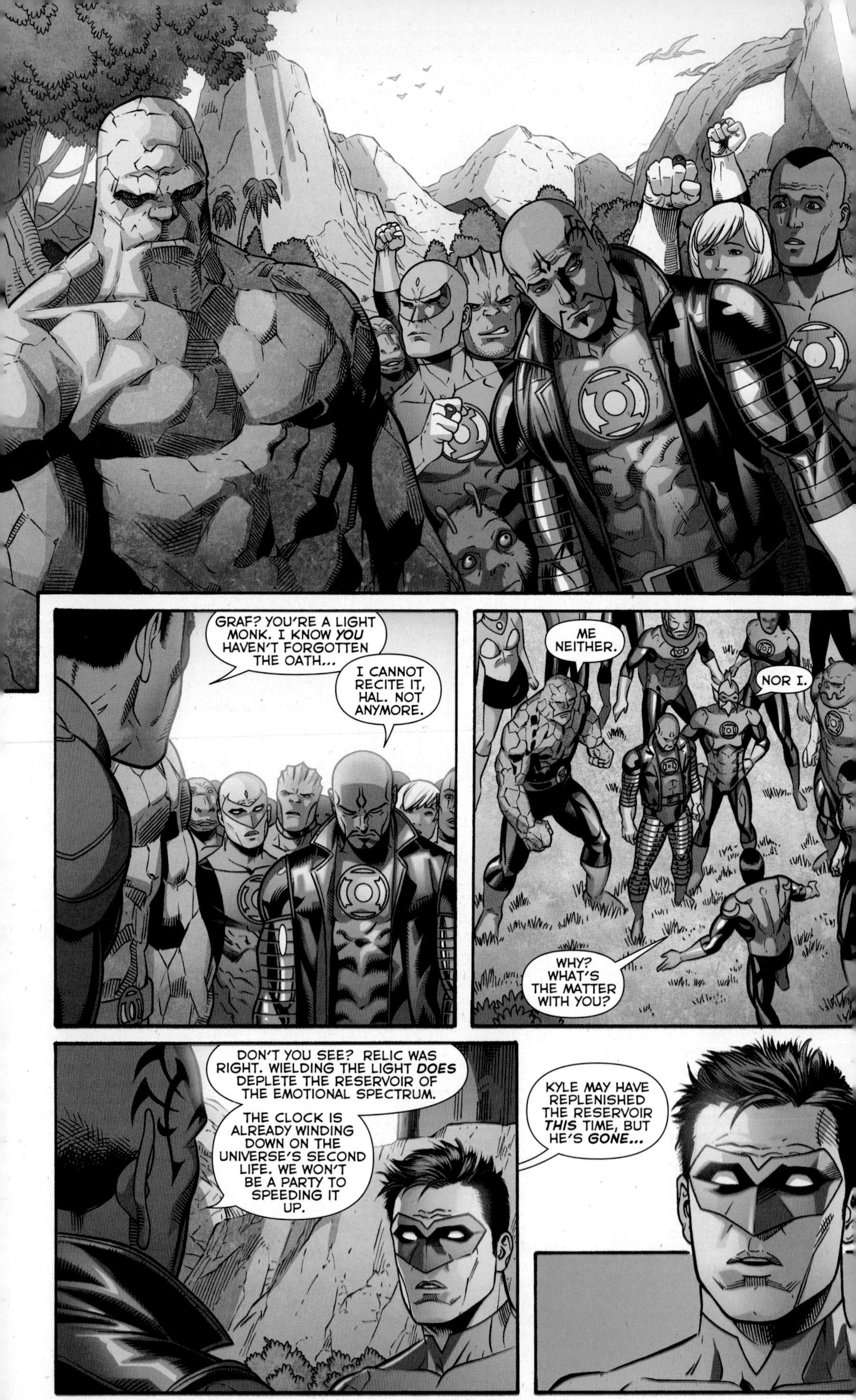
GRAF? YOU'RE A LIGHT MONK. I KNOW YOU HAVEN'T FORGOTTEN THE OATH...
I CANNOT RECITE IT, HAL. NOT ANYMORE.
ME NEITHER.
NOR I.
WHY? WHAT'S THE MATTER WITH YOU?
DON'T YOU SEE? RELIC WAS RIGHT. WIELDING THE LIGHT DOES DEPLETE THE RESERVOIR OF THE EMOTIONAL SPECTRUM.
THE CLOCK IS ALREADY WINDING DOWN ON THE UNIVERSE'S SECOND LIFE. WE WON'T BE A PARTY TO SPEEDING IT UP.
KYLE MAY HAVE REPLENISHED THE RESERVOIR THIS TIME, BUT HE'S GONE...

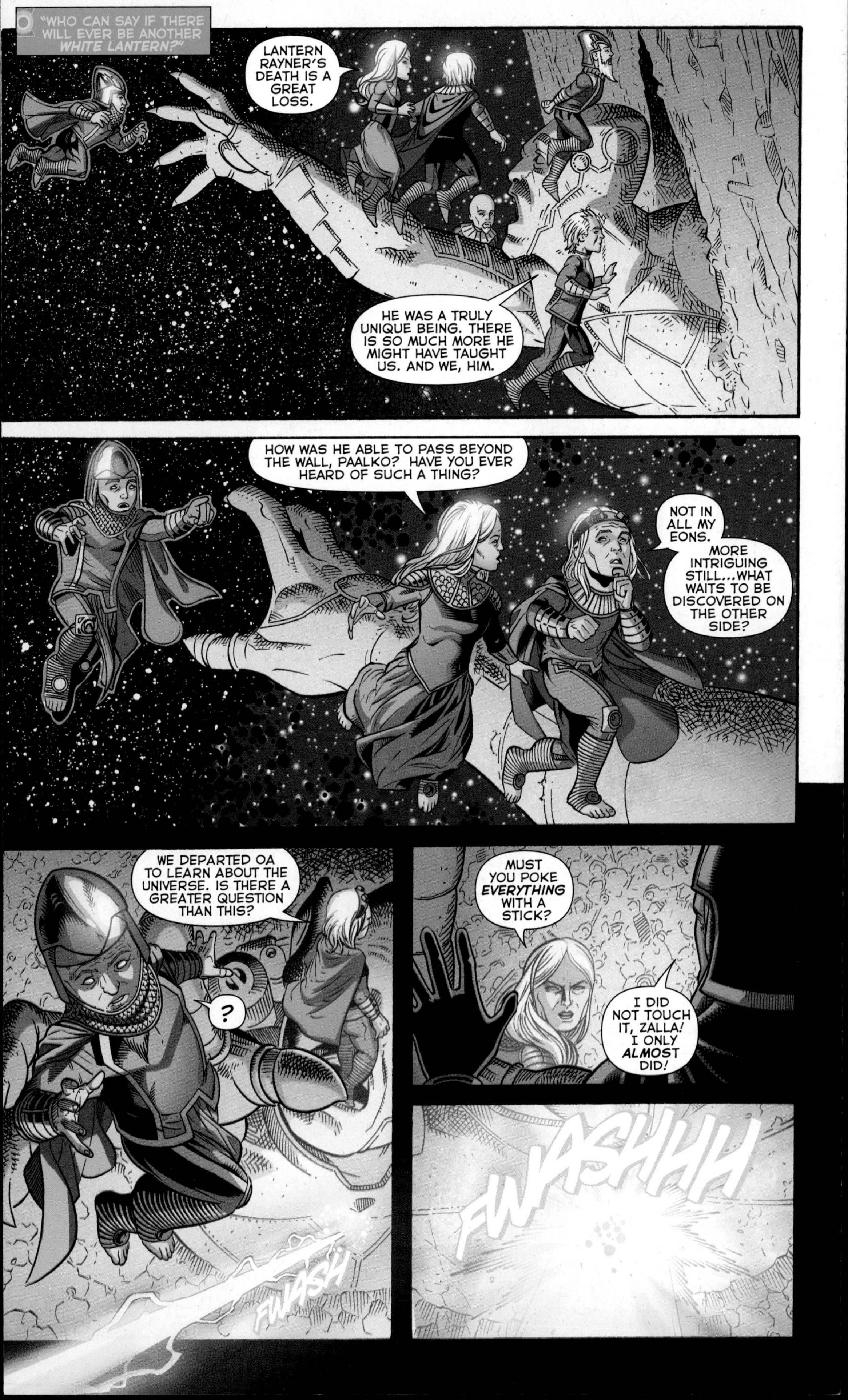
"WHO CAN SAY IF THERE WILL EVER BE ANOTHER *WHITE LANTERN?*"
LANTERN RAYNER'S DEATH IS A GREAT LOSS.
HE WAS A TRULY UNIQUE BEING. THERE IS SO MUCH MORE HE MIGHT HAVE TAUGHT US. AND WE, HIM.
HOW WAS HE ABLE TO PASS BEYOND THE WALL, PAALKO? HAVE YOU EVER HEARD OF SUCH A THING?
NOT IN ALL MY EONS.
MORE INTRIGUING STILL...WHAT WAITS TO BE DISCOVERED ON THE OTHER SIDE?
WE DEPARTED OA TO LEARN ABOUT THE UNIVERSE. IS THERE A GREATER QUESTION THAN THIS?
?
FWASH
MUST YOU POKE *EVERYTHING* WITH A STICK?
I DID NOT TOUCH IT, ZALLA! I ONLY ***ALMOST*** DID!
FWASHHH

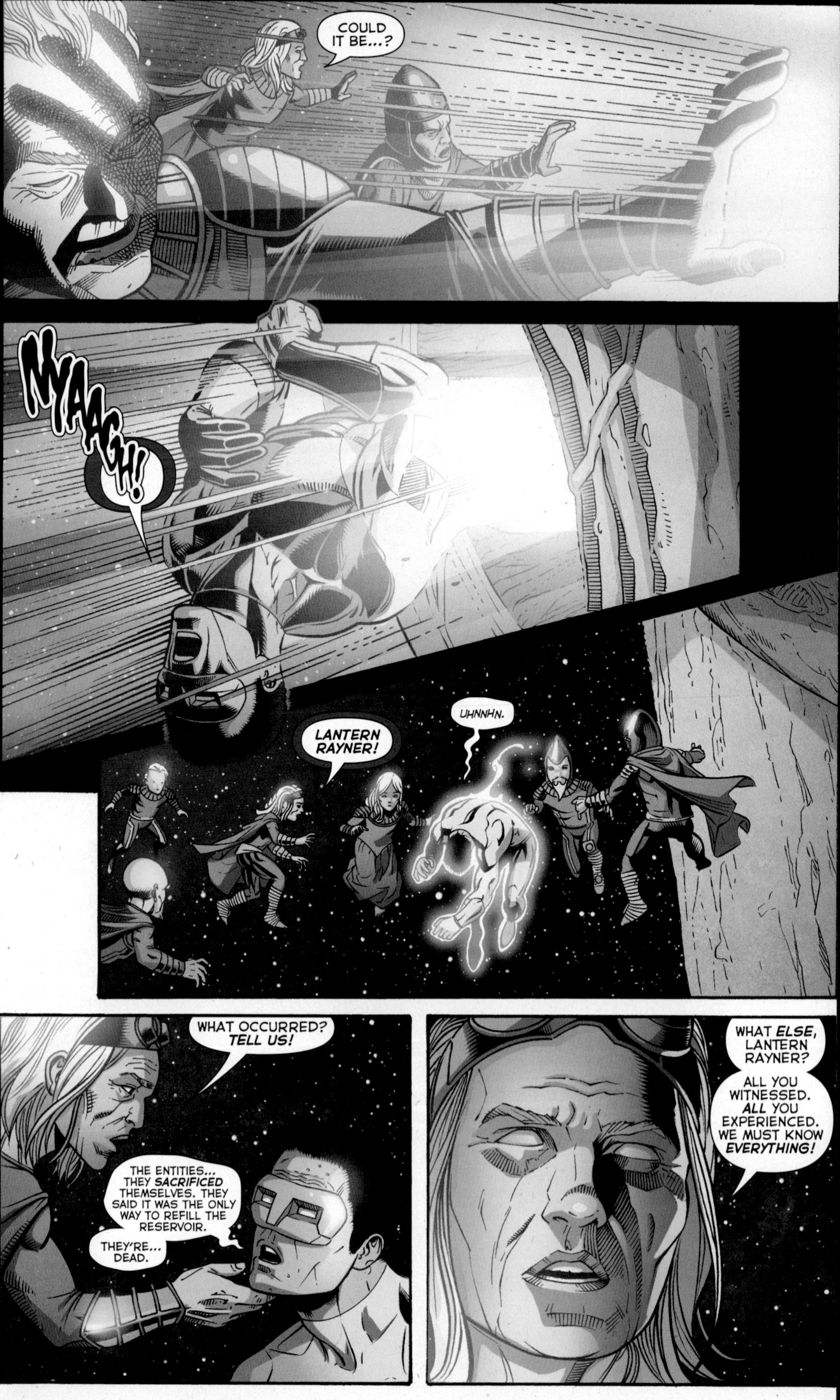
COULD IT BE...?
NYAAAGH!
LANTERN RAYNER!
UHNNHN.
WHAT OCCURRED? TELL US!
THE ENTITIES... THEY SACRIFICED THEMSELVES. THEY SAID IT WAS THE ONLY WAY TO REFILL THE RESERVOIR.
THEY'RE... DEAD.
WHAT ELSE, LANTERN RAYNER?
ALL YOU WITNESSED. ALL YOU EXPERIENCED. WE MUST KNOW EVERYTHING!

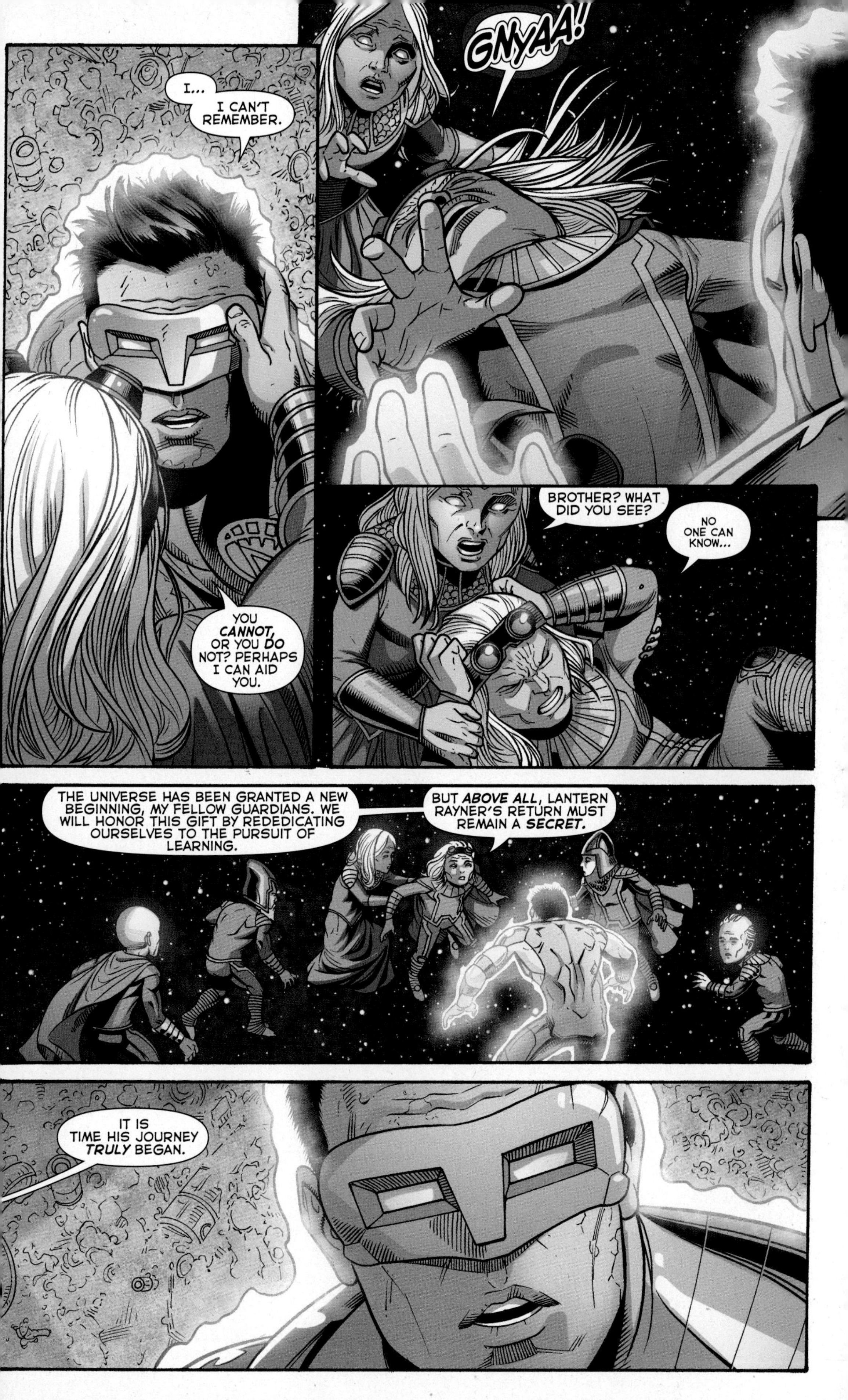
I...
I CAN'T REMEMBER.
GNYAA!
YOU CANNOT, OR YOU DO NOT? PERHAPS I CAN AID YOU.
BROTHER? WHAT DID YOU SEE?
NO ONE CAN KNOW...
THE UNIVERSE HAS BEEN GRANTED A NEW BEGINNING, MY FELLOW GUARDIANS. WE WILL HONOR THIS GIFT BY REDEDICATING OURSELVES TO THE PURSUIT OF LEARNING.
BUT ABOVE ALL, LANTERN RAYNER'S RETURN MUST REMAIN A SECRET.
IT IS TIME HIS JOURNEY TRULY BEGAN.

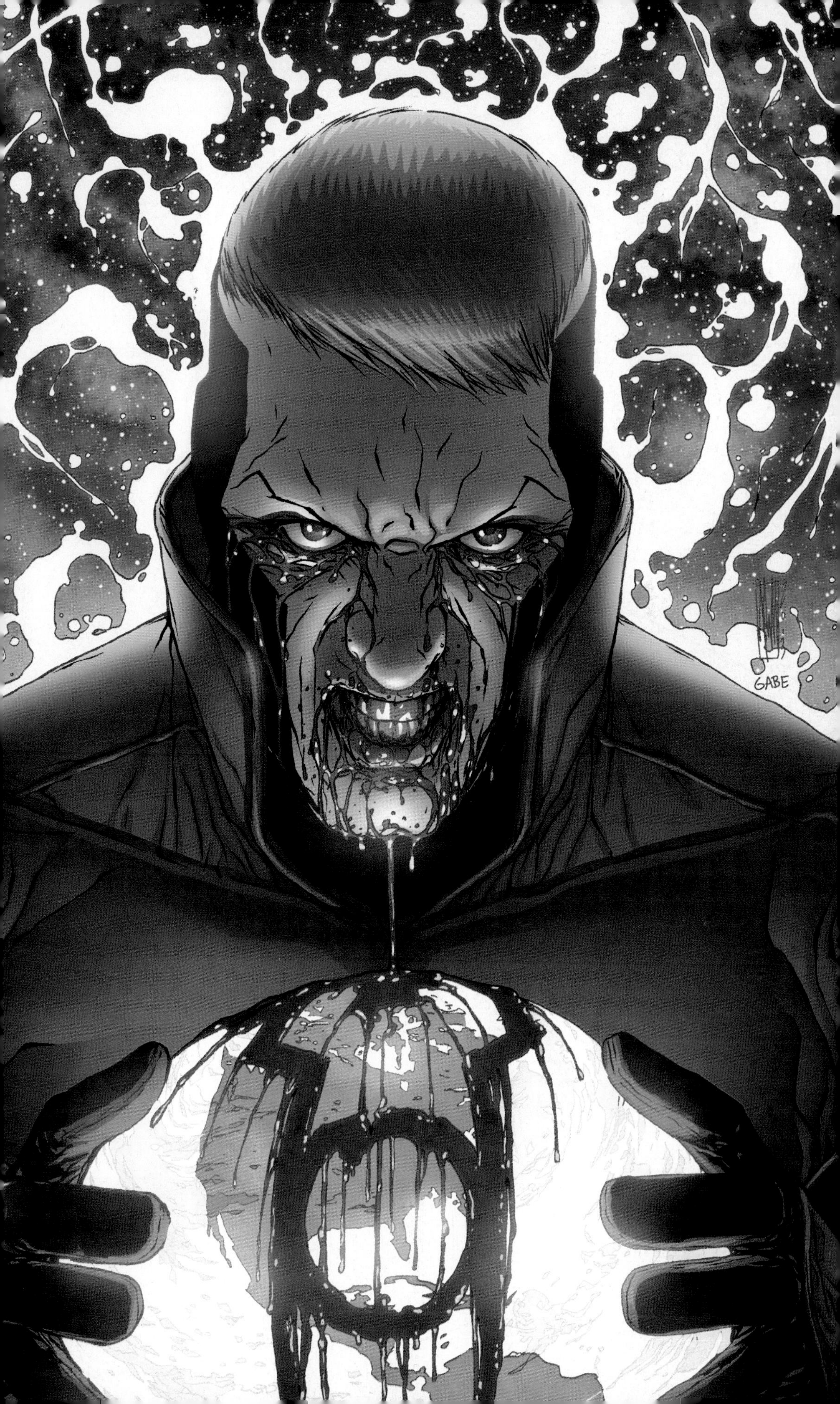
GABE

SPHERE OF INFLUENCE

CHARLES SOULE writer ALESSANDRO VITTI artist GABE ELTAEB with HI-FI colorists cover art by ALESSANDRO VITTI with GABE ELTAE

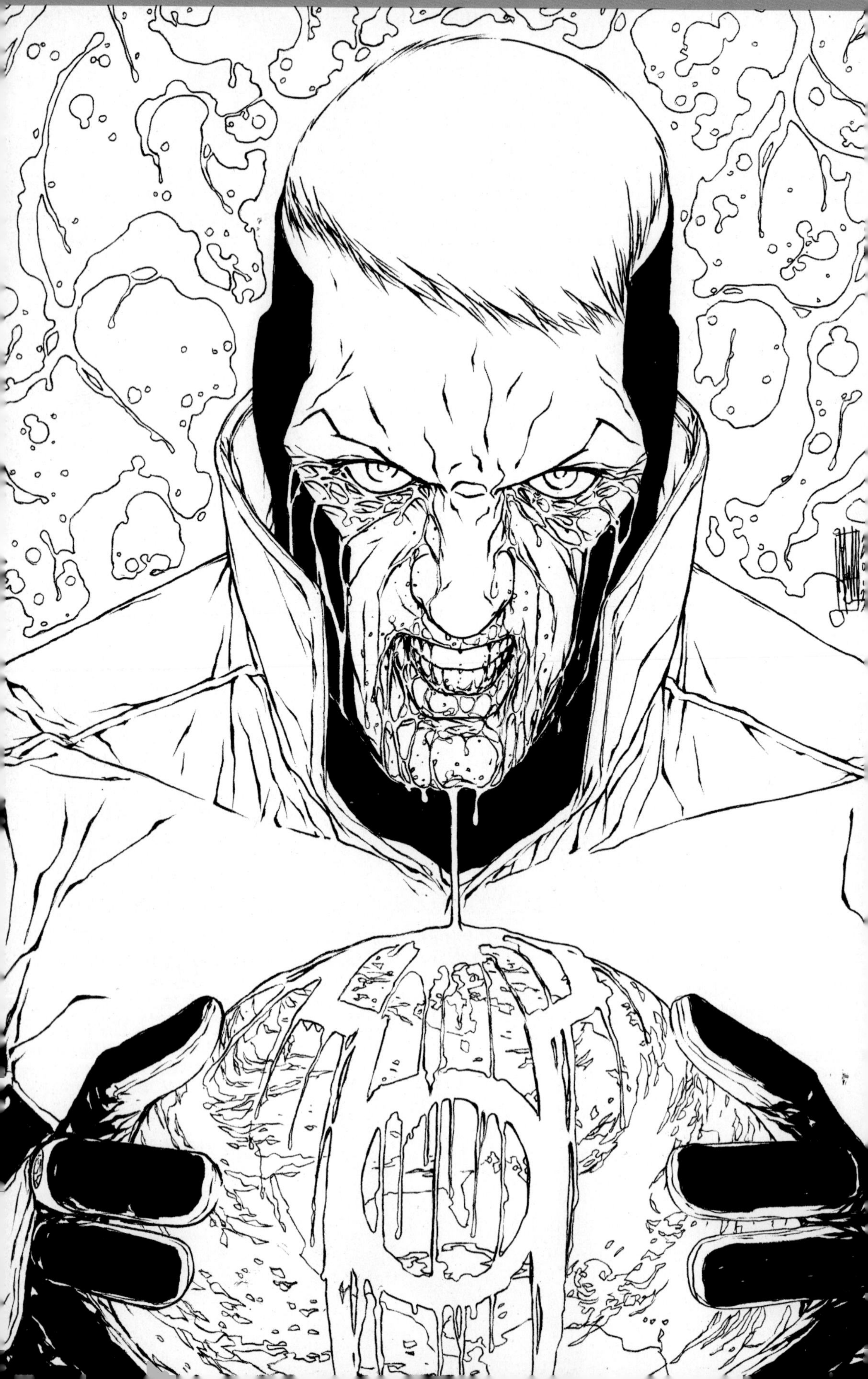

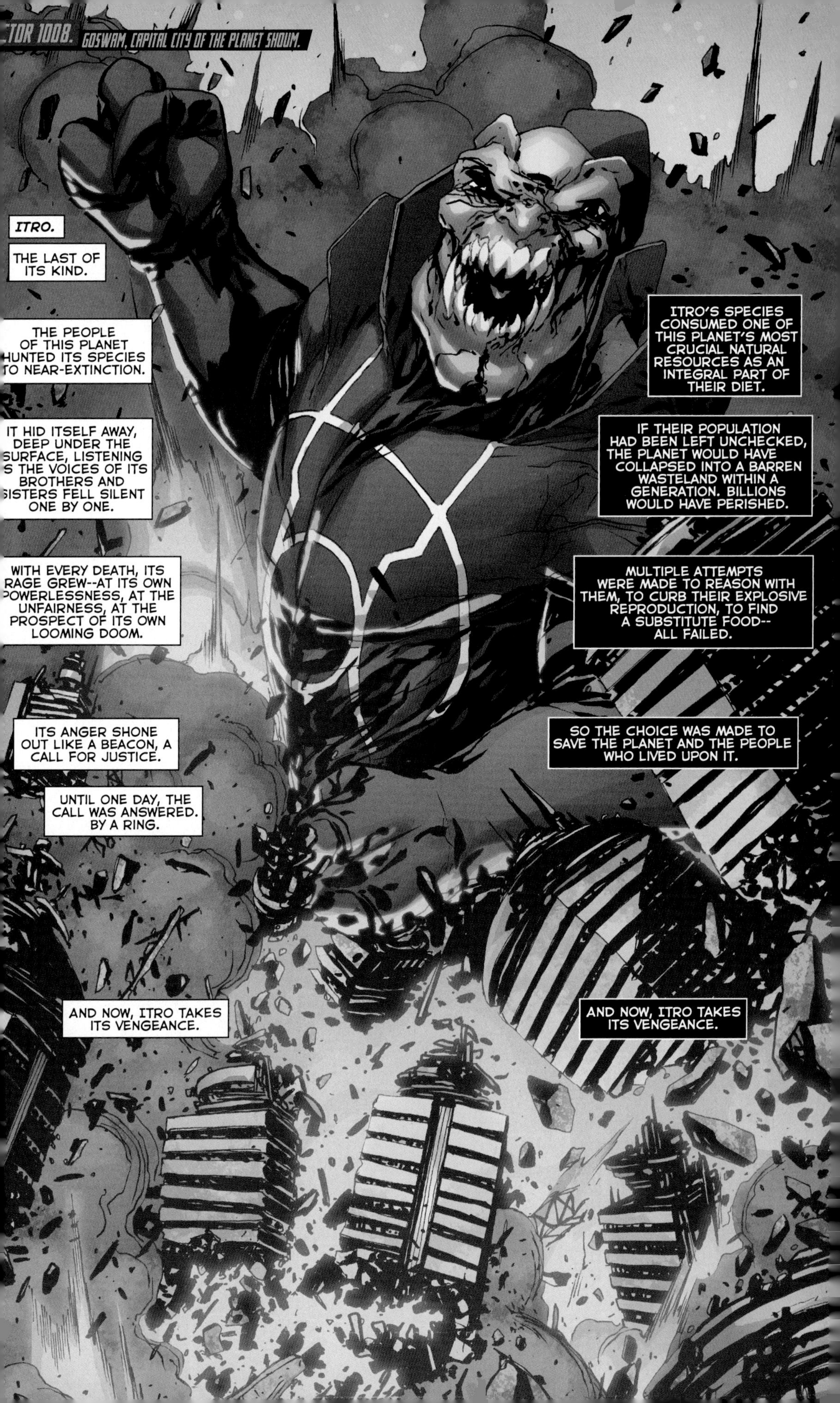

TOR 1008. GOSWAM, CAPITAL CITY OF THE PLANET SHOUM.
ITRO.
THE LAST OF ITS KIND.
THE PEOPLE OF THIS PLANET HUNTED ITS SPECIES TO NEAR-EXTINCTION.
IT HID ITSELF AWAY, DEEP UNDER THE SURFACE, LISTENING AS THE VOICES OF ITS BROTHERS AND SISTERS FELL SILENT ONE BY ONE.
WITH EVERY DEATH, ITS RAGE GREW--AT ITS OWN POWERLESSNESS, AT THE UNFAIRNESS, AT THE PROSPECT OF ITS OWN LOOMING DOOM.
ITS ANGER SHONE OUT LIKE A BEACON, A CALL FOR JUSTICE.
UNTIL ONE DAY, THE CALL WAS ANSWERED. BY A RING.
AND NOW, ITRO TAKES ITS VENGEANCE.
ITRO'S SPECIES CONSUMED ONE OF THIS PLANET'S MOST CRUCIAL NATURAL RESOURCES AS AN INTEGRAL PART OF THEIR DIET.
IF THEIR POPULATION HAD BEEN LEFT UNCHECKED, THE PLANET WOULD HAVE COLLAPSED INTO A BARREN WASTELAND WITHIN A GENERATION. BILLIONS WOULD HAVE PERISHED.
MULTIPLE ATTEMPTS WERE MADE TO REASON WITH THEM, TO CURB THEIR EXPLOSIVE REPRODUCTION, TO FIND A SUBSTITUTE FOOD-- ALL FAILED.
SO THE CHOICE WAS MADE TO SAVE THE PLANET AND THE PEOPLE WHO LIVED UPON IT.
AND NOW, ITRO TAKES ITS VENGEANCE.

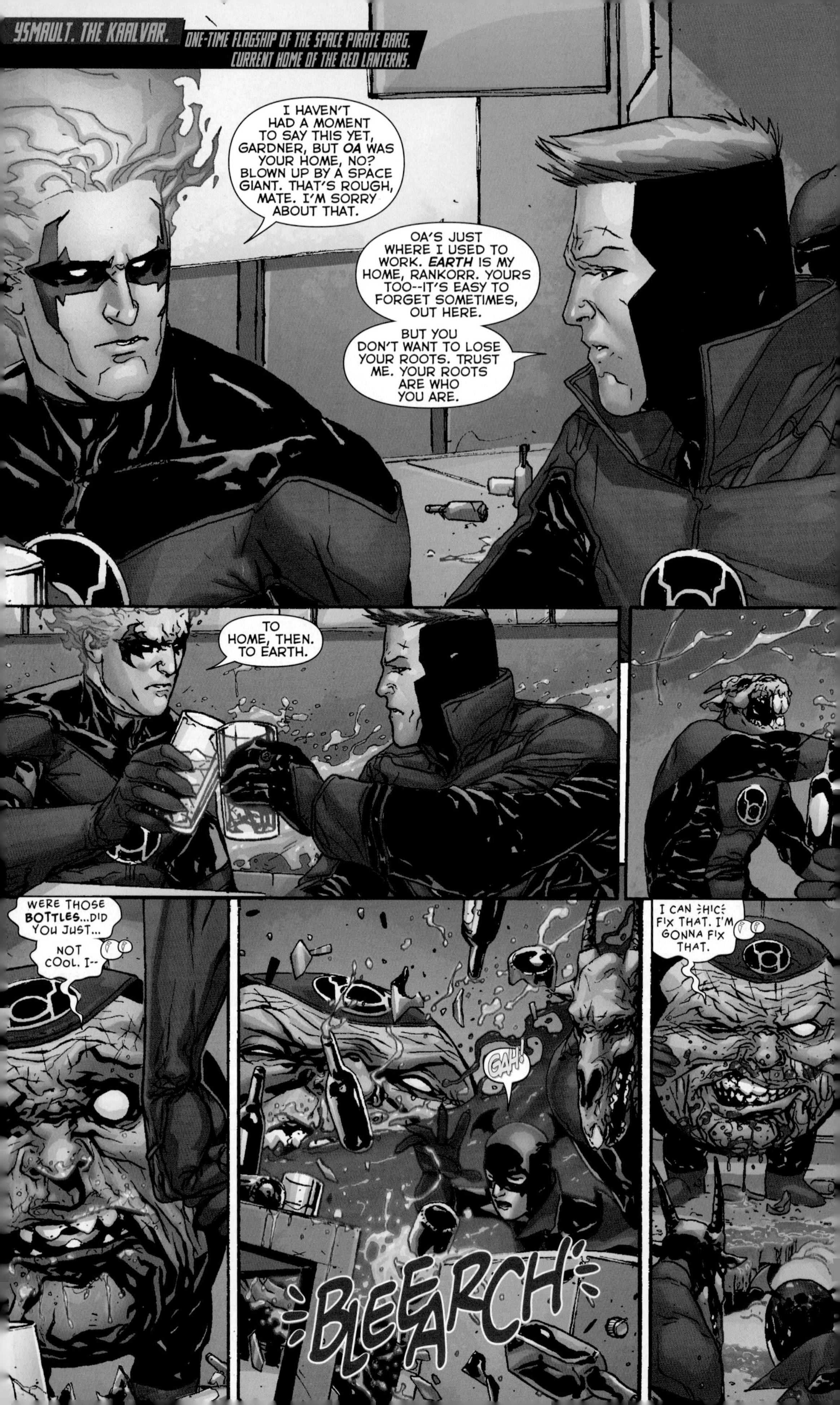
YSMAULT. THE KAALVAR.
ONE-TIME FLAGSHIP OF THE SPACE PIRATE BARG. CURRENT HOME OF THE RED LANTERNS.
I HAVEN'T HAD A MOMENT TO SAY THIS YET, GARDNER, BUT OA WAS YOUR HOME, NO? BLOWN UP BY A SPACE GIANT. THAT'S ROUGH, MATE. I'M SORRY ABOUT THAT.
OA'S JUST WHERE I USED TO WORK. EARTH IS MY HOME, RANKORR. YOURS TOO--IT'S EASY TO FORGET SOMETIMES, OUT HERE.
BUT YOU DON'T WANT TO LOSE YOUR ROOTS. TRUST ME. YOUR ROOTS ARE WHO YOU ARE.
TO HOME, THEN. TO EARTH.
WERE THOSE BOTTLES...DID YOU JUST...
NOT COOL. I--
GAH!
BLEEARCH
I CAN HIC FIX THAT. I'M GONNA FIX THAT.

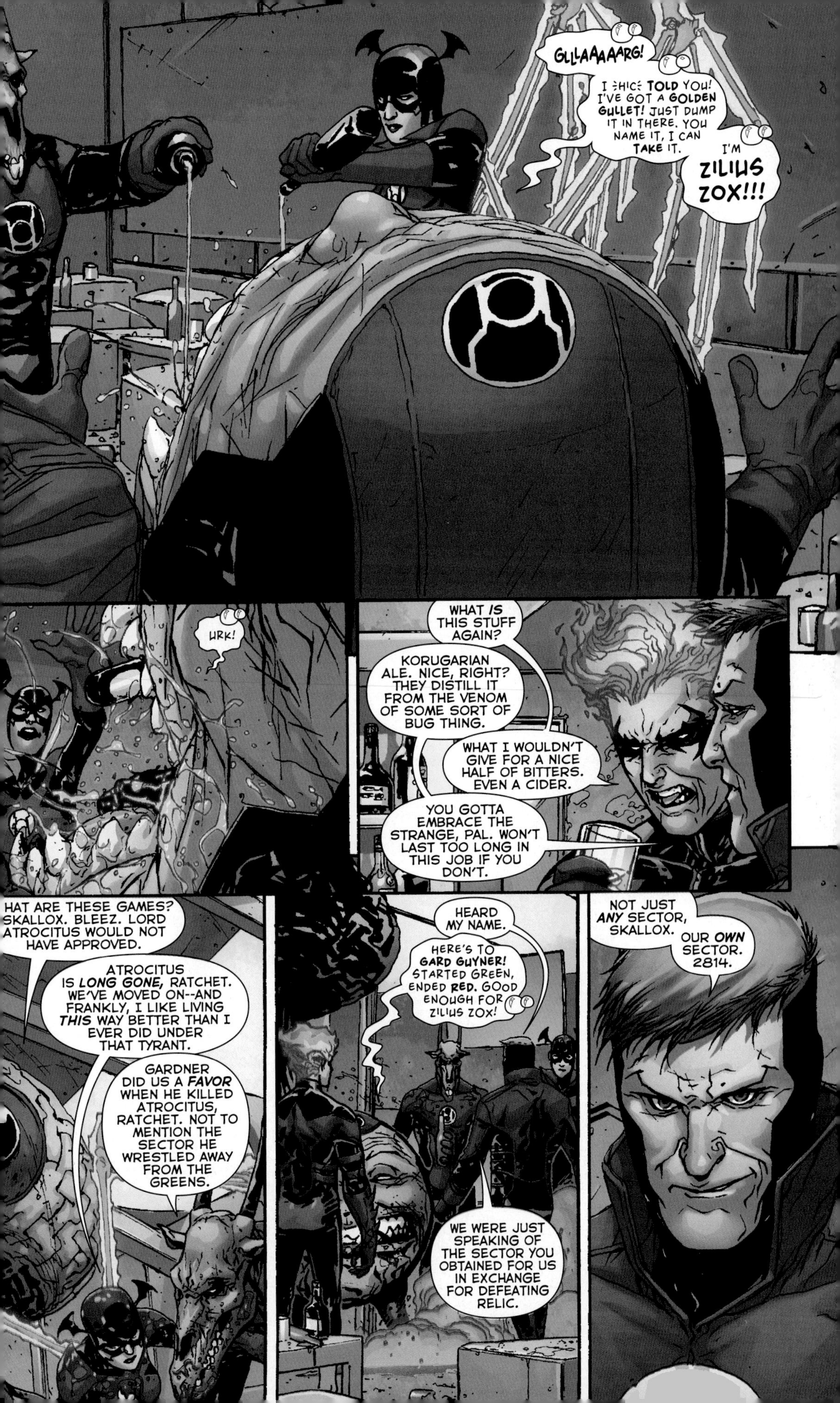
GLLLAAAAAARG!
I «HIC» TOLD YOU! I'VE GOT A GOLDEN GULLET! JUST DUMP IT IN THERE. YOU NAME IT, I CAN TAKE IT.
I'M ZILIUS ZOX!!!
URK!
WHAT IS THIS STUFF AGAIN?
KORUGARIAN ALE. NICE, RIGHT? THEY DISTILL IT FROM THE VENOM OF SOME SORT OF BUG THING.
WHAT I WOULDN'T GIVE FOR A NICE HALF OF BITTERS. EVEN A CIDER.
YOU GOTTA EMBRACE THE STRANGE, PAL. WON'T LAST TOO LONG IN THIS JOB IF YOU DON'T.
HAT ARE THESE GAMES? SKALLOX. BLEEZ. LORD ATROCITUS WOULD NOT HAVE APPROVED.
ATROCITUS IS LONG GONE, RATCHET. WE'VE MOVED ON--AND FRANKLY, I LIKE LIVING THIS WAY BETTER THAN I EVER DID UNDER THAT TYRANT.
GARDNER DID US A FAVOR WHEN HE KILLED ATROCITUS, RATCHET. NOT TO MENTION THE SECTOR HE WRESTLED AWAY FROM THE GREENS.
HEARD MY NAME.
HERE'S TO GARD GUYNER! STARTED GREEN, ENDED RED. GOOD ENOUGH FOR ZILIUS ZOX!
WE WERE JUST SPEAKING OF THE SECTOR YOU OBTAINED FOR US IN EXCHANGE FOR DEFEATING RELIC.
NOT JUST ANY SECTOR, SKALLOX.
OUR OWN SECTOR. 2814.

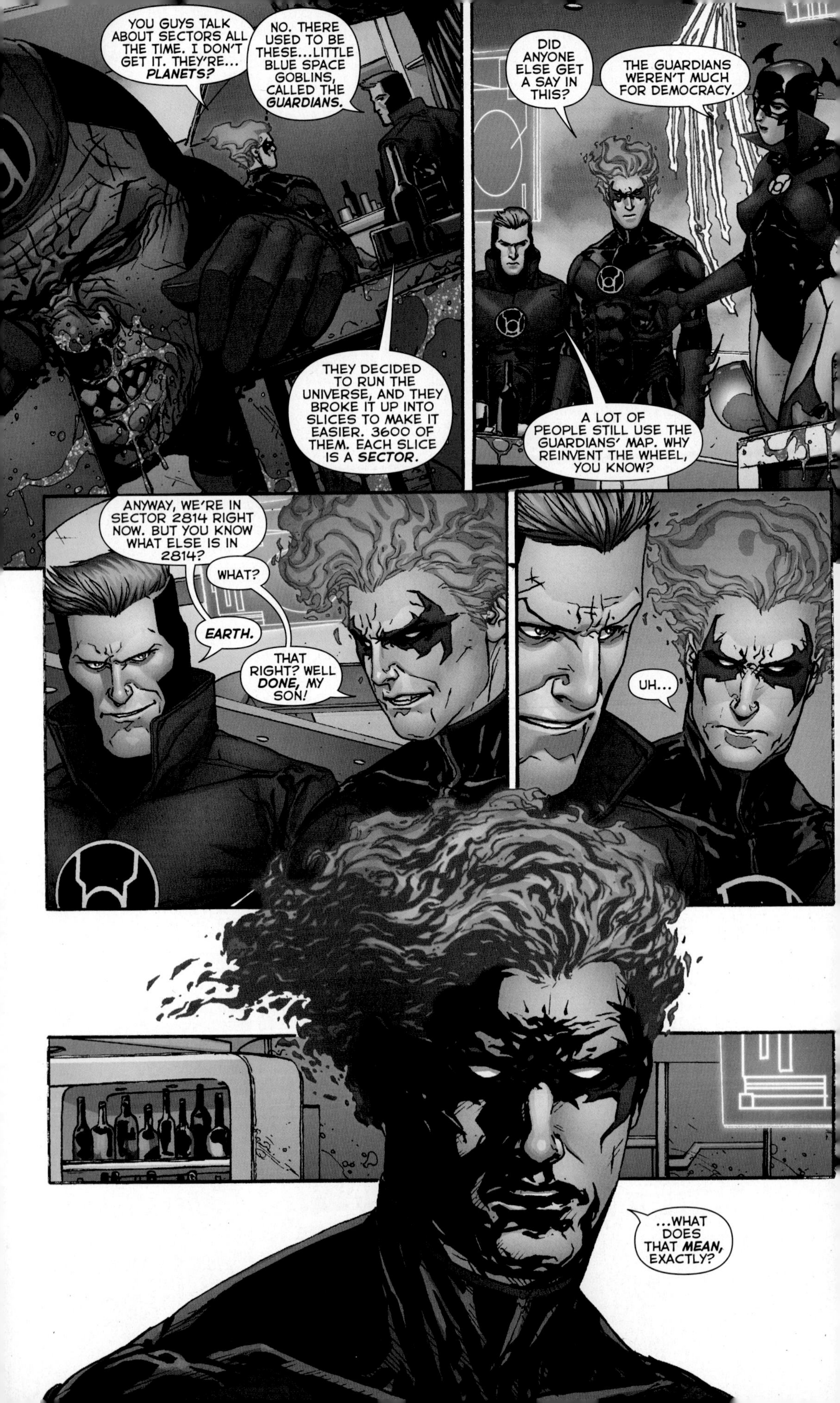
YOU GUYS TALK ABOUT SECTORS ALL THE TIME. I DON'T GET IT. THEY'RE... PLANETS?
NO. THERE USED TO BE THESE...LITTLE BLUE SPACE GOBLINS, CALLED THE GUARDIANS.
THEY DECIDED TO RUN THE UNIVERSE, AND THEY BROKE IT UP INTO SLICES TO MAKE IT EASIER. 3600 OF THEM. EACH SLICE IS A SECTOR.
DID ANYONE ELSE GET A SAY IN THIS?
THE GUARDIANS WEREN'T MUCH FOR DEMOCRACY.
A LOT OF PEOPLE STILL USE THE GUARDIANS' MAP. WHY REINVENT THE WHEEL, YOU KNOW?
ANYWAY, WE'RE IN SECTOR 2814 RIGHT NOW. BUT YOU KNOW WHAT ELSE IS IN 2814?
WHAT?
EARTH.
THAT RIGHT? WELL DONE, MY SON!
UH...
...WHAT DOES THAT MEAN, EXACTLY?

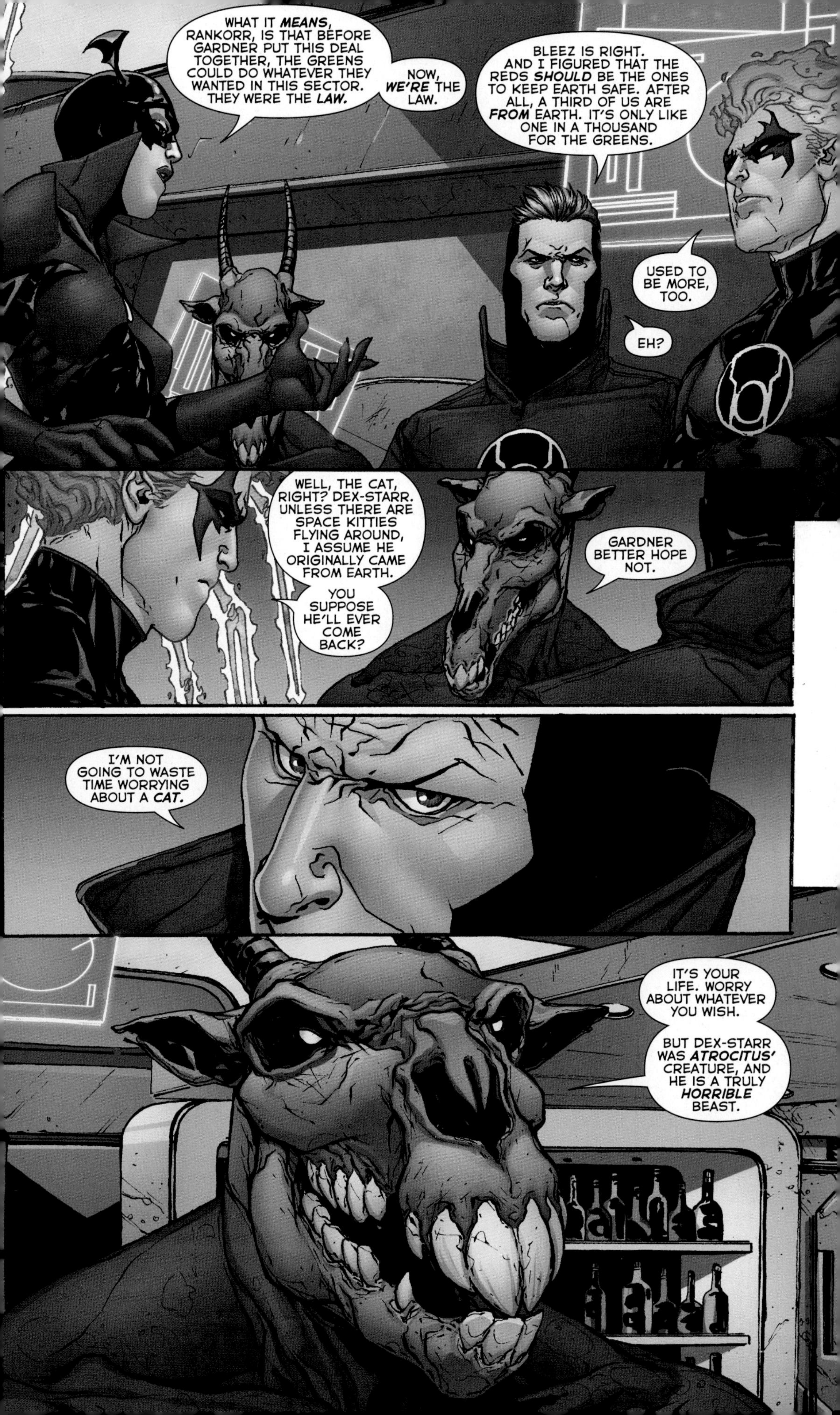
WHAT IT MEANS, RANKORR, IS THAT BEFORE GARDNER PUT THIS DEAL TOGETHER, THE GREENS COULD DO WHATEVER THEY WANTED IN THIS SECTOR. THEY WERE THE LAW.
NOW, WE'RE THE LAW.
BLEEZ IS RIGHT. AND I FIGURED THAT THE REDS SHOULD BE THE ONES TO KEEP EARTH SAFE. AFTER ALL, A THIRD OF US ARE FROM EARTH. IT'S ONLY LIKE ONE IN A THOUSAND FOR THE GREENS.
USED TO BE MORE, TOO.
EH?
WELL, THE CAT, RIGHT? DEX-STARR. UNLESS THERE ARE SPACE KITTIES FLYING AROUND, I ASSUME HE ORIGINALLY CAME FROM EARTH.
YOU SUPPOSE HE'LL EVER COME BACK?
GARDNER BETTER HOPE NOT.
I'M NOT GOING TO WASTE TIME WORRYING ABOUT A CAT.
IT'S YOUR LIFE. WORRY ABOUT WHATEVER YOU WISH.
BUT DEX-STARR WAS ATROCITUS' CREATURE, AND HE IS A TRULY HORRIBLE BEAST.

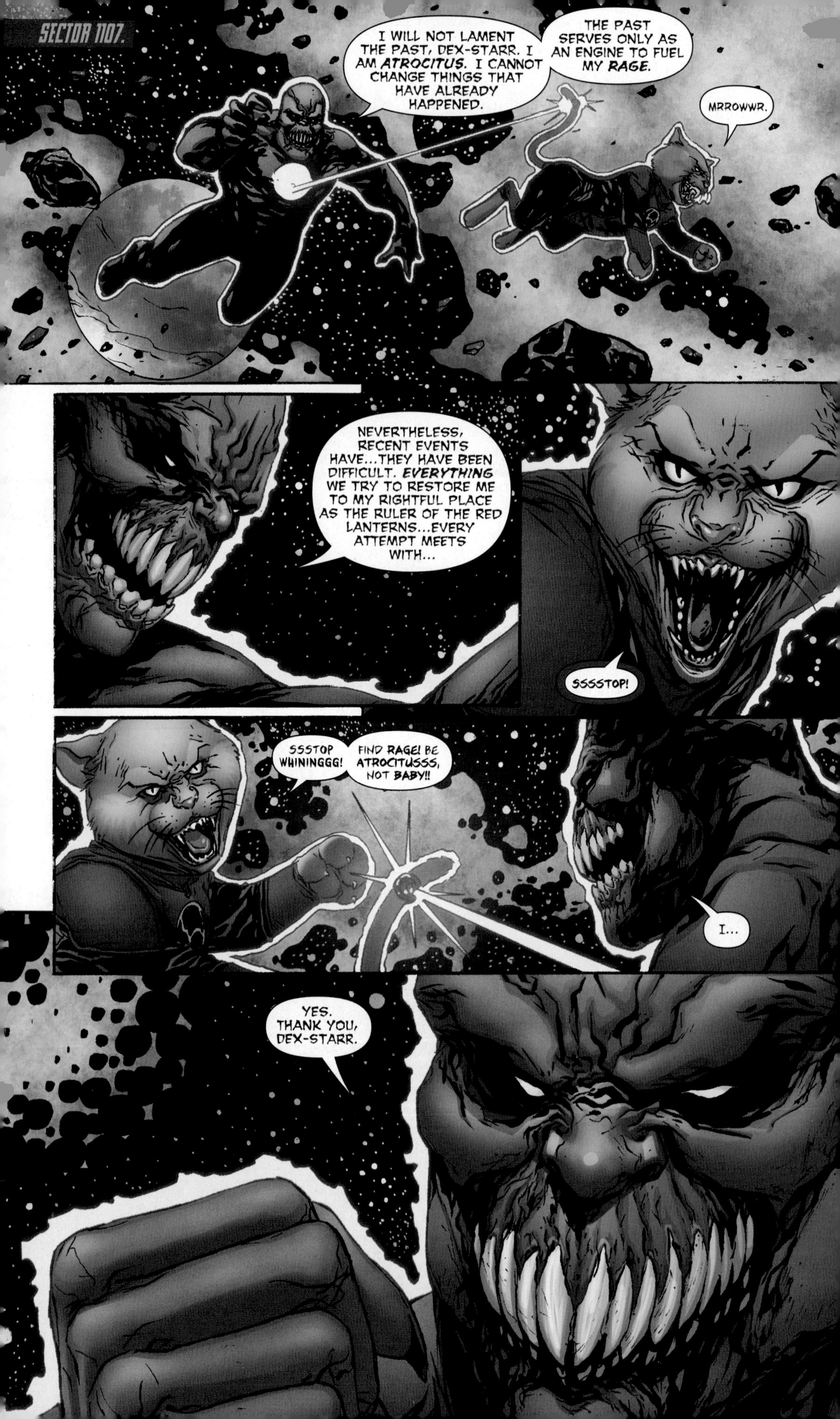
SECTOR 1107.
I WILL NOT LAMENT THE PAST, DEX-STARR. I AM ATROCITUS. I CANNOT CHANGE THINGS THAT HAVE ALREADY HAPPENED.
THE PAST SERVES ONLY AS AN ENGINE TO FUEL MY RAGE.
MRROWWR.
NEVERTHELESS, RECENT EVENTS HAVE...THEY HAVE BEEN DIFFICULT. EVERYTHING WE TRY TO RESTORE ME TO MY RIGHTFUL PLACE AS THE RULER OF THE RED LANTERNS...EVERY ATTEMPT MEETS WITH...
SSSSTOP!
SSSTOP WHININGGG!
FIND RAGE! BE ATROCITUSSS, NOT BABY!!
I...
YES. THANK YOU, DEX-STARR.

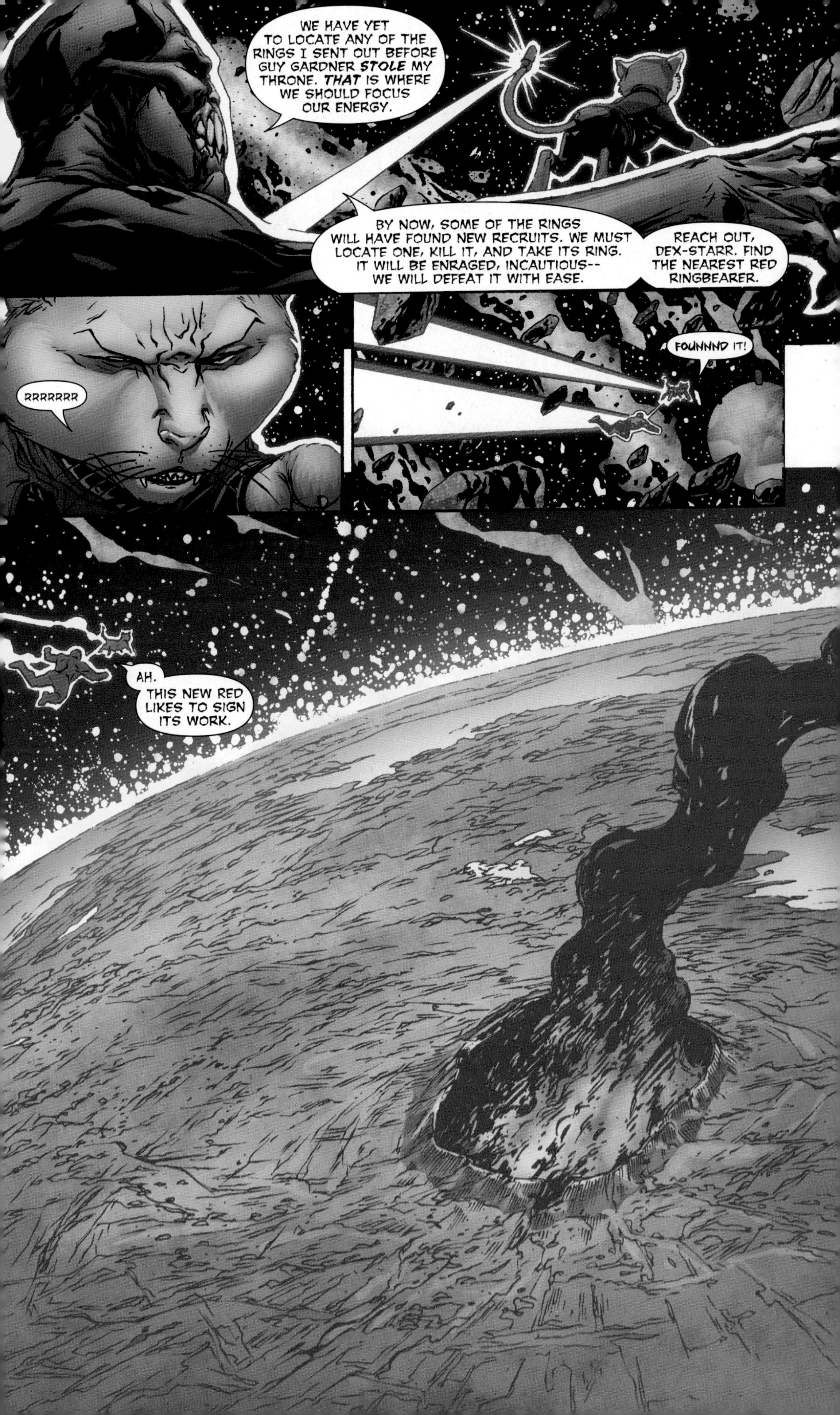
WE HAVE YET TO LOCATE ANY OF THE RINGS I SENT OUT BEFORE GUY GARDNER STOLE MY THRONE. THAT IS WHERE WE SHOULD FOCUS OUR ENERGY.
BY NOW, SOME OF THE RINGS WILL HAVE FOUND NEW RECRUITS. WE MUST LOCATE ONE, KILL IT, AND TAKE ITS RING. IT WILL BE ENRAGED, INCAUTIOUS-- WE WILL DEFEAT IT WITH EASE.
REACH OUT, DEX-STARR. FIND THE NEAREST RED RINGBEARER.
RRRRRRR
FOUNNND IT!
AH.
THIS NEW RED LIKES TO SIGN ITS WORK.

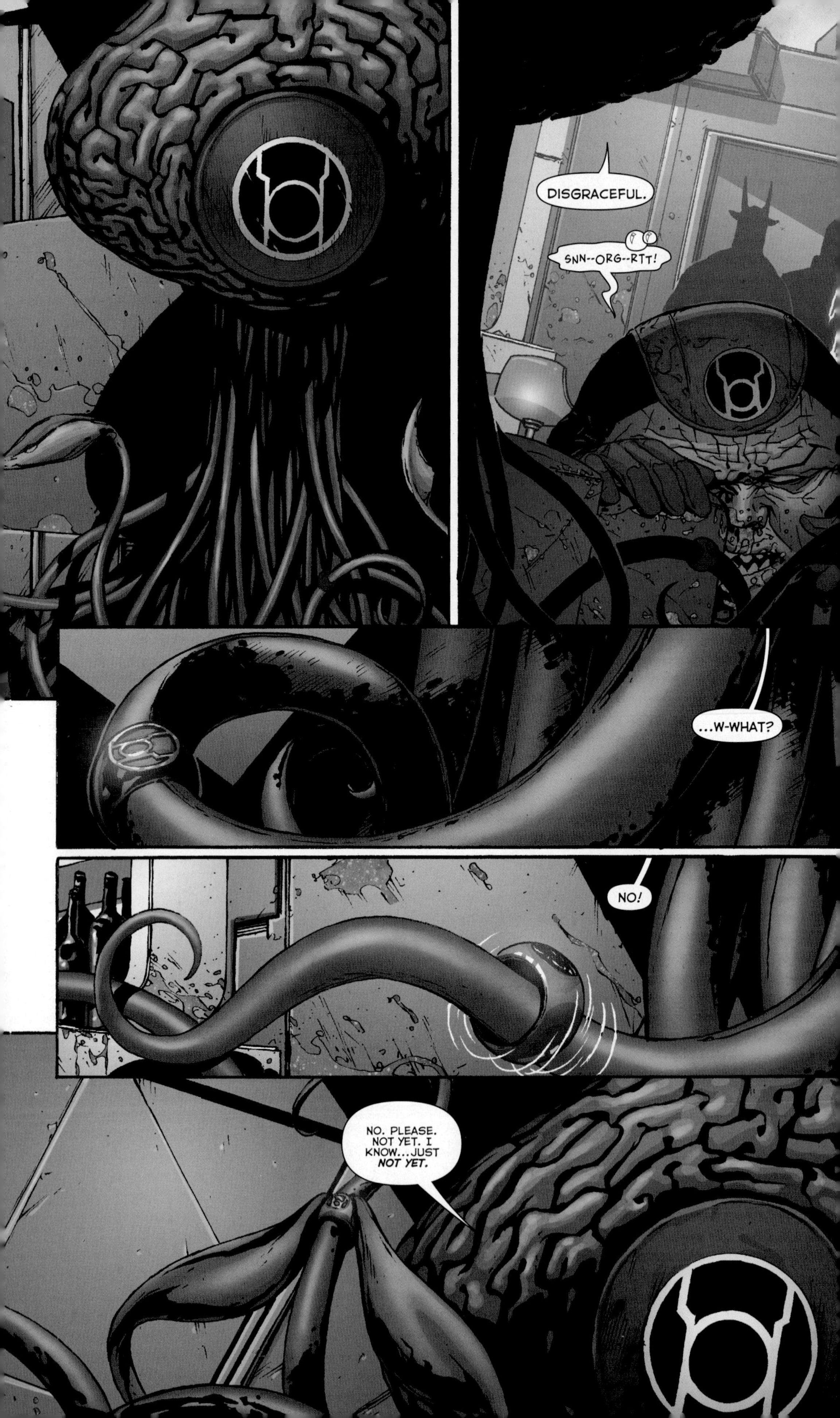
DISGRACEFUL.
SNN--ORG--RTT!
...W-WHAT?
NO!
NO. PLEASE. NOT YET. I KNOW...JUST *NOT YET.*

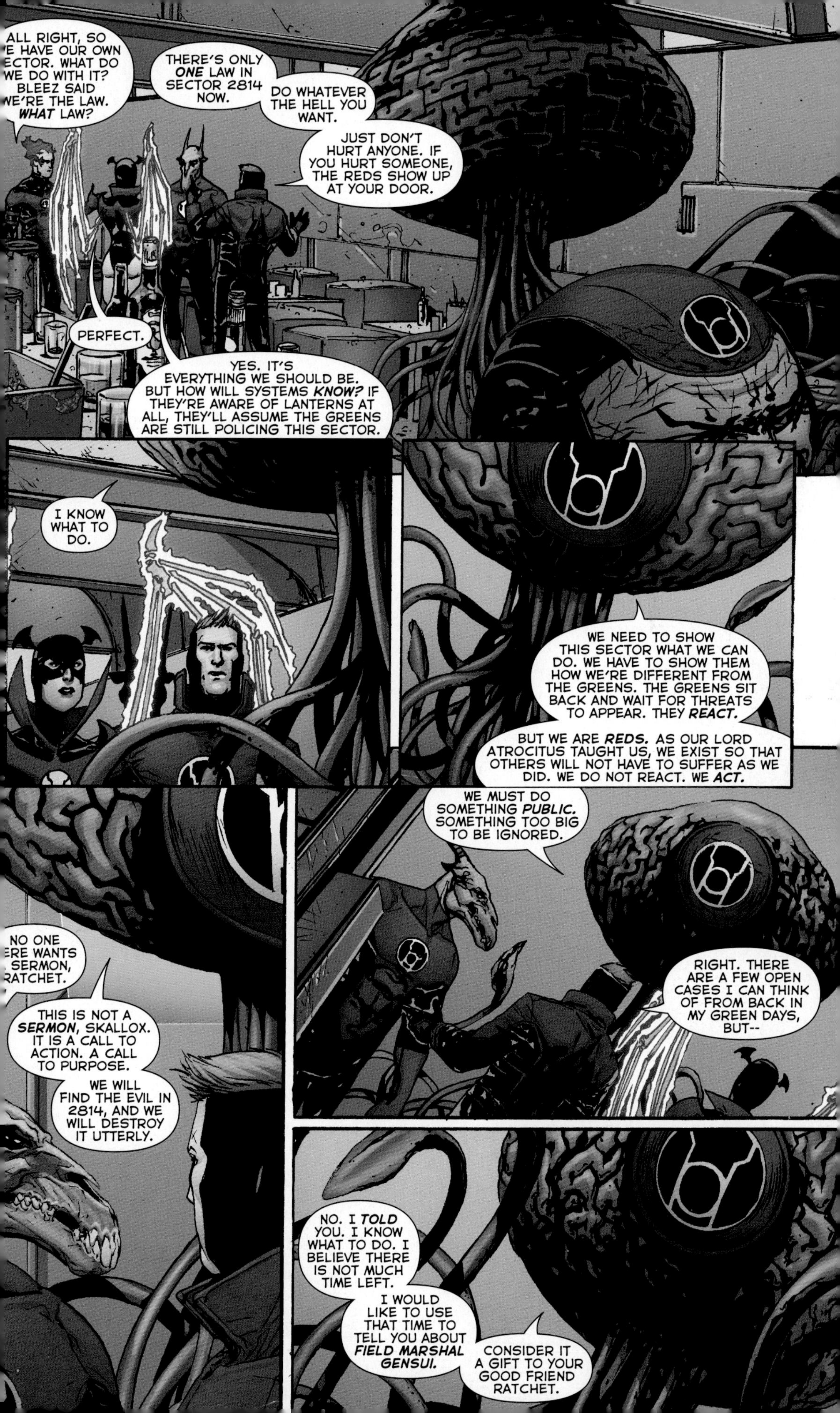
ALL RIGHT, SO WE HAVE OUR OWN SECTOR. WHAT DO WE DO WITH IT? BLEEZ SAID WE'RE THE LAW. *WHAT* LAW?
THERE'S ONLY *ONE* LAW IN SECTOR 2814 NOW.
DO WHATEVER THE HELL YOU WANT.
JUST DON'T HURT ANYONE. IF YOU HURT SOMEONE, THE REDS SHOW UP AT YOUR DOOR.
PERFECT.
YES. IT'S EVERYTHING WE SHOULD BE. BUT HOW WILL SYSTEMS *KNOW?* IF THEY'RE AWARE OF LANTERNS AT ALL, THEY'LL ASSUME THE GREENS ARE STILL POLICING THIS SECTOR.
I KNOW WHAT TO DO.
WE NEED TO SHOW THIS SECTOR WHAT WE CAN DO. WE HAVE TO SHOW THEM HOW WE'RE DIFFERENT FROM THE GREENS. THE GREENS SIT BACK AND WAIT FOR THREATS TO APPEAR. THEY *REACT.*
BUT WE ARE *REDS.* AS OUR LORD ATROCITUS TAUGHT US, WE EXIST SO THAT OTHERS WILL NOT HAVE TO SUFFER AS WE DID. WE DO NOT REACT. WE *ACT.*
NO ONE HERE WANTS A SERMON, RATCHET.
THIS IS NOT A *SERMON*, SKALLOX. IT IS A CALL TO ACTION. A CALL TO PURPOSE.
WE WILL FIND THE EVIL IN 2814, AND WE WILL DESTROY IT UTTERLY.
WE MUST DO SOMETHING *PUBLIC.* SOMETHING TOO BIG TO BE IGNORED.
RIGHT. THERE ARE A FEW OPEN CASES I CAN THINK OF FROM BACK IN MY GREEN DAYS, BUT--
NO. I *TOLD* YOU. I KNOW WHAT TO DO. I BELIEVE THERE IS NOT MUCH TIME LEFT.
I WOULD LIKE TO USE THAT TIME TO TELL YOU ABOUT *FIELD MARSHAL GENSUI.*
CONSIDER IT A GIFT TO YOUR GOOD FRIEND RATCHET.

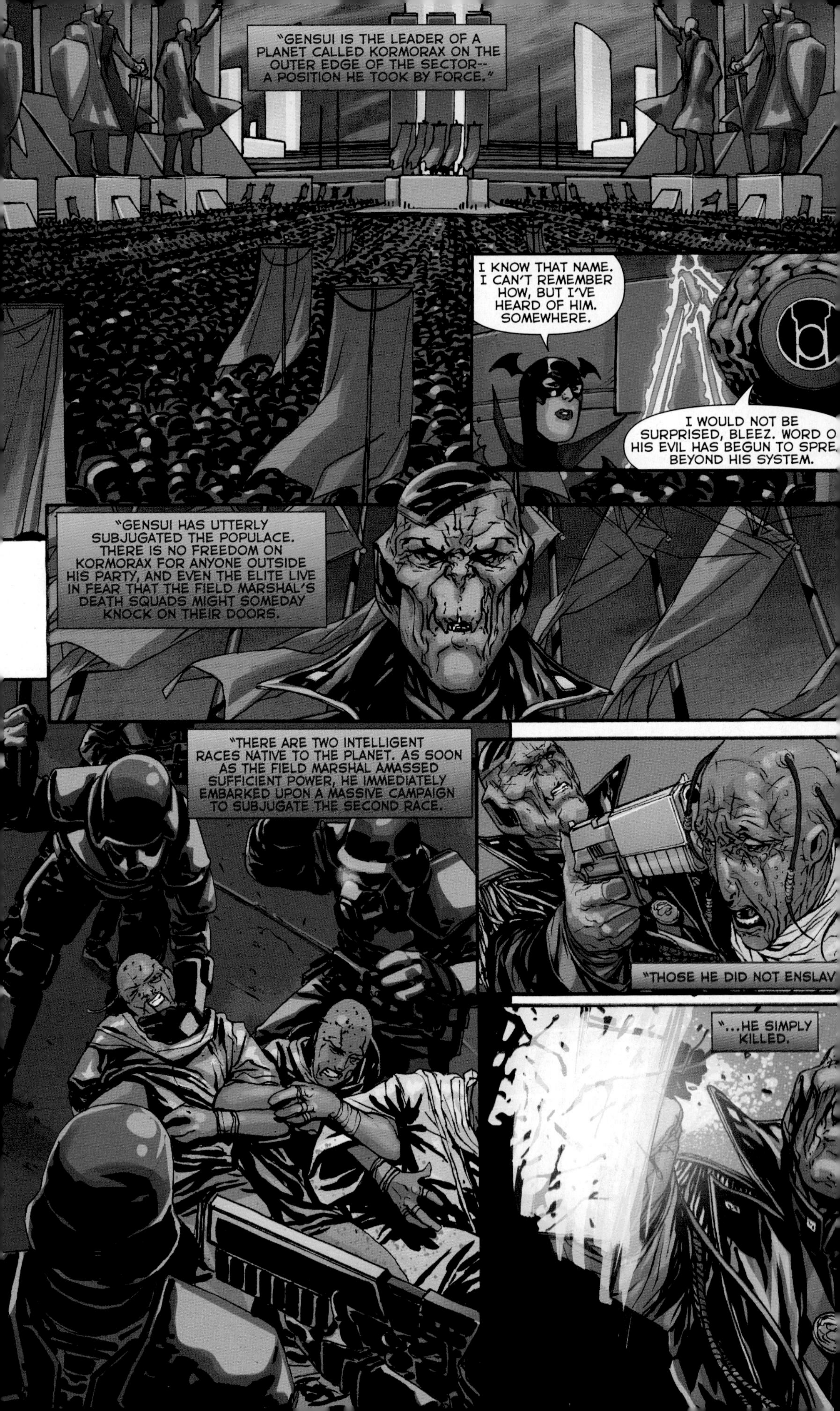
"GENSUI IS THE LEADER OF A PLANET CALLED KORMORAX ON THE OUTER EDGE OF THE SECTOR-- A POSITION HE TOOK BY FORCE."
I KNOW THAT NAME. I CAN'T REMEMBER HOW, BUT I'VE HEARD OF HIM. SOMEWHERE.
I WOULD NOT BE SURPRISED, BLEEZ. WORD O HIS EVIL HAS BEGUN TO SPRE BEYOND HIS SYSTEM.
"GENSUI HAS UTTERLY SUBJUGATED THE POPULACE. THERE IS NO FREEDOM ON KORMORAX FOR ANYONE OUTSIDE HIS PARTY, AND EVEN THE ELITE LIVE IN FEAR THAT THE FIELD MARSHAL'S DEATH SQUADS MIGHT SOMEDAY KNOCK ON THEIR DOORS.
"THERE ARE TWO INTELLIGENT RACES NATIVE TO THE PLANET. AS SOON AS THE FIELD MARSHAL AMASSED SUFFICIENT POWER, HE IMMEDIATELY EMBARKED UPON A MASSIVE CAMPAIGN TO SUBJUGATE THE SECOND RACE.
"THOSE HE DID NOT ENSLAV
"...HE SIMPLY KILLED.

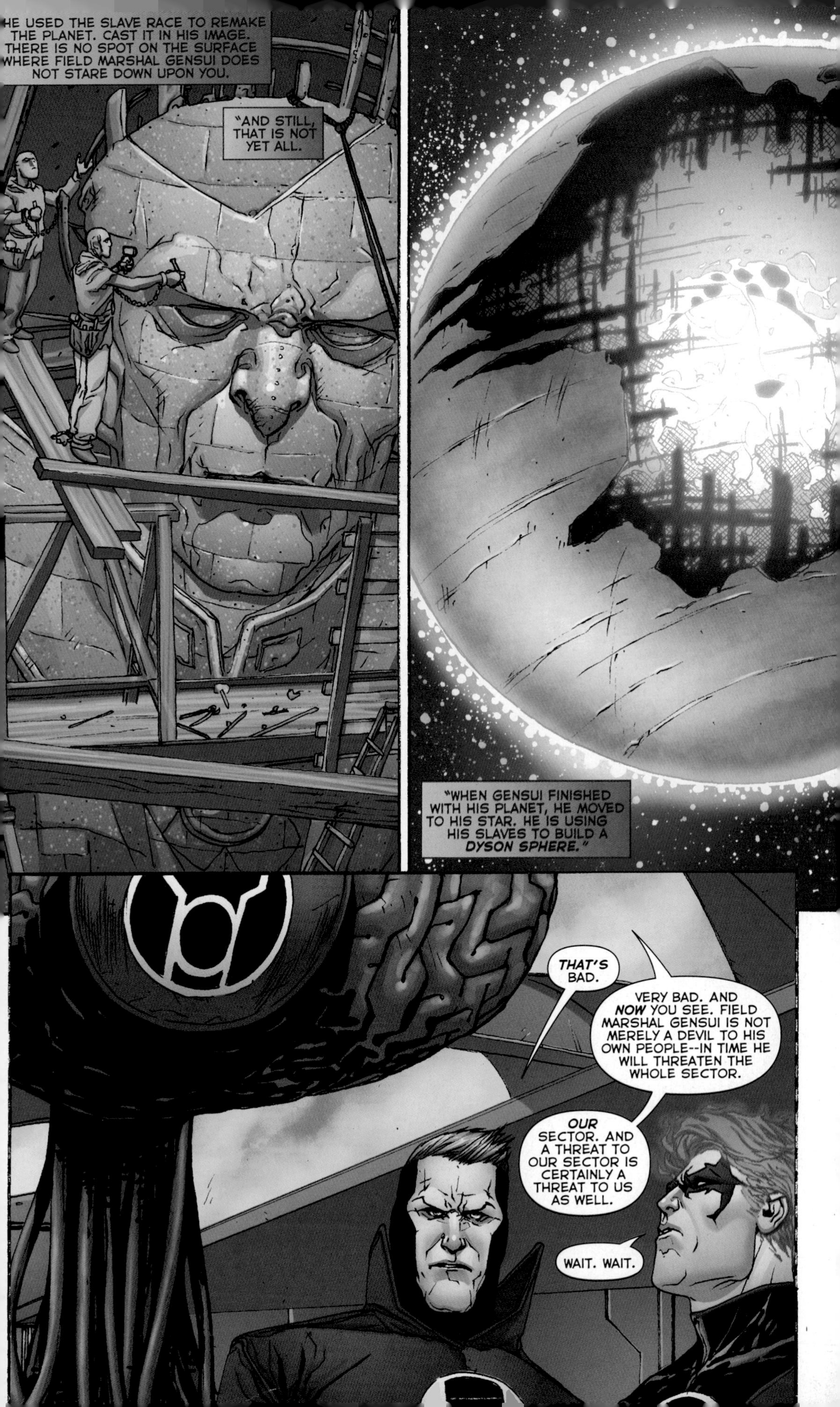
HE USED THE SLAVE RACE TO REMAKE THE PLANET. CAST IT IN HIS IMAGE. THERE IS NO SPOT ON THE SURFACE WHERE FIELD MARSHAL GENSUI DOES NOT STARE DOWN UPON YOU.
"AND STILL, THAT IS NOT YET ALL.
"WHEN GENSUI FINISHED WITH HIS PLANET, HE MOVED TO HIS STAR. HE IS USING HIS SLAVES TO BUILD A *DYSON SPHERE.*"
THAT'S BAD.
VERY BAD. AND *NOW* YOU SEE. FIELD MARSHAL GENSUI IS NOT MERELY A DEVIL TO HIS OWN PEOPLE--IN TIME HE WILL THREATEN THE WHOLE SECTOR.
OUR SECTOR. AND A THREAT TO OUR SECTOR IS CERTAINLY A THREAT TO US AS WELL.
WAIT. WAIT.

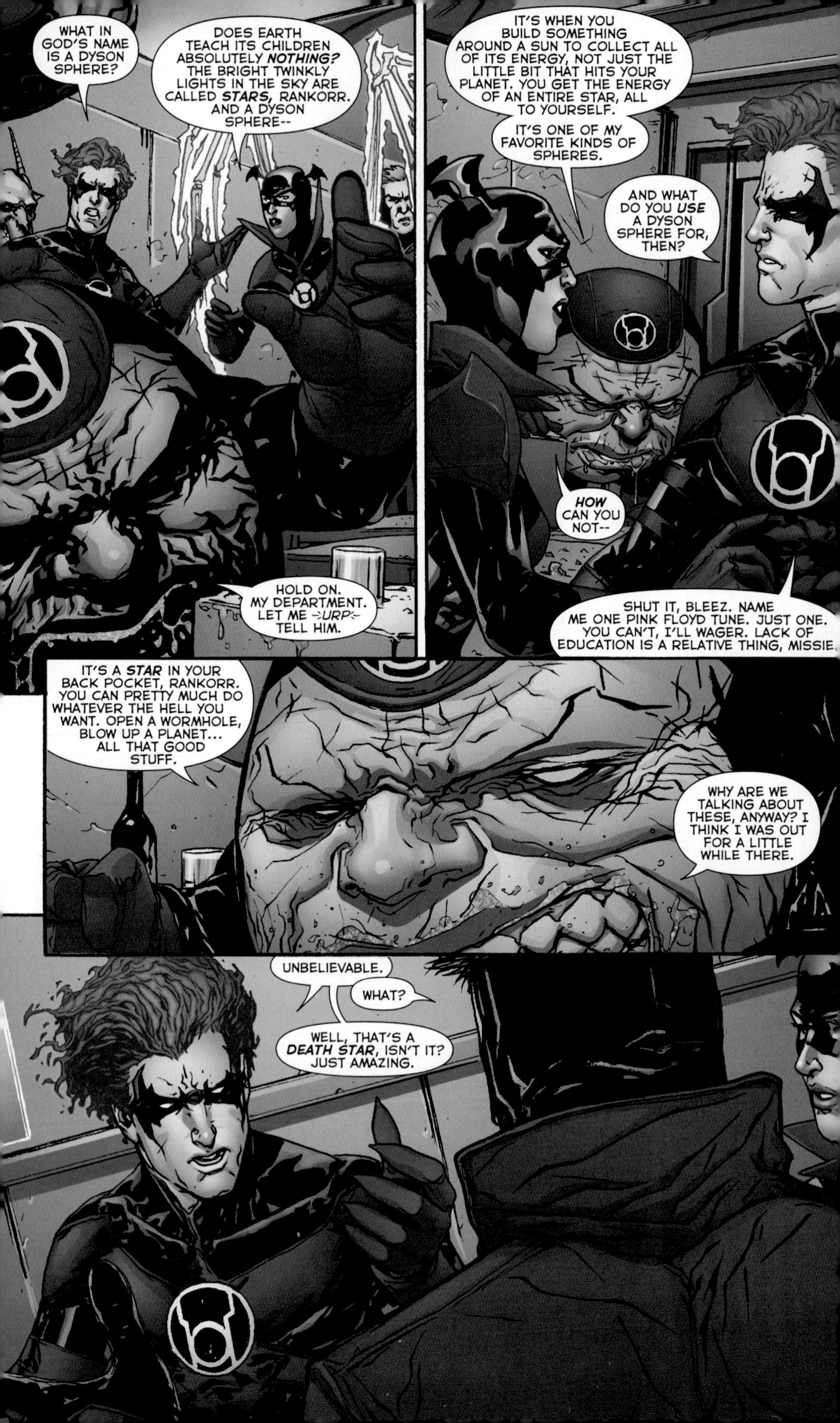
WHAT IN GOD'S NAME IS A DYSON SPHERE?
DOES EARTH TEACH ITS CHILDREN ABSOLUTELY *NOTHING?* THE BRIGHT TWINKLY LIGHTS IN THE SKY ARE CALLED *STARS,* RANKORR. AND A DYSON SPHERE--
HOLD ON. MY DEPARTMENT. LET ME *-URP-* TELL HIM.
IT'S WHEN YOU BUILD SOMETHING AROUND A SUN TO COLLECT ALL OF ITS ENERGY, NOT JUST THE LITTLE BIT THAT HITS YOUR PLANET. YOU GET THE ENERGY OF AN ENTIRE STAR, ALL TO YOURSELF.
IT'S ONE OF MY FAVORITE KINDS OF SPHERES.
AND WHAT DO YOU *USE* A DYSON SPHERE FOR, THEN?
HOW CAN YOU NOT--
SHUT IT, BLEEZ. NAME ME ONE PINK FLOYD TUNE. JUST ONE. YOU CAN'T, I'LL WAGER. LACK OF EDUCATION IS A RELATIVE THING, MISSIE.
IT'S A *STAR* IN YOUR BACK POCKET, RANKORR. YOU CAN PRETTY MUCH DO WHATEVER THE HELL YOU WANT. OPEN A WORMHOLE, BLOW UP A PLANET... ALL THAT GOOD STUFF.
WHY ARE WE TALKING ABOUT THESE, ANYWAY? I THINK I WAS OUT FOR A LITTLE WHILE THERE.
UNBELIEVABLE.
WHAT?
WELL, THAT'S A *DEATH STAR,* ISN'T IT? JUST AMAZING.

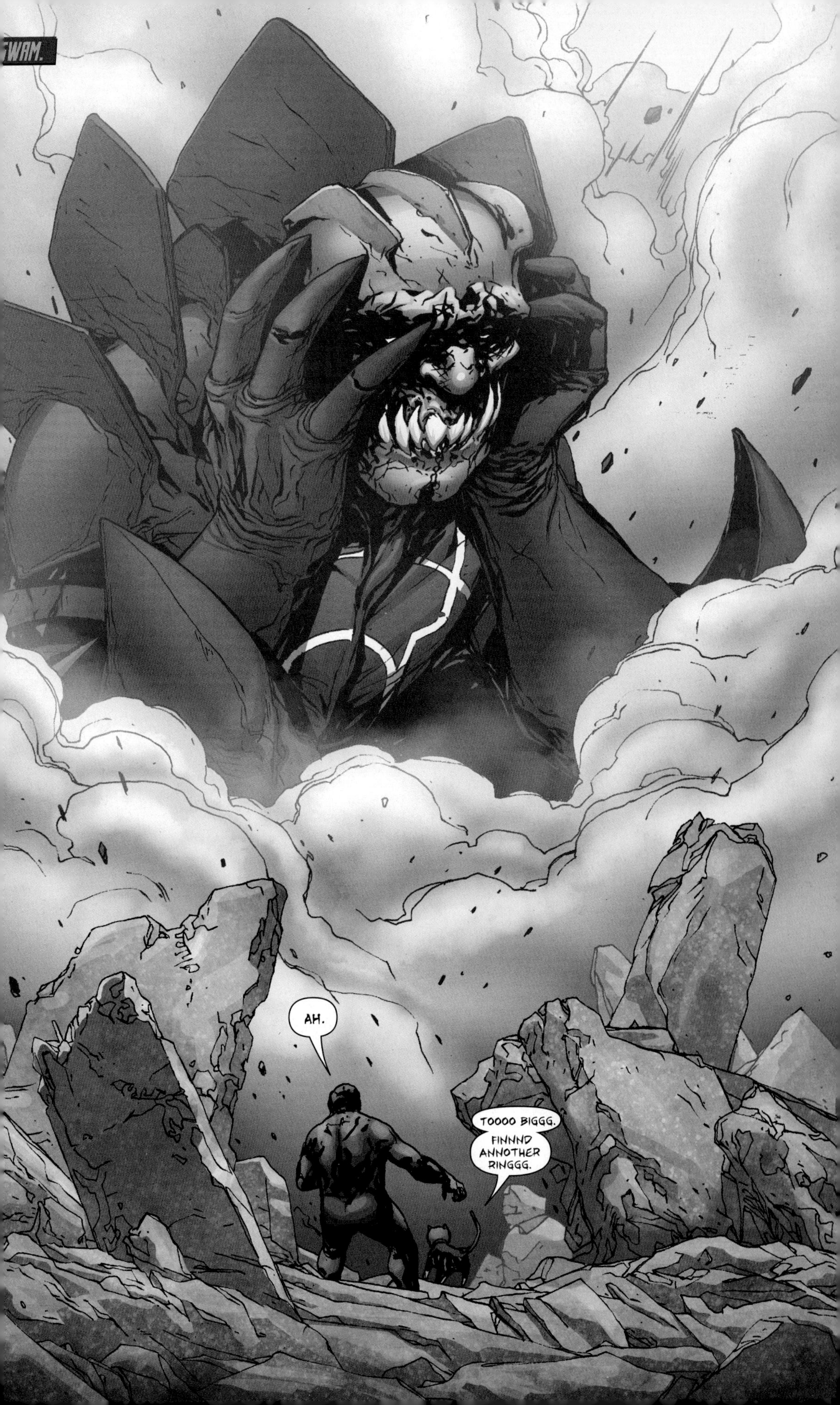
WAM.
AH.
TOOOO BIGGG.
FINNND ANNOTHER RINGGG.

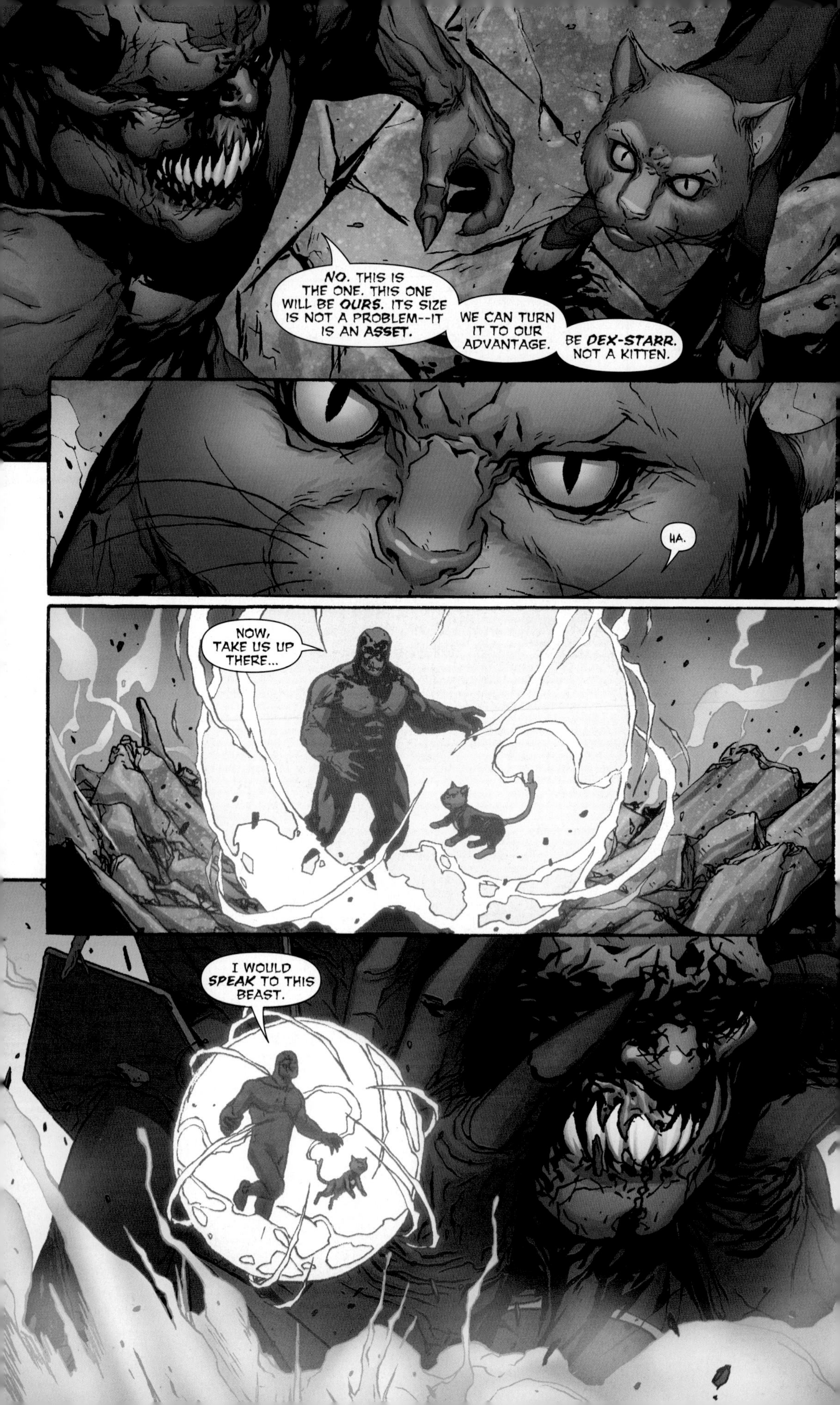

NO. THIS IS THE ONE. THIS ONE WILL BE OURS. ITS SIZE IS NOT A PROBLEM--IT IS AN ASSET.
WE CAN TURN IT TO OUR ADVANTAGE.
BE DEX-STARR. NOT A KITTEN.
HA.
NOW, TAKE US UP THERE...
I WOULD SPEAK TO THIS BEAST.

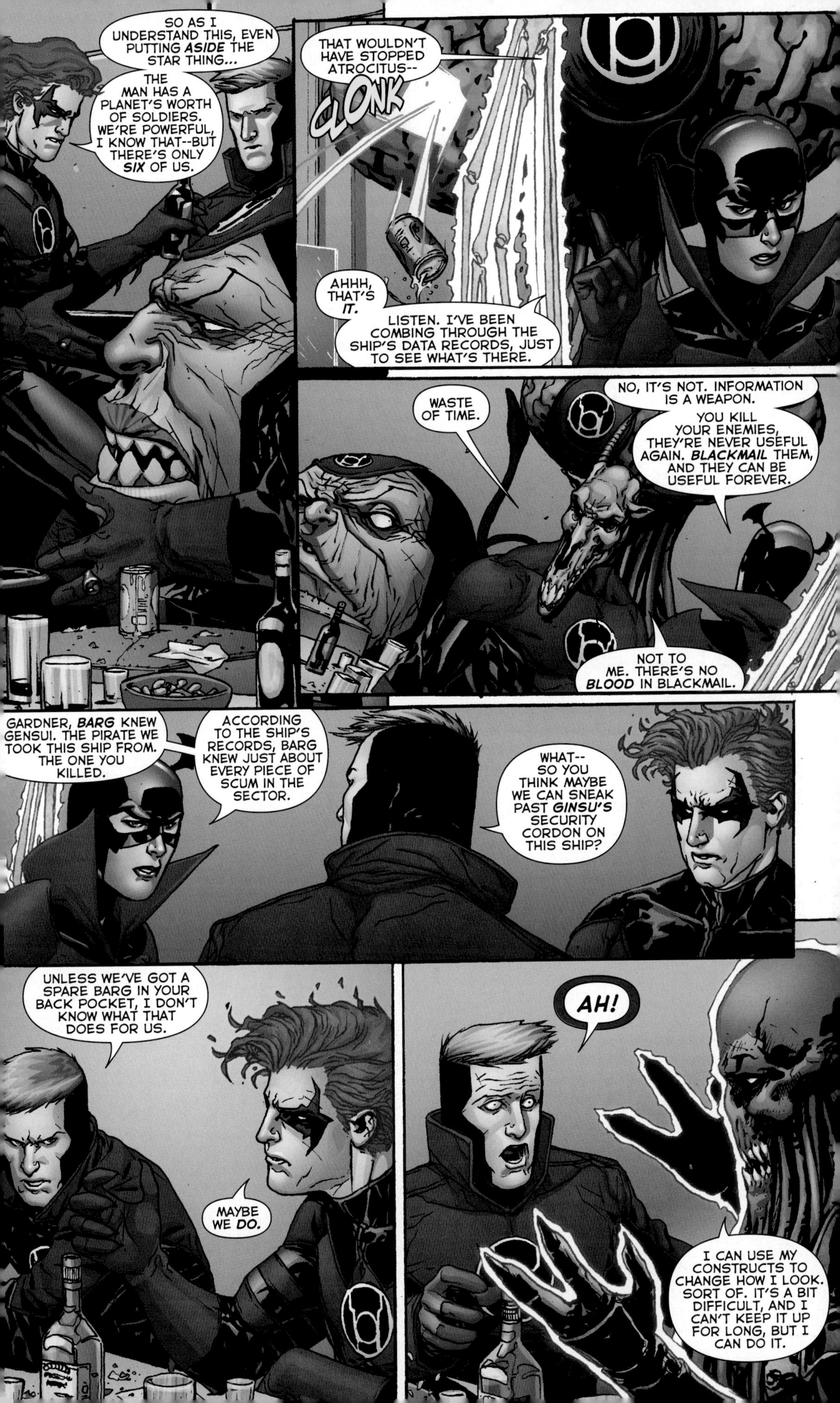
SO AS I UNDERSTAND THIS, EVEN PUTTING ASIDE THE STAR THING...
THE MAN HAS A PLANET'S WORTH OF SOLDIERS. WE'RE POWERFUL, I KNOW THAT--BUT THERE'S ONLY SIX OF US.
THAT WOULDN'T HAVE STOPPED ATROCITUS--
CLONK
AHHH, THAT'S IT.
LISTEN. I'VE BEEN COMBING THROUGH THE SHIP'S DATA RECORDS, JUST TO SEE WHAT'S THERE.
WASTE OF TIME.
NO, IT'S NOT. INFORMATION IS A WEAPON.
YOU KILL YOUR ENEMIES, THEY'RE NEVER USEFUL AGAIN. BLACKMAIL THEM, AND THEY CAN BE USEFUL FOREVER.
NOT TO ME. THERE'S NO BLOOD IN BLACKMAIL.
GARDNER, BARG KNEW GENSUI. THE PIRATE WE TOOK THIS SHIP FROM. THE ONE YOU KILLED.
ACCORDING TO THE SHIP'S RECORDS, BARG KNEW JUST ABOUT EVERY PIECE OF SCUM IN THE SECTOR.
WHAT-- SO YOU THINK MAYBE WE CAN SNEAK PAST GINSU'S SECURITY CORDON ON THIS SHIP?
UNLESS WE'VE GOT A SPARE BARG IN YOUR BACK POCKET, I DON'T KNOW WHAT THAT DOES FOR US.
MAYBE WE DO.
AH!
I CAN USE MY CONSTRUCTS TO CHANGE HOW I LOOK. SORT OF. IT'S A BIT DIFFICULT, AND I CAN'T KEEP IT UP FOR LONG, BUT I CAN DO IT.

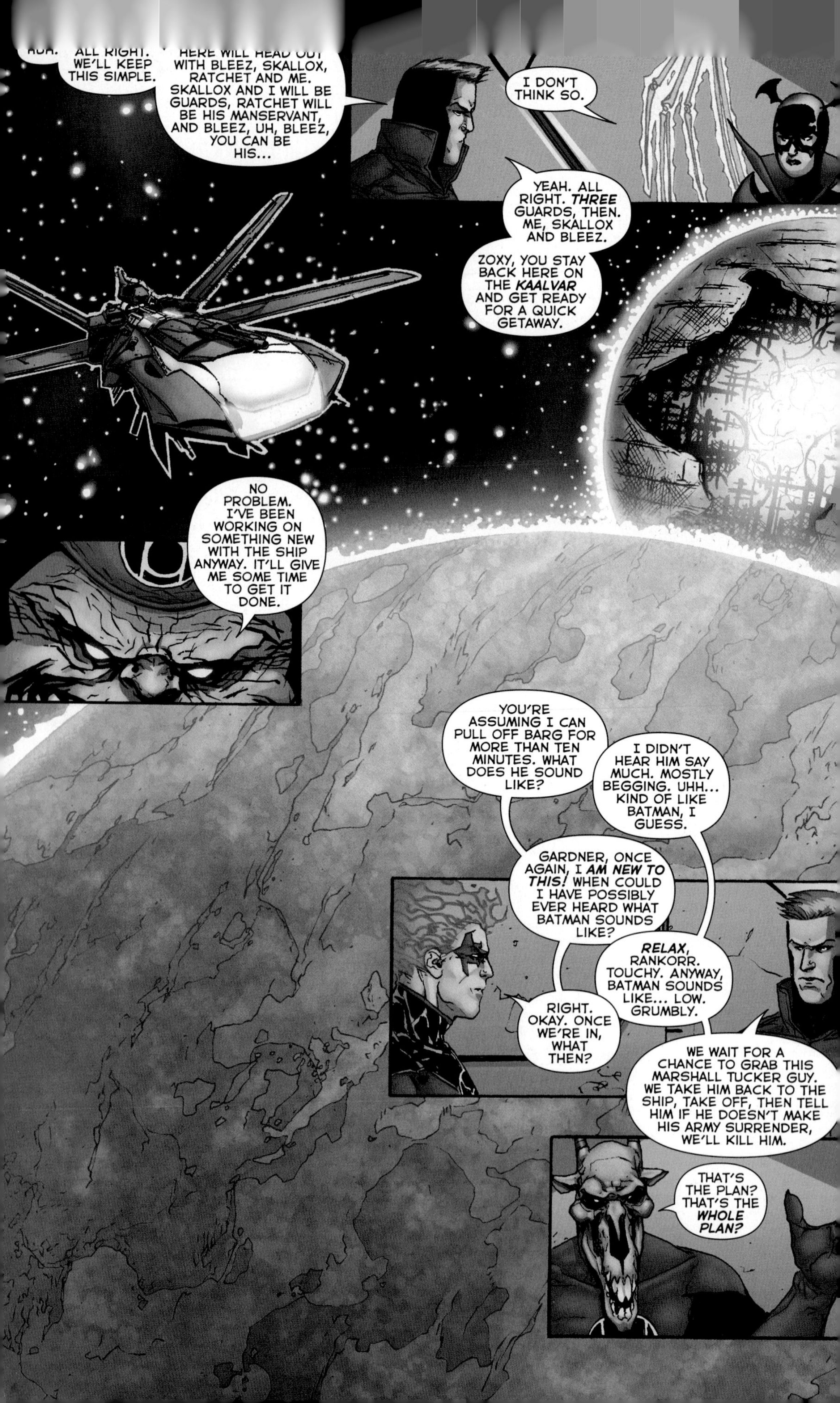
ALL RIGHT. WE'LL KEEP THIS SIMPLE.
HERE WILL HEAD OUT WITH BLEEZ, SKALLOX, RATCHET AND ME. SKALLOX AND I WILL BE GUARDS, RATCHET WILL BE HIS MANSERVANT, AND BLEEZ, UH, BLEEZ, YOU CAN BE HIS...
I DON'T THINK SO.
YEAH. ALL RIGHT. *THREE* GUARDS, THEN. ME, SKALLOX AND BLEEZ.
ZOXY, YOU STAY BACK HERE ON THE *KAALVAR* AND GET READY FOR A QUICK GETAWAY.
NO PROBLEM. I'VE BEEN WORKING ON SOMETHING NEW WITH THE SHIP ANYWAY. IT'LL GIVE ME SOME TIME TO GET IT DONE.
YOU'RE ASSUMING I CAN PULL OFF BARG FOR MORE THAN TEN MINUTES. WHAT DOES HE SOUND LIKE?
I DIDN'T HEAR HIM SAY MUCH. MOSTLY BEGGING. UHH... KIND OF LIKE BATMAN, I GUESS.
GARDNER, ONCE AGAIN, I *AM NEW TO THIS!* WHEN COULD I HAVE POSSIBLY EVER HEARD WHAT BATMAN SOUNDS LIKE?
RELAX, RANKORR. TOUCHY. ANYWAY, BATMAN SOUNDS LIKE... LOW. GRUMBLY.
RIGHT. OKAY. ONCE WE'RE IN, WHAT THEN?
WE WAIT FOR A CHANCE TO GRAB THIS MARSHALL TUCKER GUY. WE TAKE HIM BACK TO THE SHIP, TAKE OFF, THEN TELL HIM IF HE DOESN'T MAKE HIS ARMY SURRENDER, WE'LL KILL HIM.
THAT'S THE PLAN? THAT'S THE *WHOLE PLAN?*

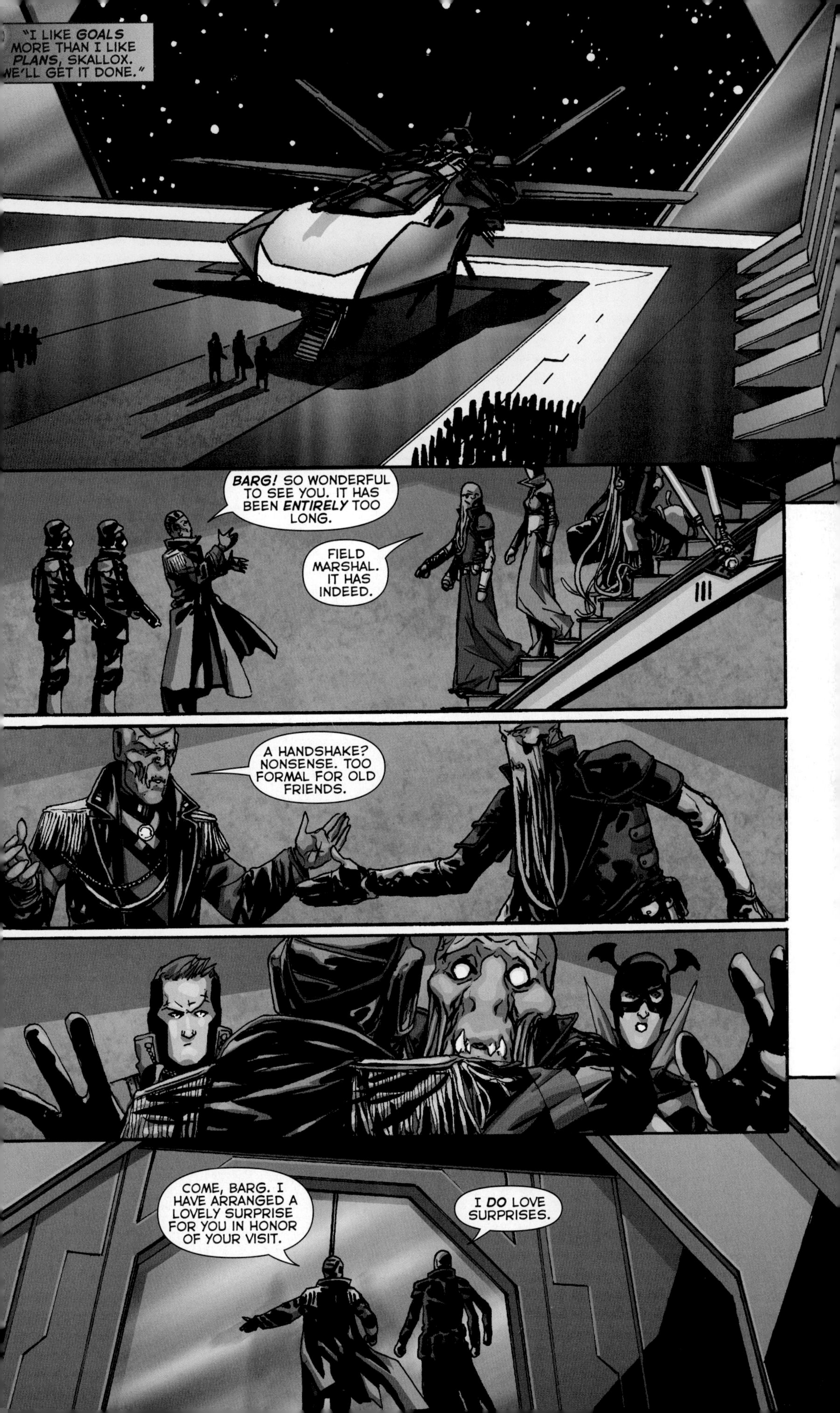
"I LIKE GOALS MORE THAN I LIKE PLANS, SKALLOX. WE'LL GET IT DONE."
BARG! SO WONDERFUL TO SEE YOU. IT HAS BEEN ENTIRELY TOO LONG.
FIELD MARSHAL. IT HAS INDEED.
A HANDSHAKE? NONSENSE. TOO FORMAL FOR OLD FRIENDS.
COME, BARG. I HAVE ARRANGED A LOVELY SURPRISE FOR YOU IN HONOR OF YOUR VISIT.
I DO LOVE SURPRISES.

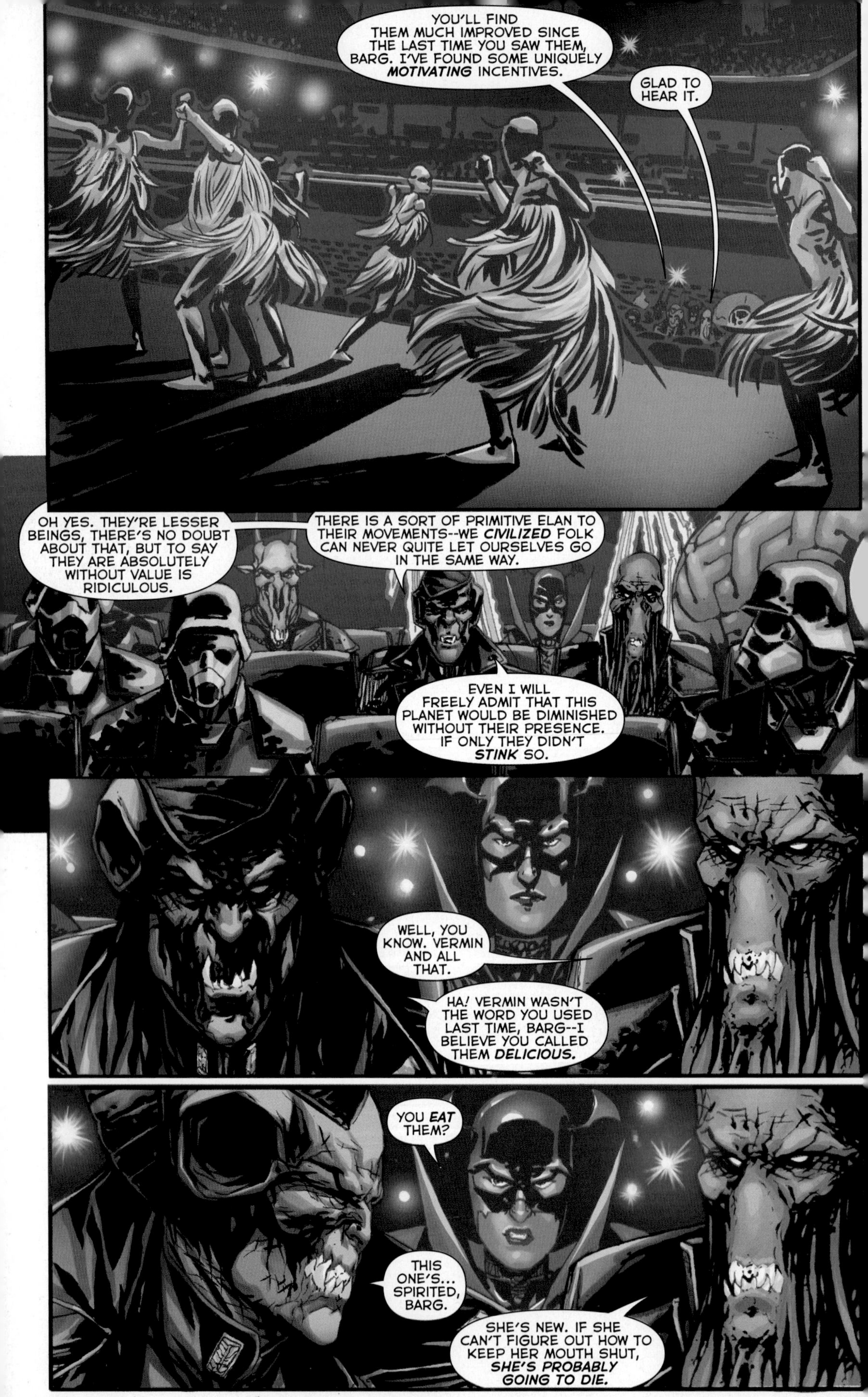
YOU'LL FIND THEM MUCH IMPROVED SINCE THE LAST TIME YOU SAW THEM, BARG. I'VE FOUND SOME UNIQUELY MOTIVATING INCENTIVES.
GLAD TO HEAR IT.
OH YES. THEY'RE LESSER BEINGS, THERE'S NO DOUBT ABOUT THAT, BUT TO SAY THEY ARE ABSOLUTELY WITHOUT VALUE IS RIDICULOUS.
THERE IS A SORT OF PRIMITIVE ELAN TO THEIR MOVEMENTS--WE CIVILIZED FOLK CAN NEVER QUITE LET OURSELVES GO IN THE SAME WAY.
EVEN I WILL FREELY ADMIT THAT THIS PLANET WOULD BE DIMINISHED WITHOUT THEIR PRESENCE. IF ONLY THEY DIDN'T STINK SO.
WELL, YOU KNOW. VERMIN AND ALL THAT.
HA! VERMIN WASN'T THE WORD YOU USED LAST TIME, BARG--I BELIEVE YOU CALLED THEM DELICIOUS.
YOU EAT THEM?
THIS ONE'S... SPIRITED, BARG.
SHE'S NEW. IF SHE CAN'T FIGURE OUT HOW TO KEEP HER MOUTH SHUT, SHE'S PROBABLY GOING TO DIE.

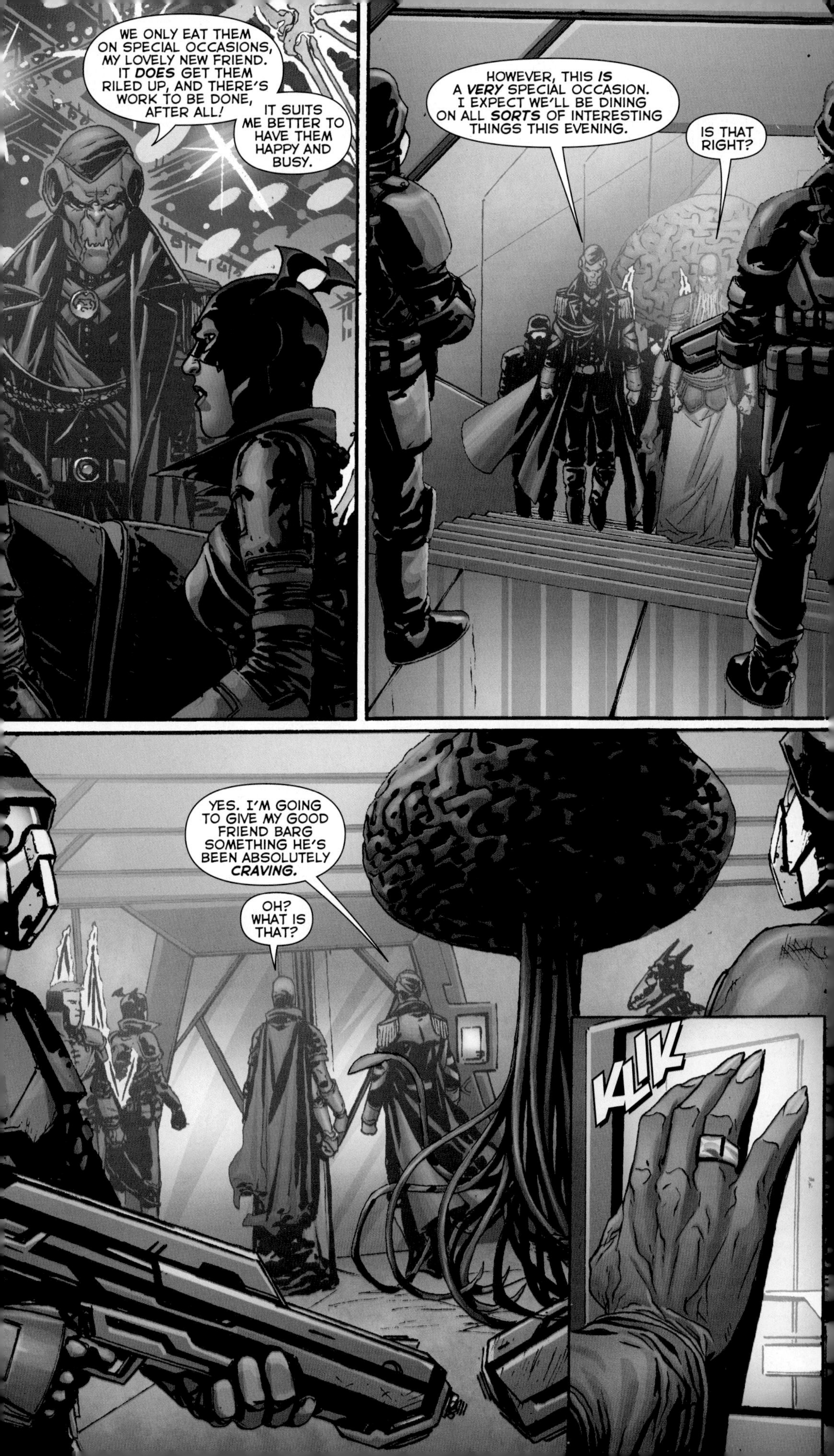
WE ONLY EAT THEM ON SPECIAL OCCASIONS, MY LOVELY NEW FRIEND. IT DOES GET THEM RILED UP, AND THERE'S WORK TO BE DONE, AFTER ALL!
IT SUITS ME BETTER TO HAVE THEM HAPPY AND BUSY.
HOWEVER, THIS IS A VERY SPECIAL OCCASION. I EXPECT WE'LL BE DINING ON ALL SORTS OF INTERESTING THINGS THIS EVENING.
IS THAT RIGHT?
YES. I'M GOING TO GIVE MY GOOD FRIEND BARG SOMETHING HE'S BEEN ABSOLUTELY CRAVING.
OH? WHAT IS THAT?
KLIK

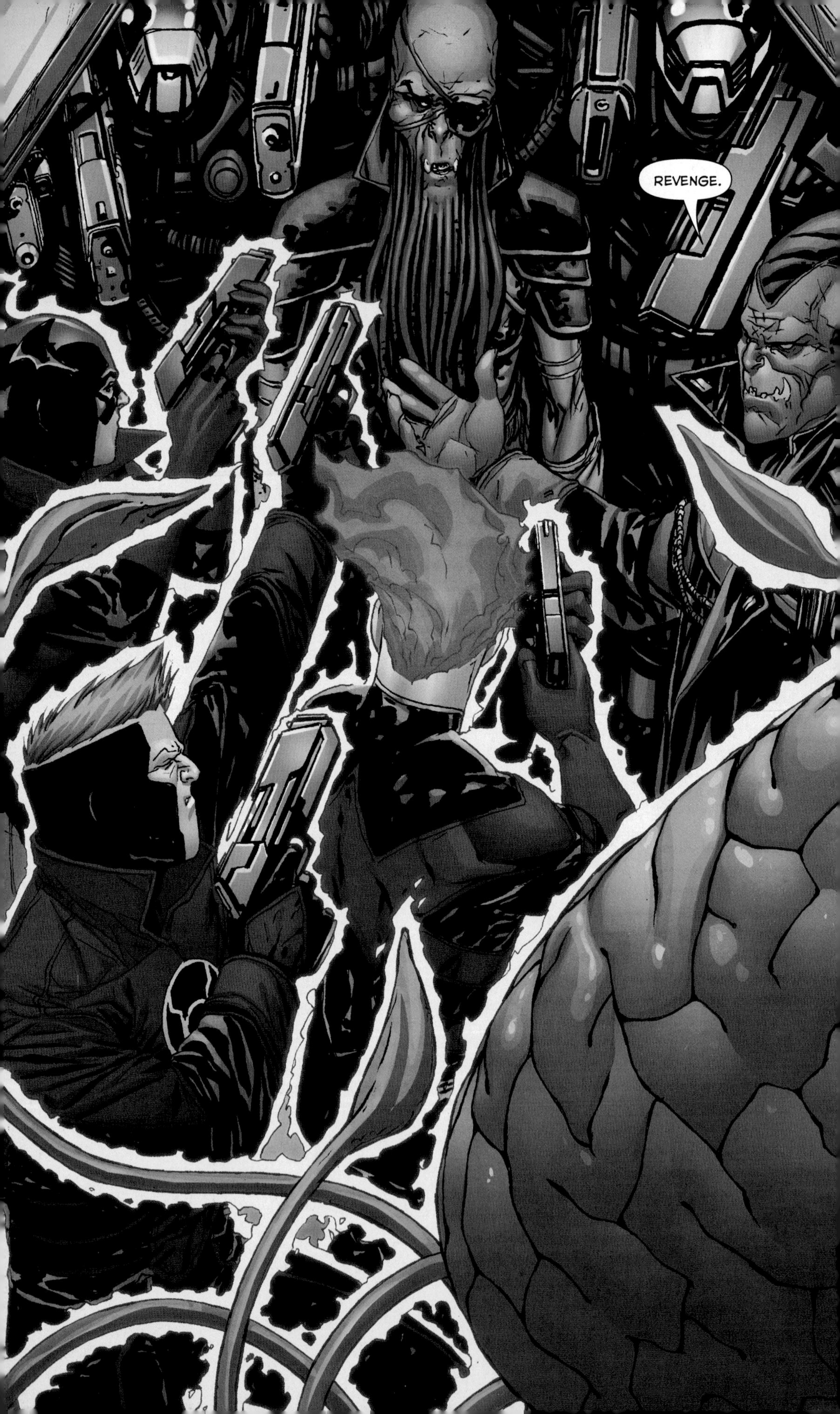
REVENGE.

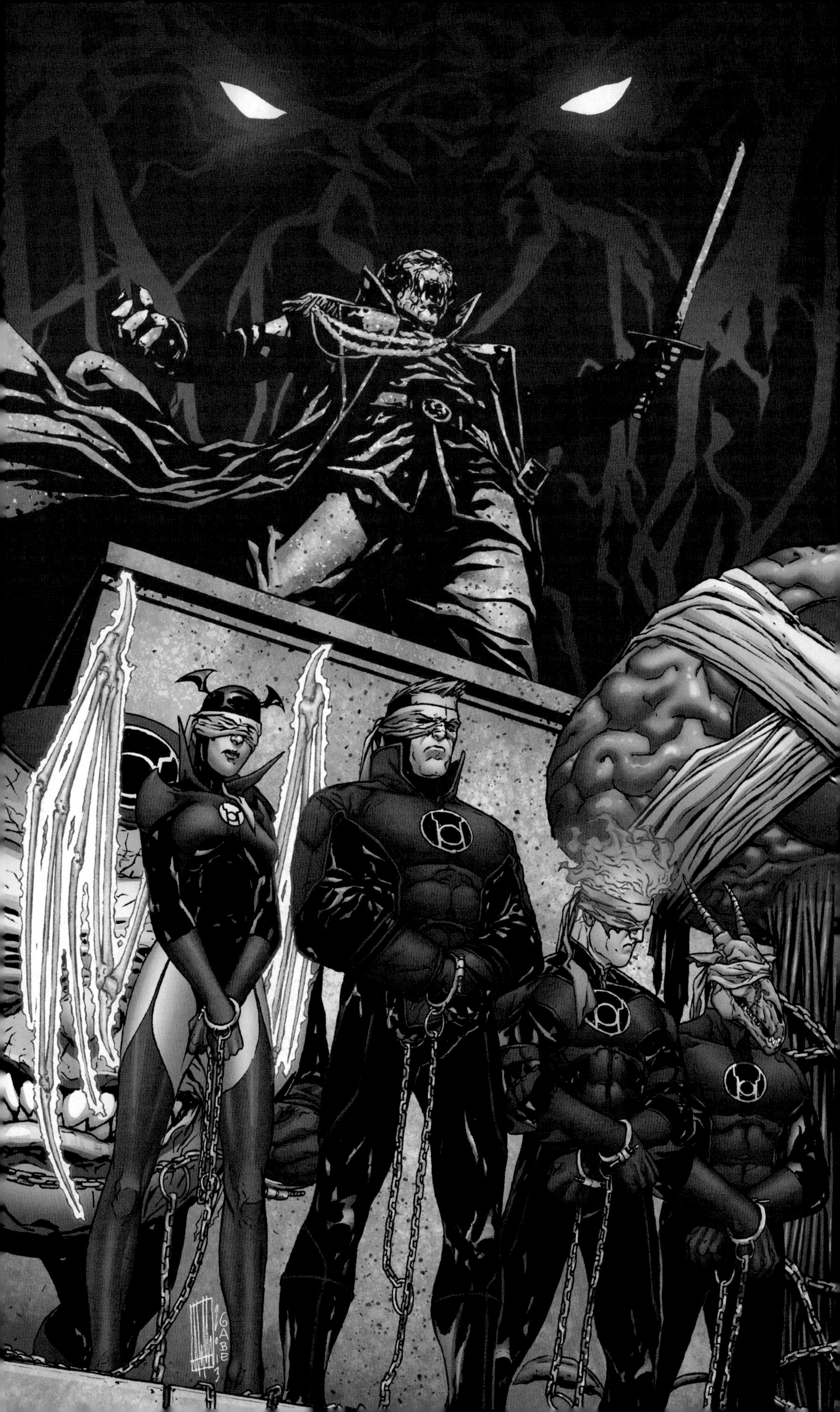

RED. DEAD.

CHARLES SOULE writer J. CALAFIORE artist GABE ELTAEB colorist cover art by ALESSANDRO VITTI with GABE ELTAEB

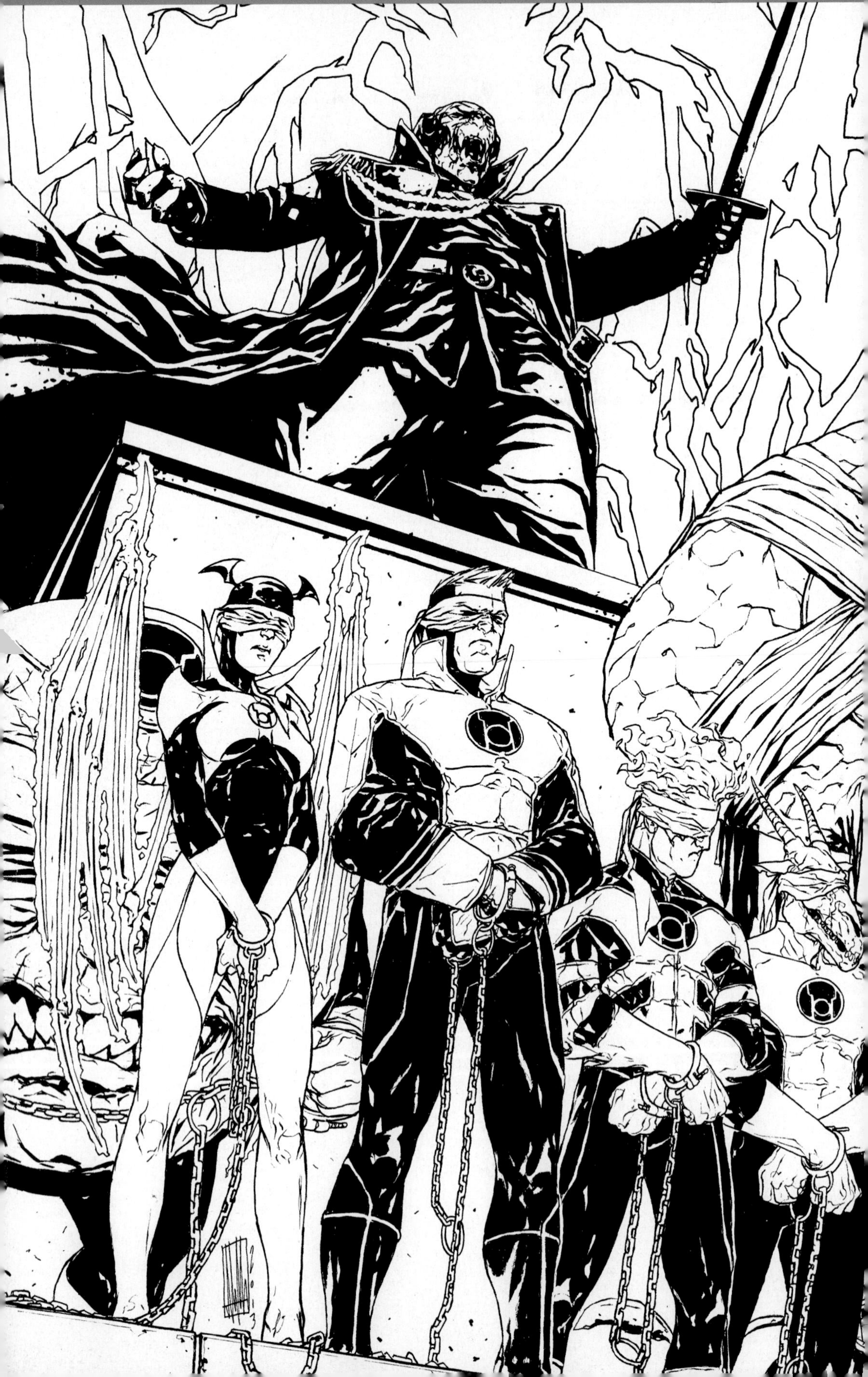

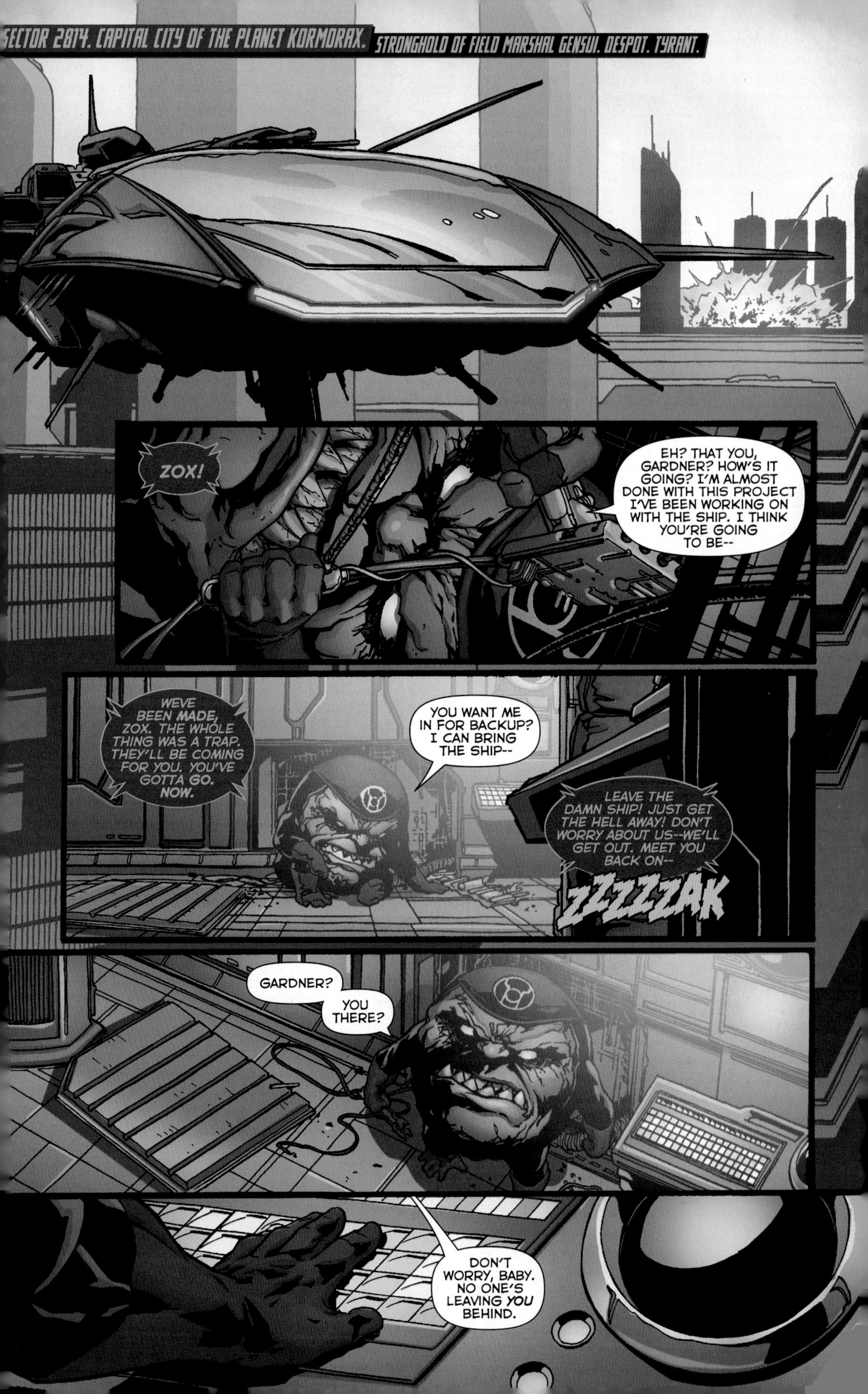
SECTOR 2814. CAPITAL CITY OF THE PLANET KORMORAX.
STRONGHOLD OF FIELD MARSHAL GENSUI. DESPOT. TYRANT.
ZOX!
EH? THAT YOU, GARDNER? HOW'S IT GOING? I'M ALMOST DONE WITH THIS PROJECT I'VE BEEN WORKING ON WITH THE SHIP. I THINK YOU'RE GOING TO BE--
WEVE BEEN MADE, ZOX. THE WHOLE THING WAS A TRAP. THEY'LL BE COMING FOR YOU. YOU'VE GOTTA GO. NOW.
YOU WANT ME IN FOR BACKUP? I CAN BRING THE SHIP--
LEAVE THE DAMN SHIP! JUST GET THE HELL AWAY! DON'T WORRY ABOUT US--WE'LL GET OUT. MEET YOU BACK ON--
ZZZZZAK
GARDNER?
YOU THERE?
DON'T WORRY, BABY. NO ONE'S LEAVING YOU BEHIND.

RANKORR! HOW LONG CAN YOU HOLD THAT SHIELD?

NOT LONG. THESE CONSTRUCTS PULL MORE POWER THAN--

ALL RIGHT. LISTEN.

THE GREENS, THE SAPPHIRES, ALL OF 'EM. THEY'RE TERRIFIED OF US. THEY THINK WE'RE MONSTERS. THAT WE CAN'T BE STOPPED.

WHAT I'M SAYING IS WE GOT A REPUTATION TO UPHOLD.

SO IF WE GOTTA GO OUT, LET'S GO OUT LIKE REDS.

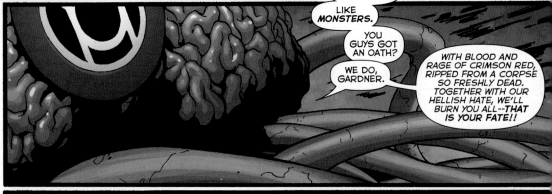

LIKE MONSTERS.

YOU GUYS GOT AN OATH?

WE DO, GARDNER.

WITH BLOOD AND RAGE OF CRIMSON RED, RIPPED FROM A CORPSE SO FRESHLY DEAD. TOGETHER WITH OUR HELLISH HATE, WE'LL BURN YOU ALL--THAT IS YOUR FATE!!

THAT'S THE RED OATH, RATCHET? THAT'S THE LEAST INSPIRING THING I'VE EVER HEARD.

LORD ATROCITUS WROTE IT.

I BET I GOT A BETTER ONE.

WE'RE RED.

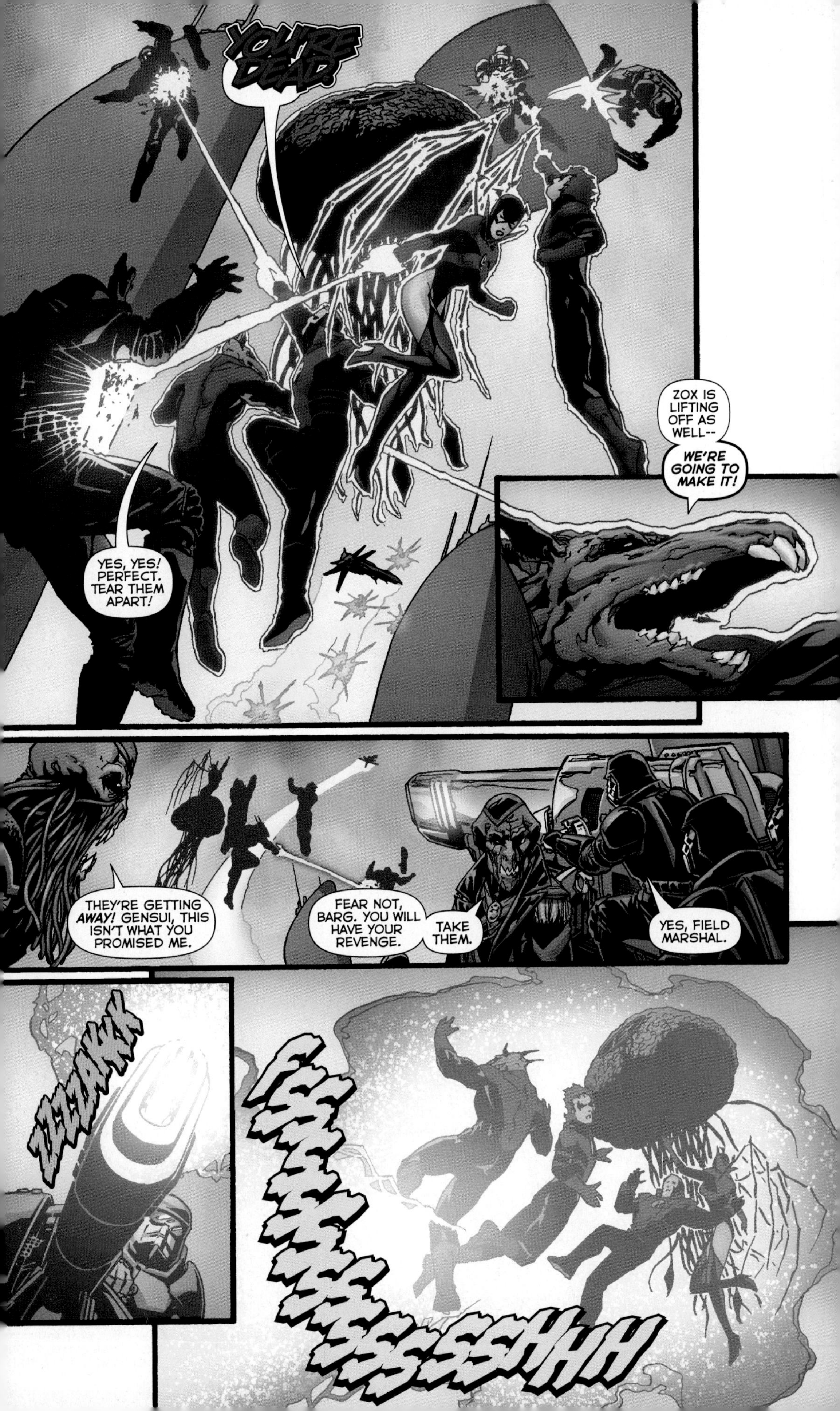
YOU'RE DEAD.
ZOX IS LIFTING OFF AS WELL--
WE'RE GOING TO MAKE IT!
YES, YES! PERFECT. TEAR THEM APART!
THEY'RE GETTING AWAY! GENSUI, THIS ISN'T WHAT YOU PROMISED ME.
FEAR NOT, BARG. YOU WILL HAVE YOUR REVENGE.
TAKE THEM.
YES, FIELD MARSHAL.
ZZZOWKK
FSSHHHHHSSSSSSHHH

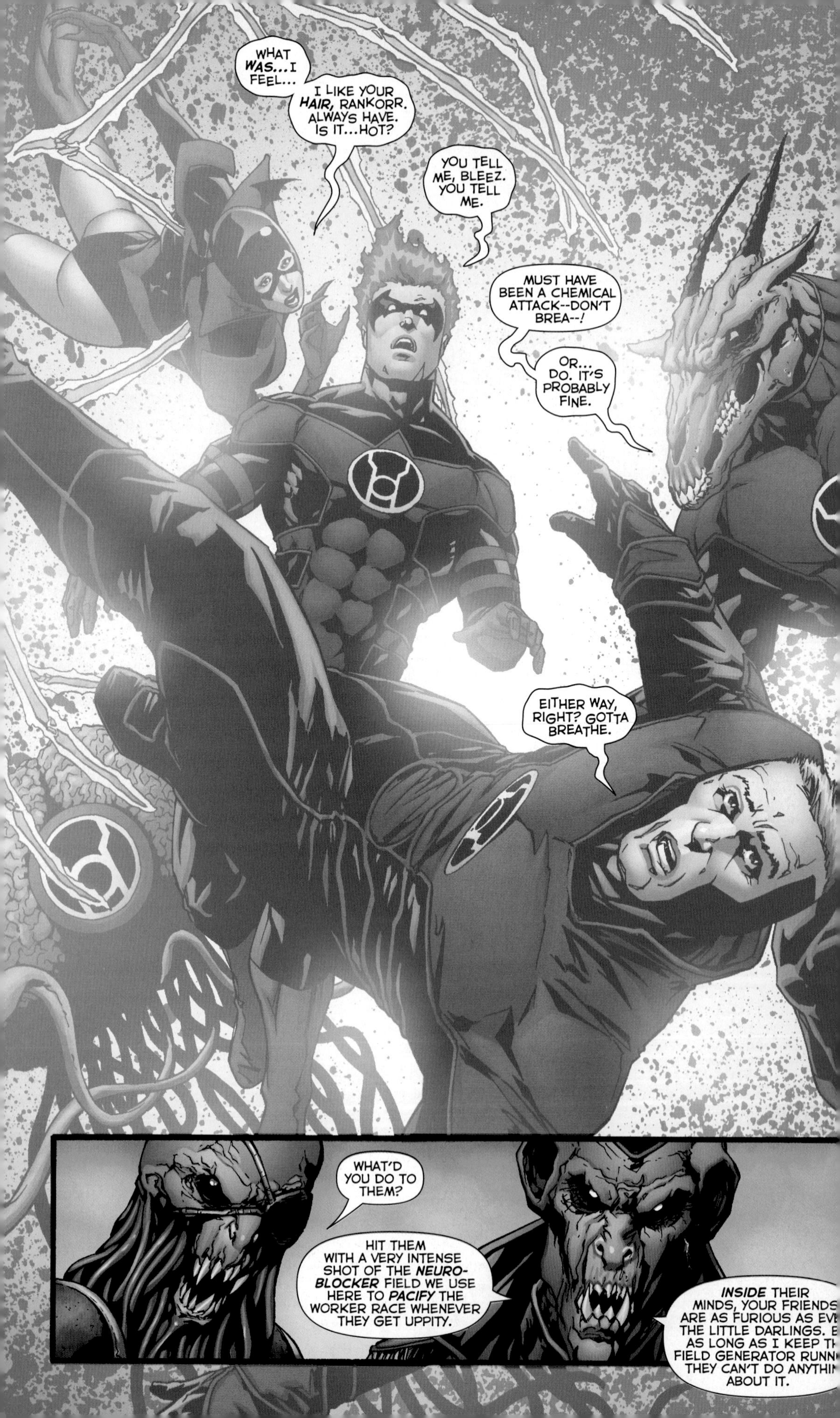
WHAT WAS...I FEEL...
I LIKE YOUR HAIR, RANKORR. ALWAYS HAVE. IS IT...HOT?
YOU TELL ME, BLEEZ. YOU TELL ME.
MUST HAVE BEEN A CHEMICAL ATTACK--DON'T BREA--!
OR... DO. IT'S PROBABLY FINE.
EITHER WAY, RIGHT? GOTTA BREATHE.
WHAT'D YOU DO TO THEM?
HIT THEM WITH A VERY INTENSE SHOT OF THE NEURO-BLOCKER FIELD WE USE HERE TO PACIFY THE WORKER RACE WHENEVER THEY GET UPPITY.
INSIDE THEIR MINDS, YOUR FRIENDS ARE AS FURIOUS AS EVE THE LITTLE DARLINGS. B AS LONG AS I KEEP TH FIELD GENERATOR RUNN THEY CAN'T DO ANYTHIN ABOUT IT.

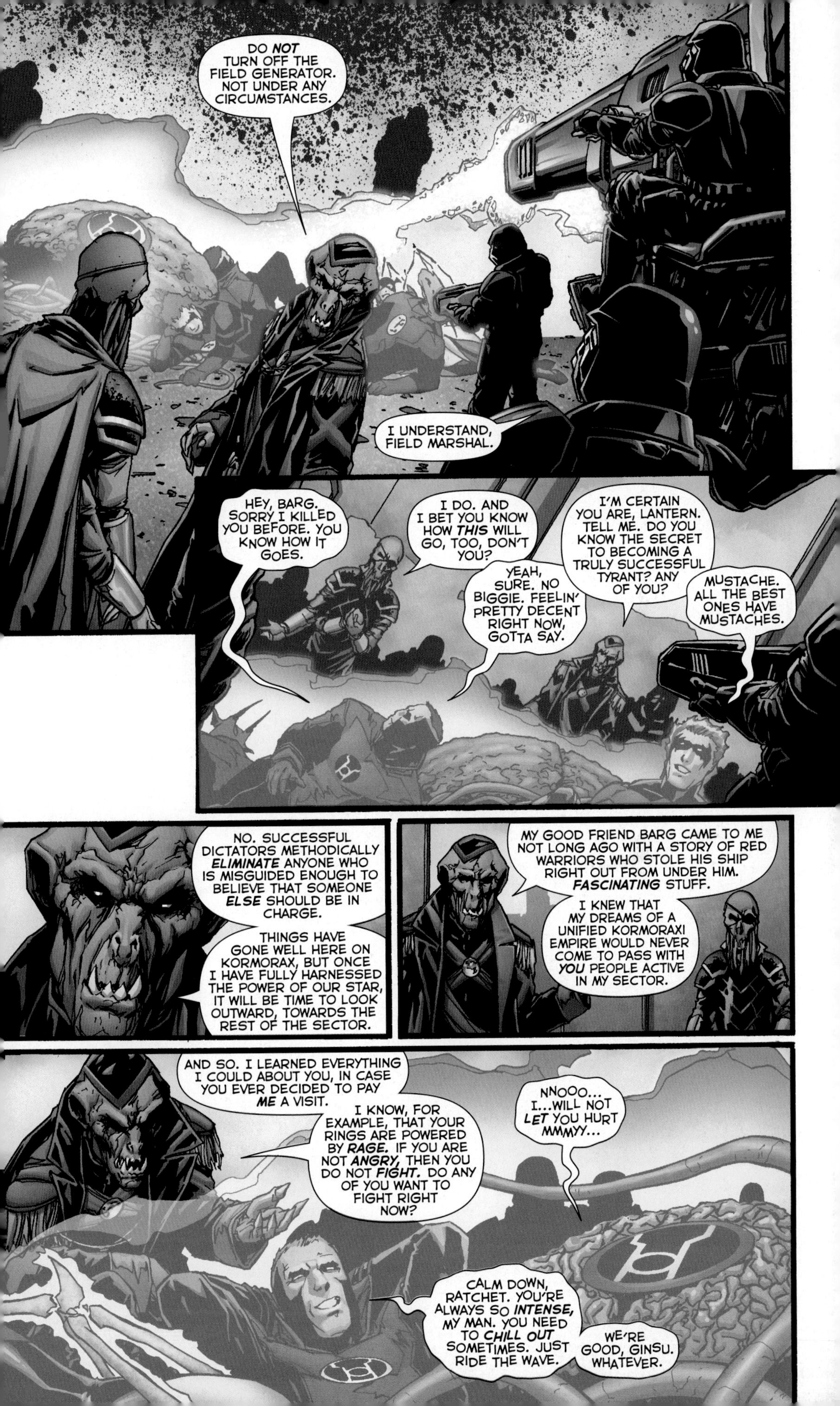
DO *NOT* TURN OFF THE FIELD GENERATOR. NOT UNDER ANY CIRCUMSTANCES.
I UNDERSTAND, FIELD MARSHAL.
HEY, BARG. SORRY I KILLED YOU BEFORE. YOU KNOW HOW IT GOES.
I DO. AND I BET YOU KNOW HOW *THIS* WILL GO, TOO, DON'T YOU?
YEAH, SURE. NO BIGGIE. FEELIN' PRETTY DECENT RIGHT NOW, GOTTA SAY.
I'M CERTAIN YOU ARE, LANTERN. TELL ME. DO YOU KNOW THE SECRET TO BECOMING A TRULY SUCCESSFUL TYRANT? ANY OF YOU?
MUSTACHE. ALL THE BEST ONES HAVE MUSTACHES.
NO. SUCCESSFUL DICTATORS METHODICALLY *ELIMINATE* ANYONE WHO IS MISGUIDED ENOUGH TO BELIEVE THAT SOMEONE *ELSE* SHOULD BE IN CHARGE.
THINGS HAVE GONE WELL HERE ON KORMORAX, BUT ONCE I HAVE FULLY HARNESSED THE POWER OF OUR STAR, IT WILL BE TIME TO LOOK OUTWARD, TOWARDS THE REST OF THE SECTOR.
MY GOOD FRIEND BARG CAME TO ME NOT LONG AGO WITH A STORY OF RED WARRIORS WHO STOLE HIS SHIP RIGHT OUT FROM UNDER HIM. *FASCINATING* STUFF.
I KNEW THAT MY DREAMS OF A UNIFIED KORMORAXI EMPIRE WOULD NEVER COME TO PASS WITH *YOU* PEOPLE ACTIVE IN MY SECTOR.
AND SO. I LEARNED EVERYTHING I COULD ABOUT YOU, IN CASE YOU EVER DECIDED TO PAY *ME* A VISIT.
I KNOW, FOR EXAMPLE, THAT YOUR RINGS ARE POWERED BY *RAGE.* IF YOU ARE NOT *ANGRY,* THEN YOU DO NOT *FIGHT.* DO ANY OF YOU WANT TO FIGHT RIGHT NOW?
NNOOO... I...WILL NOT *LET* YOU HURT MMMYY...
CALM DOWN, RATCHET. YOU'RE ALWAYS SO *INTENSE,* MY MAN. YOU NEED TO *CHILL OUT* SOMETIMES. JUST RIDE THE WAVE.
WE'RE GOOD, GINSU. WHATEVER.

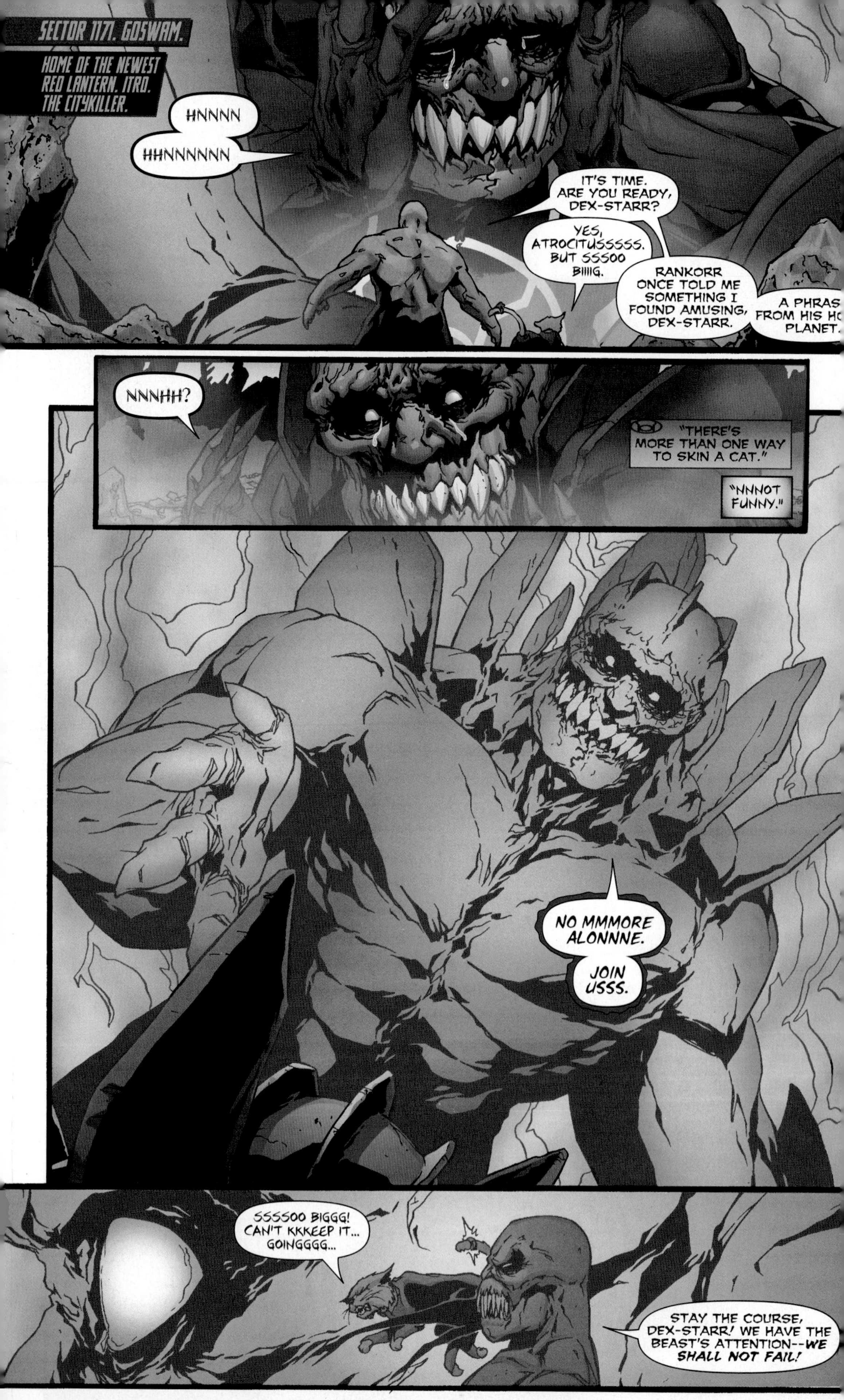
SECTOR 1171. GOSWAM.
HOME OF THE NEWEST RED LANTERN. ITRO. THE CITYKILLER.
HNNNN
HHNNNNNN
IT'S TIME. ARE YOU READY, DEX-STARR?
YES, ATROCITUSSSSS. BUT SSSOO BIIIIG.
RANKORR ONCE TOLD ME SOMETHING I FOUND AMUSING, DEX-STARR.
A PHRAS FROM HIS H PLANET.
NNNHH?
"THERE'S MORE THAN ONE WAY TO SKIN A CAT."
"NNNOT FUNNY."
NO MMMORE ALONNNE.
JOIN USSS.
SSSSOO BIGGG! CAN'T KKKEEP IT... GOINGGGG...
STAY THE COURSE, DEX-STARR! WE HAVE THE BEAST'S ATTENTION--WE SHALL NOT FAIL!

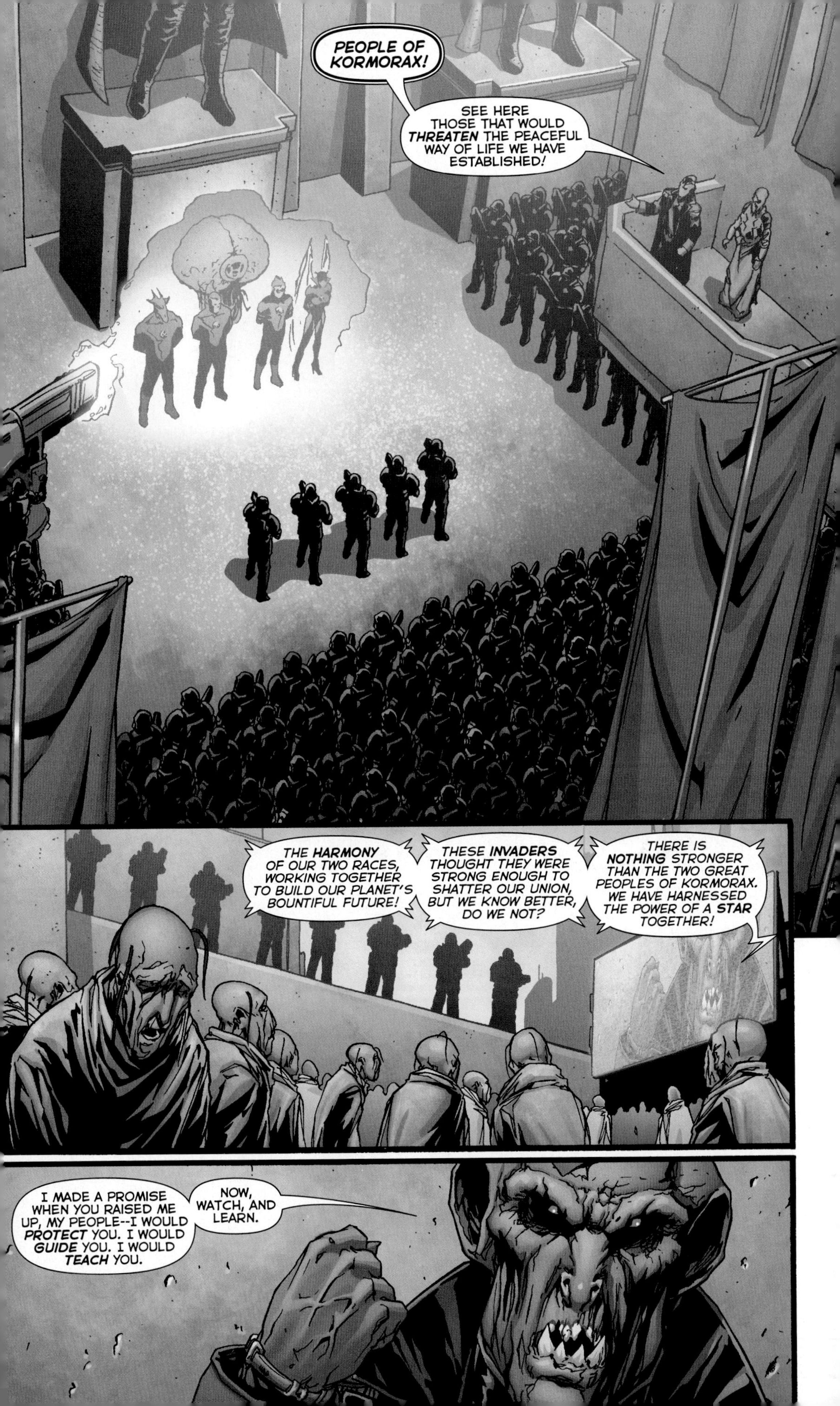
PEOPLE OF KORMORAX!
SEE HERE THOSE THAT WOULD THREATEN THE PEACEFUL WAY OF LIFE WE HAVE ESTABLISHED!
THE HARMONY OF OUR TWO RACES, WORKING TOGETHER TO BUILD OUR PLANET'S BOUNTIFUL FUTURE!
THESE INVADERS THOUGHT THEY WERE STRONG ENOUGH TO SHATTER OUR UNION, BUT WE KNOW BETTER, DO WE NOT?
THERE IS NOTHING STRONGER THAN THE TWO GREAT PEOPLES OF KORMORAX. WE HAVE HARNESSED THE POWER OF A STAR TOGETHER!
I MADE A PROMISE WHEN YOU RAISED ME UP, MY PEOPLE--I WOULD PROTECT YOU. I WOULD GUIDE YOU. I WOULD TEACH YOU.
NOW, WATCH, AND LEARN.

NO, NO-- ALL GONE WRONG. I SHOULD NOT HAVE BROUGHT US HERE. I THOUGHT...I WAS SELFISH--WANTED ONE LAST...

CALM YOUR JETS, CHIEF. NOBODY *MADE* US DO ANYTHING. WE'RE REDS. AND NOW WE'RE DEAD. THAT'S THE WAY IT GOES SOMETIMES.

I LIKE YOUR WINGS, BLEEZ. THEY LOOK LIKE...HANDS. BIG, GRABBY BONE HANDS. I WANT TO SHAKE YOUR BIG, GRABBY BONE HANDS.

THEY [...] LOOK L[...] BIG, GRA[...] BONE HA[...] THEY [...]

PREPARE YOURSELVES, INTERLOPERS, AND TAKE COMFORT IN THE FACT THAT YOU DO NOT DIE IN VAIN.

YOU WILL SERVE AS A VALUABLE LESSON TO THOSE WHO WOULD THREATEN MY RULE.

BUT WAIT. WASN'T THERE ANOTHER ONE OF YOU? OH YES. THE ONE IN THE *SHIP*.

PERHAPS YOU THINK HE'LL RETURN TO *RESCUE* YOU.

WE SHOULD *DO* SOMETHING ABOUT THAT. HMM. OH, OF COURSE. I KNOW *JUST* THE THING.

WAIT. WHAT ARE YOU GOING TO DO TO THE *KAALVAR?*

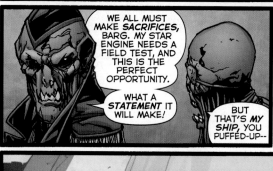

WE ALL MUST MAKE *SACRIFICES*, BARG. MY STAR ENGINE NEEDS A FIELD TEST, AND THIS IS THE PERFECT OPPORTUNITY.

WHAT A *STATEMENT* IT WILL MAKE!

BUT THAT'S *MY* SHIP, YOU PUFFED-UP--

EASY, FRIEND BARG. AFTER ALL, THERE'S PLENTY OF ROOM AGAINST THE WALL FOR *YOU* TOO.

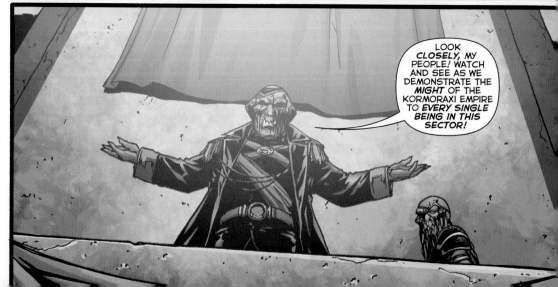

LOOK *CLOSELY*, MY PEOPLE! WATCH AND SEE AS WE DEMONSTRATE THE *MIGHT* OF THE KORMORAXI EMPIRE TO *EVERY SINGLE BEING* IN THIS SECTOR!

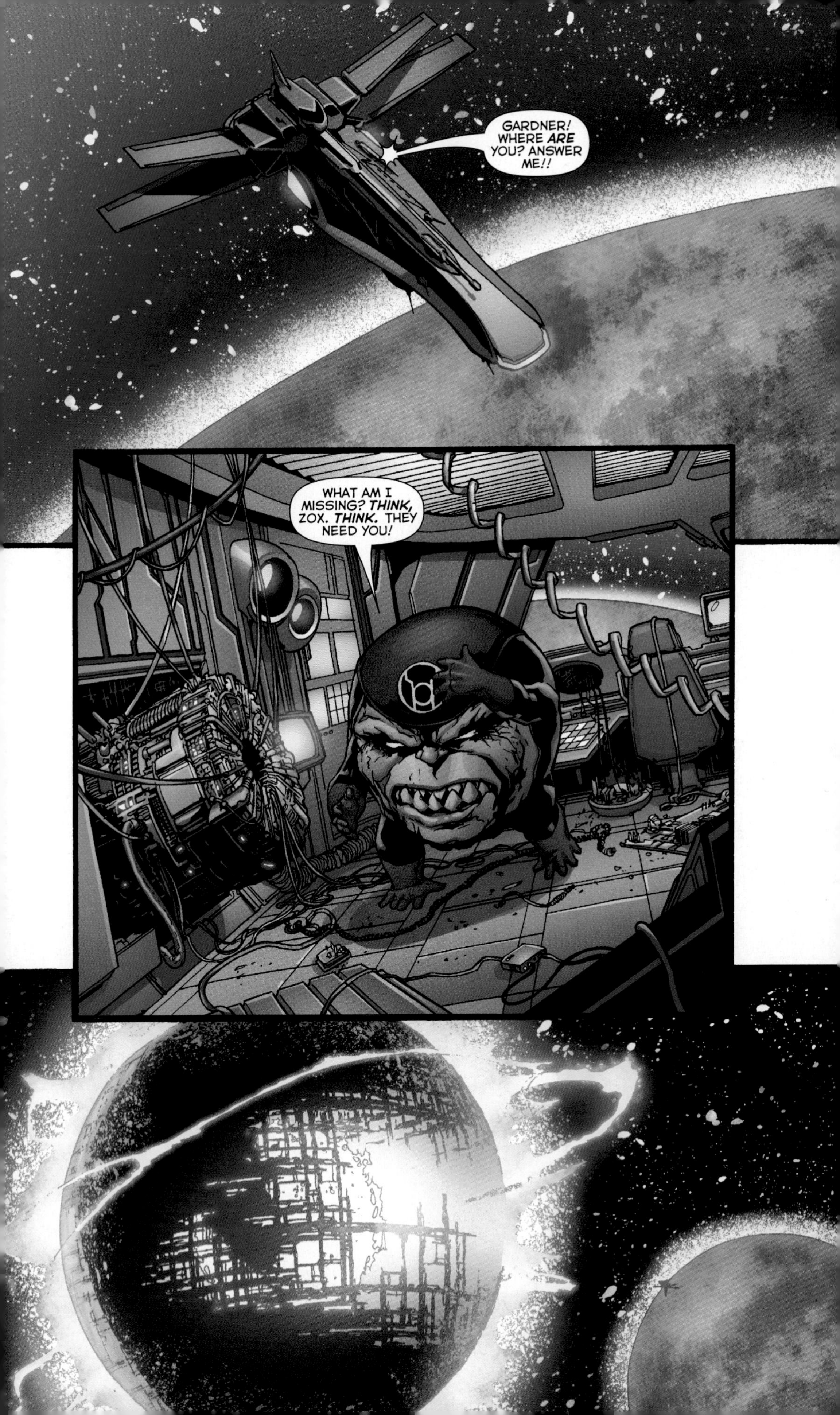
GARDNER! WHERE *ARE* YOU? ANSWER ME!!
WHAT AM I MISSING? *THINK,* ZOX. *THINK.* THEY NEED YOU!

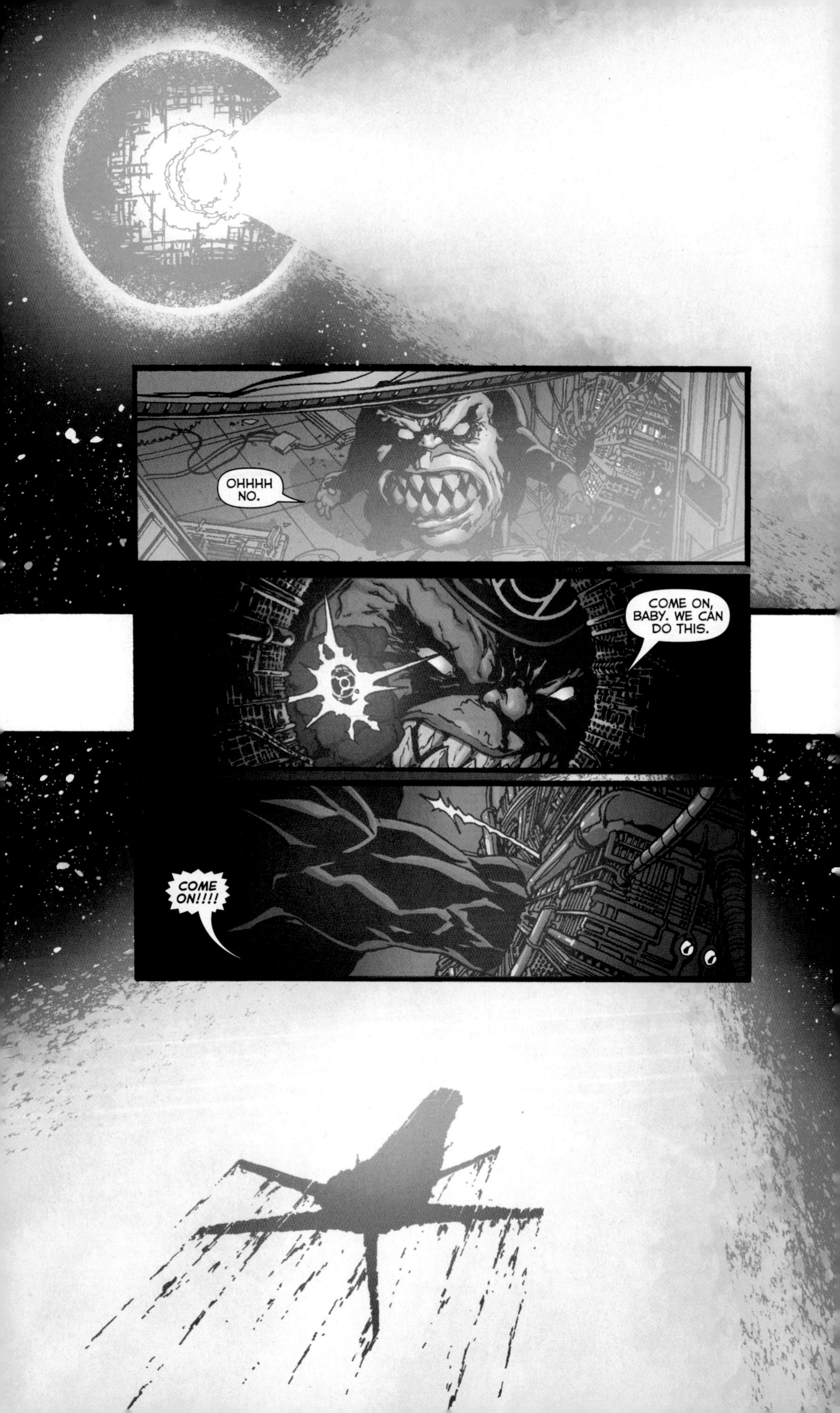
OHHHH NO.
COME ON, BABY. WE CAN DO THIS.
COME ON!!!!

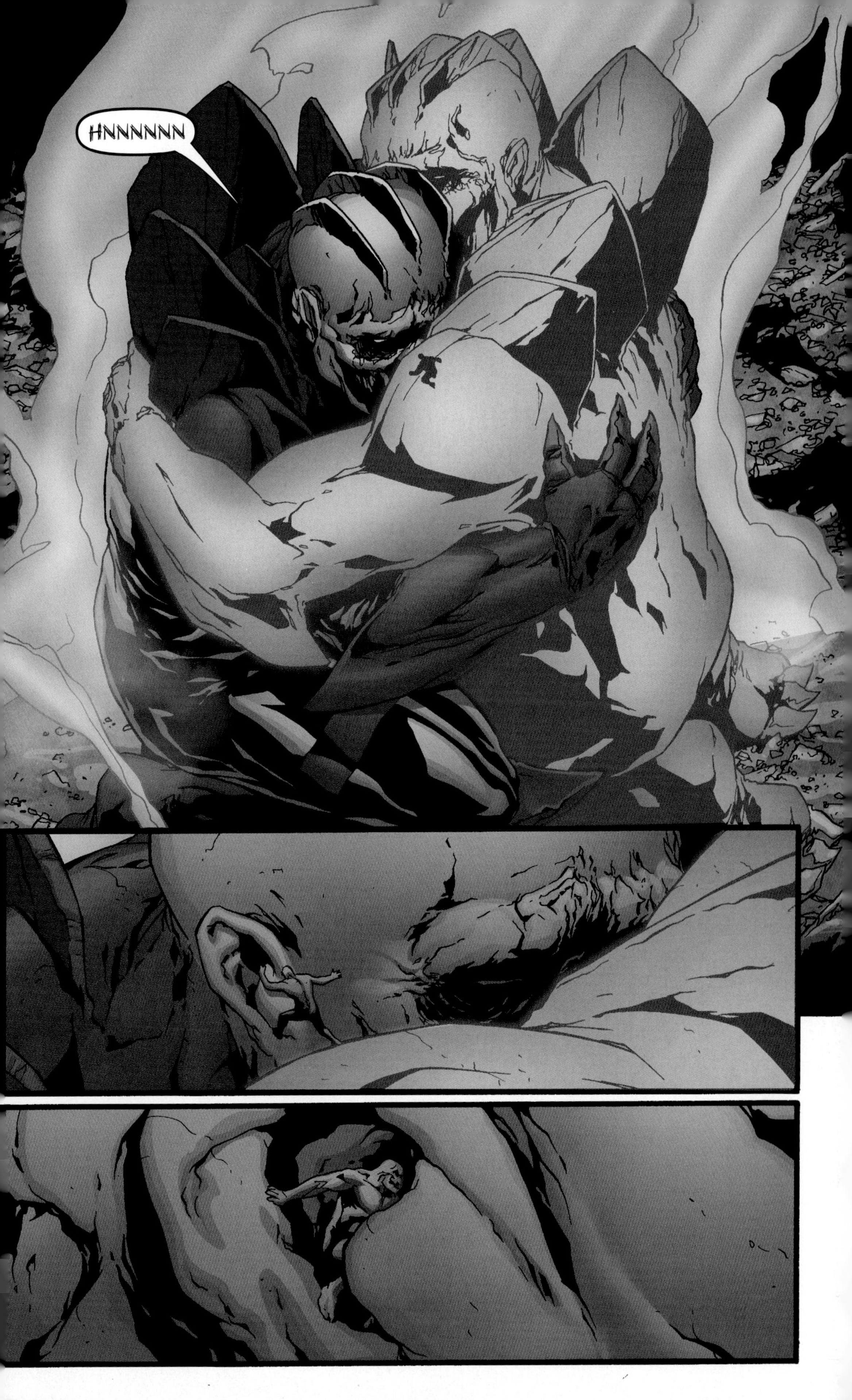
HNNNNNN

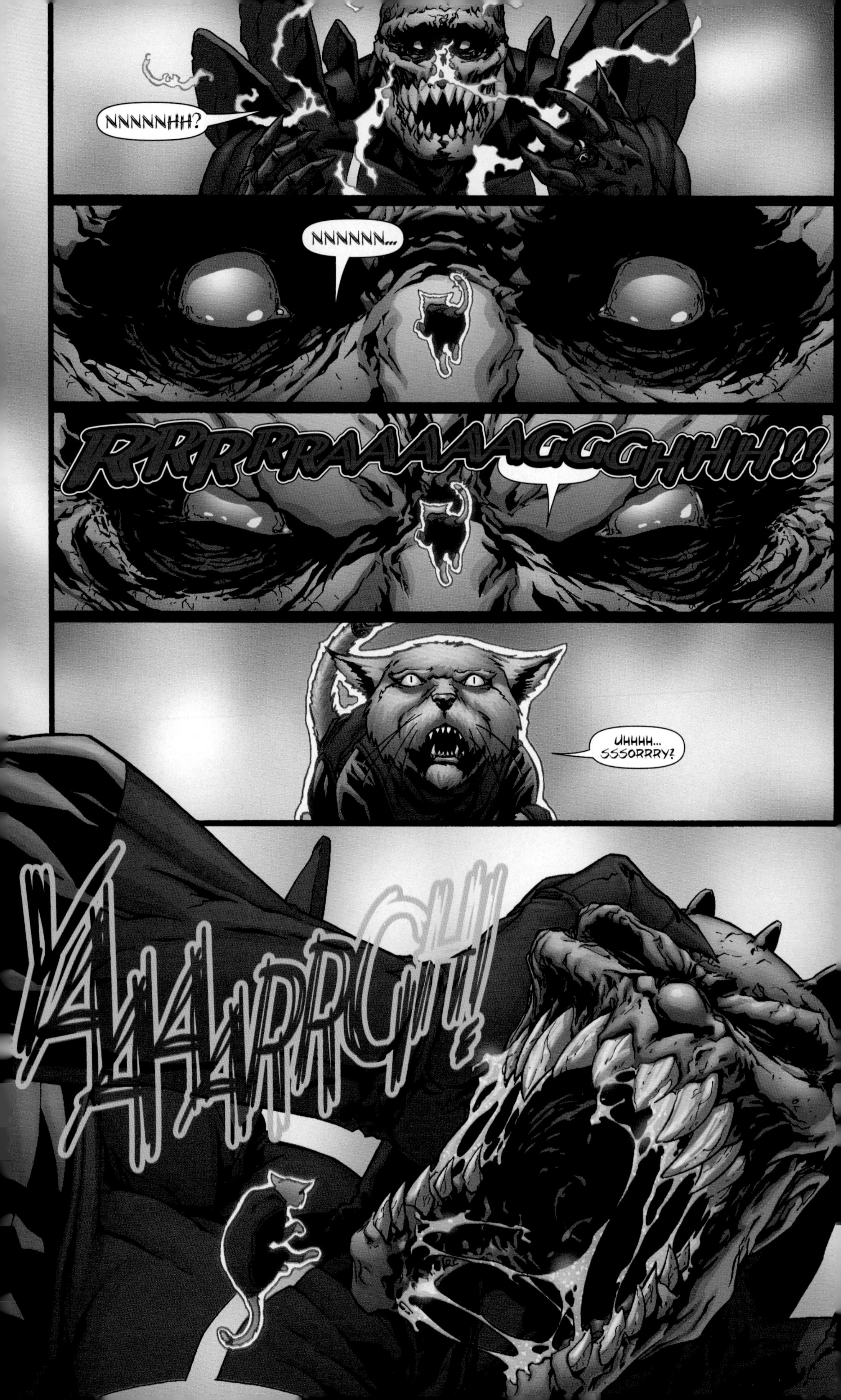
NNNNNHH?
NNNNNN...
RRRRRRAAAAAAGGGGHHHH!!
UHHHH... SSSORRRY?
YAARRGH!

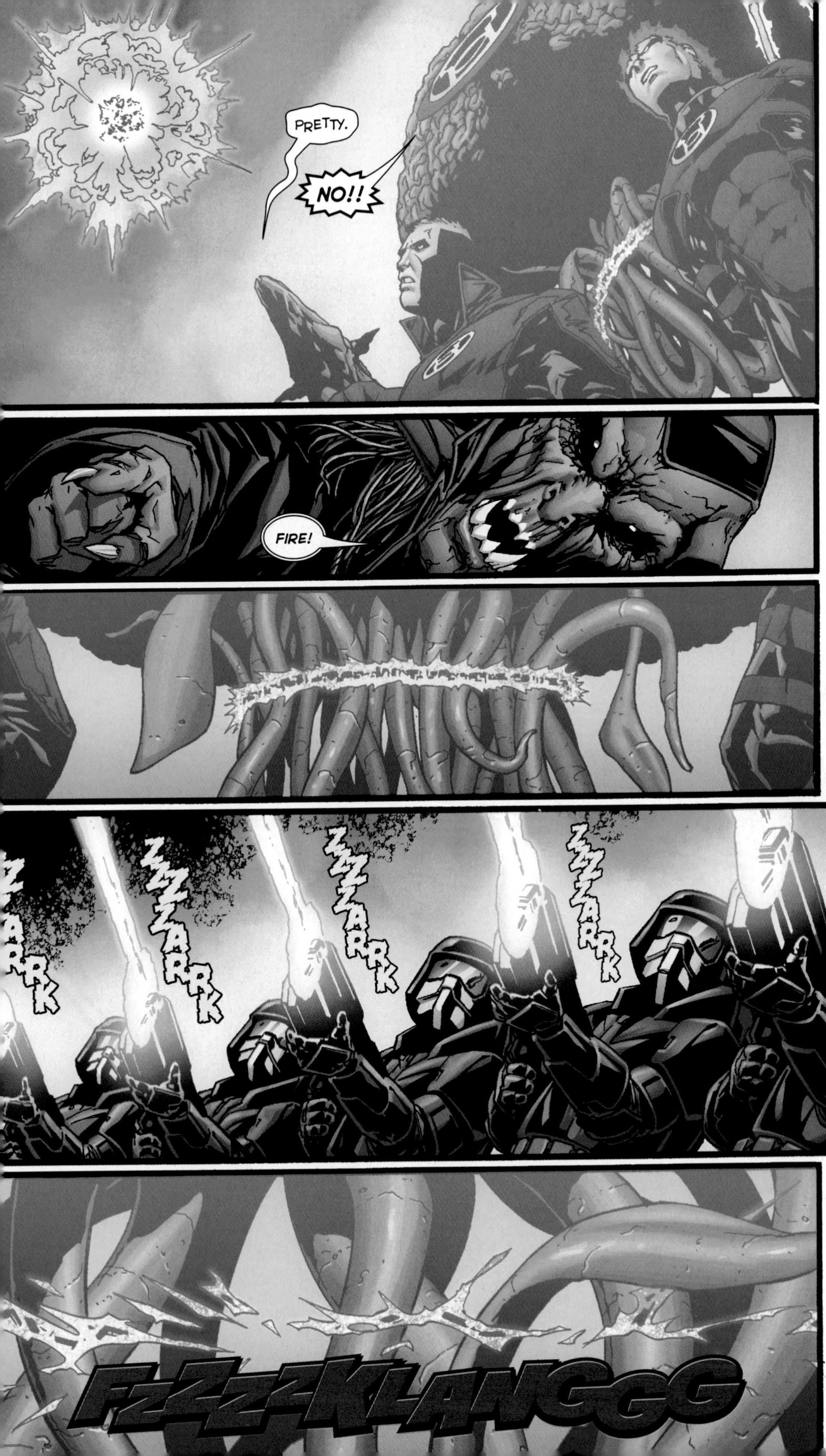
PRETTY.
NO!!
FIRE!
ZZZARRK
ZZZARRK
ZZZARRK
ZZZARRK
FZZZZKLANGGG

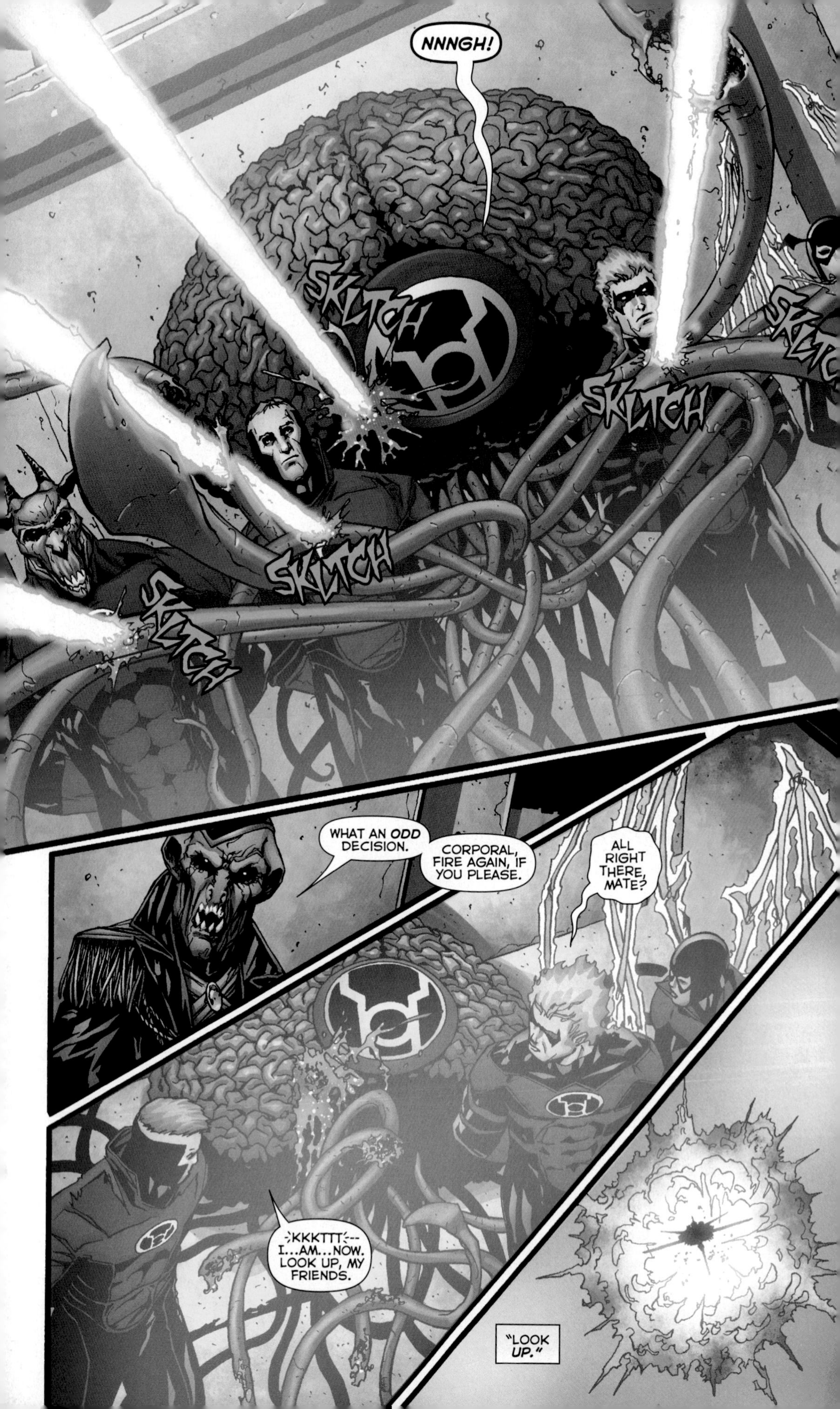
NNNGH!
SKLTCH
SKLTCH
SKLTCH
SKLTCH
SKLTCH
SKLTCH
WHAT AN ODD DECISION.
CORPORAL, FIRE AGAIN, IF YOU PLEASE.
ALL RIGHT THERE, MATE?
-KKKTTT--- I...AM...NOW. LOOK UP, MY FRIENDS.
"LOOK UP."

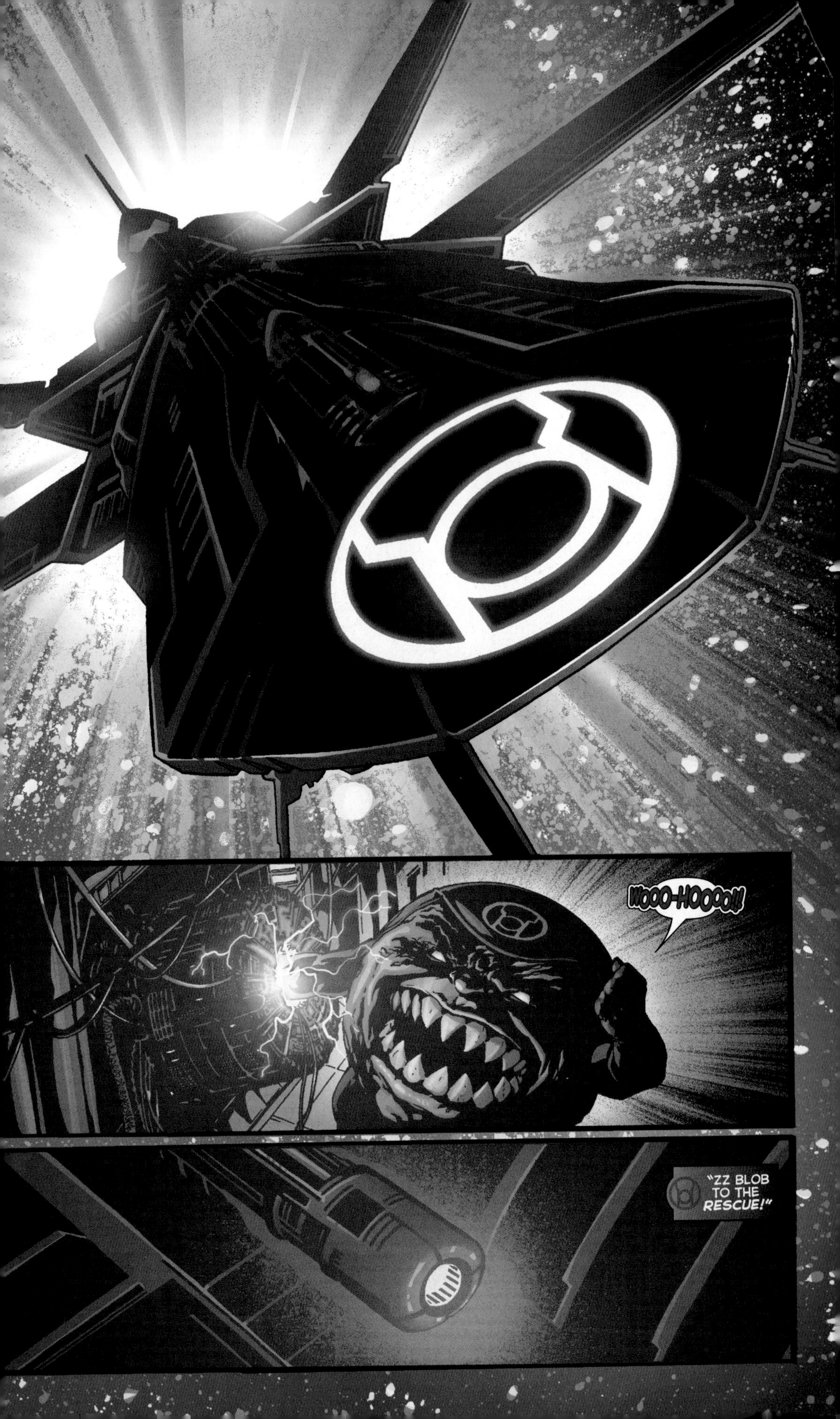
WOOO-HOOOO!!
"ZZ BLOB TO THE RESCUE!"

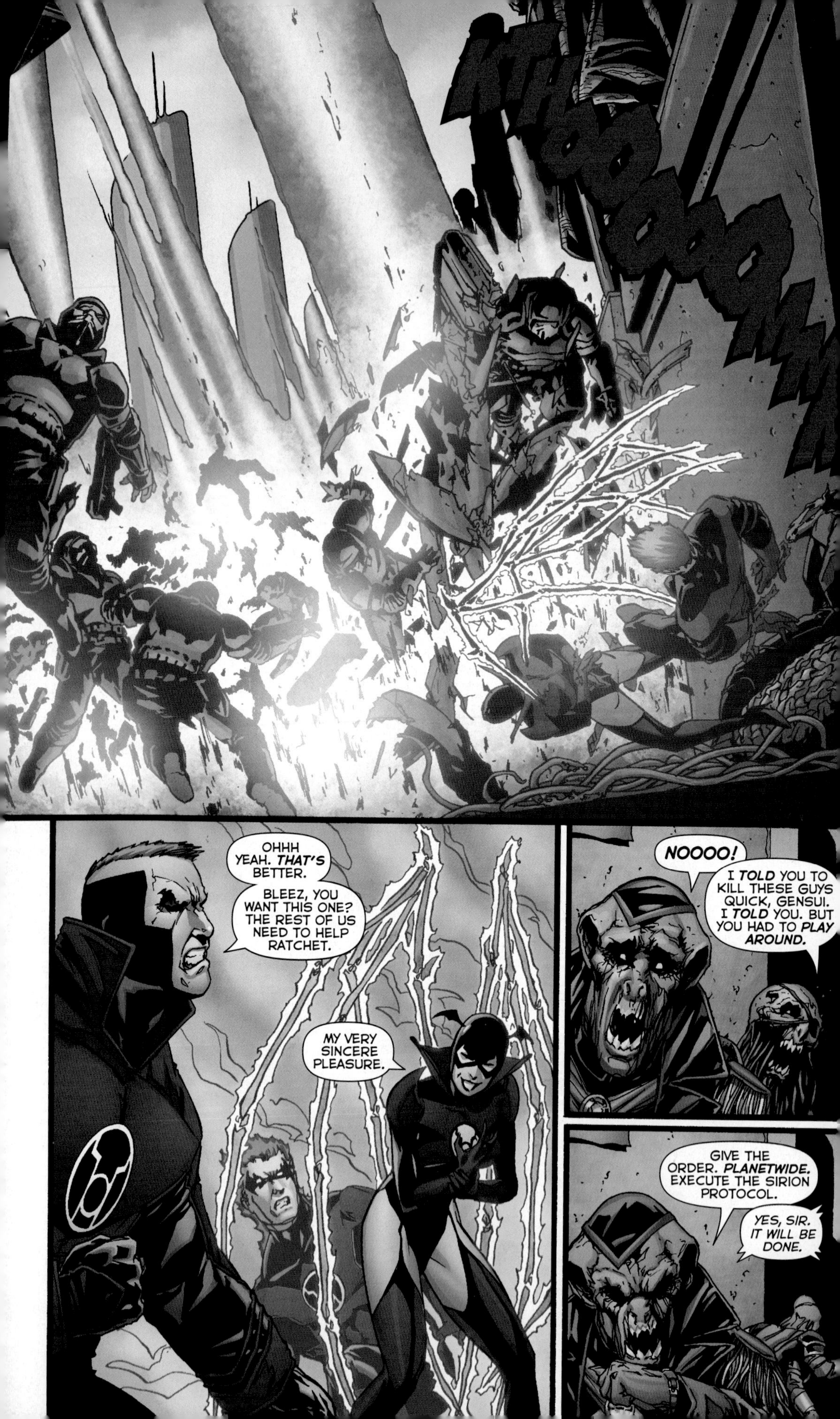
KTHOOOOOOMM
OHHH YEAH. THAT'S BETTER.
BLEEZ, YOU WANT THIS ONE? THE REST OF US NEED TO HELP RATCHET.
MY VERY SINCERE PLEASURE.
NOOOO!
I TOLD YOU TO KILL THESE GUYS QUICK, GENSUI. I TOLD YOU. BUT YOU HAD TO PLAY AROUND.
GIVE THE ORDER. PLANETWIDE. EXECUTE THE SIRION PROTOCOL.
YES, SIR. IT WILL BE DONE.

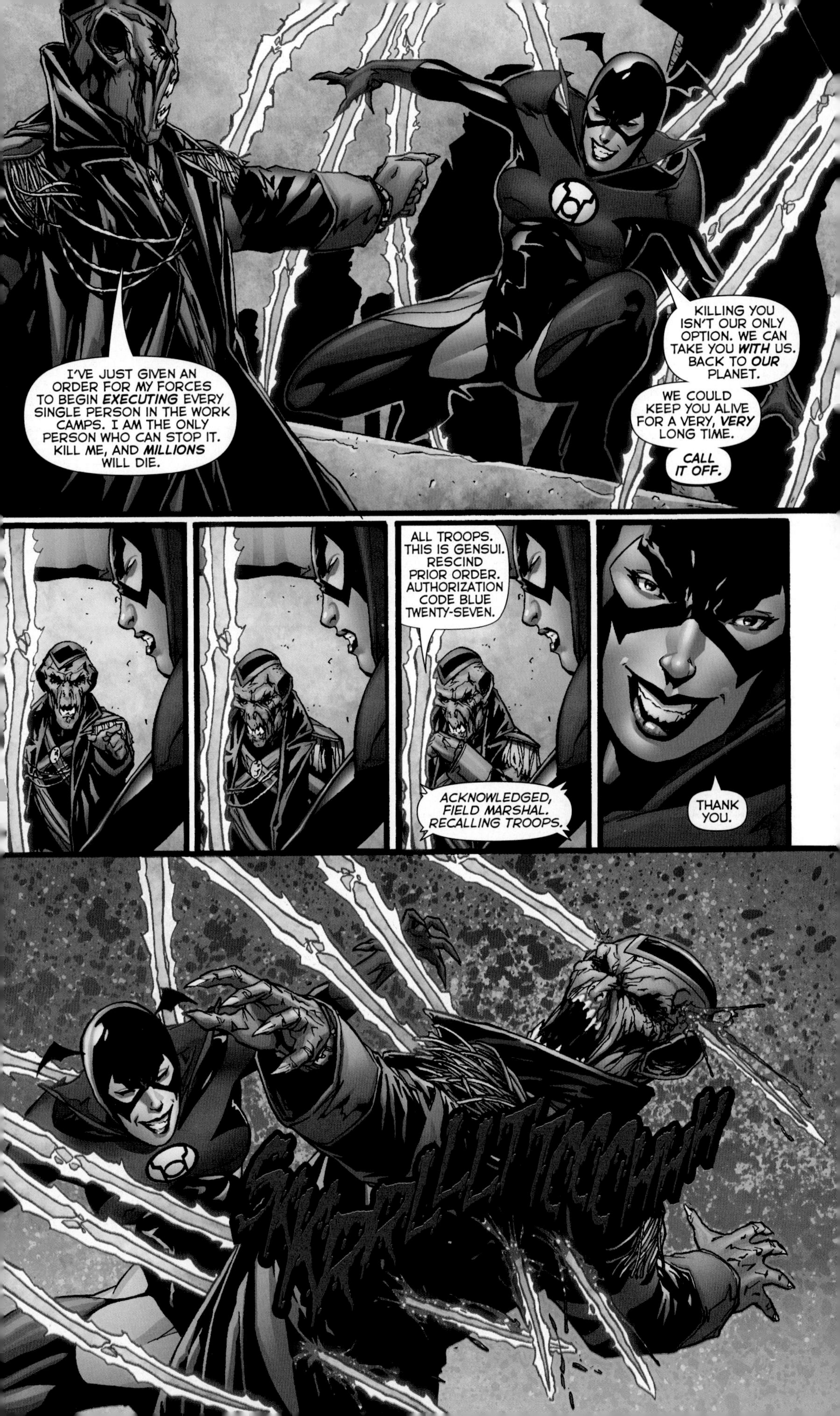

I'VE JUST GIVEN AN ORDER FOR MY FORCES TO BEGIN **EXECUTING** EVERY SINGLE PERSON IN THE WORK CAMPS. I AM THE ONLY PERSON WHO CAN STOP IT. KILL ME, AND **MILLIONS** WILL DIE.
KILLING YOU ISN'T OUR ONLY OPTION. WE CAN TAKE YOU **WITH** US. BACK TO **OUR** PLANET.
WE COULD KEEP YOU ALIVE FOR A VERY, **VERY** LONG TIME.
CALL IT OFF.
ALL TROOPS. THIS IS GENSUI. RESCIND PRIOR ORDER. AUTHORIZATION CODE BLUE TWENTY-SEVEN.
ACKNOWLEDGED, FIELD MARSHAL. RECALLING TROOPS.
THANK YOU.

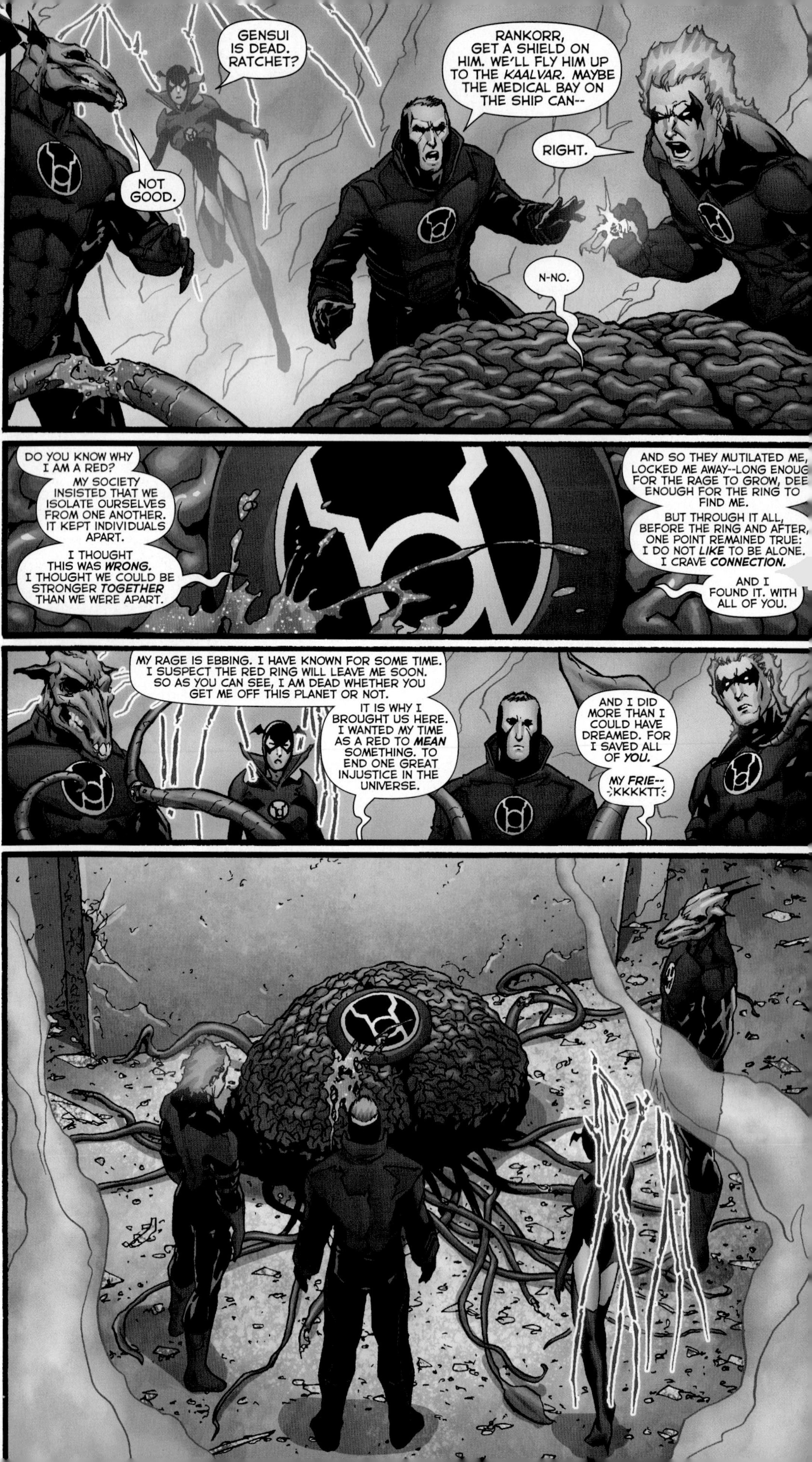
GENSUI IS DEAD. RATCHET?
NOT GOOD.
RANKORR, GET A SHIELD ON HIM. WE'LL FLY HIM UP TO THE KAALVAR. MAYBE THE MEDICAL BAY ON THE SHIP CAN--
RIGHT.
N-NO.
DO YOU KNOW WHY I AM A RED?
MY SOCIETY INSISTED THAT WE ISOLATE OURSELVES FROM ONE ANOTHER. IT KEPT INDIVIDUALS APART.
I THOUGHT THIS WAS WRONG. I THOUGHT WE COULD BE STRONGER TOGETHER THAN WE WERE APART.
AND SO THEY MUTILATED ME, LOCKED ME AWAY--LONG ENOUG FOR THE RAGE TO GROW, DEE ENOUGH FOR THE RING TO FIND ME.
BUT THROUGH IT ALL, BEFORE THE RING AND AFTER, ONE POINT REMAINED TRUE: I DO NOT LIKE TO BE ALONE. I CRAVE CONNECTION.
AND I FOUND IT. WITH ALL OF YOU.
MY RAGE IS EBBING. I HAVE KNOWN FOR SOME TIME. I SUSPECT THE RED RING WILL LEAVE ME SOON. SO AS YOU CAN SEE, I AM DEAD WHETHER YOU GET ME OFF THIS PLANET OR NOT.
IT IS WHY I BROUGHT US HERE. I WANTED MY TIME AS A RED TO MEAN SOMETHING. TO END ONE GREAT INJUSTICE IN THE UNIVERSE.
AND I DID MORE THAN I COULD HAVE DREAMED. FOR I SAVED ALL OF YOU.
MY FRIE-- KKKKTT

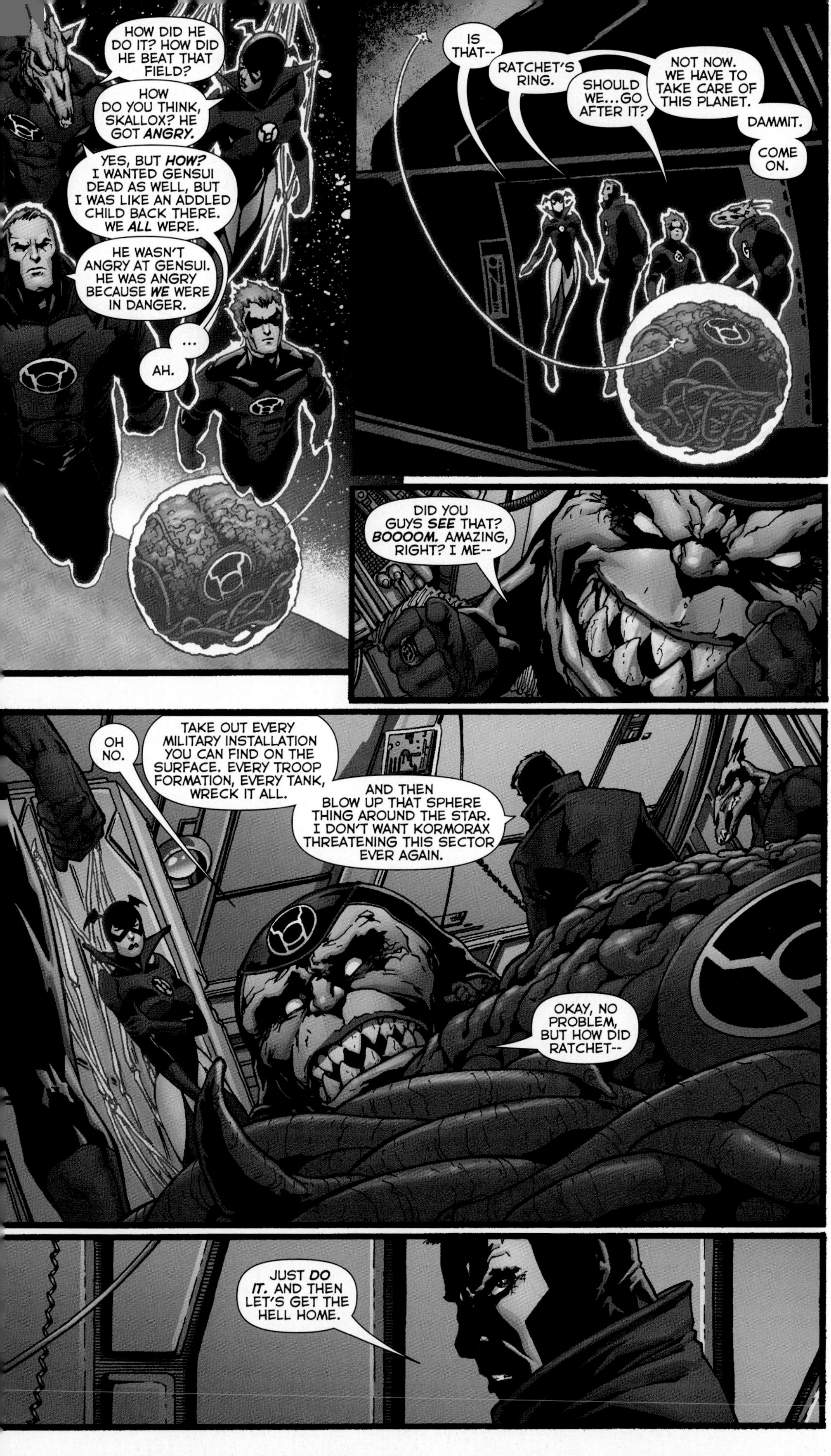

HOW DID HE DO IT? HOW DID HE BEAT THAT FIELD?
HOW DO YOU THINK, SKALLOX? HE GOT ANGRY.
YES, BUT HOW? I WANTED GENSUI DEAD AS WELL, BUT I WAS LIKE AN ADDLED CHILD BACK THERE. WE ALL WERE.
HE WASN'T ANGRY AT GENSUI. HE WAS ANGRY BECAUSE WE WERE IN DANGER.
...
AH.
IS THAT--
RATCHET'S RING.
SHOULD WE...GO AFTER IT?
NOT NOW. WE HAVE TO TAKE CARE OF THIS PLANET.
DAMMIT.
COME ON.
DID YOU GUYS SEE THAT? BOOOOM. AMAZING, RIGHT? I ME--
OH NO.
TAKE OUT EVERY MILITARY INSTALLATION YOU CAN FIND ON THE SURFACE. EVERY TROOP FORMATION, EVERY TANK, WRECK IT ALL.
AND THEN BLOW UP THAT SPHERE THING AROUND THE STAR. I DON'T WANT KORMORAX THREATENING THIS SECTOR EVER AGAIN.
OKAY, NO PROBLEM, BUT HOW DID RATCHET--
JUST DO IT. AND THEN LET'S GET THE HELL HOME.

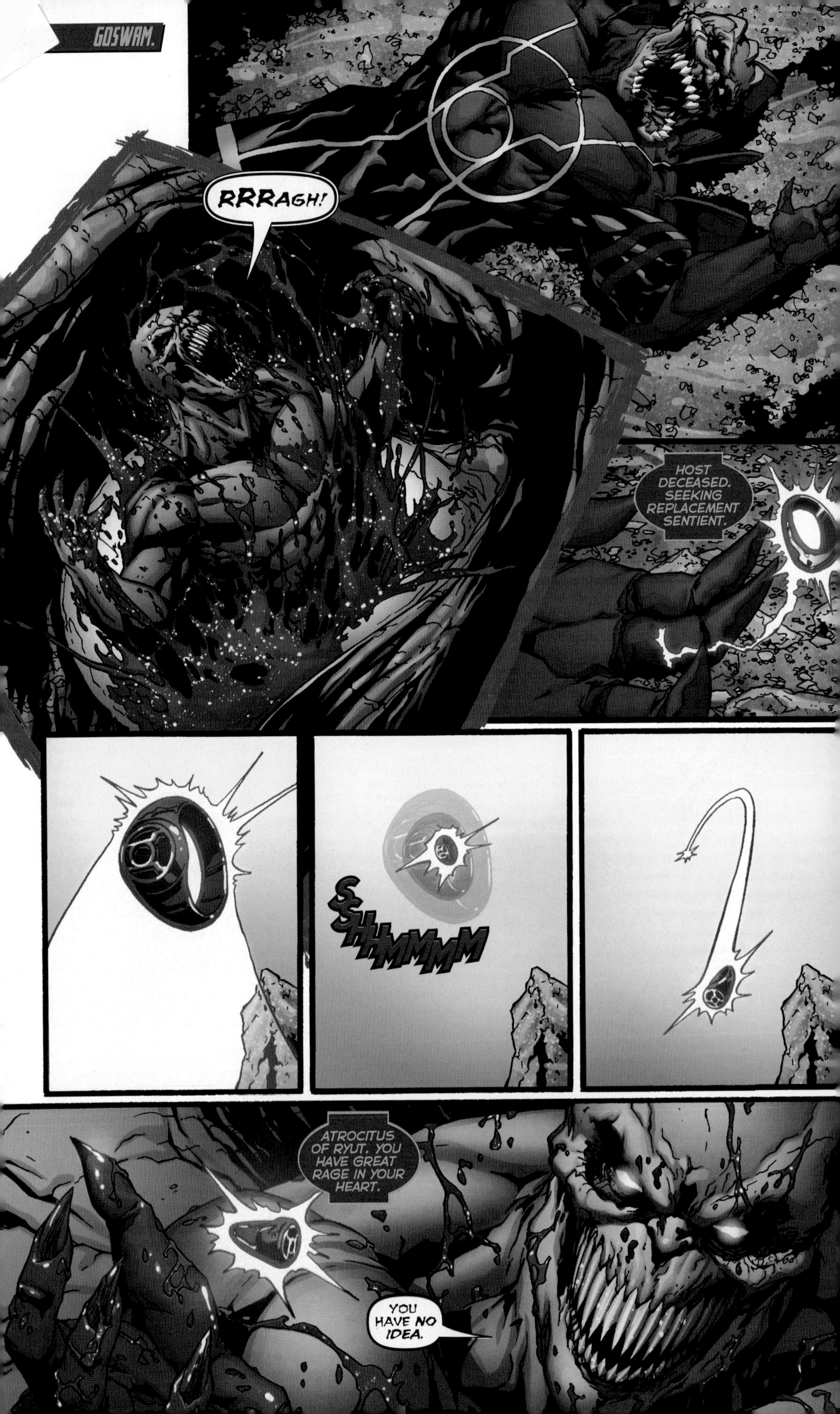
GOSWAM.
RRRAGH!
HOST DECEASED. SEEKING REPLACEMENT SENTIENT.
SSHHMMMMM
ATROCITUS OF RYUT. YOU HAVE GREAT RAGE IN YOUR HEART.
YOU HAVE NO IDEA.

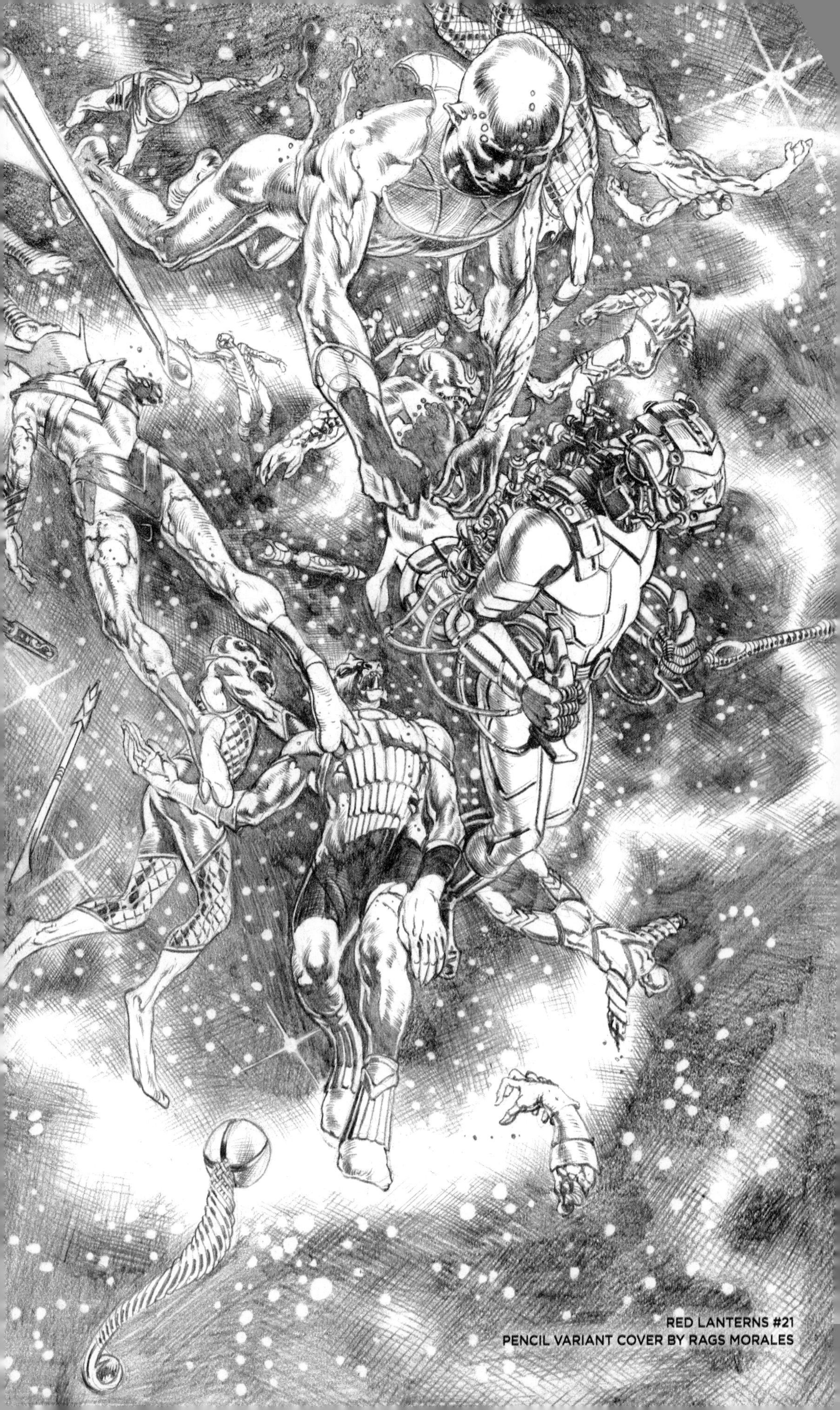

RED LANTERNS #21
PENCIL VARIANT COVER BY RAGS MORALES

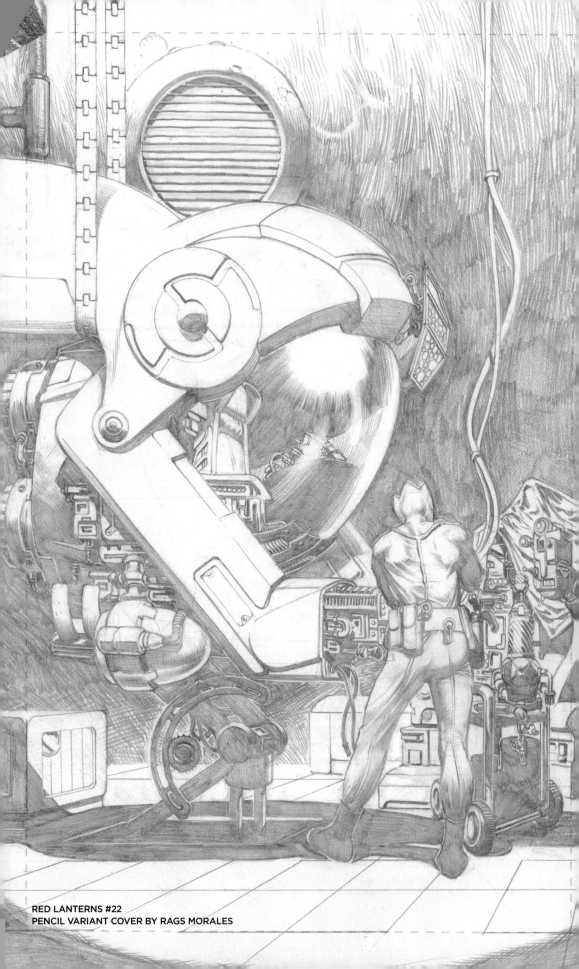

RED LANTERNS #22
PENCIL VARIANT COVER BY RAGS MORALES

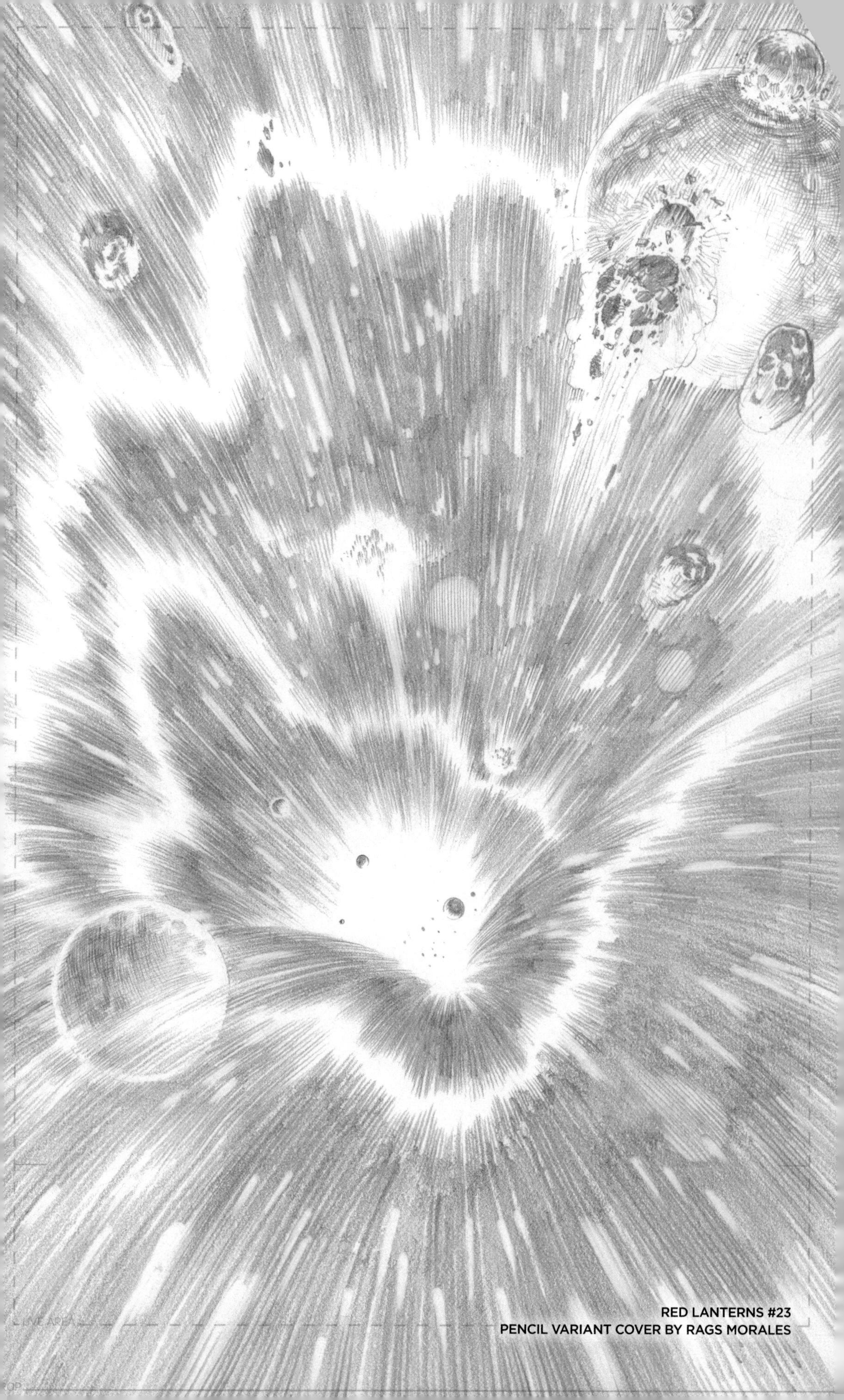

RED LANTERNS #23
PENCIL VARIANT COVER BY RAGS MORALES

RED LANTERNS
DESIGNS AND SKETCHES BY ALESSANDRO VITTI

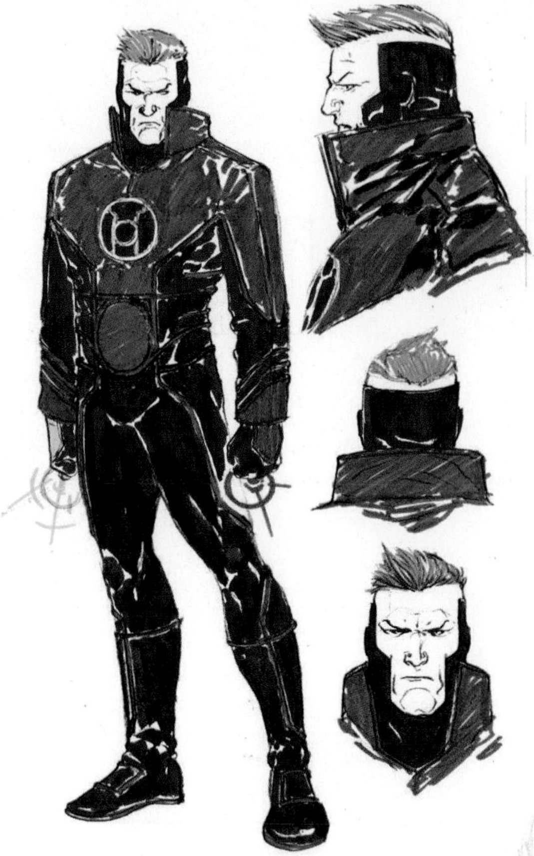

Note the presence of a green ring on these sketches — at one point in the development of the story, Guy was meant to be wearing both rings!

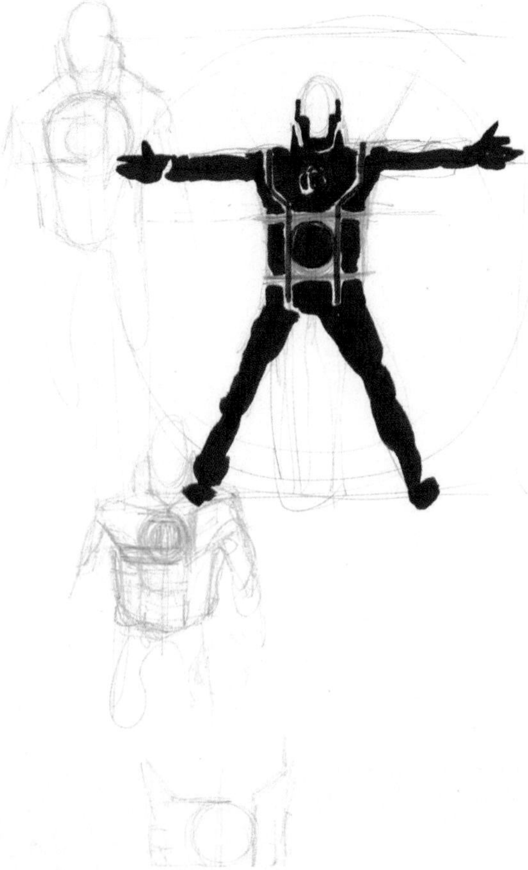

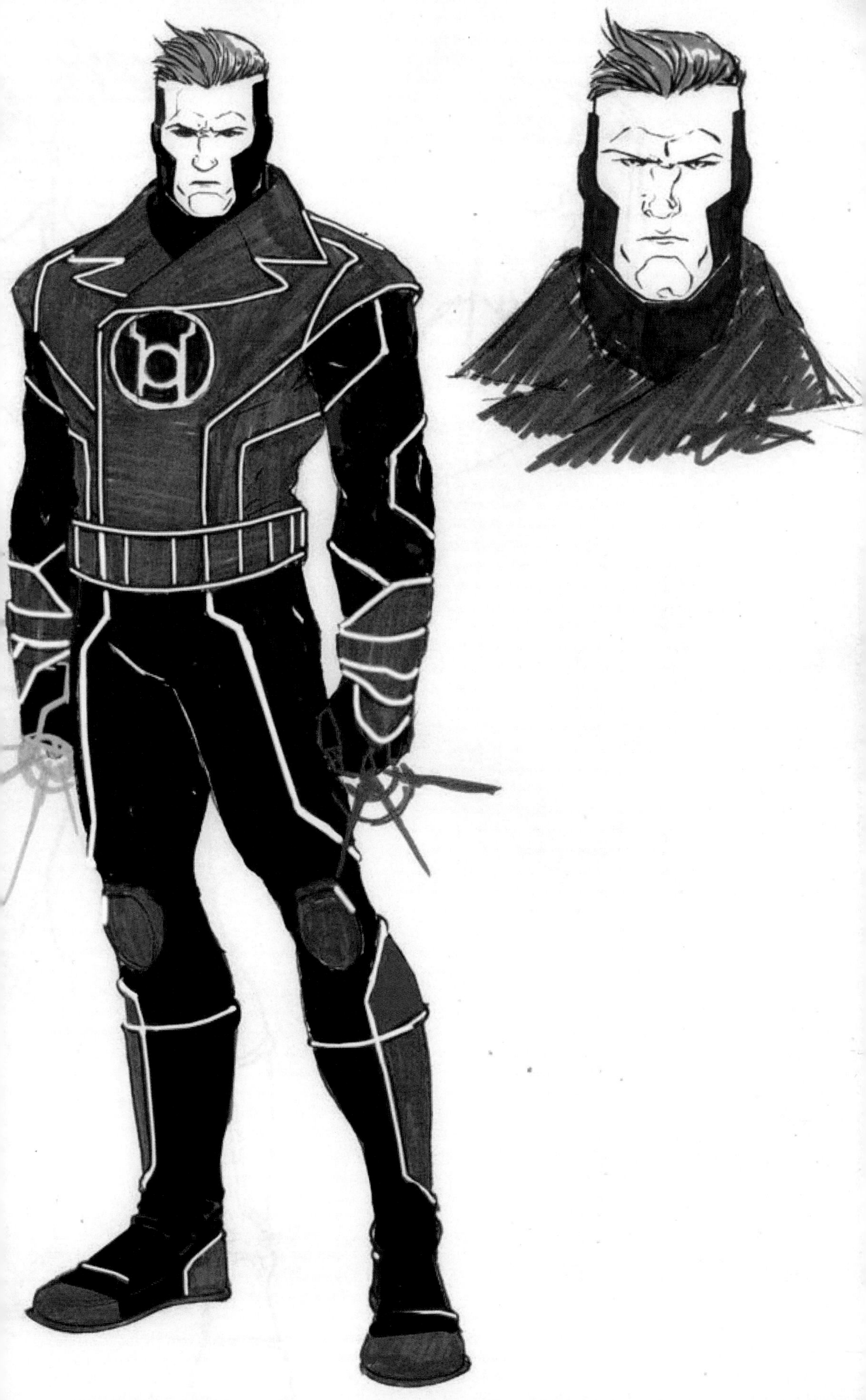

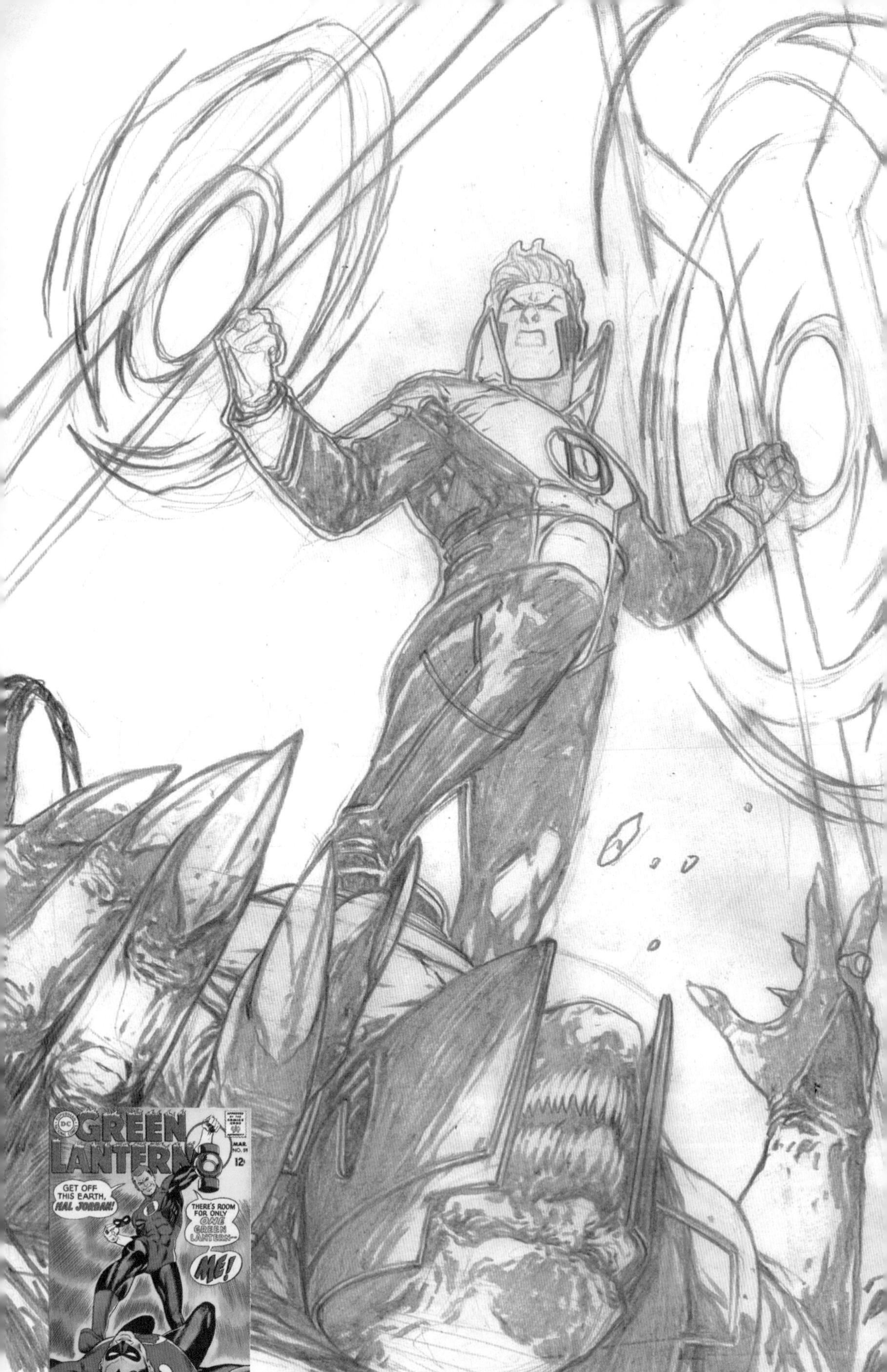

GREEN LANTERN
MAR. NO. 59
12¢
GET OFF THIS EARTH, HAL JORDAN!
THERE'S ROOM FOR ONLY ONE GREEN LANTERN—
ME!

Guy's pose on the cover of RED LANTERNS #21 intentionally mirrors the character's debut on the cover of GREEN LANTERN #59 by Gil Kane and Murphy Anderson in 1968.

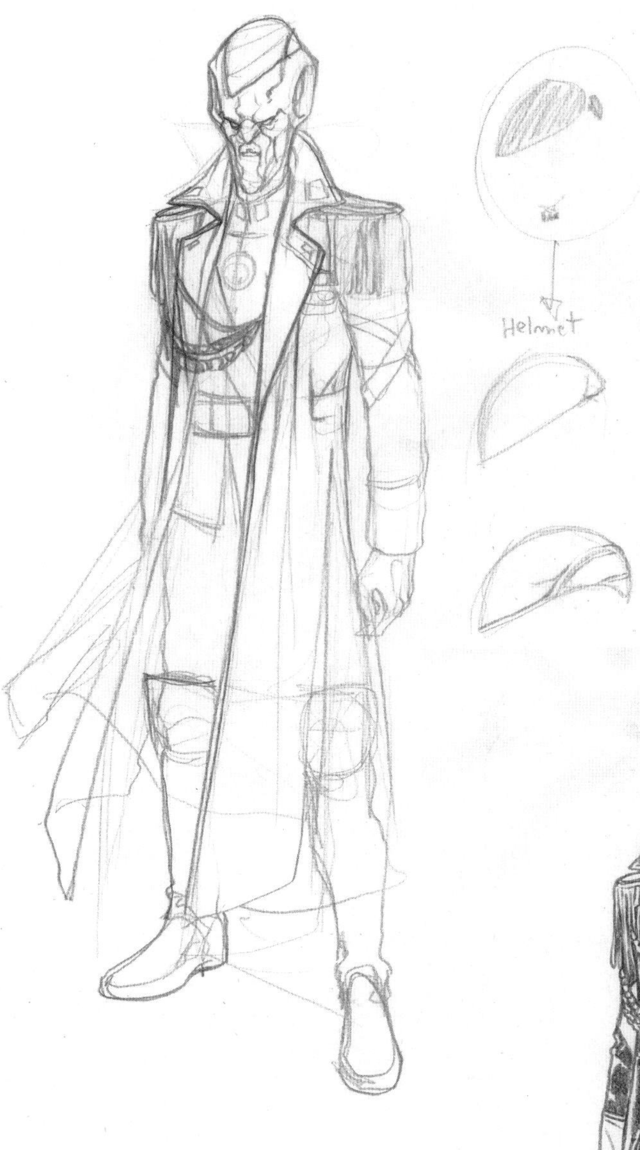
Helmet

Concept sketches for Field Marshal Gensui

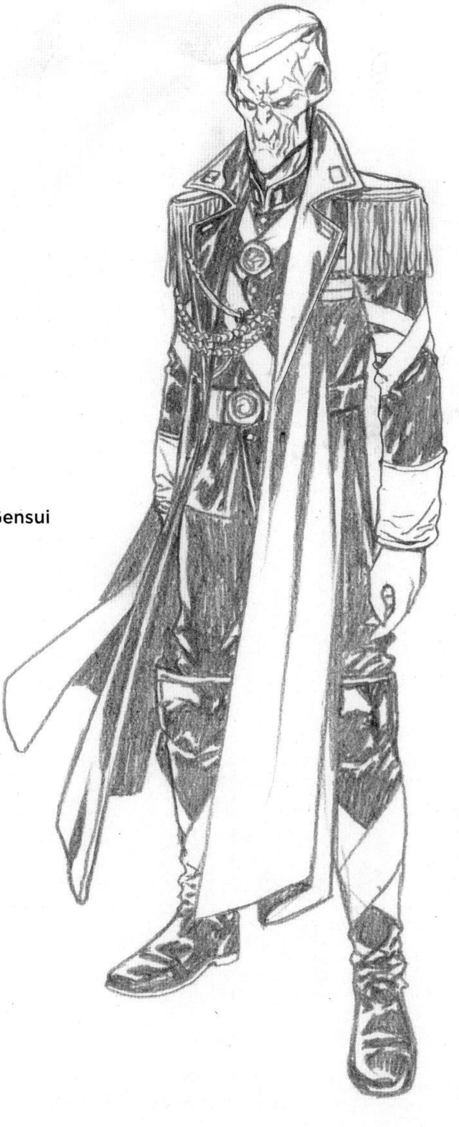

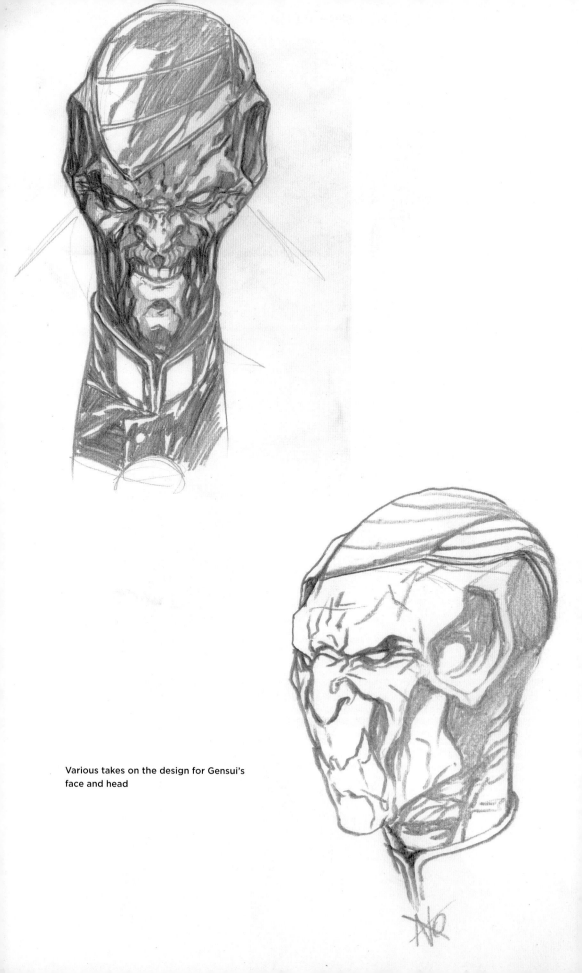

Various takes on the design for Gensui's
face and head

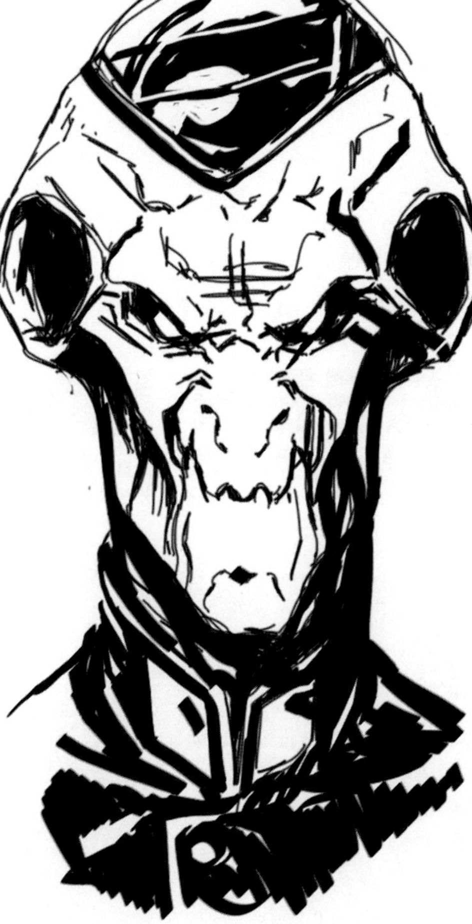

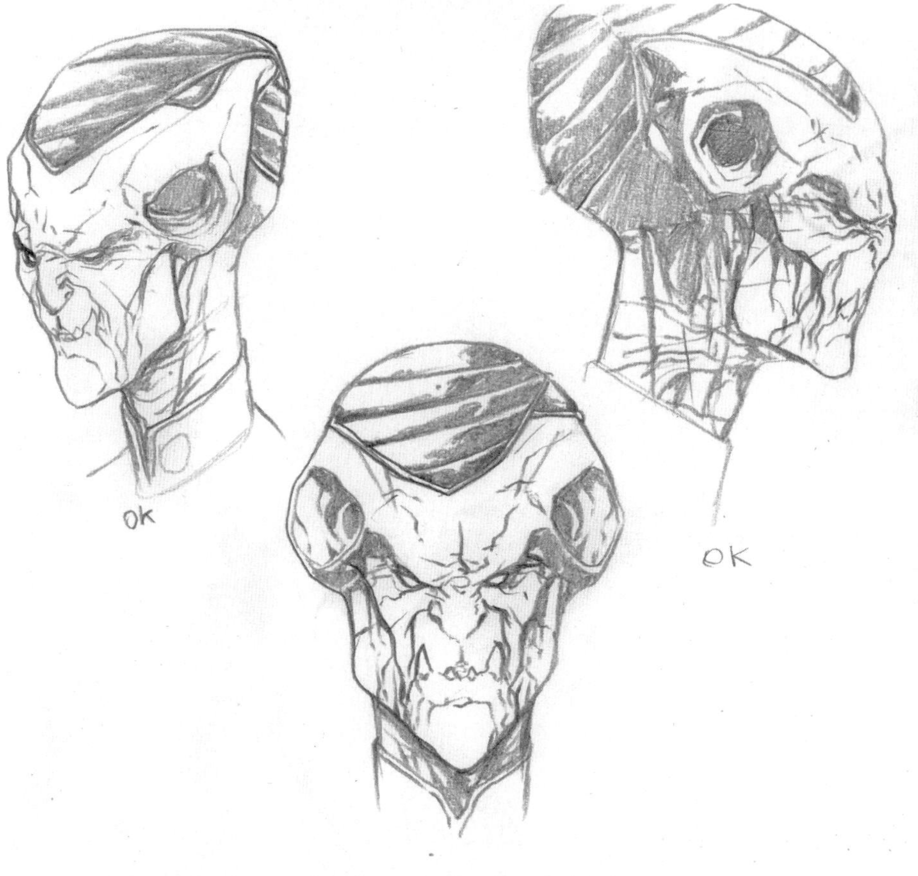
OK
OK

DC COMICS™

START AT THE BEGINNING!

GREEN LANTERN
VOLUME 1: SINESTRO

GREEN LANTERN
CORPS VOLUME 1:
FEARSOME

RED LANTERNS
VOLUME 1:
BLOOD AND RAGE

GREEN LANTERN:
NEW GUARDIANS
VOLUME 1:
THE RING BEARER

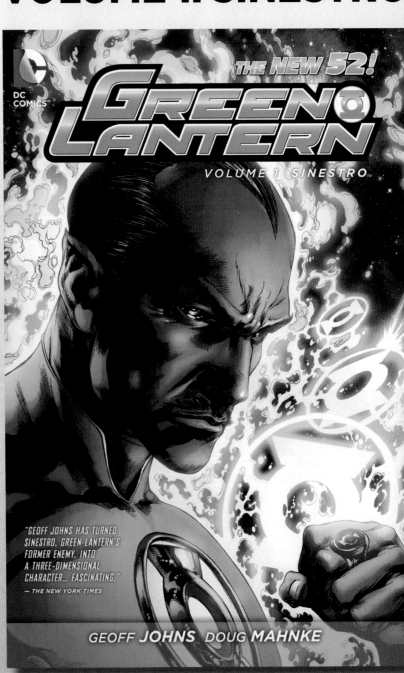

GEOFF JOHNS DOUG MAHNKE

FROM THE WRITER OF *JUSTICE LEAGUE* AND *THE FLASH*

GEOFF JOHNS
GREEN LANTERN: REBIRTH

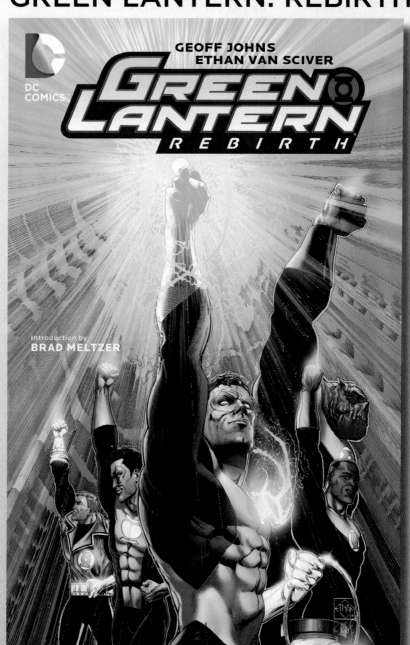

GEOFF JOHNS
ETHAN VAN SCIVER

DC COMICS

GREEN LANTERN
REBIRTH

Introduction by
BRAD MELTZER

DC COMICS™

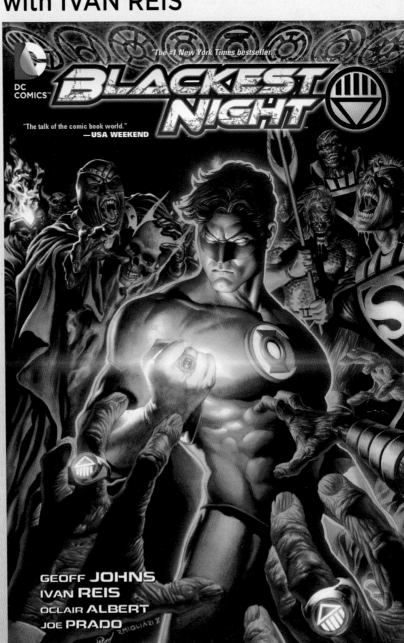

FROM THE WRITER OF *JUSTICE LEAGUE & AQUAMAN*

GEOFF JOHNS
with IVAN REIS

BLACKEST NIGHT:
GREEN LANTERN

BLACKEST NIGHT:
GREEN LANTERN CORPS

READ THE ENTIRE EPIC!

BLACKEST NIGHT

BLACKEST NIGHT:
GREEN LANTERN

BLACKEST NIGHT:
GREEN LANTERN CORPS

BLACKEST NIGHT:
BLACK LANTERN CORPS VOL. 1

BLACKEST NIGHT:
BLACK LANTERN CORPS VOL. 2

BLACKEST NIGHT:
RISE OF THE BLACK LANTERNS

BLACKEST NIGHT:
TALES OF THE CORPS